PAN-AFRICANISM RECONSIDERED

Pan-Africanism

Reconsidered

Edited by the

AMERICAN SOCIETY OF AFRICAN CULTURE

GREENWOOD PRESS, PUBLISHERS
WESTPORT, CONNECTICUT

Library of Congress Cataloging in Publication Data

American Society of African Culture.
  Pan-Africanism reconsidered.

  Reprint of the ed. published by University of Cali-
fornia Press, Berkeley.
  "Speeches, papers, and comments given at the Third
Annual Conference of the American Society of African Cul-
ture, which was held in Philadelphia at the University of
Pennsylvania from June 22 to June 26, 1960."
  Includes bibliographical references.
  1. Pan-Africanism--Addresses, essays, lectures.
2. Africa--Civilization--Addresses, essays, lectures.
3. Black race--Addresses, essays, lectures. I. Title.
[DT30.A53 1976]   301.29'6   76-3618
ISBN 0-8371-8792-3

Originally published in 1962 by University of California Press,
Berkeley

Reprinted with the permission of University of California Press

Reprinted in 1976 by Greenwood Press,
a division of Williamhouse-Regency Inc.

Library of Congress Catalog Card Number 76-3618

ISBN 0-8371-8792-3

Printed in the United States of America

Pan-Africanism Reconsidered is composed of the main speeches, papers, and comments given at the Third Annual Conference of the American Society of African Culture, which was held in Philadelphia at the University of Pennsylvania from June 22 to June 26, 1960. The subject of the conference was "African Unities and Pan-Africanism." It is our purpose in this book to reflect the nature of this significant conference and to present a record of lasting importance on a subject that is by nature constantly changing. Some attempt has been made to omit the transitory and the ceremonial which cannot be of interest to those who will turn to this volume as a source.

One major apology is made necessary by our decision to publish this volume, and this is to our African participants and guests. When we planned the conference, we had limited funds. Subsequently, we were able to raise additional money from the Cleveland H. Dodge Foundation and the Benjamin Rosenthal Foundation, which made it possible to invite African guests. Unfortunately, by this time it was too late to ask these guests to prepare papers; consequently, our African participants could only be asked to be commentators. In many instances they spoke extemporaneously and had very little time in which to preview the papers on which they were to comment. We have been able to include their contributions in this volume mainly by the use of tape recordings. The transcriptions have been edited and made into more-or-less formal papers. Where our African guests spoke in French, there has been the additional difficulty of the proper rendering of their remarks in translation. In spite of being placed under such handicaps, the contributions of our African friends stand up well in this volume.

The American Society of African Culture (AMSAC), established in 1957, is an organization of about three hunded and fifty American scholars, writers, and artists of African descent. It is an affiliate of the Société Africaine de Culture (SAC), which publishes *Présence Africaine* from its Paris headquarters. Basically, AMSAC is concerned with the study of African culture in Africa and elsewhere in the world in order to provide a bond of understanding between Africans and all Americans, especially those of African descent. AMSAC's concern with African culture includes the study of both high culture (the plastic arts, the performing arts, and the humanities) and culture and society in the sense of the social scientist's use of the term.

The first annual conference of AMSAC was held in New York in June, 1958, and was concerned largely with organizational matters. The second, in June, 1959, also held in New York, considered African literature, history, religion, arts, leadership, economy, society, and education. After long deliberations, the planning committee selected "African Unities and Pan-Africanism" as an appropriate subject for the third annual conference. It seemed to us that the role of Pan-Africanism needed a new emphasis. In the past, with considerable support and nurture from American Negroes, it had served as a rallying force against colonialism, imperialism, and racial persecution. In 1960, African states were emerging at a rapid rate and, in addition to many other problems, were facing two fearful dangers: the development of an unbridled national state system in the pre-World War II sense, and the involvement of African states in the cold war. Pan-Africanism, when properly developed, seemed to the planning committee to be a partial answer to both dangers. If the continent of Africa hopes to be neutral, then it needs the defense of Pan-Africanism just as the Western Hemisphere has had the defense of Pan-Americanism. Neutralism requires defensive strength. In the old days, this was provided by oceans, deserts, and mountains. Now that these natural barriers do not suffice, defense for neutralism can be provided for Africa by Pan-Africanism and the United Nations Organization. Pan-Africanism can also provide the motivating force to prevent political, economic, and military rivalries between African nations. There are many unities in African culture to provide a basis for a truly collective Pan-Africanism. We planned our conference in the fall of 1959 and the winter of 1959–60. The events of 1960 showed that our subject was worth considering.

Although the main work of the conference lay in the papers, the panel discussions, the commentary, and the panel reports, African high culture and its continuing creativity and contributions were demonstrated in an art exhibit, an evening of dance and music, and a tour of the University of Pennsylvania's African Art Collection. The conference opened with addresses by His Excellency Telli Diallo,

Ambassador from Guinea to the United States; Dr. Jean Price-Mars, President of the Société Africaine de Culture; and Professor Alioune Diop, Executive Director of the Société. These speeches, which explain the past and present of SAC and AMSAC, along with the keynote speech of the conference are placed in an introductory section of the volume. The book concludes with the final address of the conference by the then Speaker of the Nigerian House of Assembly, the Honorable Jaja A. Wachuku, who on the brink of his country's independence brought glad tidings to American Negroes of Africa's future and of theirs.

What the social scientist has to say about Africa is quickly eroded by time. In reading the papers of Marcum, Apter and Coleman, and Fofana, and the comments made upon them, certain events subsequent to their presentation should be kept in mind. Independence for the Congo has been threatened by regional separation. Syria has seceded from the United Arab Republic. The Mali Federation split into Senegal and Mali (the French Soudan), and the latter joined Ghana and Guinea in the Union of Africa States, a loose league involving no transfer of sovereignty. The Casablanca group of nations and the Brazzaville-Monrovia-Lagos group have emerged as representing different aspects of Pan-Africanism and certainly different attitudes toward the former European colonialists and the United States. Both Liberia and Nigeria are active in Pan-African affairs.

One final word is necessary with regard to those who made this book possible. In addition to Samuel W. Allen, the editor, Miss Cynthia Courtney, the AMSAC's Director of Publications, is mainly responsible for achieving the production of the volume. As we have already indicated, the manuscript presented a host of difficult technical problems. These were mastered by Gilman Park, Jr., who is in large measure responsible not only for copy-editing but also for the preliminary organization and format of the manuscript.

JOHN A. DAVIS

WACHUKU ABENGOWE, born in 1925 in Eastern Nigeria, is a member of the House of Assembly, Eastern Region of Nigeria, and Deputy Chief Whip for the Government. An experienced journalist, Mr. Abengowe worked for the National Council of Nigeria and the Cameroons as well as for several newspapers. He has traveled to Britain to study parliamentary procedures and is now in the United States to observe American government, education, and journalism.

RICHARD MAXIMILLAN AKWEI, born in 1923 in Ghana, is Principal Assistant Secretary, Minister of Foreign Affairs in Accra. He studied at Achimota College in Ghana and at Christ Church College, Oxford. He has served in the Gold Coast Civil Service and was attached to the British High Commission in Ottawa for foreign service training before going to Washington, D.C., where he was Acting Counsellor at the Ghana Embassy.

SAMUEL W. ALLEN, born in 1917 in Columbus, Ohio, is a graduate of Fisk University and Harvard Law School. He served as Assistant District Attorney in New York before deciding to study the humanities in New York and at the Sorbonne. A former professor of law at Southern University, Mr. Allen alternately practices law and publishes poetry. He is presently General Counsel of the United States Information Agency in Washington, D.C.

DAVID E. APTER earned his A.B. in economics at Antioch College and his Ph.D. in politics at Princeton University. He has taught in Africa and has been an associate professor of political science at the University of Chicago. He is Executive Secretary of the Committee on Comparative Study of New Nations. Mr. Apter has done much research in the social sciences and is author of *The Political Kingdom in Uganda* and *The Gold Coast in Transition*. He is now an associate professor of political science at the University of California, Berkeley.

KARL W. BIGELOW, of Bangor, Maine, is professor of higher education in the Department of Educational Administration, Teachers College,

Columbia University. He received his B.A. from Clark College, Worcester, Mass., in 1920, and his Ph.D. in economics from Harvard University in 1929. Mr. Bigelow has done an appreciable amount of work for UNESCO on education in Europe and Africa. In 1960 he became director of the coöperative Afro–Anglo-American program in teacher education and of the new unit on African education at Teachers College. He has written a number of books on education and the social sciences. He is presently codirector of the Sierra Leone Peace Corps Training Program at Teachers College.

SABURI OLADENI BIOBAKU, born in 1918 in Nigeria, earned his M.A. at Cambridge and his Ph.D. at London University. He has been Master at the Government College, Ibadan, Nigeria; Assistant Liaison Officer for Nigerian students in the United Kingdom; Secretary to the Cabinet, Western Region of Nigeria; and Registrar of University College, Ibadan. He is presently Vice Chancellor of the University of Ife.

GEORGE ERNEST CARTER, JR., born in 1925, is a graduate of Lincoln University and an M.A. of Harvard University. He was formerly Director of the Information Program at AMSAC, producing tapes for broadcast in Africa and overseeing the exchange of cultural material with East and West Africa. Independently, he is preparing a survey of the background of contemporary African social thought. A former consultant to UNESCO on government conferences and social services, he has also been a private consultant to New York agencies planning programs on Africa and Asia. He is presently based in Accra, Ghana, as supervisor of the Peace Corps in the area.

CHRISTIAN ABAYOMI CASSELL, born in 1906 in Monrovia, Liberia, received his A.B. from Liberia College in 1926 and was admitted to the bar in 1927. He has served in many capacities in the Liberian government and participated in several economic and legal conferences and commissions in Liberia and elsewhere. He has twice been a delegate to the United Nations from Liberia and is presently the chief delegate and Liberian member of the All Africa Peoples Conference Steering Committee.

JAMES S. COLEMAN studied at Brigham Young University and at Harvard University, where he received his Ph.D. He has taught political science at Harvard and at the University of California, Los Angeles, where he is the Director of the African Studies Center. In addition to his many articles based on extensive field work in Africa, he has written the book *Nigeria: Background to Nationalism*.

JOHN A. DAVIS, A.B., Williams College; Ph.D., Columbia University; has taught at Howard, Lincoln, and Ohio State universities and is now professor of government at the City College of New York. He was until 1960 a Commissioner of the New York State Commission against Discrimination. He has been a member of the Executive Council of the American Political Science Association and has written a volume in the field of public administration as well as numerous articles on civil rights. He directed the nonlegal research for the NAACP's brief in the famous education decisions and was Director of Research and Planning for President Roosevelt's FEPC. He is Executive Director of the American Society of African Culture.

TELLI DIALLO, of Guinea, was a magistrate and former Secretary General of the Grand Council of French West Africa. Since Guinea gained independence, he has been her Ambassador to the United States and permanent representative to the United Nations.

ALIOUNE DIOP, born in Senegal, now lives in Paris. He is Secretary General of the Société Africaine de Culture (SAC). Mr. Diop was the prime mover in organizing the first world congress of Negro Writers and Artists (held in Paris in 1956), which led to the founding of SAC, and in the formation of the American Society of African Culture. He is director and editor of the journal *Présence Africaine*.

ANTHONY ERONSELE OGEGHALE ENAHORO, born in 1923 in Nigeria, the son of Chief Enahoro of Uromi, has reported for and edited several African newspapers. In 1954 he became Minister of Home Affairs in the Western Region of Nigeria and Leader of the House. He is now the Action Group member of the Federal House of Representatives from Ishan East in the Western Region, holding ministries for internal affairs, foreign affairs, and legislature in the Action Group's

"Shadow Cabinet." He has attended both conferences of the All Africa Peoples Conference.

LATTEE ADEES FAHM, born in 1930 in Lagos, Nigeria, received his A.M. in economics from the University of California and is now a doctoral candidate at Massachusetts Institute of Technology. He has served as a teaching assistant and research assistant in economics at the University of California and at M.I.T. His research includes work on economic and political studies of sub-Saharan Africa.

ABDOULAYE FOFANA, born in 1917 in Senegal, has served as a civil servant at Diourbel, Senegal. A former member of the Grand Council of French West Africa, he became Minister of Education and Health for the Mali Federation. He is now Minister of Transport in Senegal.

WILLIAM T. FONTAINE, born in 1907 in Chester, Penn., studied at Lincoln and Harvard universities and the University of Pennsylvania, where he received his Ph.D. in 1936. He has taught at Lincoln, Southern University, and Morgan State College, and is now associate professor of philosophy at the University of Pennsylvania. He has published articles in several scholarly ·journals, and is Secretary of AMSAC.

KWA O. HAGAN, born in 1913 in Ghana, earned his B.A. at Adisadel College. He is National Secretary of the People's Educational Association of Ghana. He has taught at Adisadel and at the University College of Ghana (now the University of Accra). He is a member of the UNESCO International Committee for the Advancement of Adult Education and a panel consultant for Africa on the Adult Education Committee, World Confederation of the Organization of Teaching Professions.

J. NEWTON HILL is former Dean of the College, Lincoln University, and has been a member of the Lincoln faculty in the English and art history departments since 1933. He has lectured at Howard and Atlanta universities. Mr. Hill has published numerous articles and lectures on art and has been the director of several little theater groups. He is now director of the Lagos office of the African-American Institute.

VINCENT IKEOTUONYE, born in Nigeria, was educated at Christ the King College, Onitsha, Nigeria, and Lincoln University. He is now Headmaster of Zixton Grammar School, Onitsha. He has been Principal of Africa College and Vice Principal of Priscilla Memorial Grammar School, Oguta, Nigeria. He is a member of the Federal Parliament of Nigeria.

WENDELL P. JONES graduated from Elizabeth City Teachers College, North Carolina, earned his M.A. at Atlanta University and his Ph.D. at the University of Chicago. In 1958 and 1959 he made a field study of education in tropical Africa, and in 1961 he served as program specialist for the UNESCO-sponsored Development of Education in Africa project. He is now a specialist in African education in the field of comparative education at the University of California, Los Angeles, where he is presently program director of the Peace Corps "Teachers for Nigeria" training project.

JOSEPH KI-ZERBO, a history professor from Upper Volta, is Secretary General of the *Mouvement Africain de Libération Nationale*. He was educated in France, receiving a diploma from the Institut d'Etudes Politiques of the University of Paris, and is an *agrégé* in history. He has taught history at the Lycée Vollenhoven in Dakar and at the Lycée in Cona. He was a delegate to the 1958 All Africa Peoples Conference in Accra.

RAYFORD F. LOGAN, a graduate of Williams College, received his Ph.D. in history from Harvard University. He has been for many years the head of the History department at Howard University. After service in World War I, he was secretary and interpreter at three Pan-African Congresses, and Deputy Secretary of the Pan-African Association in Paris. As a Fulbright Research Fellow, Mr. Logan has studied the administration of the French Overseas Territories and has traveled under the auspices of the U.S. State Department in Africa. He is the author of numerous books and articles in the fields of American history, American Negro history, and the diplomatic history of Negro nations.

JOHN ARTHUR MARCUM studied at Stanford and Columbia universities and at the Institut d'Etudes Politiques, University of Paris. He received his Ph.D. from Stanford after completing a dissertation on "French North Africa in the Atlantic Community," based on field work in Paris and North Africa. He has been an assistant professor of political science at Colgate University and has published several articles on North Africa. He is now associate professor of political science at Lincoln University.

ACHKAR MAROF, born in 1930 in Coyah, Guinea, studied at *Ecole Breguet* in Paris. A former director of *Ballets Africains*, he is now a Guinean delegate to the United Nations.

SAIDI MASWANYA is Deputy Organizing Secretary General of the Tanganyika National Union (TANU).

EZEKIEL MPHAHLELE of South Africa is an author, critic, and teacher who majored in English, psychology, and native administration at the University of South Africa. While acting as literary editor of *Drum*, the African weekly, he earned his M.A. in English. He was a resident tutor at University College, Ibadan, Nigeria; the author of *Down Second Avenue;* and is presently the Director of the Congress of Cultural Freedom in Paris. Mr. Mphahlele lectured at Massachusetts Institute of Technology during the fall of 1961.

DUNCAN NDERITO NDEGWA, born in 1925 in Nyere, Kenya, studied at Makerere College, in Uganda and earned his M.A. in economics at the University of St. Andrews in Scotland. He is now the Assistant Secretary of the Kenya Treasury and participated in the Foreign Specialist Exchange Program of the Office of Cultural Exchange sponsored by the U.S. State Department.

TRALAPUYE O. NA ORUWARIYE, of Nigeria, is a physician and the founder of Oke-Ado Hospital in Ibadan. He studied at Igbodi and Yaba College in Lagos and is an M.B.B.S. of the University of London.

JAMES A. PORTER, B.S., Howard University; A.M., New York University; has studied at New York University, the Institut d'Art et

Archéologie in Paris, and the Art Students League in New York. He is the author of *Modern Negro Art* and of several monographs and articles, and is presently an associate professor of art at Howard University.

JEAN PRICE-MARS, of Haiti, is President of the *Société Africaine de Culture*. He is a pioneer Haitian anthropologist and ethnologist who received an honorary doctorate at the inauguration of the University of Dakar. He has served as Ambassador from Haiti to the United States, to the United Nations, and to France.

WALT WHITMAN ROSTOW is a professor of economic history at Massachusetts Institute of Technology. He studied at Yale (B.A.), Oxford (Rhodes Scholar, M.A.), and Cambridge (M.A.), receiving his Ph.D. in 1940 at Yale. He taught at Columbia College, Oxford, and Cambridge before joining the Massachusetts Institute of Technology faculty in 1950. Mr. Rostow has done extensive research, lecturing, and writing on Soviet Russia, Communist China, Great Britain, and the United States. His many significant contributions in economics include lectures and writing on "Non-Communist Manifesto," the book *The Stages of Economic Growth,* plus several other important publications. He is now on the White House staff in Washington, D.C.

MAIDA SPRINGER, International Representative with the Department of International Affairs, AFL-CIO, has been an officer of the International Ladies Garment-Workers Union. She has represented the AFL-CIO at conferences in Africa and was the AFL-CIO Special Representative for the Trade Union Program in Africa in 1957.

STANLEY SUMLIN graduated from Lincoln University and attended the University of Pittsburgh Law School. He earned his M.A. at New York University and is now a doctoral candidate there. He has been a research assistant at the National Bureau of Economic Affairs and is now in charge of the Near East and Africa desk at the Federal Reserve Bank of New York.

JAJA ANUCHA WACHUKU, born in 1918 in Aba, Eastern Nigeria, studied at the Higher College in Yaba, Lagos, and at the New Africa University College in Ghana. He received his B.A. and M.A. in Legal Science at Trinity College, Dublin University. He has been chairman of the National Council of Nigeria and Cameroons, and is the founder of the New Africa Party. Mr. Wachuku, previously Speaker of the Nigerian House of Assembly, is now Minister of Foreign Affairs and Commonwealth Relations for Nigeria.

IMMANUAL WALLERSTEIN is an assistant professor of sociology at Columbia University. He studied at Columbia and received his Ph.D. in 1959. He has published several articles on French West Africa.

ARTHUR NUTULTI LUBINDA WINA, born in Northern Rhodesia, received his B.A. from Makerere College and his M.Ed. from the University of California, Los Angeles. He is now engaged in studies in international relations and is the United States representative of the United National Independence Party of Northern Rhodesia.

EMILE ZINSOU, born in 1918 in Dahomey, has served in the French Union Assembly, the French Council of the Republic, and the Territorial Assembly of Dahomey. For a short time he was Minister of General Economy in the Apithy government, but resigned and became leader of the Dahomey section of the *Parti de le Fédération Africaine*. He is now federal Vice President of the party and Dahomey's Ambassador to France.

CONTENTS

IV ECONOMICS

V EDUCATION

VI SOCIAL THOUGHT

VII ART

VIII AFRICAN CULTURE AND NEGRITUDE

IX CLOSING ADDRESS

INTRODUCTION

IT WAS ON THE EVE of a critical phase of African liberation—the formation of the Republic of the Congo—that the Third Annual Conference of the American Society of African Culture was held in Philadelphia at the University of Pennsylvania in June, 1960. The sessions took place in historic Houston Hall—the same setting where, at the beginning of World War II, Kwame Nkrumah, then a teaching fellow at the university, had shared the platform with Justice William H. Hastie, Congressman Adam Clayton Powell, and AMSAC's Executive Director, John A. Davis, to consider the subject of African freedom. Alioune Diop, the Senegalese Secretary General and founder of the parent organization, the Société Africaine de Culture, could not remain after the Philadelphia sessions for the tour of American cities with other African visitors because of his scheduled flight to attend what proved to be that crucial event in African resurgence, the inauguration of the Republic of the Congo. In a sense, the Belgian Congo experience—or, more precisely, what at the time of writing still threatens to be the Belgian Congo disaster—reflects in microcosm the clash of forces inherent in the theme of the conference, "African Unities and Pan-Africanism." The divisive aspect of nationalism is there, threatening to splinter the Congo hopelessly into its several constituent parts; and the influence of an embattled Pan-Africanism is also manifest even in secessionist Katanga in demonstrations supporting the Republic.

Pan-Africanism is a timely subject. It has been the rallying slogan, the springboard, the ideological vehicle for the common efforts of exiled Africans, West Indians, and American Negroes to advance the cause of Africa and of Africans. But Pan-Africanism, like Joseph's coat, is described in many colors; at no time have these variegated hues been more significant than now. These are the years—1960 is in a large measure *the* year—of Africa's liberation. The drive toward freedom has, or shortly will have, succeeded, with certain reluctant exceptions at the extreme ends of the continent. That very success has, in large degree, automatically eliminated this source of psychological energy, of unity and effort, generated in the struggle *against* France, England,

and Belgium, *against* political disenfranchisement, *against* the un-numbered facets of a common colonial oppression. The more difficult question of the ordering of that freedom is imminent. In a new and changing context the delegates to the conference examined the major theme of Pan-Africanism—what it has been, what it is, and, in an awakening continent, what it is most likely to become. Their views, some prepared beforehand, others given extemporarily, are recorded in this volume.

The chapters of the volume correspond to the organization of the conference into panels dealing with the various sub-topics. Owing to the wide range of material covered and the diversity of views presented in these papers, I have found it convenient to present my summary of and comments upon the conference in several parts. The introduction proper concerns mainly the chapters on Pan-Africanism and African politics. Further introductory remarks precede the chapters on economics, education, social thought, and African culture and negritude. In the chapter on African art my remarks are included with a synopsis of the round-table discussion.

❁   ❁   ❁

In his keynote speech, John A. Davis, Executive Director of AMSAC, poses the problem that confronts Africa in the initiation of her independence: Is the virus of nationalism to infect a newly freed Africa with the same attendant ills of Balkanization, tariff wars, military alliances, and boundary quarrels which for centuries afflicted Europe so heavily? Or will a mature Pan-Africanism manage to resolve the divisive tensions that threaten not only the continent but the peace of the world? Davis graphically states the urgency of the matter: "Yet they and we together dare not fail, for the blast of nuclear fusion blows hot on our necks as we hurry along the path of human reconciliation." Subsequent events have proved his imagery no mere rhetoric, and it is increasingly evident that difficulties facing the newly independent African states have implications far beyond their impact within the limits of the continent.

A complete understanding of the actual and potential range of influence of contemporary Pan-Africanism is afforded only by a knowledge of its origin and the course of its early growth. The first panelist to speak at the Philadelphia sessions was Rayford Logan, one of the handful of pioneers in the development of the Pan-African movement. In this pioneer phase, Logan was one of the principal colleagues of W. E. B. Du Bois, the generally acknowledged father of the Pan-African movement. In his address Logan traces the origin of Pan-Africanism in the early part of the century in the activity of Sylvester Williams in the West Indies and of Du Bois in the United States. By coincidence, it was in response to a request from a group of American Negroes from Philadelphia, the site of this year's deliberations, that Du Bois issued his first call for a Pan-African conference before World War I. A series of such conferences was held in the first half of the century, meeting, for the most part, in European capitals. Logan takes issue with Du Bois's belief that the conference held in Paris at the close of World War I through the assistance of Blaise Diagne, the Senegalese member of the French Chamber of Deputies, as the Allies hammered out the clumsy Treaty of Versailles, was responsible for the mandate system. He points to the growing force of Pan-Africanism, however, in the historic culminating sessions held in Manchester in 1945 at the close of World War II, and presided over by the elder statesman Du Bois. Among the participants in this session were the men who were shortly to move to the forefront in the explosive development of African independence: Nkrumah, George Padmore, Kenyatta, Nnamdi Azikiwe, Wachuku, and others.

Logan's thesis may be termed either an exercise in realism or in cynicism, depending on the vintage of one's disenchantment. He attributes the success of the Pan-African movement neither to the influence of libertarian ideas nor, in any substantial measure, to the efforts of the early Pan-Africanists, but rather to two debilitating world wars which left Europe prostrate and powerless to maintain her empires. The colonial powers themselves were unwittingly the gravediggers of colonialism, he maintains; and rather than to the egalitarian ideals of pronouncements such as the Magna Carta, the Rights of Man, and the Atlantic Charter, it is to the suicidal struggles of two world wars and the interim stupidities of the great powers that Pan-Africanism owes its growth. Paramount Chief Anthony Enahoro, a member of the Nigerian parliament, rose in opposition to this analysis. Garbed in his traditional tribal robes, speaking in precise, lucid English, he insisted upon the guiding influence of Western ideals and of Western institutions.

Without doubt, the assessment of the relative weight of such intangibles is, at best, an art; yet through the close consideration of the pattern of interaction of forces in the political field, through a selective comparison with other areas, the historian is not helpless. There are elements of truth in both positions. War's destruction of the old is the classic occasion, of course, for the formation of the new. There is little doubt that Europe's grip upon her colonies could never have been so loosened without the impact of those internecine conflicts which were the two global struggles. An imperialist West's extremity was, in great measure, the opportunity for every vassal state and territory around the earth. The full historic truth, however, would certainly comprehend not only the shattering impact of these conflicts but also the complementary and directive force of liberal Western ideas. It is Western narcissism that holds that Europe taught an indifferent Africa to want to be free. There is the other side of the coin, however—the *possibility* of Africa's freedom. Here, Enahoro does well to point out that there was no inevitability in the successful implementation of that desire, that there was no predestined course of political events following the two world wars, and that the attendant dislocations might conceivably have been superseded by a renewal rather than a relaxation of Europe's hold upon her African colonies. It is necessary only to consider the close balance of forces in the Weimar Republic, and the almost fortuitous circumstances that determined the monstrous successor finally to emerge from the Weimar ruins, to realize that the course of liberal progress by no means runs in a straight line, and is certainly not inevitable. It is impossible to ignore the circumstances, favorable or unfavorable, attendant on its advance. It is to the English conscience, as shaped by centuries of its poets, essayists, and other writers, that Gandhi, in considerable measure, owed the inspiration for his program of passive resistance. It would be enlightening to contemplate a similar movement under a genocidal Third Reich. Although it required the stunning blows of the two wars to persuade Europe to loosen a rapacious grip upon Africa, the advance of African freedom and of Pan-Africanism, as Enahoro rightly insists, is attributable in great degree to the libertarian ideals of that same Western civilization.

Considerable attention was given at the conference to a definition of Pan-Africanism and to its changing significance over the course of half a century. Again, the conflict in the remarks of Logan and Enahoro graphically points up the transformation in the nature of the movement. In its initiation, its supporters were interested simply in an amelioration of the wretched conditions under which most Africans lived. The influence of Du Bois succeeded in transforming Pan-Africanism into a more militant program of nationalism and ultimate African independence. It was a "pan" movement in the sense that it sought vindication of the rights of all Africans and the establishment ultimately of Africa's rightful place in the political sun; yet, in a sense paradoxically, its instrumentality was the independent national state. Logan correctly indicates that throughout World War II the immediate objective of the Pan-Africanists was the independence of the several prospective African nations. In the postwar period, however, and with political independence increasingly becoming a fact, Pan-Africanism, while retaining essentially the same motivation, has taken on new tactical objectives. Marcum of Colgate, Coleman of the University of California, Los Angeles, and Apter of the University of Chicago [now at the University of California, Berkeley], in their prepared papers, and Cassell of Liberia, Enahoro and Wachuku of Nigeria, Akwei of Ghana, Zinsou of Dahomey, and others, through panel participation, all contribute to the mosaic of this evolving force in African affairs. Emphases differ, but there is general agreement that modern Pan-Africanism envisages, among other goals, the development of forms of association beyond the present boundaries of independent states in a manner that will strengthen and enrich the fabric of African life. The major discussion concerns the prospect of some kind of *political* union between or among the various African states.

The discussion seems to reveal two basic attitudes toward political unity. One appears motivated by fear of Balkanization, and advocates immediate measures to achieve political unities larger than those inherited from the chance boundaries of Europe's original conquests; the other approach would accept the legacy of such colonial boundaries as *fait accompli* and would endeavor within that framework to achieve economic and cultural coöperation and eventually, perhaps, closer political union. This latter attitude, as Apter points out, is the one urged upon African leaders by the major theorist in the era of English influence in Africa, the late George Padmore. Pan-Africanism is to be achieved, according to the "Padmore Dictum," by the realization first of national states, staked out by present political realities. These states are to be made strong and viable, and the formation of larger regional political entities is not feasible until this preliminary development has been achieved.

Apter and Coleman delineate in considerable detail the factors in colonial Africa—internal and external—which have made for the establishment of separate national states, determined geographically and politically by the boundaries of the old colonial units. Coleman finds the causes for this Balkanizing tendency in three aspects of Africa's development. The first he calls the legacy of colonialism: "It can be stated as a general proposition that during the colonial period the policy and actions of the colonial powers in Africa tended to preserve and to emphasize the separate existence of each artificial administrative entity created during this scramble for Africa." Further: "The crux of the matter is that the net effect of European colonialism in Africa has been to create—albeit unwittingly—embryonic nations coterminous with boundaries of the colonial administrative units." He examines the policies of Britain and France in Africa and finds that they fostered separateness and failed to seize the opportunity to create large political unities after World War II, when Africa was on the threshold of liberation. Akwei of Ghana later specifically referred to the "carving" habits of "our friends, the English," who, presiding over the increasingly speedy liquidation of an empire, resorted to what was conceivably the path of least resistance by carving successive pieces of that empire into small nations.

Second, the very mechanics of the struggle for independence tended to perpetuate the existing political entities. Except for certain eruptions of violence in those areas that, in Enahoro's euphemism of reverse perspective, are "burdened with a settler problem," the nationalist movements generally have been committed to constitutional and nonviolent change. Obviously, the goals of these movements could be prosecuted much more efficiently within the framework of an existing political entity of a single language area, unafflicted by customs barriers or other political and economic barriers.

Finally, once independent statehood is achieved, as Coleman points out, the imperatives of nation-building make it impossible to wait upon the liberation of other areas; the state must move immediately to create a stable political community, to inculcate loyalty and respect for the nation and the laws of the government, and to instill in the people a sense of shared purpose and of national identity. Thus, the factors inherent in the struggle for national independence militate sharply against the suprastate of the larger political unity.

The actual history of the present achievement of independence by African states indicates that these and other obstacles to broad political union are extremely powerful, and suggests the correctness of the "Padmore Dictum" that the first goal is separate national independence. Of the more than a score of nations gaining independence within the past three or four years, there have been only two examples of the larger political union we are contemplating; namely, the Ghana–Guinea Union and the Mali Federation. The first has been described as more a potentially meaningful political union than an actual operative example. The situation in the Mali Federation brings us to a consideration of another approach detected in the discussions on Pan-Africanism; that is, the urgency of achieving larger union before the rigidity of national interest sets in.

Marcum describes how Léopold Senghor, as a member of the French delegation to the Consultative Assembly of the Council of Europe in Strasbourg, was impressed with the extreme jealousy of national sovereignty of states whose separate existence had been established. Senghor thus urged, and his sense of urgency is shared by some at the Philadelphia conference, that every effort be made to achieve a broad political union *before* rather than *after* independence —the converse of Padmore's injunction. Senghor's 1959 proposal of federation of all the territories of French West Africa met defeat, and the Upper Volta and Dahomey withdrew from a prospective four-nation Mali Federation. A reduced Mali Federation, however, did eventually emerge—a union of Senegal and Sudan; it was, during its survival, the only example of political union formed prior to independence. It has therefore been signally disappointing to the adherents of Pan-Africanism to observe the recent disintegration of that union and the apparently irreconcilable differences between Senegal and Sudan.

The remarks of Zinsou of Dahomey are in substantial agreement with those of Senghor in his key study, *African Socialism*. He, like Senghor, strongly insists upon a fairly loose federal type of union, rather than a unitary state with power strongly concentrated in a central government. But federal or unitary, the sentiment was expressed more than once during the conference that Africa, by rare historic fortune, finds herself possessed of a fleeting chance to forge strong meaningful unions between nation states. One of the younger members of the Nigerian Parliament, Ikeotuonye, who indicated he had discussed the matter with his political chief Azikiwe before coming to the conference, strongly urged from the floor that the conference go on record as favoring the formation of a federation of most of the states of West Africa. Zinsou of Dahomey deplores the lack of greater awareness on the part of Africans of the dangers of Balkanization. He emphasizes the absolute necessity of African unity, and the unhoped-for historic chance that would permit this unity before the independent African states become fossilized in their nationalism. Apter of Chicago suggests a revision of the "Padmore Dictum," and an undertaking, despite the apparent obstacles, to form interstate unions *before* independence or, at least, within the still fluid period immediately thereafter. The trend, however, as the speakers point out, is otherwise, as was the preponderance of opinion expressed during the conference. Some measure of the medium-sized union has been achieved—in the Ghana-Guinea-Mali union, in what is actually multi-state Nigeria, and temporarily in the apparently ill-fated Mali Federation—but there has been resistance to further union, and those alliances that have been achieved are threatened.

It was clear from observations made by the African delegates that they will not be captured by slogans. They cautioned that the question is not the academic one of what Pan-Africanism is; and they did not feel themselves beholden there in the Quaker City to commit themselves to that construction of the "professors"—the suprastate. (The academic world, which supplied most of the American participation, was the object of considerable tongue-in-cheek deference on the part of the African delegates.) The issue was rather, they said, a practical one of what Africa needs.

Biobaku of Nigeria, whose remarks constituted perhaps the most distinguished prose of the occasion, puts his finger upon the continent's basic unresolved problems: poverty, ignorance, and disease. Pan-Africanism, he says, must be considered in the light of the answers it holds, or fails to hold, for these acute and pressing matters. Biobaku agrees with most of the African participants, particularly those from

Nigeria, that the immediate objective is the political consolidation of the individual states and an attack on the basic problems through what Marcum earlier called "functional," as opposed to political, coöperation. Under this or a similar nomenclature, most of the participants mapped out an area of coöperation on economic, cultural, and educational levels (and political levels short of surrender of sovereignty) where genuine coöperation appears increasingly possible. Marcum points to the proposal of Tubman of Liberia for a West African council for economic coöperation and for councils for coöperation in education, health, and nutrition. Biobaku makes similar suggestions. And in view of the tendency for political entities in the new Africa to take shape on the basis of European language groups, mainly English and French, Zinsou's suggestion of compulsory bilingualism is an excellent one. In time, the indigenous African languages may become the vehicle of communication in the African states; but for a substantial period European languages in daily usage will blanket practically all of the continent. To promote the unities of Pan-Africanism, bilingualism, as Zinsou urges, will be essential.

An examination of the contributions of Enahoro and Wachuku, along with those of Biobaku, reveals, however, the essential Nigerian caution concerning political union, as well as their receptivity to coöperation in the economic and cultural spheres. It is evident that they feel the imposing task is the formation of a stable political community and a strong national state—not the establishment of wider political unities. This position is not necessarily a rejection of Pan-Africanism. It fits Padmore's timetable. Furthermore, it fits well within Enahoro's broader definition of Pan-Africanism as a movement that promotes larger unities, but which remains fundamentally and more generally concerned with the advancement of the African cause, the liberation of its people, and the improvement of the quality of their lives. The title of the study by Coleman and Apter tends to suggest Pan-Africanism and nationalism as opposites from which the ultimate choice is to be made. The reaction of the African delegates, however, established a different perspective, implicit in Enahoro's definition—a Pan-Africanism broad enough to embrace both nationalism *and* the suprastate, or internationalism, as instrumentalities of the ultimate aim of African progress. In this more searching perspective, Pan-Africanism is, rather than simply a movement toward a suprastate, an application in a wider scope of that same concern that in the United States inspired the abolitionists, the Niagara movement, and the National Association for the Advancement of Colored People.

The way of wisdom, perhaps, is suggested by Akwei of the Ghana Embassy, who warns of the dangers of too rigid definitions and of system building. Complaining that it is difficult "to assess the confusions" of his platform predecessors who erred in that direction, Akwei confides that he personally is not given to this sort of unprofitable activity. He proceeds, however, to defend the initiative taken by Ghana in rallying the African people. The need is clear, he says; and as a pioneer in the hour of African freedom, Ghana feels it her duty to assume leadership in matters of continental concern.

It was much later in the conference when, as a banquet speaker, Jaja Wachuku, Speaker of the Nigerian House and veteran of the Dublin bar, finally entered the lists. His remarks, however, are pertinent here in that they focus distinctly upon several of the prominent issues of the conference. Perhaps nothing expresses more sharply the development of the Pan-African idea than the contrast between the assertion of Blaise Diagne, Senegalese Deputy to Paris, made at the close of World War I—"I am first a Frenchman; I am a Negro afterwards"—and Wachuku's unequivocal "We are Africans first! Everything else is secondary." The shift in emphasis is even more pronounced when we realize that Wachuku does not even bother to disclaim European citizenship—he obviously feels it unnecessary; he is concerned rather with the ideological camps which may threaten to attract primary African allegiances.

Wachuku, like most Nigerians, takes the more deliberate approach to interstate political organizations. His position, again, is in marked contrast to that expressed by Davis in the keynote speech. He does not share the latter's alarm at the prospect of Balkanization of African nations. It will not be as it was in Europe, he says. These are different times. Africa will learn from the mistakes of others. It is, moreover, unrealistic and unwise, he contends, to expect internationalism before a strong nationalism is assured. He points to the seventy years required to achieve the organization of American states. Internationalism is the apex, not the foundation, of political growth. Employing an African figure, he resists what he terms the inverted pyramid. Let there be first economic unity, a Pan-African airways, a West African currency;

let there be a cultural unity; let there be achieved through these unities strong, separate national states. Only then will it be realistic to attempt the apex of political internationalism.

Before leaving this issue, we should consider again Professor Apter's questioning of this strategy. With Africa's profound industrial and technological weakness, the larger political union is, he implies, the means by which economic strength is to be achieved. The large market—whether in a state or a private economy—undivided by numerous custom barriers, is a prerequisite to economic growth. Wallerstein of Columbia supports him in this emphasis, citing the hypothetical case of the Ivory Coast industrialist who finds the area's three million inhabitants insufficient to generate a demand equal to his productive capacity. Apter, in his prepared paper, states that the younger Africans are, in contrast to their elders, passionately concerned with greater political union, and find present African leadership, though able and necessary to the struggle for independence, perhaps not equally so suited to the task of working out political union. In this light, Ikeotounye's proposal of federation is doubly interesting, as are the remarks of Arthur Wina of Northern Rhodesia, who briefly but explicitly states his disappointment in his fellow African speakers—leaders in public life—regarding what he feels was their undue emphasis upon the obstacles to unification.

There were certain other large issues around which the discussion of political Pan-Africanism shaped itself. Probably the most pronounced, if one examines the African participation carefully, is not the East-West ideological conflict, but the effect of the African liberation upon the plight of African peoples the world over. Pan-Africanism, as we have seen, had in its origin a distinctly international flavor —its protagonists being American Negroes, West Indians, and African exiles in Europe. Pan-Africanism was repatriated. It went home to Africa and was embodied to a great degree in the nationalism that served as the vehicle of the African thrust toward freedom. Now that this freedom is being achieved, Africa looks with increasing concern— as speaker after African speaker testified—at the proscriptions against African descendants scattered by the slave trade to the various sectors of the earth.

Cassell of Liberia, a member of the steering committee of the All Africa Peoples Conference (that honor guard of Pan-Africanism, as

Marof of Guinea terms it), led off in this phase of the discussion. In a voice halting, seemingly indifferent, but rising always at the last moment to articulate some especially appropriate phrase, Cassell said that Pan-Africanism is concerned with the lot of persons of African origin beyond, as well as within, her borders. "I want to be generous about this matter and say that I think that in historical retrospect we shall find that the men who, from the late nineteenth and early twentieth century, have been struggling for us in Africa have also been struggling for—if you would like to confine it to race—the people of African origin all over the world." Maswanya, Deputy Organizing Secretary General of the Tanganyikan National Union, continues the theme by asking, rhetorically, just what was the motivation for the beginning of Pan-Africanism in the West Indies and the United States, if not the extant disabilities of persons of African descent in those areas. Enahoro implies that despite the continentalization of Pan-Africanism, and despite the charge of racism, the condition of Negroes of the Western Hemisphere should be an object of its concern. Raymond Pace Alexander of the Philadelphia bench, in his welcome on behalf of Mayor Dilworth, set the stage for Wachuku's culminating remarks by alluding to the powerful voice of the increased African representation in the United Nations, which may rise in behalf of the forces of "liberalism and democracy." Wachuku, betraying no sign of the diffidence he lamented in his cousins across the sea, hammered out the case for collaboration. In contrast to a frequent emphasis upon Africa's weaknesses and in a manner suggestive of the oratory of another day (leaving some of his audience happy, and others perhaps less so), he sketched the mural of African strengths: her practically untapped mineral resources, her tremendous power potential, her human resources. In a speech little inclined to indulgences, on no point was he less prone to restrain his displeasure than in his expression of Africa's concern for the condition of persons of African origin in the Americas. He pointed to the great increase in representation which Africa is to enjoy in the United Nations Assembly; and, intimating without revealing things to come, he assured his audience of the approaching sharp impact of that faction within the international arena: he said it would be a bombshell.

The unrealism of any attempt to compress the dynamics of Pan-Africanism within the logical confines of definition was apparent in the contrast between the expressed concern over the plight of Negroes in the Americas and the assertion of solidarity with the North Africans. Wallerstein of Columbia was sensitive to the contradiction: What is the role of negritude if, as Apter and Coleman and Enahoro indicate, Pan-Africanism has been continentalized? More explicitly: Is Pan-Africanism basically racial or continental? If the former, how would it embrace Algeria? If the latter, of what concern is Little Rock? Realism would again remind us of the words of Mr. Akwei, who, we recall, is personally no champion of definitions. A social force never follows with logical consistency an a priori conceptual pattern. And so with Pan-Africanism. It addresses itself primarily to the continent, but projects its concern across the Atlantic. It seeks to vindicate the human dignity of the black African in particular, but it senses and cultivates solidarity among all Africans. Pan-Africanism is broad enough to embrace both the continental and the racial concern. Enahoro expressed perhaps not only his own sentiments when he stated his apprehensions regarding the objectives of Nasserism; but numerous African speakers thereafter —including Marof of Guinea, Diop of SAC and Senegal, Maswanya of Tanganyika (to whom an Algerian speaker from the floor responded)—expressed the solidarity of black Africa with the African nations of the north, and particularly with Algeria in her long, bloody drive toward freedom.

There was a similar expression of concern over other areas of the continent where liberation is not yet in sight—primarily, of course, South Africa but also Spanish and Portuguese Africa. There was no equivocation here. If Pan-Africanism has any agreed goal, it is the liberation of the continent in its entirety. The unity of attitude here is especially significant in view of the intention in those areas of Africa "burdened," as Enahoro puts it, "with the settler problem," to establish a line against further African independence—roughly across the southern triangle of the continent. Coleman and Apter have referred to the dubious efforts of the settlers to establish federation in Southeast Africa, which would assure them of continued control. Curiously, in the earlier part of the century an essentially identical effort to make Africa safe for a white man's oligarchy was termed "Pan-Africanism" by the late Smuts and other promoters. This inverted Pan-African development, however, was an anachronism, and was shortlived.

The delegates to Philadelphia were not unreasonable; none made the assertion, heard in recent years in the crescent to the north, that because of the long duration of the Moorish conquest the line of African advance should again embrace Cordova. Nor, on the other hand, did sympathy for the plight of the South African or Rhodesian settler or appreciation for his seniority on the job lead to any expression of support for his special privileges. The African members of the Philadelphia conference, and even the American professors, considered the liberation of South Africa and the other colonial areas as a necessary task of the Pan-African movement. Cassell of the All Africa Peoples Steering Committee, and Mphahlele, South African refugee from the infamous treason trials, were among others who sought condemnation of the inhumanity to which the South African government has descended in its official policy for treatment of the African people. It will loom as a signal failure of the West (which, after all, holds the power) if it proves unable to develop a *modus operandi* for the relinquishment of her special prerogatives in the difficult and explosive settler areas without such violence as that which erupted in Kenya, in Algeria, in the Union of South Africa, and in the Congo.

There was remarkably little controversy over the East-West issue; from the panel discussions, it would appear that the cold war constitutes no serious threat to the unity of the Pan-African movement. The African position in that war is neutralism, and African leaders appear to be firm in their refusal to allow that controversy to divide them. Wachuku appears to state the case when he says, as we have noted: "We are Africans first." There does develop, however, a brief dialogue on this issue, as on some others, between Enahoro of Nigeria and Akwei of Ghana. Enahoro agrees that Nigeria preferred not to align herself with either of the two great world powers, but cannot admit neutrality where the fundamental issues of liberty of the individual and the rule of law are at stake. In essence, certain fundamental decisions must be made about the nature of the political state, and Nigeria cannot enter into any type of federation or union that would place these basic civil guarantees in jeopardy. As with definitions, Akwei cautions against the temptation to make unnecessary "fundamental decisions." Africa is in need of all the friends she can win, he urges, and it scarcely serves her true interest to make gratuitous pronouncements upon controversial issues which are the subject of contention among those who might otherwise come to her aid.

Zinsou of Dahomey, although on a different level than that of Enahoro, urges the necessity of a basic preliminary choice. While abstracting the cold war, Zinsou strongly affirms that socialism, which Coleman and Apter designate as one of the major intellectual currents in the Pan-African movement, is the only hope for an Africa that cannot afford the long unencumbered trek of Western free enterprise toward industrialization. He reminds his audience that he has recommended socialism, not a Marxist state; Africa has its own kind of socialism in the solidarity of the traditional African society. Cassell observes that the new African nations are generally influenced by and associated with the liberal democracies of the West, but that it is nevertheless difficult to comprehend how the West, and the United States in particular, could remain silent on the oppression of the African people in the still unliberated areas. Professor Apter suggests that perhaps the African leadership is not so monolithic vis-à-vis the cold war issue as it may diplomatically appear. He throws what some consider to be his own bombshell by arguing that competition in Africa between East and West might be a good thing for Africa; he chides the United States for being in favor of it only when we are certain to win.

In retrospect, we may observe that a strong sense of rivalry exists between Nigeria and Ghana. If any strong common effort is to develop in West Africa, it will depend in great measure upon these two nations and their ability to accommodate their differences. It will be necessary to find some formula—some ingenious federal formula—giving proper weight on the one hand to Ghana's pioneer role and relative economic security afforded by her natural wealth, and on the other hand—this is without doubt ultimately more important—to Nigeria's position as the colossus of the West African hegemony. Cassell is correct; it is impossible to impose a United States of America upon Africa. But, as Nkrumah has recently said, Africa must find some means of integrating her efforts, or she will disintegrate.

SAMUEL W. ALLEN

August 29, 1960

I BACKGROUNDS

AIMS, ACCOMPLISHMENTS, AND A KEYNOTE

STATEMENT BY DR. JEAN PRICE-MARS
President, Société Africaine de Culture

To YOU of the American Society of African Culture I bring the fraternal best wishes of the Société Africaine de Culture, which in our twentieth century is the source and point of departure for spiritual Pan-Africanism.

It was in 1956, was it not, that our friends of *Présence Africaine* (whose tireless and indispensable center of attraction, Alioune Diop, is with us today) called together Negro artists and writers from every corner of the world to discuss the various aspects of their problems. And was it not during that congress at the Sorbonne that we decided, among so many other things, to form groups everywhere in the Negro community with the mission of explaining to the world the value and originality of our culture?

And it was this movement that gave birth to AMSAC, whose growth, influence, and success are a cause of pride and joy for your members as well as for yourselves, gentlemen of the board of directors —and also for all of us who are committed to the pursuit of the same ideal of the grandeur of Negro and African culture.

How we would like to see the entire Negro community of the American continent and of the Caribbean, as well as that of the African continent itself, become inflamed with the same creative enthusiasm and develop movements such as ours! How we would like to join their discussion of the problems involved in their social, political, and economic existence!

It is evident from an examination of the history of the Negro in America—a minority so often threatened, so gravely harassed in the attainment of your most legitimate aspirations as well as in the simple enjoyment of the rights of man (though these same rights are nevertheless guaranteed by the federal Constitution)—that only in a perpetual atmosphere of bitter struggle, in an unceasing battle of values, have you conquered the privilege to cultivate your intelligence.

And yet after less than a hundred years of liberty you have furnished the American community with scientists and men of letters, with scholars and artists who have enriched American civilization with their contribution of new life.

And if it were necessary to illustrate my idea with a concrete example, could I not say—after so many others—that the suffering of the Negro, his unconquerable optimism, and his natural emotional qualities have given American music a poignancy the charm and power of which is universally acknowledged?

This is because the Negro—formed originally over thousands of years under the specific conditions of an earth ablaze with light and drenched with a torrential rain from a heaven illuminated with an incomparable brilliance by intense solar rays and often streaked by terrible electric storms—this Negro has within him a soul molded by endurance, receptive to belief, and constantly open to impressions.

Even when mixed with other human varieties—a very ordinary phenomenon since the beginning of the world—the Negro is always ready to break the borrowed mold to mark his general humanity with that certain quality that distinguishes him wherever he is to be found.

Is this the reason why, despite the inadequacy of any attempt to define, despite the cultural deformations imposed by forced immigration, despite integration into Western or Eastern civilizations, despite the repudiations and the compromises of history, there is indeed a Negro culture whether we like it or not?

We bear an indelible imprint wherever we dwell—like the Israelites of prehistoric times who carried their teraphim as a sort of self-protection in their ceaseless wanderings. Wherefore, far from grieving over our condition as we did of old when the facts of history gave us good reason, now we should take pride in our race. In fact, if my premises are correct, we have serious obligations toward the masses of our fellow men.

This is why the mission we have assumed—you of AMSAC, we of SAC—is by our fraternal association to make everyone understand that we have not the slightest opposition to other cultural groups, that we are not in arms against the universality of human nature. We intend—at a moment when Africa, of old dominated by colonial conquest, is rising in defense of her right to self-determination—to proclaim the stormy vitality of the Negro among the more than a billion human beings on our planet.

This is the message we like to think we are bringing to an apprehensive world, avoid the disputes of nations at work, with the help of science and its conquests, on new arms of self-destruction. As if the destiny of man resided in this tragic dilemma: the wider the horizon of life is opened by science, the greater are the means of annihilating all human life by the diabolical mechanism of that same science.

Fortunately, there exists a fraction of humanity to which we belong; we Negroes, torn between wretchedness and hope, have no other vocation but that of living in peace with the rest of mankind—thanks to the love and the sense of brotherhood that are the cardinal virtues of the Negro.

AFTER THE STIRRING MESSAGE just delivered by our dear president, Dr. Price-Mars, in which he expressed the feelings of us all—both those of Société Africaine de Culture and, I am sure, those of AMSAC—there isn't much left for me to say except to bring you the message from the Paris Committee.

It is a message of congratulation and of gratitude. Of congratulation in that we are particularly happy about the timeliness of your choice of a theme that occupies the center of our attention at the present time: I mean the theme of African unity.

Yesterday, to be sure, our efforts were directed against racism, in favor of racial equality; our battle was for independence—in Africa and elsewhere. Today, although we must carry on more vigorously than ever, we are convinced that one battle has already been won and that all Africa will soon be independent—from the north to the south, from the east to the west.

It remains then to consider the second step: that of our security, or the conditions under which we can give the world the message of which Léopold Senghor spoke a little while ago; the message we alone can convey and which centuries of servitude, of irresponsibility, of immobility have prevented us from conveying—namely, the message that the Negro race is a brother to the other races of the world.

But this required condition of security obliges us to commence the regrouping of African territories and the unification of Africa. As is well known, Africa is the least populated of the continents; it is a land particularly filled with riches; it is the most open, the least obstructed of continents.

And thus, naturally weak, we are threatened by a Balkanization that might transform the independence of the various states, their political independence, into another form of colonization which could be worse than the preceding. Therefore, the obligation of all of us interested in the destiny of Africa is to think seriously about the problem of regrouping the country, so as to hasten the unification of the various territories of Africa. Thus possessed of the strength of our unity and sense of solidarity, we can properly appreciate our organized economic power, accurately analyze our situation in the world, and usefully intervene on the international level in the solution of the great problems facing humanity.

Congratulations, therefore, from our friends in Paris for having chosen the most timely topic possible. But also, as I said, I bear a message of gratitude because we feel, we should feel, the profound solidarity that binds the Negro community across the Atlantic to the Negroes of Africa.

Some people haven't much faith in this solidarity. I think they are wrong. As you were told just a minute ago, we Africans are particularly grateful to you Americans as well as to the West Indians for having been able, by your exploration of all the dimensions of human suffering, to give to the world a great number of poets, artists, and scholars of whom America and the entire world are obliged to take account.

And whatever honors the American Negro community is, you can be sure, a source of pride for us—just as we are pained whenever this American Negro society is affected in one of its members. When a Negro somewhere in America is lynched or is the victim of injustice, often the news reverberates throughout Africa and moving poems are written—poems of which many Americans are unfortunately unaware; poems of solidarity.

We are grateful, therefore, that we have so many great men who make up our common Pantheon. We are likewise grateful to you for having set in motion across the world certain currents of thought. Everyone knows that our very successful Pan-Africanism of today had its origin in America.

I thus take this occasion to render homage not only to the entire Negro community but also in particular to certain of its very great men. (I mention Dr. Du Bois, who a few generations ago organized a number of international congresses from which developed the basic elements of Pan-Africanism.) I say we are grateful because many of these men—your poets, novelists, thinkers—have become, as it were, classics of the Negro spirit.

There are, perhaps, certain American Negroes who are not well enough known, but your poets, your writers, and your artists are read with admiration and gratitude by many Negroes throughout the world.

Allow me in passing to render homage to our brothers of the West Indies to whom we owe so much, and perhaps in the very first place to our President, our Dean, the man we are wont to call *Uncle* in the Negro world, because he was the first many decades ago to demand recognition for the dignity of Negro culture and the first to see to it that the particular qualities of this culture were made known—and all this under very difficult conditions.

It is likewise well known that this notion of negritude which causes so much feeling in certain Western circles was born in a corner of the globe where there were many more West Indians than Africans, and that we owe this idea more particularly to the West Indian spirit— the spirit of people who have twice been uprooted and whose situation is particularly serious.

We are grateful, then, to these Negro communities of the United States and the West Indies because this negritude (about which we will have something to say later on), which is one of the marks of creations of the Negro genius and which arouses so many different feelings in the West, really deserves to be studied by the West. It will be, I believe, a source of enrichment for human culture and for the human spirit. It is the result of painful experience; it is a form of awareness conditioned by history; it is revolutionary; it is a culture in itself; it designates irreplaceable values. It is also in a sense political, or rather the spirit of a politics.

For all of us, I think, it is finally a question not simply of getting our human dignity known and recognized, but of having our conception of this dignity admitted as well. And our peoples, our own peoples, would they not be in the best position to reveal this conception by their very living of it? And how will they do this except by the daily exercise, in their own way, of the responsibilities that modern life assigns to all peoples and all individuals? How are we to teach and spread the richness of the Negro spirit (this has nothing to do with racism) unless our poor underrated people are given the responsibility for attacking with their own cultural and moral resources, their own problems and the problems of our time?

As we have been told by one of the most remarkable leaders of the modern world, Sékou Touré, the human domain, which is growing and expanding beyond the limits of the earth, could never tolerate, except under force and constraint, these special areas called "colonies" reserved for the rivalries of the "great" powers.

The situation of modern man demands that there be everywhere on earth complete solidarity and full participation in humanity's works and enterprises. But negritude cannot flow into the great sea of the universal until it is itself accepted without complexes and with pride and conviction.

THE SESSIONS of the annual conference of AMSAC are an important event which will permit Africa in this historic year of its evolution once more to present for consideration certain of its problems. By means of the important questions you plan to consider, she will be able—in your person—to analyze the sources of her strength as well as the hopes she cherishes in the various domains of Pan-Africanism: culture, politics, economics, and social organization.

It already seems certain that the year 1960 will stamp history with the mark of Africa—already 1960 has been called Africa's Year. And in fact, besides the more than nine sovereign states whose stars already glitter in the firmament of Africa, more than fifteen new nations were born or will be born this year. And their stars will be added to those of their sisters to form the grand constellation that henceforth will guide the people of Africa irresistibly toward the light.

This conference has the merit of being held at the very moment when Africa, like a giant long held captive, begins to break its chains one by one in order finally to enter the grand family of free nations as an element of concord and peace. As such, Africa intends to play to the full the important role assigned to it by the very fact of its youth and its moral, cultural, and economic potential.

The conference will have the privilege of hearing some of Africa's most qualified and alert sons—I mean both those suckled by the African motherland herself and those nourished by America and other lands. These sons of Africa will explain, with the greatest talent and authority, the most important and diverse aspects of this continent which today has the sustained attention of the entire world.

It is easy to understand why we Africans at all meetings of this importance put so much emphasis on the glorious struggle waged by our peoples, why we take the liberty—whenever and wherever we have the chance—of insisting on the importance of this struggle. As President Sékou Touré said in a message addressed to representatives of Negro culture meeting in Rome in March, 1959: "Any free and sovereign people is in a better position for the expression of its cultural values than a colonial people, deprived of all liberty, whose culture suffers the harmful consequences of its state of subjection."

Nevertheless, despite the state of servitude in which she was kept during the last few centuries and though she has not been able to develop her culture in a normal fashion, Africa has had at least the merit of preserving her culture to a great extent and even of spreading it throughout the world. This remarkable phenomenon stems not only from the African's profound identification with his culture but from his ability to continue to incarnate Africa's most original cultural values even when he is transplanted.

And now our rebirth in this domain of cultural values is developing rapidly, thanks to the positive action and the initiative of organizations such as the American Society of African Culture. Founded only three years ago, this organization has already done for Africa what the best of her sons could do for her and for her growing influence in the world. Moreover, let us not forget the decisive and tireless action of the parent organization, the Société Africaine de Culture, which since its inception has devoted itself entirely to the difficult struggle for the affirmation of the personality of Africa. We must pay homage to these numerous men throughout the world who played the important role of studying and diffusing Negro and African culture.

It is a privilege to have among us some of the most important representatives of the Société Africaine de Culture, among whom there is one we are especially happy to greet as a friend, as a brother in the good fight, as a great African: Mr. Alioune Diop.

In homage to his great contribution to the African cause, the Republic of Guinea has made him an honorary citizen of one of our most beautiful cities. The President and people of Guinea thus testified in a concrete manner to their sympathy and gratitude for the work of Alioune Diop in the Société Africaine de Culture, and therefore for the work of AMSAC. The activities of AMSAC have helped greatly to acquaint the American people with the African culture and with the aspirations of the African people.

We owe it to these successful efforts that today we can proceed to an inventory of the African heritage in areas at once so varied and so important; that we can study the main lines of its evolution and draw lessons therefrom which will be most useful in the exciting task that awaits us all.

Really, this action goes far beyond the domain of culture. For, in making Africa and her cultural heritage better known, these organizations are aiding that necessary understanding between Africa and the other countries of the world—above all the United States—which remains the only sure basis for sincere friendship and fruitful coöperation.

In reality, Africa, which has already given so much to the world and has received so much from the world (often, alas, in connection with force and constraint), desires more than ever to bring to this same world a still greater effective contribution, both material on the one hand and moral and intellectual on the other—but under the more favorable conditions henceforth provided by her regained liberty.

Ladies and gentlemen, the government and the people of Guinea, having resolutely embarked upon the process of the liberation and the unification of Africa, feel obliged to express here publicly the esteem and active sympathy that they feel for your conference and its organizers.

KEYNOTE ADDRESS

PAN-AFRICANISM: NASCENT AND MATURE

JOHN A. DAVIS

Executive Director, American Society of African Culture

IN TERMS of the rapidity of events in Africa, the American Society of African Culture (AMSAC) is a very old organization. We began in 1957—a few scant months after some five of us returned from the first International Congress of Negro Writers and Artists called by Alioune Diop and his Paris Committee of *Présence Africaine* in September of 1956. It was agreed at that original conference:

1. That an international society devoted to African culture should be formed, together with national and local organizations;
2. That such organizations should undertake to make an inventory of black African culture everywhere in the world; and
3. That all of those present would work for African freedom as a necessary prerequisite to cultural freedom and cultural contribution.

While we were present in Paris in those far-off days of September, 1956, the British announced that in the following March the Gold Coast would become free and the French announced autonomy for Togoland. The times were pregnant and exciting. Long-delayed ambitions seemed at last capable of realization. The next year, 1957, the Société Africaine de Culture was formed in Paris and AMSAC was formed in this country.

Since that year the American Society of African Culture has earnestly followed the dictates of the First International Congress of Negro Writers and Artists. We have presented to America, and to a lesser extent, to the world, the contributions of black African sculpture, dance, music, art and literature—the high culture of the African Negro as it has existed in Africa, in this country, and indeed in this hemisphere. We have done this through publications, exhibitions, demonstrations, conferences, seminars, lectures, visits, and promotions.

Our aim has been to provide an understanding of the validity of African and Negro cultural contributions in order to provide a basis for mutual respect between Americans and Africans, and indeed between Africans and other citizens of the world. Believe me, there is still a great need for this work, which in essence is the basis upon which all peace efforts must be built. Recently, according to the *New York Times*, one of our leading poets testified before Congress that Africa had no culture, and the television industry in this country has now followed the lead of the movies in making money out of the "me, Tarzan–you, Jane–plus Clever-Ape" picture formula.

But I should certainly be remiss if I failed to point out that this work with regard to the validity of African culture, as carried out by SAC and AMSAC, is also of great importance to the African nations themselves. It provides the basic qualifications for national freedom— the capacity to contribute to the culture of man, to beauty and to truth—and it provides a basis for unity among African nations, not only in the struggle for independence, but also in the more difficult task of later adjustment between new sovereign and equal African nations.

Many persons have labored diligently in AMSAC, but the main burden has fallen on the five who went to Paris in 1956: Mercer Cook, Horace Bond, James Ivy, William Fontaine, and the present speaker— and one additional person, James Theodore Harris. Our extensive work has been made possible by generous grants from devoted philanthropists, among whom you will recognize the well-known names of Lehman, McCloskey, Waddell, Dowling, Benton, Beaumont, Rosenthal, Burroughs, Bynoe, Cabot, and Dodge. These men have followed the great American tradition of making their private wealth available for national and international peace and goodwill—a tradition to which Andrew Carnegie gave so much.

I would be misleading indeed if I did not confess that those of us who labor in AMSAC are mindful also of the political implications of our work. If we fail, the world has taken one more step toward disorder and destruction. It is for this reason, especially, that AMSAC has always concerned itself with the study of African culture in the sense of the social scientist—with the study of society, and hence with the economic, social, and political problems of Africa. The image of the new African states in the eyes of America and the world will also depend on their success as states when judged against the social, political, and economic factors they must face. All of AMSAC's annual conferences have examined such problems.

The present conference, therefore, is in truth a blending of AMSAC interests. It examines a major factor in the political development of Africa in terms of political, economic, social, and cultural imperatives and unities.

The interest of the American Negro in Pan-Africanism is of long standing. It goes back to 1900 when Du Bois involved himself with the First Congress of persons of black African descent, called in London by Sylvester Williams. Pride in racial origins, similarity of caste status between African Negroes and American Negroes, and the desire for a free and respected homeland—a desire shared with other Americans in the past—have all made the American Negro an ardent advocate of black Pan-Africanism as a springboard for African independence. It was largely William E. Burghardt Du Bois, Rayford W. Logan, and Walter White who sparked collectively the Pan-African movement from the beginning of World War I to 1924. The first Pan-African Congress called by Du Bois in Paris, February 19–21, 1919, certainly had some influence on the establishment of the mandates system under the League of Nations. Although American Negro leadership in the Pan-African movement waned after 1927, at a conference in 1942 in this very room the current speaker, Kwame Nkrumah—then a graduate student and instructor at this university—Justice William H. Hastie, and Congressman Adam Clayton Powell all noted that should success attend America's arms in the then raging conflict, the resultant political situation would mean the inevitable freedom of all those living under a caste system within or outside of colonialism.

In view of the past, it is then altogether fitting that the Third Annual Conference of AMSAC should examine Pan-Africanism in the Africa of today. Pan-Africanism's major contribution has been to forge African solidarity in the demand for independence for all African nations and has therefore been the motivating force in the continuing appearance of new states. It is, however, precisely the emergence of new states that places Pan-Africanism in crisis by presenting it with its severest task. The course of history makes plain that the virus of nationalism can destroy international unity and subvert pan-movements to its purposes.

It is our fervent hope that the new nations of Africa will not repeat the sorry history of the national state system that in Europe and in Asia has brought so much grief, disorder, and slaughter to mankind. Yet the problems are already upon us: national states that are too small and too poor in natural endowment to offer their people the material advantages of independence and free government or to maintain their independence against outside influence; irredentist quarrels over populations unredeemed—quarrels that frighten those who remember Lombardy and Venetia, Alsace-Lorraine, the Polish Corridor, and the Sudetenland through the whole weary history of Europe in the later part of the nineteenth century and during the first half of this century; quarrels over water resources and the movement of peoples; and restrictions on the movement of goods and persons.

What of the national state system tomorrow in Africa? Are there to be tariff wars and dumping and all the rest? In some new economic depression, will autarchy raise its head? Are we soon to face in Africa the old aggressive nationalism and the fear of aggression with consequent demands for offensive-defensive alliances, the quest for natural military boundaries, the never-ending search for security through a chain of military bases? Is Pan-Africanism to be subverted to the national interests of a single state, as was the racist Pan-Slavism of old Russia or the racist Pan-Asianism of old Japan? Will Pan-Africanism be politically subordinated to Asian interests or economically subordinated to European interests? If the national state system in Africa is to develop all of these characteristics, all of these ancient discouraging characteristics, then the freeing of Africa may well have increased rather than reduced the threat of general war.

There is little time left for us in which to head off the formation of the traditional state system in Africa. A geographic area with no conceivable basis for unity except colonial happenstance or the presence of a river or a mountain range, will quickly develop a sense of mission once it becomes a national state. In this country, North Dakota and South Dakota were the creations of a surveyor's line running east and west, but they are semi-sovereign states of these United States today. Patriotism, common rights and privileges of citizenship, common dangers and enemies, common security, public benefits, and the development of a common literature and language, can all quickly create a state where none was before.

On the brighter side, the outlook for the national state system in Africa is certainly not without hope if we act now. There are strong forces in Pan-Africanism today which give us a chance for the orderly development of a national state system in Africa. These may be noted as follows:

1. The tendency to form larger state units through annexation, federation, executive coördination, and the pre-independence association of territories.
2. The present tendency of African states to form all-African functional organizations for political or economic reasons with and without international sponsorship.
3. The tendency to form all-African nongovernmental organizations for all-African political purposes.
4. The continual fear of a new imperialism from the old colonial areas, the United States, and Russia.
5. The presence of a common enemy in the Union of South Africa, if not in French Algeria.
6. Ethnic solidarity resulting, in part, from oppression in the past on ethnic grounds.
7. The resurgence of a belief in African culture, in African social ideas, sculpture, dance, music, and literature—the belief, in short, in a common cultural mission for all of Africa.
8. The world climate of internationalism.
9. The chance to mold educational institutions so that they will train for a mature Pan-Africanism.

With such hopes in mind, it is our purpose in this conference to examine all the complex problems that a mature Pan-Africanism must resolve, even while nascent Pan-Africanism carries on to its finish the war for independence. Pan-Africanism, emergent and mature, now has the twofold task of providing on the one hand the basis for prosperity and order in the new African national state system, and on the other hand of guiding the world role of Africa so that its impact will strengthen the cause of world peace.

The tasks of the new African statesmen are formidable, and they must operate from the base of fragile societies. Yet they and we together dare not fail, for the blast of nuclear fusion blows hot on our necks as we hurry along the path of human reconciliation. Man has discovered the eternal sources of energy, and in so doing has unlocked a portion of the infinite truth of the material world. He explores God's universe with thundering rockets. Yet with truth and knowledge almost in his grasp, with literally new worlds to know in God's universe, man is on the brink of destroying this world and himself, for he fails to understand and to control himself. The beauty of God's grace escapes him. On this note, I close and commend you at this Third Annual Conference of AMSAC to the proper study of mankind—man: man, the citizen of Africa; man, the citizen of the world.

II PAN-AFRICANISM

THE HISTORICAL ASPECTS OF PAN-AFRICANISM, 1900–1945

RAYFORD W. LOGAN

Department of History, Howard University

THE HISTORICAL ASPECTS of Pan-Africanism, 1900–1945, reveal fascinating reciprocal relationships between ideas and events, men and events. The more important ideas and men will emerge in their appropriate places in this paper. At the outset, however, I emphasize the two main events that enabled these men to crystallize, publicize, and, in some measure, gain increasing support for their ideas. These events were World War I and World War II. Without these acts of supreme folly on the part of the "superior races," it is unlikely that in 1945 Pan-Africanism would have laid the foundations that made possible its mighty leap forward. By Pan-Africanism I mean self-government or independence by African nations south of the Sahara.[1] The role of certain African and Western institutions in promoting this Pan-Africanism must be adumbrated. A "United States of Africa" was so nebulous as late as 1945 that it did not deserve serious consideration.

William Edward Burghardt Du Bois oriented modern Pan-Africanism to mean the self-government or independence of the "black" peoples of Africa. H. Sylvester Williams, a young West Indian barrister in London, did not have these aims in mind when he conceived the idea for the Pan-African Conference that met there during July 23–25, 1900.[2] Two of his aims were to bring peoples of African descent

---

[1] The nomenclature for the peoples of Africa is very confusing. The concept of "races" is, of course, largely unscientific. Many so-called "black" peoples are blue-black, black, dark-brown, brown, copper-brown, light-brown, colored, and "white." In this paper, Africans denotes non-Europeans and non-Asians. "Africa south of the Sahara" is a misnomer, for the Sahara now extends to the Niger-Nigeria border. See, especially, UNESCO, *The Race Concept: Results of an Inquiry* (Paris: UNESCO, 1951); Lord Hailey, *An African Survey, Revised, 1956* (Oxford, 1957), pp. 1049–1050.

[2] One must speculate why Williams conceived the idea of a Pan-African congress and why he did so in 1900. The beginning of a century has often generated a *mystique* that foresees new blessings for mankind. For example, Booker T. Washington, N. B. Wood, and Mrs. Fannie Barrier Williams (she, incidentally, attended the London conference) wrote in 1900 *A New Negro for a New Century*. Perhaps a more rational explanation for Williams's proposal was the Anglo-Boer War.

throughout the world into closer touch with each other and to establish more friendly relations between the Caucasian and African races. That he did not envision self-government or independence in Africa is evident in his third aim; namely, "to start a movement looking forward to the securing to all African races living in *civilized countries* their full rights and to promote their business interests." [3]

A memorial addressed by the conference to Queen Victoria deplored the plight of Africans in South Africa, especially the compulsory labor, segregation, the curfew, the passes, and the restrictions on their right to vote. The Queen's Secretary replied that she had commanded the Colonial Secretary, Joseph Chamberlain, to assure the members of the conference that, "in settling the lines on which the administration of the conquered [South African] territories is to be conducted, Her Majesty's Government will not overlook the interests and welf∍re of the native races." [4]

But Du Bois, Chairman of the Committee on Address to the Nations of the World, transformed Williams' aims to mean self-government or independence. In language that he repeated three years later in his classic *Souls of Black Folk*, he warned: "The problem of the Twentieth Century is the problem of the color line." [5] He then urged:

> Let the British Nation, the first modern champion of Negro freedom, hasten to crown the work of Wilberforce, and Clarkson, and Buxton, and Sharpe [*sic*], Bishop Colenso, and Livingstone, and give, as soon as practicable, the rights of responsible government[6] to the Black Colonies of Africa and the West Indies.

Du Bois said nothing about the Spanish and Portuguese colonies, and he did not explicitly demand "responsible government" for the German and French colonies. He did propose, however, that the Congo Free State should become "a great central Negro state of the world." He then advocated respect for "the integrity and independence of the free Negro states of Abyssinia, Liberia, Haiti, etc." He also expressed

[3] Bishop Alexander Walters, *My Life and Work* (New York: Revell, 1917), pp. 251–253. Italics mine.
[4] *Ibid.*, p. 257.
[5] W. E. B. Du Bois, *The Souls of Black Folk*. Chicago: McClurg, 1903.
[6] Evidence is lacking that "responsible government" meant a cabinet that held office as long as it had a majority in a legislature elected by the people. But there is little doubt that in his mind "responsible government" meant self-government or independence.

the hope that the inhabitants of these states, "the independent tribes of Africa, the Negroes of the West Indies and America, and the black subjects of all nations [would] take courage, strive ceaselessly, and fight bravely, that they may prove to the World their incontestable right to be counted among the great brotherhood of mankind." [7] Thus, while Du Bois made a plea for the inclusion of Negroes in all parts of the world in "the great brotherhood of mankind," he specifically urged self-government or independence for at least some Africans. Hence, in my judgment, this Address to the Nations of the World includes the first modern published exposition of my definition of Pan-Africanism.

To be sure, the world paid little heed to his address. Du Bois has written that the 1900 conference put the word "'Pan-African' in the dictionaries for the first time." But the concept had no deep roots in Africa itself; the movement and the idea died for a generation. [8] Du Bois turned to more urgent tasks: his controversy with Booker T. Washington, the Niagara Movement, teaching and writing—especially the publication of his still indispensable Atlanta University Studies. In 1910 he became editor of *The Crisis* and director of publications and research for the National Association for the Advancement of Colored People. Bishop Walters, who had presided at the 1900 conference, devoted most of his attention to the Afro-American Council and the activities of the African Methodist Episcopal Zion Church. "A thrill of joy possessed" him when in 1910 he stepped on the shores of his "fatherland" in Africa. But his two main concerns were whether Islam or Christianity would conquer Africa and whether a "Negro Cecil Rhodes" would emerge to reap "untold wealth and glory in Africa." In 1915 he wondered whether China, India, and Africa would follow the rising nation of Japan. But he left it to God to answer the question. [9]

In the history of ideas, it is frequently difficult to determine origins, changes, continuity, discontinuity and revival, and influence. Du Bois formulated his concept of the world-wide aspects of race as early as 1892 while he was a student at the University of Berlin. Von Treitschke, Sering, Weber, and Schmoller made him "see the race problem

---

[7] Walters, *op. cit.*, pp. 257–260.
[8] Du Bois, *The World and Africa* (New York: Viking, 1947), pp. 7–8.
[9] Walters, *op. cit.*, pp. 151–172, 239.

in America, the problem of the peoples of Africa and Asia and the political development of Europe as one." [10] His published works,[11] do not, however, make clear the extent to which this concept germinated the aims he expressed in his Address to the Nations of the World. In 1906 the eminent American anthropologist Franz Boas gave a new dimension to Du Bois's thinking; namely, the history of the black kingdoms in Africa south of the Sahara.[12] But at the Races Congress in London in July, 1911, Du Bois appears not to have developed either the theme of the world-wide aspects of race or the history of the black African kingdoms.[13] On the other hand, an ominous event occurred on the eve of the Races Congress which revealed dramatically the importance of Africa in world affairs: the German cruiser *Panther* arrived at Agadir, Morocco, on the west coast of Africa. Lloyd George in his famous Mansion House speech of July 21, 1911, in effect warned that Germany could not presume to rearrange the map of Africa without consulting England.[14] Agadir drew Britain and France closer together and transmuted the Entente Cordiale into a virtual military and naval alliance. Agadir was thus an important African prelude to World War I.

That the Races Congress did not receive serious consideration is evident in the tone of an anonymous article in the London *Times* on "Science and the Milennium." This was a masterpiece of spoofing, even for the *Times*, which has had few peers in the art of destruction by ridicule. One gem stated: "It has slowly been borne in on me that the old friends I meet (always with the surprised 'What, you here?' of Congress *rencontres*) have some unusual idiosyncracy; one subsists entirely on cold cucumbers; another is founder of a secret society for regenerating the world by a new method on theosophic principles; . . . There are men with long hair, women with short hair; women very small, or praeternaturally tall; women with rings on the wrong fin-

[10] Du Bois, *Dusk of Dawn: An Essay Toward an Autobiography of a Race Concept* (New York: Harcourt, Brace, 1940), pp. 32, 47.

[11] After the indictment and acquittal in 1951 of Dr. Du Bois on the charge of failure to register as the "principal" of a foreign government, Soviet Russia, he closed his private papers to investigators. Francis Broderick had gone only as far as 1910. See Broderick, *W. E. B. Du Bois [sic], Negro Leader in a Time of Crisis* (Stanford: Stanford University Press, 1959), p. vii.

[12] Du Bois, *Black Folk Then and Now* (New York: Holt, 1939), p. vii.

[13] Du Bois, *The World and Africa*, p. 3.

[14] Viscount Grey of Fallodon, *Twenty-Five Years, 1892–1916* (New York: Stokes, 1925), pp. 216–217.

gers."[15] Reports in the London *Times* also indicate that no speaker discussed Pan-Africanism: Du Bois's address had the title "The Negro Race in the United States."[16] But the outbreak of World War I led to a restatement of his Pan-Africanism.

Du Bois's *Atlantic Monthly* article "The African Roots of War"[17] emphasized particularly the economic aspects of imperialism, both with respect to the war then raging and to possible future wars. This was all the more true because, he prophesied, "Africa is the Land of the Twentieth Century." Moreover, if a lasting peace were to be achieved, "we must extend the democratic ideal to the yellow, brown and black peoples." Africans must have land, and they must be trained in modern civilization. "Lastly, the principle of home rule must extend to groups, nations, and races. The ruling of one people for another people's whim or gain must stop. . . . The domination of one people by another without the other's consent, be the subject people black or white, must stop." Du Bois did not use the words Pan-African or Pan-Africanism, but he developed more clearly than he had since 1900 the concept of self-government or independence for black Africans. Thus, World War I not only furthered the movement; it also revived Du Bois's quest for African freedom, and it gave him the opportunity to reach, through one of the most influential magazines in the United States, an audience that had probably not heard of the Pan-African Conference or the Races Congress.

In the same year, 1915, Du Bois's little book *The Negro* popularized the history of the African kingdoms south of the Sahara, and Dr. Carter G. Woodson founded the Association for the Study of Negro Life and History. Two of the four articles and one of the four book reviews in the first issue of the *Journal of Negro History* (January, 1916) dealt with Africa. Dr. Woodson, until his death in 1950, insisted through the *Journal*, the *Bulletin of Negro History*, the annual meetings of the Association, and Negro History Week upon a revision of African historiography.[18] His book *The African Background Outlined* (1936)

---

[15] *The Times* (London), July 28, 1911, p. 8a.
[16] *Ibid.*, pp. 29, 4f.
[17] Du Bois, "The African Roots of War," *Atlantic Monthly*, May, 1915.
[18] Ulysses Lee, "The ASNLH, *The Journal of Negro History* and American Scholarly Interest in Africa," in *Africa Seen by American Negroes* (Dijon: Bourguignonne, 1958), pp. 401–418. This is a special issue of *Présence Africaine*, under the auspices of AMSAC.

gave an excellent summary of the African kingdoms and included an excellent bibliography. Probably more than any other one man, Dr. Woodson inspired among Negro Americans pride in their African past and a desire to know more about it. During World War I, William Leo Hansberry was beginning his studies of ancient and medieval African history, which he taught to a large number of students, notably at Howard University. Melville J. Herskovits began his teaching of anthropology in 1924 and made his first trip to Africa in 1931.

Thus, Negro and other Americans became increasingly interested in Africa at the same time that the colonial powers were beginning to dig the grave of imperialism. My major conclusion that these gravediggers aided Pan-Africanism is, of course, not original. It is related to the well-known thesis of Professor Samuel Flagg Bemis that Europe's distress was America's gain. The sale of Louisiana by Napoleon Bonaparte to the United States is a classic example[19]; another is the role of this distress in the winning of Haitian independence.[20] The converse has also been true: during the American Civil War, Britain and France supported the Confederacy (but not because of enthusiasm for slavery), and Spain temporarily destroyed the independence of the Dominican Republic. Sumner Welles was to say on May 31, 1943, that the colonial powers had been so weakened and impoverished by two world wars that they were no longer able to hold their colonial peoples in subjection.

Du Bois, who at a Washington conference of Negro organizations in May, 1917, had further developed the African roots of the war and the relationship between permanent peace and the principle of the consent of the governed for Africans as well as other peoples, convened the First Pan-African Congress in Paris, February 19–21, 1919. I do not accept the contention of Du Bois that the establishment of the Mandates Commission resulted from this congress.[21] George Louis Beer, Chief of the Colonial Division of the American Delegation to Negotiate Peace in 1919, had prepared as early as 1917 a memorandum

[19] Samuel Flagg Bemis, *A Diplomatic History of the United States* (rev. ed.; New York: Holt, 1942), pp. 64, 94–95, 137.
[20] Rayford W. Logan, *The Diplomatic Relations of the United States with Haiti, 1776–1891* (Chapel Hill: North Carolina, 1941), pp. 112–151.
[21] Du Bois, *Dusk of Dawn*, p. 248; *The World and Africa*, p. 11.

on the subject which greatly influenced the thinking of Woodrow Wilson, the real architect of the mandate system.[22] More important than this alleged role of the First Pan-African Congress in the establishment of the mandate system was one of the resolutions adopted by this congress. It stated:

The natives of Africa must have the right to participate in the government as fast as their development permits, in conformity with the principle that the government exists for the natives, and not the natives for the government. They shall at once be allowed to participate in local and tribal government, according to ancient usage, and this participation shall gradually extend, as education and experience proceed, to the higher offices of the State; to the end that, in time, Africa shall be ruled by the consent of the Africans.[23]

The proposal for self-government or independence was premature, since the colonial powers were not prepared to grant it and since the concept of the inherent inferiority of the Negro still prevailed. George Louis Beer, for example, wrote in a memorandum that "the negro race has hitherto shown no capacity for progressive development except under the tutelage of other peoples." Nonetheless, he did not fully agree with "many scientists" that "it is an established physiological fact that the cranial sutures of the negro close at an early age, which condition, it has been contended, prevents organic intellectual progress thereafter." [24] Wilson believed in the inherent inferiority of the Negro.[25] His principal coadjutor in the establishment of the mandate system, Jan Smuts, held even stronger convictions than did Wilson; Smuts was to say in Town Hall, New York City, on January 9, 1930, that "the Negro is the most patient of all, next to the ass." [26]

The mandate system mirrored the views of Beer, Smuts, and Wilson. Article XXII clearly provided for the independence of the former Turkish communities, which, apparently, were presumed to be white.

[22] George Louis Beer, *African Questions at the Paris Peace Conference* (New York: Macmillan, 1923), pp. xix, 57–67; Logan, *The African Mandates in World Politics* (Washington: Public Affairs Press, 1948), pp. 1–19.
[23] Du Bois, *The World and Africa*, pp. 11–12.
[24] Beer, *op. cit.*, p. 179.
[25] See especially the Wilson Papers in the Library of Congress.
[26] *New York Times,* Jan. 10, 1930, p. 2.

But it is impossible to find in the provisions pertaining to the former German colonies in Africa an implied recognition of the possibility that they would one day be able to stand alone. In 1945 all the former Turkish communities that had been placed under the mandate system, with the exception of Palestine, were independent. In 1945 not one of the former German colonies in Africa had gained self-government or independence; indeed, no colony in Africa had gained independence.

One is therefore forced to conclude that the Pan-African congresses after World War I had failed to achieve the aim of self-government or independence for black Africa. The Second met in London, Brussels, and Paris in 1921; the Third in London and Lisbon in 1923; the Fourth in New York in 1927. Like the London Pan-African Conference of 1900, these had no deep roots in Africa. Blaise Diagne, black Deputy from Senegal who had helped to prevent Wilson from impeding the First Congress and who presided at the Paris session in 1921, declared on that occasion: "I am a Frenchman first, and a Negro afterward." The Pan-African Association, which met periodically in Paris during 1921–1924, had for its officers three black Frenchmen and one Negro American, the writer of this paper.[27] Nor did the movement have deep roots in the United States; although the NAACP contributed to the costs of the First and Second congresses—it established a fund of 3,000 dollars for the Second[28]—thereafter its organizational support dwindled. The first postwar depression reduced the revenues of the NAACP; the circulation of The Crisis declined; the NAACP devoted most of its resources to an attempt to obtain the passage of an anti-lynching bill.[29] The Fourth Congress resulted in large part from the determined interest of a group of women headed by Mrs. Addie W. Hunton and Mrs. Addie Dickerson.

Meanwhile, the interest of Dr. Du Bois waned. Following the Third Congress of 1923, he met in Sierra Leone members and promoters of the Congress of West Africa, founded by the Gold Coast lawyer and elder statesman Joseph Casely Hayford in 1920. But there seems to have been little rapport between the Pan-African Congress and the Congress of West Africa. The latter became inactive after Hayford's

[27] Diagne's statement and the observation about the officers of the Pan-African Association are based upon the writer's reminiscences.
[28] James W. Ivy, "Traditional NAACP Interest in Africa (as Reflected in the pages of The Crisis)," in Africa Seen by American Negroes, pp. 229–246.
[29] Du Bois, Dusk of Dawn, pp. 265–266, 275.

death in 1930.[30] The opposition of the French government to a Fifth Congress in Tunisia in 1929,[31] followed by the stock-market crash later in the year, virtually silenced the Pan-African movement in the United States. Dr. Du Bois had asked me to serve, in his place, as Executive Secretary in Tunisia. Even before his resignation from the NAACP in 1934, he had become professor of sociology at Atlanta University. There I repeatedly urged him, in vain, to call a new Pan-African congress. In 1935 appeared his *Black Reconstruction in America*. From 1931 to 1945, he was editor and co-editor of a projected encyclopædia of the Negro, which eventuated only in a *Preparatory Volume* of proposed topics and bibliographies. His strained application of Marxism to reconstruction made him increasingly interested in the Soviet Union.

One of the most important obstacles to Du Bois's Pan-Africanism resulted from the meteoric rise of Marcus Garvey, who arrived in the United States on March 23, 1916. The death of Booker T. Washington on November 14, 1915, the migration of large numbers of Negroes and whites from the south to the north, and the bitterness of Negro soldiers who had served in France provided Garvey with the opportunity to use his demagogic power for the exploitation of black chauvinism. But his Back-to-Africa Movement foundered on the secular opposition of Negro Americans to seek a solution of their problems by flight to Africa; on the divisiveness that he fomented between black and light Negroes; on his acceptance of support by leaders of the Ku Klux Klan; and on his conviction in 1924 for alleged perjury and income-tax evasion.[32]

Above all, Garvey's Back-to-Africa Movement encountered the opposition of colonial powers and the United States. When Dr. Du Bois asked me to organize the Paris meeting of the Pan-African Congress in 1923, I went to the summer home of Blaise Diagne near Saint Nazaire and persuaded him to return to Paris to preside at the meeting. But a French newspaper reporter gave the *coup de grâce* to that session by writing that Du Bois was a disciple of Garvey! [33] When

[30] *Ibid.*, pp. 278, 279; George Padmore, *Pan-Africanism or Communism: The Coming Struggle for Africa* (London: Dobson, 1946), pp. 128, 129, 142, 173.
[31] Du Bois, *Dusk of Dawn*, pp. 279–280.
[32] Edmund David Cronon, *Black Moses: The Story of Marcus Garvey and the Universal Negro Improvement Association*. Madison: Wisconsin, 1955.
[33] Personal recollections of the author.

Garvey in 1924 tried to establish a colony of Negro Americans in Liberia, Ernest Lyon, the Liberian Consul General in Baltimore, declared: "I am authorized to say that no person or persons leaving the United States under the auspices of the Garvey movement will be allowed to land in the Republic of Liberia." Garvey accused Du Bois, whom he derided as "'purely and simply a white man's nigger,'" of sabotaging the work of the Garvey movement.[34] Du Bois, in turn, charged that Garvey was "'either a lunatic or a traitor.'"[35]

Garvey's most important specific contribution to Pan-Africanism was probably his influence on the thinking of Kwame Nkrumah. Nkrumah has given credit to Dr. Kwegyir Aggrey, assistant vice-principal and the first African member of the staff of Prince of Wales College, for first arousing in him the idea of African nationalism. But even then, about 1926, Nkrumah rejected Aggrey's famous analogy about the need to play both black and white keys on a piano in order to achieve harmony. Nkrumah, influenced by Garvey, chose to play only on the black keys: he accepted Garvey's principle of "Africa for the Africans." On the other hand, it was Nkrumah's great admiration for Aggrey that first led him to think of continuing his studies in the United States. The white-man's folly also contributed to his desire to play his part in bringing about the downfall of colonialism. While Nkrumah was en route to the United States in 1935, headlines in London newspapers about Mussolini's invasion of Ethiopia spurred this ambition,[36] which Italian brutalities probably enflamed.

In the United States, Nkrumah not only pursued his studies at Lincoln University and at the University of Pennsylvania; he also fortified his own thinking on Pan-Africanism and measurably increased interest in the movement. He helped to organize an African studies section at the University of Pennsylvania and the African Students' Association of America and Canada. The association published a newspaper, the *African Interpreter*, in order to revive a spirit of African nationalism. The philosophy of Marx and of Lenin impressed him as being best adaptable to the solution of colonialism. But it was *The Philosophy and Opinions of Marcus Garvey*, published in 1926,

[34] Cronon, *op. cit.*, pp. 128–131, 190.
[35] Broderick, *op. cit.*, p. 190.
[36] Kwame Nkrumah, *Ghana: The Autobiography of Kwame Nkrumah* (Edinburgh, Toronto, and New York: Nelson, 1957), pp. 17, 29.

which most inspired his enthusiasm for "Africa for the Africans." [37] When one reads today this balderdash, based in part upon Garvey's opposition to "social equality" and upon his fears that the Negro in the United States would not be able to ameliorate his plight, one wonders that Nkrumah could have accepted Garvey's aberrations as fully as he did. Nkrumah evidently brushed aside these aberrations because they were necessary to Garvey's fixed idea of "Back to Africa."

During his sojourn in the United States, Nkrumah supported the concept of West African unity as a necessary prelude to a Pan-African movement for the liberation of the whole African continent.[38] In a debate at Howard University on February 10, 1943, he derided the mandate system and demanded the independence of all Africa at the end of the war. I derided the belief that all Africa would become independent at the end of the war, and I continued, along with Raymond Leslie Buell and Clement Attlee, to ride the hobbyhorse of the mandate system for all African colonies. Nkrumah and I were partly right and partly wrong. His own Gold Coast did not become independent until March 6, 1957 (one hundred years to the day, incidentally, after the Dred Scott decision). The trusteeship system of the United Nations left it to each responsible power whether it would place any of its mandates, territories "detached from the enemy," or any of its own colonies under trusteeship. At the Fifth Pan-African Congress in Manchester, England (October, 1945), Nkrumah derided not only mandates and trusteeships but also "partnerships." [39] I leave it to other historians and political scientists to determine whether the trusteeship system furthered independence or self-government.

I have selected a relatively unknown factor in the Pan-Africanism of Nnamdi Azikiwe, whose studies at Lincoln University in Pennsylvania and at Howard University contributed to the crystallization of his views on Pan-Africanism. On the eve of World War II, Azikiwe expressed his "love" for British institutions. But England's apparent desire to appease Hitler by dangling before him the bait of the return of some of the former German colonies in Africa disillusioned him. This disillusionment increased as the result of rumors that England might even cede Nigeria to Hitler. Even though the details of these

[37] *Ibid.*, p. 33–34, 43–45.
[38] *Ibid.*, p. 44.
[39] Padmore, *op. cit.*, pp. 163–164.

Hitler-Chamberlain negotiations were not fully known to Azikiwe, and the negotiations terminated by Hitler's invasion of Poland, Azikiwe remained suspicious of Chamberlain. "Zik" also feared possible aggression by Mussolini against African territories, especially after Il Duce's invasion of Ethiopia. Thus, Zik's Pan-Africanism stemmed in considerable measure from his fear that European diplomats might use a new "rape of Africa" to maintain or restore peace in Europe.[40]

Azikiwe, like many other African nationalists, also based his Pan-Africanism upon the first part of the third clause of the Atlantic Charter of August 24, 1941, which stated: "They [Roosevelt and Churchill] respect the right of all peoples to choose the form of government under which they live."[41] Even though Churchill later made a statement in the House of Commons which seemed to exclude British colonial peoples from the ideals of the Charter,[42] African nationalists and their supporters insisted that "all" meant all. There comes to mind almost instantly the insistence by Negro Americans that when slaveholders signed the Declaration of Independence, they, however inconsistently, must have included Negroes in the statement that "all men are created equal."

The English Magna Carta and Bill of Rights; the Declaration of Independence; the Thirteenth, Fourteenth, and Fifteenth Amendments; *Liberté, Égalité, Fraternité*—these and other great libertarian principles have influenced in varying degrees the ideas of African nationalists. Many of them also absorbed some of their ideas, directly or indirectly, from Greek and Roman philosophers; Bodin, Descartes, Voltaire, and Rousseau; Milton, Locke, Hobbes, Burke, and Mill; Marx; Jefferson, and Lincoln. Nehru, Eric Williams, Norman Manley, and Sir Grantley Adams are all Oxford men, as was the late S. W. R. D. Bandaranaike. Habib Bourguiba is a Paris-trained lawyer. Nkrumah, Azikiwe, George Padmore, Jones Quartey, and other Africans studied in the United States, and Nkrumah studied also in England. Obafemi

[40] Babalola Cole has made a perceptive analysis of these fears in "Analysis of the West African *Pilot* from November 23, 1937 to December 31, 1941"; unpublished M.A. thesis, Howard University, 1957. For a detailed analysis of Chamberlain's negotiations with Hitler and an account of a proposal for the redistribution of African colonies after Hitler's invasion of Poland, see Logan, *African Mandates*, pp. 150–204.

[41] Padmore, *op. cit.*, pp. 152–153.

[42] T. Walter Wallbank, *Contemporary Africa: Continent in Transition* (Princeton: Van Nostrand, 1956), pp. 126–127.

Awolowo likewise pursued studies in England and became a barrister; Kojo Botsio took his B.A. at Oxford, J. B. Danquah holds a doctorate from Cambridge, and K. A. Busia, one from Oxford. Jomo Kenyatta studied in London and Tom Mboya spent a year at Oxford. Julius K. Nyerere is a graduate of Edinburgh University; Dr. Hastings Banda, of Fisk University, the University of Chicago, and Edinburgh University. Dr. Du Bois received his doctorate from Harvard University in 1895 and Dr. Woodson, his in 1912. Léopold Senghor is a graduate of the Sorbonne.

African tribal and district councils, and even the British system of indirect rule, gave a few Africans apprenticeship in self-government or administration. Although Padmore has criticized the scrambling by middle-class professional elements for membership in the Legislative Councils in British West Africa,[43] and although French Africans told me that black French members of the Chamber of Deputies and of the Territorial Assemblies were "stooges," I firmly hold the belief that participation in these legislative bodies provided even more valuable training in preparation for self-government or independence. Professor Rupert Emerson, in a provocative chapter, "Colonialism as a School for Democracy," has emphasized legislative councils, executive councils, political parties, the suffrage, and a rationalized system of public administration as important institutions introduced or developed by colonial powers in the development of self-government.[44] Many writers have discussed the importance of industrialization and urbanization in the nationalist movements, for such movements develop in cities and large villages rather than in rural areas.

Western ideas and institutions contributed less, however, to Pan-Africanism than did World War I and World War II. Pan-Africanism is writ in the slaughter of ten million brave men on the bloody fields of Ypres, Verdun, and Château-Thierry, to name the most famous battles. About forty million men were wounded; the colonial powers were so impoverished that they could not measurably promote the welfare of their colonial or mandated subjects. Analogies do not prove anything, but they are sometimes revealing. The failure of the Southern states in the United States after *Plessy* and even after *Gaines* to provide

[43] Padmore, *op. cit.*, p. 173.
[44] Rupert Emerson, *From Empire to Nation: The Rise to Self-Assertion of African and Asian Peoples* (Cambridge, Mass.: Harvard, 1960), pp. 227–237.

substantially equal though separate facilities within the States for Negro school children almost inexorably drove Negro leaders to demand the abolition of segregation itself. The failure of the colonial powers to make colonialism sufficiently palatable drove a few nationalists to demand the abolition of colonialism.

The bitter lessons of World War I were soon forgotten by victors, vanquished, and neutrals. At the end of the war, thousands of earnest seekers after peace—practically none of whom were Communists or even labeled Communists—marched through the streets of European cities with banners: "No More War"; "À bas la guerre"; "Nicht wieder Krieg." But the balance of power in Europe had to be restored and the capitalistic system preserved. It has long been an axiom of British foreign policy that Britain has no eternal allies, Britain has no eternal enemies; Britain has only eternal interests. Most other major powers—especially the United States, France, Russia, and Japan—predicate their foreign policy upon similar principles of Realpolitik. In a few years, the United States, Britain, and France were rebuilding Germany as a bulwark against Bolshevik Russia. This policy was dangerous enough under the Weimar Republic; it became vicious and almost suicidal after Hitler's advent to power. Rarely in modern times have such sadistic perverts as Hitler, Goering, Goebbels, Himmler, and Roehm received such unswerving support from the three great democracies—the United States, Britain, and France. What difference did it make that Hitler and his megalomaniac practitioners of hate and homosexuality were slaughtering millions of Jews? After all, they were only Jews; and American, British, and French investments in Germany produced handsome profits, and Hitler was manning the bastions against the Bolsheviks. Who cared that Mussolini (a normal person by comparison with his counterpart German thugs) strutted like a small-town Napoleon, suppressed civil liberties, caused his opponents to be murdered, brutally invaded Ethiopia, and ranted about a "New Empire of the Caesars"? After all, he "made the trains run on time" (though not infrequently to the wrong destination), constructed public works, protected private investments, and stood guard, at long distance, on the ramparts against the Russian Communists. What did it matter, at the time, that the United States permitted the sale of scrap iron to the Japanese warlords? Pan-Africanism owes a great debt to the "inter-wars" policy of Britain, France, and the United States; of Germany, Russia, Italy, and Japan.

This *Realpolitik* of the democracies, in the words of Talleyrand, one of its most cynical practitioners, was worse than a crime; it was a blunder. On August 23, 1939, Germany and Russia signed a pact of nonaggression, the immediate prelude to World War II. This war tolled the deathknell of colonialism, not only in Africa but also in many other parts of the World. This conclusion, which is not original and which seems to me inescapable, should not make us forget the tens of millions of men, women, and children who died, suffered wounds, and lost their homes because of a madman's belief that German "Aryans" were a master race who would rule the world for a thousand years. Nor should we forget the brave survivors of the Blitzkrieg in Poland, the gallant heroes of Dunkirk, Pearl Harbor, Stalingrad, Bastogne, and other epic battles; the Free French Fighters in the Resistance and the Yugoslav Partisans. I salute also the indomitable leaders, Churchill, Roosevelt, and Stalin (after June 22, 1941); Sir Robert Watson-Watt who perfected radar, and other scientists. Above all, I salute the pilots of the English Hurricanes and Spitfires whose supreme sacrifices and magnificent courage and airmanship deprived the Luftwaffe of the air supremacy that Hitler deemed necessary for an invasion of England.[45]

Nor should one forget Félix Eboué, the black French colonial governor who first declared allegiance to General de Gaulle's Free France and helped to organize black troops who fought across Africa into Europe and aided the liberation of Paris. These and other black colonial troops not only played a not insignificant role in the overthrow of Italy and Germany; they, like French colonials and like Negro Americans in World War I and World War II, also lost most of their illusions about the "superior races." This disillusionment, plus the weakening and impoverishment of the colonial powers and a growing demand in some of these powers for a new colonial policy, presaged the demise of colonialism.

The Fifth Pan-African Congress in Manchester, England, in October, 1945, where Du Bois, Nkrumah, Padmore, Jomo Kenyatta, and

[45] Peter Fleming, *Operation Sea Lion* (New York: Simon and Schuster, 1957), especially pp. 218, 219, 228–237.

others drafted resolutions for self-government or independence in Africa had,[46] therefore, a greater impact on world opinion than had the previous conference and congresses. Imperialism had dug deeper its own grave. But the almost unbelievable rapidity with which African nations have become and will become self-governing or independent would hardly have been possible without the maturation of Pan-Africanism from 1900 to 1945.

[46] Padmore, *op. cit.*, especially pp. 152–170; Nkrumah, *Ghana*, pp. 52–56.

PAN-AFRICANISM: PRESENT AND FUTURE

JOHN MARCUM

Department of Political Science, Colgate University

PAN-AFRICANISM is one of the forces fashioning modern Africa. In the past it was activated by a sense of African solidarity and has prompted a "we" feeling among Africans. It has emphasized common interests and the similarities of African culture and experience. Now with each grant of independence Africans are afforded new opportunities to implement Pan-Africanism and thus to realize the ideal of African unity. Africans may now work together on common problems of education and social change, economic development and planning, boundary adjustments, political coöperation, and external pressures.

As Independence Days follow, one after the other, and the map changes to reflect new names and boundaries, Pan-Africanism becomes more than an idea, a mystique, or a sentiment to be realized in the distant future. It suddenly comes alive with possibilities for practical realization. It enters a new dynamic phase, and while it is impossible to predict with accuracy just what its impact upon the African Revolution will be, it does promise to be important. Pan-Africanism will assert itself at two levels, governmental and nongovernmental.

I. GOVERNMENTAL: BACKGROUND

African colonies, though carved out artificially, were developed as separate political entities. Most appear to be gaining independence separately. A number of factors have tended to fragment Africa into a host of petty states. The political society of each territory has a distinct history covering the period of colonial control, the growth of nationalism, and the struggle for self-government. Differing responses by colonial regimes to African nationalism have led to differing paces of political evolution. Also, technological limitations, notably in com-

NOTE: Certain events subsequent to the presentation of this paper should be kept in mind. Independence for the Congo has been threatened by regional separation. Syria has seceded from the United Arab Republic. The Mali Federation split into Senegal and Mali (the French Soudan), and the latter joined Ghana and Guinea in the Union of African States, a loose league involving no transfer of sovereignty. The Casablanca group of nations and the Brazzaville-Monrovia-Lagos group have emerged as representing different aspects of Pan-Africanism and certainly different attitudes toward the former European colonialists and the United States. Both Liberia and Nigeria are active in Pan-African affairs.

munications and transportation, have tended to hold down the geographical scope of precolonial and colonial political organization.

The possibility that Africa would emerge from colonialism with large independent states formed by extensive groupings of territories is fading. Even though French colonial policy more than any other worked to destroy precolonial political frameworks and to superimpose a political uniformity upon its territories, the administrative federation of French West Africa has broken up. With the decision of the four states of the Conseil de l'Entente to opt for separate independence, former French West Africa is scheduled to be transformed into a total of seven sovereign states. Elsewhere, the Central African Federation of Rhodesia and Nyasaland, dominated by a white-settler government, faces African demands for dissolution, and to the north, British East African territories are scheduled to attain their independence separately.

Some new African governments may have their hands full in the near future in just holding together that unity that was created and imposed by colonial regimes. The (Belgian) Congo faces grave ethnic, regional, and political cleavages. The Sudan, Uganda, Ruanda-Urundi, and even Nigeria—the most promising and populous experiment in African federation—must overcome serious centrifugal forces and particularist loyalties.

What is being achieved, however, is the creation of a number of medium-sized states, representing the merger of from two to three smaller colonial territories. Senegal and French Sudan have united to form the Mali Federation. The Somalia trusteeship and British Somaliland are scheduled to form one state. The Chad, Central African (Ubangi-Shari), and Congo Republics of former French Equatorial Africa have agreed to unite within a Union of Central African Republics (UCAR). Such mergers may at least reduce the proliferation and increase the general size of African political units.

Will such medium-sized units tend to evolve into still larger states? It may be expected that political offices, social services, and economic progress will lead them to a natural preoccupation with domestic affairs. As they are politically integrated, popular loyalties will focus increasingly upon the source of political order, economic mobilization, and social welfare—that is, upon the national government. Local patriotism may soon militate against political unification with other states whose political and economic orientations differ, and interest in larger mergers may lessen to the degree that new states prove economically viable.

Recent history fails to provide an instance of successful political amalgamation uniting two or more previously sovereign states that have reached the stage of modern social-service government.[1] Léopold Senghor has said that his membership in the French delegation to the Consultative Assembly of the Council of Europe (Strasbourg) impressed him with the difficulty of persuading independent states to give up any facets of their national sovereignty. The transferability of loyalty becomes increasingly difficult as political independence solidifies. Accordingly, Senghor urged, though without success, that a far-flung federation of the former territories of French West Africa be reconstructed before independence. Yet may there not remain a certain period even after independence during which time new national loyalties will be sufficiently flexible to permit their transfer to enlarged units?

The Pan-African ideal may be strongest in those states ruled by mass political parties. For example, in building broad popular followings, the Convention Peoples' Party (CPP) of Ghana and the Democratic Party of Guinea (PDG), combated tribalism and stressed the general concept of African solidarity. Yet states governed by such parties tend to develop the program and apparatus of a modern welfare state most rapidly, and in the process they inevitably mobilize national sentiments. Their very dynamism may cause their less militantly organized or "progressive" neighbors to shy away from political union for fear of being absorbed.

One may not, on the other hand, rule out the possibility of further political mergers during the early flexible period of African political development (e.g., Mali and the Conseil de l'Entente?)—the period before conflicting national loyalties have grown strong. The leaders of monolithic, single-party states may be able to subordinate personal ambitions, respond to old school ties and friendships with leaders of other states and contract political mergers of their states which their parties will then implement. Furthermore, predictions of fragmentation may not allow sufficiently for the psychological strength of the

---

[1] Unless the merger of Egypt and Syria into the United Arab Republic be so construed.

quest for African unity. This quest is optimistically articulated by Article Two of Ghana's new constitution: "In the confident expectation of an early surrender of sovereignty to a union of African states and territories, the people now confer on Parliament the power to provide for the surrender of the whole or any part of the sovereignty of Ghana."

Political "Balkanization" could seriously compromise the political, economic, and social aspirations of the African Revolution. The history of Latin America warns of the dangers of conflict arising from territorial and boundary disputes (already difficulties have arisen between Ethiopia and Somalia over Ogaden, and between Ghana and Ivory Coast over Sanwi). Conflict may develop out of uncontrolled economic competition and duplication; for example, competition between West Coast cocoa- and coffee-producing states that are slated for privileged access to the European Economic Community and those that are not. Conflict may be produced by political and military subversion, as foreshadowed by the recent discovery of arms caches in Senegal destined for use against the Sékou Touré government in Guinea. In addition, conflict may develop if Africa is enticed into cold-war politics by means of propaganda, trade, arms sales, and competitive diplomacy. These dangers require early, vigorous, and imaginative measures on the part of African governments to order their relations within a clearly defined continental code.

II. GOVERNMENTAL: PROJECTS AND PROSPECTS

Proposals for implementing African unity at the governmental level take the form of (1) schemes for full political merger (amalgamation) under common federal or unitary governments, and (2) projects for more limited functional (pluralist) union. With southern Africa held tightly under colonial and settler rule and the North African scene dominated by the continuing Algerian War, current moves for African unification are restricted to West, East, and Central Africa.

A. WEST AFRICA: POLITICAL OR FUNCTIONAL UNION?

Prepared by its pioneer role among new African states and the Pan-African convictions of its leadership, Ghana has made two moves toward enlarged political union. First, in November, 1958, Ghana joined with Guinea to form a "political entity" designed to be the nucleus of a broad Union of West African States. The two countries exchanged resident ministers whom they accorded the status of cabinet member in each other's government. The Ghana-Guinea Union, however, stopped short of full political merger. It remained a loose alliance or "union of potentialities" to be given constitutional substance if and when the two partners overcome language barriers, lack of communications and contiguous borders, differing external commitments, and rival political ambitions.

Second, Ghana has proposed to extend African unity by expanding its own borders. Ghana's new constitution has been officially described as "designed to enable peoples who are at present outside Ghana but who are linked by racial, family and historic connections with Ghanaian peoples to join them in one integrated state.[2] Its authors clearly have in mind the Ewe people who inhabit both Ghana and Togoland. This is an example of the natural tendency to encourage the unification of traditional African groups where such unification promises to expand one's own territory. Prime Minister Kwame Nkrumah has invited Togoland to become a province of Ghana. Premier Sylvanus Olympio has rejected the invitation. Indeed, the latter is busy consolidating the tribally mixed entity of French Togoland into a new, independent nation.

There has been one other noteworthy effort to achieve amalgamated political union in West Africa—Mali. Though restricted to a federation of Senegal and French Sudan at present, Mali's federalist founders would like to extend it to cover all French-speaking Negro African states. In the words of the president of the Mali legislative assembly: "If Mali succeeds, it will serve as an example and a magnet. Then we will be able to create a single federation which may extend—why not?—from Dakar to Brazzaville."[3]

Both Mali and the Ghana-Guinea Union appear to be faced with desires on the part of relatively self-sufficient Nigeria, mineral-rich Mauritania, traditionally independent Liberia, and independent-minded Sierra Leone, Togoland, and the Entente countries of Dahomey,

---

[2] *Government Proposals for a Republican Constitution.* Accra: Government Printing Office, March 7, 1960.

[3] Léopold Senghor, *African Socialism: A Report to the Constitutive Congress of the Party of African Federalism* (New York: American Society of African Culture, 1959), p. 33.

Ivory Coast, Niger and Upper Volta to preserve their separate African personalities. There is strong resistance to further political amalgamation in West Africa. Hope for progress toward unification may lie instead with proposals for functional integration, such as the close economic, administrative, and technical coöperation being developed among members of the Conseil de l'Entente.

President William Tubman of Liberia and Premier Sylvanus Olympio of Togoland have urged that the problem of West African unity be approached through concrete measures to develop functional coöperation. The Liberian president has proposed the creation of a West African Council for Economic Coöperation to expand and stabilize regional exports and commerce and to spur industrialization. He has also called for the creation of councils for coöperation in education, health, and nutrition. Such functionalism can accommodate separate national sovereignty, with all its symbols, offices, and glories, while attempting to preserve and develop common markets, postal and customs services, and educational facilities. It may produce institutions, habits, and services that will facilitate eventual political union.

Federalists and functionalists might well view their respective roles as being complementary as well as competitive. French West Africa is a case in point. Whereas the Mali Federation and Conseil de l'Entente may not be able to agree upon merger within a common federation now, they may develop flexible confederate ties both between their two groupings and also with Mauritania, Togoland, and perhaps even Guinea, thus contributing to the unity of French-speaking Africa. In the same fashion, the federal Union of Central African Republics (Chad, Congo, and Ubangi-Shari) expects to preserve and expand functional ties with its former associate in French Equatorial Africa, Gabon, and might extend these ties to include Cameroon and the Conseil de l'Entente.

B. EAST AND CENTRAL AFRICA: POLITICAL OR FUNCTIONAL UNION?

East Africa is behind West Africa in the race to independence, and all proposals for political integration must await such independence. The Pan-African Freedom Movement of East and Central Africa (PAFMECA), supported by nationalist leaders such as Julius K. Nyerere of Tanganyika and Dr. Hastings Banda of Nyasaland, foresees a three-stage political evolution: first, regional coöperation among the nationalist movements of Kenya, Uganda, Tanganyika, Nyasaland, and Zanzibar; second, independence for each territory; and third, formation of a Greater East African Federation stretching from Somalia to Rhodesia. Kenneth Kaunda of Northern Rhodesia recently expressed the view that upon attaining self-goverment, he would like to see Northern Rhodesia, Tanganyika, Nyasaland, the Congo, Kenya, Uganda, and Ruanda-Urundi merge into one state—"one big powerful state in Central East Africa." It is too early, of course, to predict the fate of such proposals. Yet political amalgamation would appear to have the greatest chance for being realized among those territories that have shared the experience of British rule.

It would appear, on the other hand, that the Congo, Ruanda-Urundi, Ethiopia, Sudan, Somalia (British and Italian), Angola, and Mozambique are following distinct political paths that are not likely to lead to mergers with their neighbors. Patrice Lumumba of the Mouvement National Congolais has expressed the view that a state the size of the Congo ought to integrate itself ultimately within a full continental union, but not within an intermediate regional federation.

In East and Central Africa, as in West Africa, the functional approach may offer the most immediate hope for limiting the effects of fragmentation and for paving the way for later political amalgamations. It could preserve and develop common services such as railroads, postal administration, harbors, and universities existing among the territories of British East Africa and the Central African Federation respectively. Furthermore, if Ethiopia, Somalia, and Sudan could agree upon instituting a functional union among themselves, the dispute over Ogaden might take on more manageable proportions.

C. PROSPECTS FOR OVERALL CONTINENTAL UNION

Flexible, supple, and permissive of subregional arrangements, the Sanniquellie Declaration seems to be a most likely formula for Pan-African coöperation. Meeting at Sanniquellie, Liberia, in July, 1959, the government heads of Ghana, Guinea, and Liberia called upon representatives of independent African states, or states with fixed dates for independence, to hold a special conference in 1960 to elaborate a charter for a Community of Independent African States (CIAS). The declaration suggested that member states of such a regional organization should maintain their "own national identity and constitutional structure." Furthermore, the declaration stated that the Community should not be designed "to prejudice the present or future international policies, relations and obligations of the States involved." With the motto "Independence and Unity," it should respect the principle of noninterference in the internal affairs of other members, but at the same time the Community should help African populations still under colonial rule to speed up their progress toward independence.[4]

Hopefully, the Community of Independent African States might serve several important functions. It might promote and coördinate nonviolent and collective action to "finish the job" by dislodging hardcore colonial control in Portuguese, French (i.e., Algeria), Spanish, and Boer areas. It might help to develop an African personality in world diplomacy, possibly through the proclamation of an African Monroe Doctrine proscribing foreign military bases and alliances that would involve Africa in the cold war. It might sponsor agreements, machinery, and processes for pacific settlement and arbitration of disputes, demilitarization of frontiers, and mutual limitations on armed forces. It might oversee and harmonize relations among the regional organizations and common markets that may develop in various parts of Africa. It might promote cultural coöperation, pooling of educational resources, exchanges of technical and administrative personnel, language training in English and French, and exchanges of scientific information.

Finally, the Community might foster coöperation in economic development and planning. To avoid duplication, however, it might defer to the United Nations Economic Commission for Africa (UNECA) as the primary body concerned with economic coöperation. At its second session, held at Tangier in February, 1960, UNECA gave evidence of having become an important body in the eyes of African governments. The Tangier meeting initiated economic studies on the present state and potentialities of intra-African trade and industry and on measures necessary to stimulate the coöperative movement in Africa. It directed UNECA's executive secretary, Mekki Abbas, to assist in the preparation of a 1961 conference of African businessmen which will consider ways in which private enterprise may promote African

[4] *Joint Declaration and Communique by the Governments of Liberia, Ghana and Guinea* (July 19, 1959). Accra: Government Printer, 1959.

trade, and it established a committee on community development with instructions to work out a UNECA program in this field. Tangier revealed a strong feeling among African states that UNECA should play an important role in any new (Western) proposals for economic assistance, and confirmed an African preference for multilateral over bilateral aid. In particular, African delegations urged that UNECA not be bypassed or rivaled by any other organization for aiding Africa. Clearly, when formed, the Community of Independent African States would find the institutional framework for continental economic collaboration already in place. By promoting economic diversification, joint marketing arrangements, transportation and communication links, and raw material processing industries, UNECA may help to develop a modern, integrated African economy. Both the Sanniquellie and Tangier meetings give hope that African governments will embrace regional organization and the innovating spirit of common-market functionalism in early efforts to build a peaceful African community.

III. NONGOVERNMENTAL

Behind governmental moves for political and functional union lies the role of nongovernmental associations, the series of Pan-African conferences, and the work of *Présence Africaine* and the international Société Africaine de Culture. A growing web of contacts among intellectuals, youth, labor, political and business leaders is vital to the realization of African unity. The All Africa Peoples Conference (AAPC) now embodies the tradition of earlier Pan-African conferences. Following its first meeting in 1958, when for the first time politically active Africans from most areas of the continent gathered and deliberated together, the AAPC established a permanent secretariat in Accra. At its second meeting in Tunis in January, 1960, it reiterated African demands for equality and independence and pledged itself to "mobilize the African masses" around the idea of unity. Most significantly, it made a series of specific recommendations, which, if implemented, could do much to further African unity. These recommendations include the development of exchange scholarships in Africa in order to intensify human and cultural contacts; the exchange of agriculturists to demonstrate and diffuse techniques; the emission of radio programs on regional African cultures; the organization of inter-African sports, cultural events, and art exhibits; the organization of an African youth festival in Conakry in 1961 and the establishment of a coördinating body for all African youth and student movements; the suppression of visa requirements and customs barriers among African states; the unification of the African trade union movement; and the encouragement of joint economic enterprises, inter-African companies and coöperatives.

Cohesion built upon the negative force of anti-colonialism will not suffice to build lasting unity. Hence it is important that the Pan-African movement as embodied in the AAPC not limit itself to the destruction of colonialism and the assertion of racial equality. To realize its positive potentials the AAPC must assume the functions of an umbrella organization for numerous and varied nongovernmental associations that are working for the unification of Africa. Much as the European movement has furthered the unification of Europe, it may be the task of an "African movement" to mobilize popular support for African integration and to propagate the ideals of tolerance and peaceful coöperation among the new societies of Africa. An "African movement" might help youth, labor, nationalist and intellectual groups to imagine, invent, and improvise the construction of an African community.

IV. ALTERNATIVES: EUR-AFRICANISM AND AFRO-ASIANISM

In recent years, the Pan-African movement has faced two rival approaches to political unification: Eur-Africanism and Afro-Asianism. The first, Eur-Africanism, has been European-centered. It resulted from desires to reconstruct Europe as a major power center by joining to it the human and material resources of Africa. Coincident with the failure of France to assimilate its African territories, however, geopolitical schemes for Eur-African unification have fizzled.

Though underlying motives may not have been neocolonial as is sometimes charged, the extension of certain provisions of the European Economic Community (EEC) to cover sections of Africa under the administration of its members (France, Italy, and Belgium) has proved controversial. It is feared that this association with Europe may hinder African unity by offering special market advantages and investment funds to certain states, leaving other states to orient their trade, and by implication their diplomacy, toward the Commonwealth, Eastern Europe, or elsewhere. The controversial implications of the EEC association and the growth of a rival European Free Trade Zone have prompted African governments to request UNECA to make a broad study of the effects of economic groupings in Europe upon African trade and development. The object of the study will be to develop measures to offset any effects prejudicial to the over-all interests of Africa.

Afro-Asianism as a concept has much more appeal than Eur-Africanism in a continent only partially freed from colonial control. Broadly speaking, supporters of Afro-Asianism reject Pan-Africanism as "separatism" and emphasize the common interest of all Asian and African peoples in the struggle against colonialism and racialism. They argue that African unity should be sought within the broad framework of the Afro-Asian Solidarity Committee in Cairo. On the other hand, its critics contend that the Afro-Asian approach contains at least three disadvantages as compared with straight Pan-Africanism. First, Asian interests are not always those of Africa. For instance, relatively tepid Asian attitudes toward colonial issues in Africa (e.g., southwest Africa) contrast with the attitudes of African delegations at the United Nations. Second, the Afro-Asian framework may be used to involve African states in conflicts extraneous to their interests. For example, the United Arab Republic used the second Afro-Asian Conference at Conakry in April, 1960, as a sounding-board against Israeli "imperialism." Israel has developed substantial commercial relations and a technical assistance program in a number of West African countries, and Africans might only compromise such economic advantages if they become associated with resolutions condemning Israel. Third, the Soviet Union, excluded from Bandung as an essentially "European power," has joined Communist China in the Afro-Asian Solidarity Committee. The Communist partners use the committee as a propaganda and contact vehicle for extending their influence and introducing the cold war into Africa.

In general, the Eur-African and Afro-Asian approaches involve the risk of subordinating African interests to those of European, Middle Eastern, and Communist powers. At the present stage of their political evolution, Africans might better avoid ensnarling alliances with outside powers and concentrate instead upon their own intra-African relations and upon working through neutral organs such as the United Nations Economic Commission for Africa.

V. ASSESSMENT OF PAN-AFRICANISM, 1960

Historically, pan-movements have contributed little to the enrichment of man's material and spiritual condition. Some have been exclusivist and racist, notably Pan-Germanism. Yet one can find within the unachieved aspirations of Pan-Arabism and the modest accomplishments of Pan-Americanism a noble striving toward inclusive political, economic, and cultural coöperation. Perhaps the constructive tone of the pragmatic functionalism applied in European integration represents a modern approach to "pan" aspirations which is consistent with a world of social-service states and global interdependence.

Pan-Africanism is entering a decisive stage. Its success will depend upon the vision and realism of its architects and activators. It could be sterile if only aimed against colonialism and past indignities. It would be vain if only rhetorical. It would be tragic if distorted into a counter-racism. In this light, it is heartening to note that at the All Africa Peoples Conference of 1958, most delegates rejected any form of racialism and embraced "residential" Pan-Africanism; that is, the idea that all persons born or naturalized in African states, irrespective of race, creed, or color are "African" provided they believe in full economic and social equality and in "one man, one vote." To realize its potential human impact upon Africa, and upon society at large, Pan-Africanism must remain open to the world so as to open new worlds to Africa.

There is as yet no general agreement as to whether Pan-Africanism must embrace an "African socialism," or promote a homogeneous, as distinct from a variegated, African personality or cultural pattern. Pan-Africanism, after all, is an ideology and a movement that is changing with Africa. On the other hand, it does reflect a general and growing desire for African unity. One of Africa's most responsible newspapers recently commented: "Along paths that logic cannot always explain, African Unity is being realized a little more each day. Slowly, perhaps, but surely, African wisdom is triumphing over egoism and personal ambitions. And despite the Cassandras, a preoccupation with

the Common Good is gaining over that of particular interests."[5]
Through its achievements, Pan-Africanism could become an inspiration
to all those men in all places and of all origins, who are laboring to
construct a more just, dignified, and humane world.

[5] *L'Afrique Nouvelle*, No. 668, May 25, 1960, p. 1.

COMMENTS

ABOYAMI CASSELL

Liberian Delegate, All Africa Peoples Conference Steering Committee

THOSE OF us who have been designated as commentators are at a distinct disadvantage in discussing such brilliant expositions as those of Drs. Logan and Marcum. It is especially difficult for us to make fair evaluations, since we have had so little time in which to study their papers. The paper by Dr. Logan—one of the *dramatis personae* in the historical development of Pan-Africanism—is brilliant without doubt. I am convinced that he has grasped in breadth and depth the problems that face us in Africa.

However, I would prefer, with your permission, to broaden our subject momentarily to include the question of equality for peoples all over the world. That is, we in Africa are not only concerned about our own lot and fate; we are equally concerned about the lot and fate of all people who have been or who are oppressed at the moment. In consideration of that fact, I would like to include in our discussion the problems of your own country—and I am sure that any discussion at this level by intelligent men and women can be conducted with frankness. Thus, we would assume that Dr. Du Bois, who dedicated most of his life to the development of Pan-Africanism, was equally interested in the development of total independence for every man living under the constitution of your great country, under the constitution of our great country, and under all the other constitutional systems. I want to be generous about this matter and say that I think the men who, from the late nineteenth and early twentieth centuries, have been struggling for us in Africa have also been struggling for— if you wish to confine it to race—people of African origins all over the world. And we must not forget that there are people in the Caribbean and other parts of the world who still need to be emancipated from one type of domination or another.

In what form will independence emerge on the continent of Africa? Isolation is impossible. There are ideological battles on the continent of Africa as there are everywhere else. There is no way to isolate ourselves from this ideological struggle. We who align ourselves with the Western democracies believe that the struggle is so important, so urgent, that in considering Pan-Africanism we must also consider many questions regarding the kind of system that will evolve or emerge from it. This is important to us—I believe it is important to all who are concerned and who subscribe to Western democracy. Hence, we must observe closely the attitudes that are being assumed by the respective sides in this struggle to gain our assent to one or the other ideology. We believe, for instance, that those people who have been the main protagonists, proponents, and carriers of what we call Western democracy have been linked almost indivisibly with colonialism and—perhaps it is unnecessary to stress—imperialism. We wonder why such a great state as the United States doesn't assert its views and insist upon them in dealing with her allies—Britain and France, Spain and Portugal—who maintain a position on our continent which is distressing to us and which we can't accept as friendly.

Similarly, we must ask about South Africa—a country that is also aligned with what is called Western democracy. It is amazing that people who subscribe to Christianity and Western democracy can assume the attitudes and position that the government of South Africa has assumed. And it is more amazing that her friends—especially the Christian people of the world—have not challenged and condemned her openly. There are challenges—I am aware of them—but I think these challenges should be clearer, louder, so that all the people of the world might know where we who call ourselves Western democrats and Christians stand regarding these diabolical deeds.

I would like to close by stating briefly that a United States of Africa is not necessarily a dream; it is something that is within the competence and potential accomplishments of the African people. We who know the problems best do not believe we can import any system. For example, we can't simply borrow the history and development of the United States of America and graft them onto the continent of Africa. We feel that the African personality, to which we subscribe, and the emergence of our countries to independence will dictate the evolution of our own system of democracy. In the beginning, it may not be comparable to or even compatible with yours; but in time it will mature. We are sending many of our brilliant men and women to be exposed to the cultures and civilizations of many parts of the world.

Let us hope that when they return, we who are now laying the foundations will not have laid so firm a foundation as to make impossible the achievement of the United States of Africa. Meanwhile, we believe that sober thought and serious consideration and careful deliberation are the stances we should assume in working to unite Africa into a single political unit.

ARTHUR NUTULTI LUBINDA WINA

(*Northern Rhodesia*)

I WOULD LIKE to start my comments on the papers by expressing regret at the undue emphasis that has been placed on the obstacles to Pan-African unity and the relatively less weight that has been given to those supreme factors in Africa that make Pan-African unity not only possible but inevitable.

For over a hundred years the African people have suffered under varying forms of colonialism—from the mild Lugardian form of indirect rule in Nigeria to the Baascap dictatorships of apartheid in South Africa. Throughout this period the African people have been conscious of one dominating factor—namely, rule by a foreign regime or a minority settler community. It is, therefore, natural that our reaction to this colonialism should be one of strong opposition to those foreign forces that denied us our political freedoms. Of even greater importance is the feeling of African oneness and solidarity which developed out of common experiences of humiliation and injustice. When to this are added the common strains of African culture, personality, and physical location on one continent—a continuous sea of people from the Cape to Cairo—you have forces that irresistibly lead to cultural and political solidarity.

Admittedly we face problems in our struggle for the realization of this unity, and it would be unrealistic to ignore those disuniting elements in the present African situation: narrow territorial jealousies, suspicions regarding personal motives, competing aspirations of leaders, and more recently the intrusions of cold-war rivalries into African political life. But if we realize that Pan-Africanism serves no individual ambition or international power bloc, we will then face the future without timidity or apprehension. Africa needs disinterested leadership in her movement toward political unity—the only framework within which we will realize our national personality and cultural dignity. We of Central and East Africa realize that only under the conditions created by Pan-African unity and solidarity shall Africa make her maximum contribution to world peace and humanity.

I know that the ordinary student, the trade union member, the peasant and the intellectual throughout Africa are at heart truly disciples of Pan-Africanism. Our leaders should heed this national aspiration and consciousness. To disregard it or to attempt to suppress it is to court serious problems.

ANTHONY ENAHORO

Nigerian Action Group;
Member, All Africa Peoples Conference Steering Committee

There are one or two points in Dr. Logan's paper that invite discussion, and one in particular that certainly requires development.

First, I find it very difficult—with all due respect—to accept Dr. Logan's definition of Pan-Africanism. It seems to me that Pan-Africanism would have no future at all if that definition were correct. Self-government or independence is, after all, only one phase or stage of Pan-Africanism.

Dr. Logan, again with all due respect, may have been handicapped by a desire to formulate a compact definition. But, as I have said, if that definition were accepted, Pan-Africanism would have no purpose beyond the next five years. Yet Dr. Logan would, I believe, be the first to admit that Pan-Africanism cannot come to an end with the attainment of independence by the various states.

It is true that, historically, Pan-Africanism was little more than anti-imperialism and was concerned mainly with the African continent and the West Indies. Even in those days, however, Pan-Africanism was also concerned with the fortunes of Negroes on this continent and in other parts of the world.

Currently, Pan-Africanism seems to stand not only for anti-imperialism but also for coöperation in various fields among African states, as well as with and among organizations concerned with Negro culture. And I have no doubt that in the future, Pan-Africanism will express itself in other ways, will have other interests. I think, therefore, that a more appropriate definition would embrace all these phases of Pan-Africanism. I suggest that the purpose of Pan-Africanism may be defined as the liberation of Africa; the economic, social, and cultural regeneration or development of Africa; the avoidance of conflicts, territorial, and otherwise, in Africa; and the promotion of African unity and of African influence in world affairs. I am the first to admit that even this definition is not comprehensive enough, but I think that with it we would not have to evolve a new definition in every succeeding age to express the purposes of Pan-Africanism.

The second point I would like to make is that while it is easy to see from Dr. Logan's paper the historical importance of World Wars I and II, and to appreciate their significance, and even to accept the influence of contemporary events and ideas of Pan-Africanism as defined by Dr. Logan, it is much less easy to consider World War I, for example, a real cause, rather than merely a landmark.

The same is true, to a lesser extent, of World War II. Though it is possible to argue, as Wells and others have argued, that the colonial powers could not hold their colonies after 1946, it would be wrong, I think, to attribute this fact merely to the material effects of the war on Europe. Is it not possible that without the presence of certain other factors (which I will mention in a moment), World War II might well have been followed simply by one more redistributions of colonies, possibly accompanied by relaxation and liberalization in certain sectors, but also accompanied by an intensified exploitation of African territories, in order to assist a reconstruction and development of metropolitan states?

I think it is by no means certain that, without the factors to which I am going to refer, less than fifteen years after the war more than half of Africa should now be free. It is somewhat surprising, therefore, that Dr. Logan should seem to minimize these factors. I refer, of course, to the great libertarian principles he mentioned briefly: The Declaration of Independence, the Statute of Westminster, as well as the existence of Liberia, and so forth.

I object also to his contention, near the end of his paper, that Western ideas and institutions contributed less to Pan-Africanism, according to his definition, than did the two world wars. On the contrary, it is, I suggest, the cumulative effect of the development of liberal and progressive thinking, through the years in all the countries of the world, which created a climate of opinion, in the face of which colonialism was finally put on the defensive. It is also the influence of Western ideas and Western institutions—the impact of the great ideas of liberty, equality, fraternity, and so on—that has generated and sustained Pan-Africanism and nationalism, not only among Nationalist leaders, but also among the people. It presented them with alternatives in the fields of government, social organization, individual liberty, and public welfare which were far more attractive to them than conditions that existed in the pre-European era within their own memory.

Third, I agree completely with Dr. Logan on the advantages that participation in legislative processes, before independence, has brought African territories. It is quite clear that the territories that passed through that stage have found themselves better prepared for democratic government. And, I maintain, the very fact of seeking participation has sometimes, in itself, provided opportunities for challenging the existing system and furthering the cause of nationalism. As you may well know, in Nigeria in the last seven years, independence has been won merely by parliamentary action. And this without mass action, where there was no dominant nationalist organization or personality. Parliamentary action has proved to be a most effective weapon in the nationalist struggle.

I think that Professor Marcum's paper is very competent; I wish I had more time to consider his views. As he says, there is much thinking going on in West Africa about whether unity should be based on organic union or on functional coöperation. Perhaps we can go into this more fully when we come to Professor Coleman's paper.

On the question of the future of Pan-Africanism, and indeed of its present, there are a few points that I think ought to be made. There has been no attempt made here to examine the difficulties we face in Africa in this regard. This desire for unity must not, we think, be confused with expansionism. It would be disastrous if, on the altar of unity, we attempted to justify in any part of Africa the incidents, events, or ideas that in other parts of the world we would roundly condemn as expansionist or even imperialist. It seems to me that Professor Marcum tries in part of his paper to rationalize what some Africans, better acquainted with the situation, regard as expansionism.

Second, I agree, and I think you will find that most Nigerians agree, with Professor Marcum's view that "progress toward unification may lie instead with proposals for functional integration, such as the close economic, administrative, and technical coöperation being developed among members of the Conseil de l'Entente." This, at any rate, would be a first step toward closer association.

Third, I would like to impress on all of us the importance of the Nigerian experiment. I say this not because I am a Nigerian myself, but because I think that success in Nigeria may well point the way to peaceful development in other parts of Africa. After all, there cannot be internationalism without nationalism. The nationalism of Nigeria is, in fact, internationalism in the sense that, within our borders, Nigeria is a kind of nation of nations. There are within our borders peoples who, if they were confined within their borders, would make larger nations than at least eight of the European countries, and would surpass a good number of those in South America. In trying to weld all these people together into one nation, we are trying in Nigeria to do what on the African level we would like to do continentally.

As I said earlier, no treatment has been attempted in this paper of the difficulties confronting Pan-Africanism. I would like to enumerate a few of them. The first is the Arab problem. White, Arab, or Negro, we would like to think of ourselves as Africans. Nevertheless, some of you are no doubt aware of the controversial views put forth in President Nasser's book: views that seem to be the basis of the United Arab Republic's foreign policy. Those propagating Pan-Africanism must take notice of such views—they give grounds for hesitation, however eagerly one might want to press on.

Another point, very important to us in Nigeria, is that, for us, Pan-Africanism must not involve the surrender of the very principles that have inspired the nationalist struggle: individual liberty, the rule of law, and democracy. Do we have to surrender these in order to achieve a Pan-African union? If you cannot agree on certain principles, how can you agree on other things? In Nigeria, we think that before agreeing to a surrender of sovereignty, we must be sure that the various states of Africa are themselves as committed as we are to these principles. I think it is more important that we should nurture and develop these principles within Nigeria than that for the sake of unity we should give them up—to the damnation of our people.

Another problem is the shortsightedness of some of the European countries (Belgium and France, notably) who, without preparing the colonial territories for independence, departed without notice, leaving voids now being filled by methods and materials not always to one's liking. If this is repeated in the Congo and in the Portuguese and Spanish territories, the principles dear to us in Nigeria will, we fear, be challenged on the rest of the continent.

Next, consider the ideological conflict of which Mr. Cassell spoke: the call for neutrality or nonalignment in Africa. In Nigeria (and I think my colleagues here will agree) we accept neutrality and non-alignment—at least given the military context and the situation in the United Nations. But as to the great issues, I do not think we will accept neutrality or nonalignment. I do not think we are neutral in the great debate that is going on in the world. We are definitely committed to democracy, to individual liberty, to the rule of law. Wherever they are challenged, we think that our interests are at stake. (In the United Nations, we agree, we should not be prejudiced, nor should we join NATO and other military alliances.)

Unless we can agree on these very basic, vital, fundamental principles, we are going to have great difficulty in achieving African unity. Moreover, some of the larger states in Africa—Nigeria and Congo for example—being in themselves federations and preoccupied with internal problems, will not be as receptive to Pan-African ideas as some of the other states for whom unity would be far easier. I am sure you will not press me to develop that point any further. There are great men with whom one must, it appears, come to terms as regards certain ideas and principles. Without this agreement people will continue to misunderstand, as it seems Professor Coleman has misunderstood, the Nigerian reaction to Pan-Africanism.

I think that both of these papers have omitted two vital influences on Pan-Africanism. One is India. It was Indian independence that really inspired the national struggle in Nigeria. It was a very important landmark in the history of Pan-Africanism, this first attainment of independence by a colored nation. It was an example to us.

The second vital influence is the settler problem. It has been my experience that in all African conferences certain differences of opinion or emphasis arise generally between those African states burdened with settlers and those not so burdened. It is my opinion that what you might call "settler areas" have generally developed a broader view of Pan-African interest than the others.

Finally, these papers might well, I believe, have paid more attention to the All Africa Peoples Conference. In the last few years this conference has developed into a grand Pan-African platform, bringing together governments and peoples from various parts of Africa, as well as people of African descent. There is no doubt but that the conference has stimulated the rapid emancipation of Africa. What is to be the future of the conference after the independence of African states, when most of the problems that are now discussed at congresses of the conference are resolved at other levels between the various African states? I think this question might well have been examined.

EMILE ZINSOU

Secretary, African Federation Party, Dahomey

The two topic papers, plus the comments that have already been made, have covered our subject so well that my task has been simplified to some extent. Regarding Dr. Logan's paper, I do not have a great deal to say. I should simply like to add this: The story, the spirit of Pan-Africanism, although originating in America and France, was brought to our country by a man whose name and memory I should like to recall here. I am speaking of Marc Kodio Tovallo Queno, who—as an authentic African forerunner of the movement—claimed his negritude even before the word was coined. He brought us to know Marcus Garvey, Dr. Du Bois, and so many others; when I was a child I heard my parents speak of these names and evoke these problems. That is to say, if the first sketch of this movement was begun in America and Paris, it had, before it was publicly evident, repercussions and an extension in Africa.

Pan-Africanism, as we have heard, is many-sided. If it is primarily a movement with a cultural basis, if it is above all the rediscovery, the rehabilitation of the African—the black African—and if it is also the search for the liberation of Africa and Africans, we can see by the law of consequences that it naturally opens onto the vistas of both African independence and African unity.

It is on the question of African unity that I should like to pause a moment. Unity is an absolute necessity for us, but we must realize at the same time that it is not destined of itself. It does not arise of itself, because peoples and nations that have found themselves in situations like ours when they were approaching independence did not always achieve unity. Unity is threatened at the very time we are seeking it, and it can be compromised by new imperialisms (we saw an aspect of this in Dr. Marcum's paper), since African states may have the propensity to stretch out and envelop territories that are not at present within their boundaries. Unity can be compromised (again, as Dr. Marcum notes) by this patriotic enthusiasm which our nations are obliged to incite and which is the supporting wall of the national edifice—enthusiasm, nationalism, which at the beginning of a movement may be narrow, overpowering, and perhaps intolerant. Unity can be threatened by Balkanization, which, as our countries reach independence, each at its own time and not simultaneously, obliges us to make economic and political choices—and I might even say philosophical choices. These choices may be different from, even antagonistic to, the choices made by others. This is happening to such an extent that the necessary unity—and nothing seems to me more important than to preserve its atmosphere and the paths of its attainment—must each day be more and more sought after.

In such a difficult and grandiose task we must be idealists and realists at one and the same time. That is why I believe we must choose the way that will lead us to the end we seek. I believe that unity must be sought first of all within the framework of languages—that is to say, unity of French-speaking Africa and unity of English-speaking Africa. I believe we must then proceed to the broadest and fullest exchanges. We African people who are today in a position to make our own rules must make bilingualism obligatory, so that we may eventually have that vehicle and that powerful tie that is understanding through language. Then, when this French-speaking and English-speaking African unity has progressed through exchanges and simultaneously through bilingualism, we shall see that we will attain—I will not say naturally, but to a certain extent more easily—a United States of Africa, the supreme dream of my generation.

Obviously, when we see the difficulties with which Europe is confronted in its search for unity, we can only regret that our politics, at a given moment, facilitate the Balkanization of Africa. We can certainly regret that Africans themselves have not more clearly and completely perceived the danger and avoided falling into the trap. We had an unhoped-for historical opportunity of starting, not with a clean slate, but with a political, economic, and geographical situation that allowed a less difficult path to unity than the one faced by states fossilized by nationalism and their political situations. Must we wait until a situation similar to that of Europe crystallizes in Africa, forcing the next generation to make a severe break in order to recover unity?

Grant me a moment to express my political views and to invoke the ideals and the program of the African Federation Party. We assert, as the focal point of our activity, not only independence but also the constant search for unity. We believe that African regrouping will in fact have more chance to operate within a union of a federal nature. If frontiers are an accident of history, our various states might have had boundaries different from the present ones. This hinders Dahomians from feeling completely Dahomian; it hinders one from feeling completely Senegalese, from feeling completely Guinean; and it hinders one's disposition to fight for a nation whose frontiers were determined by others. We must, nevertheless, take these realities into account. It seems to us that the federal formula acts as a safeguard for originality and autonomy and at the same time molds the whole into a complementary and unified ensemble. It is a formula that will permit us to avoid difficulties inherent in the obviously more attractive, perhaps more effective, but erroneous and, it seems to me, unrealistic formula of complete unity.

We must begin with simple problems—with those that are so immediate and so inevitable that we are obliged to deal with them. That is why the idea of an African common market, launched by the African Federation Party, is making progress. It provides for all forms of economic coöperation that are at present under consideration. It offers the advantage—in the present situation where distinct nations are being formed which sometimes have different languages—of including the whole of Africa—French-speaking and English-speaking —and consequently of creating the first tie of unity.

We could have tried to analyze the unconscious, certainly involuntary, contributions that colonization—and even colonialism and racism —have made to Pan-Africanism. I am not speaking paradoxically. We could have tried to see how, to a certain extent, colonialism was fertile in arousing a reaction in the black man who tried to rediscover himself; we could also have seen in this a dialectic movement of history (we cannot escape the dialectic movement of history), in which our role is to act as well as to be acted upon.

The originality of our situation is that we do not have any territorial claims, that we do not claim any ideological hegemony, that we are in search of the blossoming of every dimension of man—of the human become more human, of total man. We can be, we must truly be, a fundamental element in the equilibrium of the world—a world to which we shall teach new love, charity, understanding, and generosity.

Indeed, if one wanted to prove that in spite of our color we are a power of light, it would be sufficient to imagine for a moment that the world were deprived of black faces and black people. I believe that we here would all agree that at that moment night would descend upon the earth.

VINCENT C. IKEOTUONYE

M.P., Federal Parliament, Nigeria;
Headmaster, Zixton Grammar School, Onitsha, Nigeria

Pan-Africanism, if it is to play its part as it did in the past, should take note of the wind of change across Africa. In the past it was the slogan, the emotional cry of colonial Africa and the peacefully insurgent Negro race. Its value then was the emotional ebullition that it egendered in the minds and feelings of patriotic Africans and their friends and brothers on both sides of the Atlantic. Then emotive platitudes were more useful and effective than definite programs.

But in 1960 Africa is different. Freedom, independence, and sovereignty have come to Africa, and to preserve them we must face the hard facts. We must define Pan-Africanism; we must forge out its connotation and denotation on the anvil of practical politics and historical experiences.

Pan-Africanism should not consist of philosophic flights and scholarly documents, like some I have listened to here. From Plato to this day, philosophers who have attempted to organize societies or the governments of man, have always failed, though man has always gained from one or another aspect of their social speculations. The papers we are discussing here are not the papers of men about to build a society.

Nor can Pan-Africanism be the cultural organization or confederation of the African states. We know from history that all such confederations and organizations have failed—usually destroyed by the evolutionary stresses of sovereignty in search of survival or the basic needs for food, shelter, and clothing. The African statism, the Negro world, will look ridiculous in the eyes of detractors if this melancholy chimera is the object of its political quest.

Our enemies who fear the rise of the sleeping giant will celebrate their luck and rejoice that Africa will not catch up even in the next two thousand years: its political thought, they will say, is still antediluvian.

With the wind of change blowing across Africa, with the fertilizing flow of freedom and sovereignty bathing the colonial communities of Africa, Pan-Africanism poses a relentless and ineluctable question to us all: federalism or nationalism?

My answer, and I urge this society to adopt a resolution to that effect, is that the salvation of Africa, as a part of the world community, is in the regional federation of the African states. If the African states fail to federate, when the historical cycle completes its turn Africa may again find itself a colony.

I have therefore traveled like a bird—in fact a bird is more powerful than men locked up in a crazy machine forty thousand feet above sea level, for the so-called conquest of nature is so far only the conquest of man—from Nigeria to put forward this suggestion: The only way in which Pan-Africanism can help the newly free and independent communities of Africa is by the immediate regional federation of the states.

III POLITICS

PAN-AFRICANISM OR NATIONALISM IN AFRICA[*]

DAVID E. APTER

Department of Political Science, University of Chicago,

JAMES S. COLEMAN

Department of Political Science, University of California, Los Angeles

I. INTRODUCTION

Our plan in this paper is a simple one. In addressing ourselves to the political aspects of Pan-Africanism and of nationalism, we shall first provide some overview of the issues that each presents. We shall then proceed to a more detailed analysis of the politics of Africa in order to illustrate some of the dynamism of both the forces of Pan-Africanism and the forces of nationalism. Because the internal and external political factors that shape and affect these two forces are so closely interrelated, we have decided to write this paper jointly. In this way we will be able to illuminate the relationships between Pan-Africanism, or the building of larger African political unities; nationalism, or the building of effective national polities; and international politics, or the relations both between independent African states and between those states and the world at large. Each of these—Pan-Africanism, nationalism, and international politics—has important implications for the others. These are the implications we hope to clarify.

Although both Pan-Africanism and nationalism are manifestations of the same general urge toward independence and freedom, they are by no means the same thing. Indeed, the simultaneous effort to create Pan-African political unity and to build effective national societies in Africa creates political paradoxes which, difficult to resolve, may hold the key to Africa's future. Both have in common the objective of politi-

[*] This paper was presented by Professor Coleman. Professor Apter participated in the discussion. Certain events subsequent to the presentation of this paper should be kept in mind. Independence for the Congo has been threatened by regional separation. Syria has seceded from the United Arab Republic. The Mali Federation split into Senegal and Mali (the French Soudan), and the latter joined Ghana and Guinea in the Union of African States, a loose league involving no transfer of sovereignty. The Casablanca group of nations and the Brazzaville-Monrovia-Lagos group have emerged as representing different aspects of Pan-Africanism and certainly different attitudes toward the former European colonialists and the United States. Both Liberia and Nigeria are active in Pan-African affairs.

cal unification. Yet there are several levels at which political unification can occur. It is important at the outset, therefore, that we make a clear distinction between a politically unified community that is recognized and acts as a sovereign state and one that is not.[1]

A sovereign state has two distinguishing characteristics: (1) externally, it carries on, and is recognized as having the legal capacity to carry on, diplomatic relations with other sovereign states (and it usually, but not necessarily, is a member of the United Nations); and (2) internally, the government of the state has the "last word" (i.e., sovereignty) regarding certain government functions of the political community for which it acts—the irreducible minimum being foreign relations. Structural relations within a sovereign state can, of course, vary widely—from a purely unitary to a loose federal system; but to be sovereign the state must have the recognized legal capacity to act both internally and externally as stated above. Thus, for example, the United Arab Republic, the Mali Federation, Ghana, and Guinea are sovereign states; but the Ghana-Guinea Union, Senegal, and the Conseil d'Entente are not. Pan-Africanist unification movements within or among Africa's present political entities to establish a common government endowed with "sovereignty" in the sense described above will be referred to as *suprastate political unification.*

Once this "sovereign state" legal category is distinguished, one can observe the existence, and contemplate the development, of a wide variety of other forms of political activity aimed at the creation of larger-scale, but nonsovereign, political communities. These may be either intergovernmental or unofficial in character, although in some cases lines are crossed (e.g., when the governments of sovereign African states convene conferences of representatives of unofficial associations, such as labor organizations or political parties, from other states and territories). In the intergovernmental category two types of activity stand out: (1) intergovernmental collaboration in the establishment and development of institutions and arrangements providing for common services (e.g., the Conseil d'Entente or the East African High Commission); and (2) intergovernmental consultation and collaboration in foreign affairs (e.g., the periodic Conference of

---

[1] Deutsch has made this fundamental distinction in terms of an "amalgamated security community" (i.e., federal or unitary sovereign states) versus "pluralistic security community" (i.e., confederations, alliances, or close permanent political coöperation among sovereign states). See Karl W. Deutsch, et. al., *Political Community and the North Atlantic Area* (Princeton, Princeton University Press, 1957).

Independent African States, African bloc activity in the United Nations, and such *ad hoc* events as the Accra meeting of representatives of Ghana, Guinea, and Liberia to decide whether or not their governments should recognize the Republic of Cameroon). Such coöperative functional activity can occur among African states or between those states and the former metropolitan power. The essential feature of all of these forms of intergovernmental activity, however, is that they are confined to specific functions, and there is no transfer of sovereignty to a suprastate body endowed with absolute and final authority over the governments concerned. Such action, of course, may ultimately lead to, or at least facilitate, suprastate political unification, but at the time it takes place it is not specifically so directed. For present purposes we will call this *interstate functional unification*.

The foregoing two types of unification activity involve the relationships among existing African political entities. But each of these entities are themselves artificial creations of the colonial period. Therefore, any discussion of the political aspects of African unification must include an analysis of forces and factors making for unity and disunity not only *between* but also *within* these existing entities. Indeed, in certain respects a study of the actual problems of political unification within Nigeria or Mali (Pan-Nigerianism or Pan-Maliism), for example, could be just as rewarding as efforts to analyze the problems of creating a United States of West Africa. The crucial point is that once one moves beyond Africa's traditional political communities—whether the Mali or Fulani Empire, the Buganda or Bakongo Kingdoms, or a Birom village—the problems and issues involved in unification are essentially the same—the main difference being one of scale. For our present purposes, we will refer to nationalist activity directed toward the politcal unification of existing entities (i.e., Nigeria, Congo, Tanganyika, etc.) as *intrastate political unification*.

Having distinguished between these three levels and types of unification what, then, is Pan-Africanism? If one examines critically the array of concrete proposals for political unity that have been made by African leaders, it is clear that *political* Pan-Africanism is subject to multiple interpretation. Yet, all proposals appear to have one element in common; namely, the achievement of a political unity that transcends and embraces existing political entities. For present purposes, we will interpret *political Pan*-Africanism as encompassing all forms of sentiment and activity directed toward *suprastate* political unification. In the same vein we will interpret *political nationalism* as embracing all sentiment and activity directed toward *intrastate* political unification in existing political entities. In thus defining our concepts we do not mean to suggest that efforts to achieve forms of political unity, short of the actual transfer of sovereignty to a larger scale unit, are not legitimately Pan-Africanist in character. Given our "political" terms of reference, however, we wish to focus upon a narrower and more explicitly political range of issues. In so doing we will not exclude from our discussion other aspects of Pan-Africanism that bear so importantly on those issues.

II. THE EVOLUTION OF POLITICAL PAN-AFRICANISM

There are at least three phases in the evolution of political Pan-Africanism that can be usefully distinguished. Stemming from an expatriate heritage, the first phase was the gathering of exiles in metropolitan centers of Europe and the United States. There African, West Indian, and American Negro and other groups more or less "discovered" one another. Sharing common disabilities and increasingly aware of many common elements in their heritage they convened *ad hoc* conferences, organized student groups and cultural associations, and, in the later stages, turned to explicit political agitation for African independence. The second phase was the nationalization of political Pan-Africanism, a period during which there was a progressive shift in the locus of political agitation to individual territories in Africa as the result of the formation of territorial nationalist movements. This second phase is now virtually at an end, having given way to the third and contemporary phase which is characterized by two lines of activity—political action within and among independent African states directed at the creation of a wider unity; and political action by those states, in close collaboration with nationalist leaders in the remaining colonial territories, aimed at the complete liberation of all Africa from alien rule. These second and third phases will be examined in greater detail in the succeeding two sections of this paper. Here we are concerned more generally with the early growth of political Pan-Africanism and the main elements of which it is constituted.

It would be most unwise simply to regard the history of political Pan-Africanism as a rather episodic series of events, meetings, congresses, and manifestoes, which eventually broke through colonial defenses and established successful independence movements in Africa. To do so would be to miss both the essential dignity of the movement and its more fundamental historical context. It is too coherent to be regarded episodically. Certain common themes have so deeply touched all Africans who have had contact with it that few remain unaffected by its ideals.

Pan-Africanism developed first outside of Africa. This was so not only because its founders were mainly intellectuals studying or in residence abroad who came in contact with leaders of other anticolonial pan-movements, but also because colonial authorities in Africa made it virtually impossible for Pan-Africanist political activity to be carried on in Africa itself. Indeed, if one views the cosmopolitanism of Accra today, and compares it with two decades ago, the difference between a relatively apolitical, fun-loving but backwater colonial town, and the present vibrant and lively capital of an independent nation, and center of a continental Pan-Africanism, is the whole distance between colonialism and independence.

During the formative years of Pan-Africanism there was a characteristic cosmopolitanism as reflected in both the heterogeneity of the "exiles" and in the universalistic quality of their objectives and organizational activity.[2] Most of the early associations did not, however, espouse nationalism nor did they engage in racial agitation. On the contrary, their main objective was to ameliorate the lives of colored peoples abroad by persuasion and petition. A more pronounced political spirit gradually emerged in the activities of students from the West Indies and Africa.

The first—and certainly the most durable—of the student associations was the West African Students' Union (WASU) formed by

[2] The names of the conferences and organizations, and the diverse origins of the participants illuminate this cosmopolitan and universal character. Thus, for example, in 1911 W. E. B. Du Bois (United States), Edward Blyden (Liberia), and Mojola Agbebi (Nigeria) attended the First Universal Races Congress in London. By 1919 the following organizations were active: the Bureau International Pour la Défense des Indigènes, the Welfare Committee for Africans in Europe, the African Progress Union, and the Society of Peoples of African Origin. The two last-named organizations merged to form the Union of African Peoples, which in time was succeeded by the League of Coloured Peoples and the International African Service Bureau. In addition, there was Garvey's Universal Negro Improvement Association and Du Bois's Pan-African Conference, both of which were more explicitly political in character than the other organizations.

Chief Solanke, a Nigerian lawyer, in 1924. The title of Chief Solanke's book, published in 1927, reflected a characteristic Pan-Africanist continentalism: *United West Africa (or Africa) at the Bar of the Family of Nations.* The WASU increasingly became the organizational focus for the growing political consciousness of students from Nigeria, Gold Coast, Sierra Leone, and occasionally from East Africa.[3] The London School of Economics provided a fresh focus for Pan-Africanism by bringing students into contact not only with nationalists from Asia and the West Indies, but also with Fabians, Marxists, Christian Socialists, Trade Unionists, and others. Among these groups the tradition of muscular Christianity was strong. Self-reliance and self-improvement, the twin legacies of the Victorian era, were by no means dead. Students participated both in the academic life of the universities and in the organizing efforts of the Pan-Africanists with ever greater seriousness. From 1935 onward students came to consider themselves as the future political leaders in Africa.

From its inception Pan-Africanism was led by intellectuals—men who did research on Negro and African affairs and sought to establish useful principles and perspectives for the understanding of both colonialism and the means to attack it. The thoughts and writings of these men reflect many intellectual currents, each of which has left its stamp upon that ensemble of ideas and principles making up pan-Africanism. At least four of these intellectual currents have had, and probably will continue to have, considerable influence in the development of common political perspectives as well as a common orientation to political action among African nationalists.

One dominant theme in Pan-Africanist ideology is Marxist socialism. This has been nourished from many sources: Leninist identification of

[3] This development pattern was not limited to English-speaking Africans. Although the number of prewar African students in France was small, they were more readily absorbed—perhaps because of French assimilationism—into social and Catholic cultural and political societies. Thus they participated more thoroughly in the life of the country than did their English-speaking counterparts in England. Among them were such established scholars as Senghor, as well as others from the West Indies. Their perspectives were more philosophical and historical, and the standard of intellectual effort considerably higher than those of the English-speaking groups with whom they had only limited contact. The French African students of the thirties became the leading nationalists of the immediate postwar period. Often theirs was a problem of identifying with their own cultures. In the process they gave voice to some of the more profound and spiritual elements in Pan Africanism. In addition, there was a strong infusion of Marxism of various types among the French West Africans.

the proletarian dimension of socialist thought with the struggle for independence in Africa; the argument that traditional African culture was basically communal—and therefore socialist—in character; and the conviction that socialism provided the best ethical basis for a political order combining democratic ideas with strong government. Each of these elements, and others, can be found in the polemical literature and public statements of African leaders on the subject. Whatever the source of this Marxian orientation, however, it has provided, and continues to offer, a unifying link among the politically relevant strata of the population of Arabic-, English-, and French-speaking Africa.

A second strand in the Pan-Africanist intellectual tradition is the commitment to passive resistance as the political strategy for the pursuit of independence.

The nationalist movement in India, and particularly Gandhian political ideas, has exerted no little influence. Certainly African leaders north of settler-dominated southern Africa have tended to believe—for reasons already proved valid—that the changes they desired could be accomplished through nonviolent agitation. Moreover, apart from the fact that passive resistance fortified their moral position, they were also confronted with the ever-present reality that any other type of political action could and would be smashed by the superior power of both colonial and metropolitan governments. As the freedom struggle moves south to the Rhodesias, the Portuguese territories, and the Union of South Africa it remains an open question whether the strategy of nonviolence will continue to prevail.

A third strand in the intellectual tradition of Pan-Africanism is an appreciation of and a respect for traditional African culture. It is to an older generation of lawyers, those early educated West African political leaders, that much is owed for the development of a new pride in old institutions. Their pioneering work has since been greatly enriched by the more detailed research of African scholars. The product of this research has served to illuminate elements of both unity and diversity in African culture. But there is little doubt that the idea of African cultural unity has captured the imagination of increasing numbers of Africans and that diversity is played down. Cultural Pan-Africanism keeps alive and strengthens the shared symbols and heritage of Africa.

A fourth strand in Pan-Africanism is the tolerant eclecticism characteristic of the Pan-Africanist approach to ideology, culture, and institutions. Although many are Marxists of one variety or another, few have allowed themselves to be drawn into competing factions within the church of Marxist orthodoxy. The intellectual fathers of Pan-Africanism came from many cultures—West Indian, Negro-American, West African, and East African. Although they had their differences, often profound ones, both ideological, cultural and generational, they also showed an amazing capacity to absorb one another's ideas and to be tolerant of one another's doctrines. This element of tolerance, and their eclectic attitude toward ideological and cultural borrowings has facilitated communication, compromise, and an essential spirit of understanding.[4]

Beyond the general acceptance of these dominant strands in the intellectual tradition of Pan-Africanism, most contemporary Pan-African leaders have had many shared experiences over the past two decades. Their numbers were small enough to enable their relationships to retain some of the aspects of a club. They shared their money and their possessions with one another. They had the generous expansiveness of the poor, and brought to it the casual communalism characteristic of many African societies. They worked closely together in writing and publishing pamphlets, newspapers, and propaganda sheets, many of which were financed almost from day to day. There were all-night drafting sessions, urgent efforts to pay bills, and similar activities which brought them constantly into working relations with one another. Their intellectual concerns thus developed organizational centers, which rapidly came to include holding mass rallies, fund-raising, and tactical work. Through this intimate interaction and col-

[4] In a recent article, Thomas Hodgkin argues that there are important similarities in the basic ideas held by the new political elites. These include: (1) the primacy of ethical ideas, and particularly the dignity of African man; (2) the relevance to the contemporary situation of African values inherited from the precolonial past—in particular a collectivism in which the individual defines himself by his relations with groups; (3) an emphasis upon human equality, not only in African-European relationships, but also in relations within the African community; and (4) a cluster of Pan-African ideas, such as, "the assertion, on historic grounds, of a sense of African solidarity; emphasis upon the common interest of, and need for, mutual aid between African states and peoples; and the demand for non-interference by external powers in the affairs of the African family" ("Political Forces in French-Speaking West Africa" [unpublished manuscript]).

laboration, Africa's future leaders developed common organizational skills and a wide measure of mutual responsiveness.

These various elements in thought and experience in the evolution of Pan-Africanism propel Africans toward unity. They are fundamental and go far deeper than mere verbal proclamations in favor of unity. They are crucial ingredients in the continuing urge to develop some form of political unity.

III. THE NATIONALIZATION OF PAN-AFRICANISM

It is indeed ironical that the territorial nationalist movements, which have been and remain the instrumentalities for the realization of Pan-Africanist objectives, should acquire a dynamism and an autonomy of their own sufficient to constitute a countervailing force, militating against the larger political unity envisaged by the founders and long-time exponents of Pan-Africanism. Here we are concerned with the nature of territorial nationalism and the problems it poses.

Until it became localized as a political-action movement in the political arenas of Africa, Pan-Africanism was destined to remain an esoteric affair of intellectuals and "exiles" abroad. Beginning in the early years of World War II, Pan-African organizations—such as the West African Students' Union (WASU), and the West African Secretariat, of which Nkrumah was joint secretary—concerned themselves with the task of organizing political groups in Africa. Azikiwe had already shown the way by the formation of the National Council of Nigeria and the Cameroons (NCNC). If this was not to be an isolated event, but rather part of a larger movement for liberation, then similar movements were required in Sierra Leone and the Gold Coast and other territories. Thus, the locus of political Pan-Africanism progressively shifted from Europe and America to the individual territories in Africa. This launched the process of progressive nationalization of Pan-Africanism, a process that continued unabated to the present time.

In the struggle for African liberation the general trend has been for African leaders to seek and to attain separate sovereign statehood in each of the administrative entities created by European colonialism. Their slogan has been "Independence first, then unity." There are interesting exceptions, of course, such as the integration of British Togoland

and the Gold Coast to form the independent state of Ghana, the union of Senegal and the French Sudan to form the Mali Federation, and the current moves toward some form of unity among the territories making up the Conseil d'Entente and the Union Équatoriale. In general, however, African leaders have tended to be opposed to pre-independence political unification.

In view of the fact that most of these leaders are exponents of Pan-African unity, why has this been the case? Some possible answers can be found in (1) the legacy of colonialism, (2) the special imperatives that emerged during the period of agitation for independence, and (3) imperatives of nation-building operative in the post-independence period.

THE COLONIAL LEGACY

It can be stated as a general proposition that during the colonial period the policy and actions of the European powers in Africa tended to preserve and to emphasize the separate existence of each artificial administrative entity created during the scramble for Africa. Guided by the assumption that the European presence in Africa would continue for several generations, if not forever, the European powers made few efforts to create large-scale political-economic entities capable of inde-pendent existence. Territories were not transferred or amalgamated, nor were boundaries altered, even where all rational considerations made these actions desirable. Thus, such anomalies as Gambia, Río Muni, and French Somaliland—to mention only the more obvious— were preserved as separate entities. The disinclination of the British and the French to resolve the knotty Togoland-Ewe problem in its early stages—when they still had a wide measure of discretion—is a striking example.

Although the British government made certain efforts to develop interterritorial links in West Africa (particularly during World War II), in East Africa through the East African High Commission, and in Central Africa, the net effect of its policy during the colonial period has been the maintenance of territorial separateness. Two features of that policy help to explain this effect. One has been the characteristic British policy of treating each territory as a little world unto itself through devolution of administrative responsibility to the territorial colonial bureaucracy, through territorial budgetary autonomy, and by insistence upon a distinctive pace and pattern of territorial political development. Helpful though this policy may have been in the creation of territorial consciousness and embryonic nations, it tended to militate against interterritorial integration.

A second aspect of British policy that has contributed to territorial consciousness and separateness has involved, ironically, official efforts to develop interterritorial unity. For very rational economic reasons the British have endeavored in both East and Central Africa to create larger entities—the East African Federation and the Federation of Rhodesia and Nyasaland. Yet, as originally conceived, both were destined to be failures. Why then were they proposed, and, in Central Africa, actually established? One reason is found in the historic predilection of the British government to devolve power, and the imperial responsibility for exercising "trusteeship" upon European settlers (the "kith and kin" overseas). Another is the equally historic insensitivity to African fears about settler domination. This has recently undergone fundamental change, but only after a series of rather painful events that have led them to begin to take seriously what African leaders in these areas have been telling them, namely, that Africans of Uganda and Tanganyika are not prepared to join a settler-dominated Kenya, and that Africans of Northern Rhodesia and Nyasaland will not remain in a federation dominated by Southern Rhodesia. In any event these abortive efforts to achieve political unification in these vast stretches of Africa have been largely responsible for the development of militant territorial nationalisms.

During most of the colonial period virtually every aspect of French policy was aimed at the creation of a monolithic unity throughout Afrique Noire. How, then, do we explain the politically fragmented character of this vast area as it moves toward independence? The answer is found, in part, in the French policy regarding the two large federations of Afrique Occidental Français (AOF) and Afrique Équatorial Français (AEF). Thoms Hodgkin has pointed out in a recent article that from the very beginning the government and institutions of the federations had certain inherent weaknesses.[5] The government-general of the federations never really became important in the administrative or authority structure, mainly because of the concentration of all decision-making in Paris. During the critical decade 1946–1956 the

[5] *Ibid.*

Grand Conseil in each federation remained weak; each successive administrative and political reform tended to result in an enhancement of the role of the twelve territorial governments, rather than those of the two federations. As Hodgkin observes, "'AOF,' as such, never became a focus around which African popular loyalties could be organized or symbols developed. . . . It was not possible to take pride in being an 'Aofian'—as it was in being a Ghanaian or a Nigerian."

When in 1956–1957 it became clear that certain fundamental changes had to be made in Afrique Noire, the die was cast in favor of a policy of "territorialization." In part this was in response to the demands of a few prominent African political leaders, but it also reflected a decision of the French government to acquiesce in—indeed, if not to encourage—the weakening of the federal system by devolving authority and responsibility to the territories. With the benefit of hindsight we can now say that if, beginning in 1946, the French government had, in the interest of preserving and developing large-scale units, progressively devolved authority and responsibility upon the federal governments in Dakar and Brazzaville, African leaders today would not be confronted with the painful task of seeking to create larger unities in former French Afrique Noire.

Another ironical, but given the circumstances understandable, legacy of the colonial period has been the contribution made by the anticolonial majority of the members of the United Nations to a preservation of African political fragmentation. They repeatedly refused to approve Administrative Unions (the uniting of Trust Territories with contiguous colonies ruled by the same administering authority), because of their fear this would result in an extension of colonialism in Africa. They too assumed, until quite recently, that European colonialism would continue in Africa for some time to come. Thus, for nearly ten years the United Nations refused to permit British Togoland to be integrated with Ghana (although their position changed on this issue following a plebiscite in 1956), Ruanda-Urundi with the Belgian Congo, the French Cameroons with French Equatorial Africa, and so forth.

Here our purpose is not to judge, but to explain. The crux of the matter is that the net effect of European colonialism in Africa has been to create—albeit unwittingly—embryonic nations coterminous with boundaries of the colonial administrative units. Despite the brevity of

European rule, a variety of historic integrative processes have operated within the confines of those boundaries to create, at least among certain strata of the population, a sense of national consciousness. The mere fact of establishing a common administrative and judicial system, common representative institutions, a common communication and transportation grid, a common educational system and acculturative process, and of providing a lingua franca, among many other things, served to differentiate the peoples inhabiting one territory from those in another. Territorial differentiation has been further strengthened by the consequentially greater interaction and communication among the peoples of one territory as against those in other territories. All of these factors have operated to create a "territorial" as distinguished from an "African" personality.

THE IMPERATIVES OF NATIONAL LIBERATION

There have been overwhelming practical considerations that have compelled African leaders to pursue the objective of independence within the context and boundaries of the colonial systems and territories in which they find themselves. Committed to a strategy of constitutional agitation and nonviolent change, as most of them have been, they were obliged to adapt the style, scope, and tempo of their political action to the unique situation and institutional complex with which they were confronted. Perforce they had to operate within territorial political structures. Legal and political obstacles to interterritorial movement and organization, as well as the many limitations imposed by the environment and state of technology upon the scale of political organization, were also important considerations. Thus, for very real and practical reasons African leaders have understandably felt that they could secure their objectives much more easily and quickly by confining their political action to, and by working within, the institutional framework of their respective territories. It is this fact that has made colonial policies and institutions such decisive determinants of the differential political development in Africa.

Beyond this very practical imperative of obligatory adaptation to the territorial framework, there has been the equally important need to mobilize the masses and to galvanize them into political action. This involved two types of activity, both of which strengthened the trend toward the nationalization of the political struggle. One of these was the need to politicize and harness to the nationalist movement an array of territorial interest groups. Thus, when it was first inaugurated, the NCNC in Nigeria was, from an organizational standpoint, little more than an aggregation of more than a hundred various associations ranging from the Trade Union Congress to tribal unions. Similarly, the CPP in the Gold Coast leaned heavily upon a network of almost fifty organizations already in being, and the Northern Rhodesian National Congress was at first simply a federation of pre-existing welfare societies. The crucial point is that the need to quickly establish organizational roots in the territory concerned compelled political leaders to become heavily involved in and committed to a mélange of local interests. Subsequently the nationalist movements sought to break these links and establish the principle of individual membership. By then, however, the process of nationalization of political action had already gone very far.

A second course of action requisite for effective mobilization of the population was the need to create in the popular mind some concrete image of the new community being created, to endow that community with symbols of greatness either in terms of potentialities for the future or by relating it to some historic past, as well as to inculcate a loyalty to and an affect for that nation-to-be. In short, the territory, which perforce had to be the arena of political action—artificial though it was—became *la patrie*.[6] From the following quotation it is clear that the late George Padmore, the leading architect of Pan-Africanism in the English-speaking world, recognized the priority of territorial (i.e., national) independence:

> The revolution taking place in Africa is threefold. First, there is the struggle for national independence. Second is the social revolution which follows the achievement of independence and self-determination. And thirdly, Africans are seeking some form of regional unity as the forerunner of the United States of Africa. However, *until the first is achieved the energies of the people can-*

---

[6] This was easier to achieve in British territories, for reasons already explained. But even in the French territories there was a rapid development of a "territorial personality." Thomas Hodgkin has noted that the Union Soudanaise (Sudanese branch of RDA) was built upon a sentiment of "Sudan-ness" and the Bloc Démocratique Senegalaise (BDS) upon a sentiment of being Senegalese.

not be mobilized for the attainment of the second and third stages, which are even more difficult than the first.[7]

As African leaders developed territorial political movements, Pan-Africanism receded as a practical concern. The intimacy of the club gave way to the new solidarity of the local territorial movements. This final organizational stage, which was the logical conclusion of Pan-Africanism, also exposed some of its weaknesses. Increasingly the focus became internal and the territory became the principal, if not the exclusive, political arena. Thus, the politics of Pan-Africanism became the politics of nationalism. By becoming national in its focus, it changed the essential cosmopolitanism of its origins, at least for a time. Most African leaders did not give up their Pan-African ideals, nor did they entirely lose their wider cosmopolitanism. But they did share Padmore's view that the achievement of territorial independence was an absolute precondition for the final victory of Pan-Africanism.

Another factor reinforcing the trend toward complete territorial separateness has been the imperative of *total* consummation of African freedom. The fact that the territory has been the vehicle for pursuit of this objective, coupled with the fact that independence has been achieved by different territories at different times, has meant that as a territory secures its self-government, it feels compelled to break all unifying interterritorial links established by European colonial powers during the colonial period. Thus, once Ghana and Guinea achieved their independence, both in advance of the other territories with which they had been linked during the colonial period, they proceeded to sever such connections, both horizontal with other territories and vertical with the metropolitan country.[8] After attaining its independence, for example, Ghana severed virtually all links with other West African territories. These included the West African Airways Corporation, the West African Inter-Territorial Council, and the West African Frontier Force. The crux of the point is that the drive for complete

[7] George Padmore, *A Guide to Pan-African Socialism: A Program for Africa* (Accra, 1957), p. 18 (italics ours).
[8] The establishment of a republic in Ghana was explicitly designed to extinguish all symbolism of a vertical tie because, as Prime Minister Nkrumah pointed out, the head of the Ghanaian state must also be the head of the Ghanaian government —authority must be seen to lie where in fact it does lie.

consummation of freedom from colonialism, when linked with the territorial time differential in its attainment, has led to complete disentanglement from all connections with the external world, including other African states.

THE IMPERATIVES OF NATION-BUILDING

The achievement of independent statehood brings deep emotional and spiritual satisfaction, but it also creates or reveals a host of problems which colonialism had obviated or kept hidden. The principal challenge to the leaders of the new states is one of creating a sense of common citizenship in which there are certain shared political values, a measure of common purpose, and a respect for political institutions and established authority. They confront not only the problem of consolidating and stabilizing the new society, but also the monumental task of mobilizing the human and material resources of their country in pursuit of the goal of rapid modernization. They cannot mark time awaiting the liberation of all Africa; they must address themselves immediately to meeting those challenges they confront in that part of the continent for which they are responsible. Not the least demanding of these is the need to shift from the role of agitator against government to a government official ready and willing to control agitators. Even more awesome, they must give dramatic and continuing evidence that the brave new world they and their followers envisaged is being rapidly created.

It would be quite unfair and unrealistic to regard the nation-building efforts of the rulers of Africa's independent states as petty parochialism or anti-Pan-Africanism. Rather, one should view it as a coming to grips with an age-old problem, namely, the creation of a stable political community capable of achieving its goals. Confronted with heterogeneous populations having varied interests and making conflicting demands, they must create a common political nationality and the role of participant citizen identified with that nationality. They must meet challenges to public authority and internal security, not only by the use of those coercive and punitive measures employed by all governments faced with crisis, but, more importantly, they must inculcate a positive loyalty to the new nation and a respect for the laws of the government of that nation. To achieve rapid modernization they must draw upon all the latent skills and talents of their people. This can be done only by creating a widespread feeling of shared purpose. Each of these requisites—national unity, respect for authority, positive loyalty, and a sense of shared purpose—make it absolutely essential for leaders to create national symbols, national institutions, and a sense of national identity—in other words, to build a nation.[9]

There are other factors operative in the post-independence period of nation-building which tend to reinforce national separateness. One set of these factors represents two of the most highly cherished values and goals of Pan-Africanism, namely, socialism and democracy. It is ironical that socialism, the most internationalist of political ideologies, should have become one of the strongest reinforcements for nationalism. Like Pan-Africanism, it becomes meaningful, and acquires a base in the real world only within the framework of existing states. Ideology requires power, and in the modern world the units of power are nation-states. Once socialism becomes official state doctrine, the government of the state concerned becomes ever more deeply involved in the preservation of the integrity of the state, and in protecting and maximizing the use of its resources for the achievement of socialist goals. In this respect, "nationalized" socialism has an inherent imperialist potential. All groups in the national society increasingly acquire a vested economic interest in the survival, prosperity, and wealth of their nation as distinguished from other nations. The point here is that socialism—like democracy discussed below—is not intrinsically nationalistic, but once brought down from the level of an internationalist ideology and applied in the real world, it not only becomes national, but it tends itself to strengthen nationalism and to maintain separateness.[10]

It is equally ironical that political democracy, which aims at maximizing the interests of the individual as against those of the group or of the state, is also a force that operates to preserve and strengthen the separate existence of those states in which it has become the accepted

[9] Many Westerners fail to recognize the creative and positive aspects of nationalism, partly because of ethnocentric judgments that colonial nationalism is only negative and "anti," or because of memories of such nationalist extremists as Hitler.

[10] One needs only to reflect on the "Little England" position of the Labour (socialist) government of Britain regarding all proposals for economic and political unification in Europe. The issue here is a familiar one—e.g., the struggle between Trotsky and Lenin over the nationalization of socialism (it is in point to note that Lenin won the battle).

political formula. This is so for a variety of reasons, among which are the recurrent mobilization of the population around *national* issues, the progressive habituation of the peoples to participation in the political process through a distinctive set of *national* institutions, the routinization of political strategies and channels of influence within the confines of those national institutions, and the limitations that democratic involvement in foreign policy imposes upon the freedom of national governments to carry on foreign relations, including the uniting with other countries. Autocratic governments have an infinitely greater freedom of action in defining relationships with other states. Indeed, if the rulers of Africa's new states were all autocrats and passionate Pan-Africanists, and if the African peoples had not yet become exposed to, involved in, or committed to either the ideology or the practice of democracy, suprastate political unification could be accomplished by a mere declaration of their collective will. Democracy not only mobilizes larger numbers of people around national symbols; it also complicates, and frequently obstructs, the making of foreign-policy decisions. This factor acquires special significance if it is recognized that the issue of suprastate political unification in Africa is increasingly a foreign-policy matter and will be decided only by intergovernmental agreements ratified by national parliaments.

There is another sense in which democratic competition within Africa's new states complicates, if indeed it does not militate against, the process of suprastate political unification. The argument is quite simple. Parties competing for power are divided by certain issues. As most African parties are agreed upon—or feel obliged to support—a broad *national* platform of rapid modernization, and as the postcolonial process of "sorting out" is still in progress, the issues that divide them tend not to be questions of economic or social policy, but rather questions involving both internal and external relationships and boundaries. Prominent among these key issues in territorial party politics is the question of unification with other states and territories. Apart from the different interests, attitudes, and motives that create internal party divisions on unification, there is the simple universal fact that party competition inexorably tends to compel parties to maximize their differences; that is, to take opposing positions on all of those issues on which there may be or could be divided views. To the extent that the question of unification is drawn into the political arena and made an issue forcing a party division, the chances of supra-state unification by popular consent has been lessened.

As the data in the list of party divisions show, in those states having more than one party there are few instances where there is not an internal party division on the issue of unification with other states. Some, or even most, of these divisions might prove to be false; that is,

LIST OF PARTY DIVISIONS ON UNIFICATION
IN SELECTED AFRICAN STATES
(AS OF MID-1960)

ENGLISH-SPEAKING STATES	Position on Unification
Gambia	
Gambia Muslim Congress Party	Political union with Mali
Gambia United Party	Economic union with Mali
Sierra Leone	
Sierra Leone Peoples' Party	Closer coöperation (Sanniquellie)
Peoples' National Party	Union with Guinea
Ghana	
Convention Peoples' Party	Integration of Togoland and Sanwi area of Ivory Coast into Ghana; ultimate United States of Africa
United Party	Union where appropriate, but no surrender of Ghanaian sovereignty
Nigeria	
Northern Peoples' Congress (NPC)	Opposed to West African Union and to Pan-Africanism; no surrender of Nigerian leadership
Northern Elements' Progressive Union	Ultimate United States of Africa under Nigerian leadership
Action Group	Friendship with all states; no political union
National Council of Nigeria and the Cameroons (NCNC)	Favors idea of Federation of West African States as long-term objective; first separate independence for each state
FRENCH-SPEAKING STATES	
Mauritanian Islamic Republic	
Parti du Regroupement Mauritanien	Friendship with all states; no political union with either Mali or Morocco
Union Nationale Mauritanienne	Union with Mali
Nahdet al-watni	Union with Morocco

ENGLISH-SPEAKING STATES	Position on Unification
Mali Federation	
Parti Fédéraliste Africain	Reconstitution of West African Federation (ex-AOF); confederation with France
Parti de la Solidarité Senegalaise	Opposed to Mali Federation
Guinea	
Parti Démocratique Guinéen (PDG)	Union with Ghana; ultimate United States of Africa
Ivory Coast	
Rassemblement Démocratique Africain (RDA)	No surrender of territorial sovereignty; close functional links (Conseil de l'Entente)
Voltaic Republic	
Union Démocratique Voltaique	Conseil de l'Entente with Ivory Coast, Niger, and Dahomey
Parti de la Liberté Républicaine	Union with Mali
Niger Republic	
Rassemblement Démocratique Africain	Conseil de l'Entente with Ivory Coast, Dahomey, and Upper Volta
Sawaba (PFA)	Union with Mali
Dahomey	
Regroupement Démocratique Dahoméen	Conseil de l'Entente with Ivory Coast, Niger, and Upper Volta
Union Démocratique Dahoméen (RDA)	Conseil de l'Entente with Ivory Coast
Parti Nationaliste Dahoméen (PFA)	Union with Mali
Benin Party for the Socialist Revolution	Union of Dahomey-Togoland; ultimate United States of Africa
Togoland	
Comité de l'Unité Togolaise (CUT)	Independent Togoland; links with French Community; opposed to integration with Ghana
Union Démocratique Populaire Togolaise	Same as CUT
Juvento	Union with Ghana

they may simply be the luckless product of party competition or contrived opposition. Others may be more fundamental. In any event, a brief examination of some of the possible reasons for differing positions taken on unification is in point. One type of division involves those cases where the issue of unification is viewed instrumentally in terms of the achievement of a particular goal or interest of the state or territory concerned, and not necessarily as a step toward Pan-African political unity. In such cases other factors may be operative, but the dominant consideration is how best to achieve a particular goal of the state or territory concerned. In most examples of this type the goal has been accelerated political independence. One example involves the former French Togoland, where there was a division between the Comité de l'Unité Togolaise (CUT), which agitated for unification with British Togoland as the best instrument for obtaining early freedom from France, and the Parti Togolais du Progrès (PTP), which desired continuing links with France. Another example was the division in the Sudan between the National Unionist Party (NUP), which sought union with Egypt as the quickest and most effective way of terminating British rule, and the Umma Party, which opposed such union, partly because of a more pro-British orientation.[11] These examples are now of historical interest only, but the instrumental factor is present in several contemporary unification efforts: for example, the pro-Mali (PFA) opposition parties in Mauritania, Upper Volta, Niger, and Dahomey; and the growing evidence of a design for a Nyasaland-Tanganyika union as a means of liberating Nyasaland from the Federation. As the independence movement sweeps to the southern reaches of the continent, however, the instrumental use of unification to achieve independence loses its rationale.[12]

Another type of party division over the unification issue, related to the foregoing, concerns genuine differences of view over the priority to be given political and economic objectives as well as the most effective way to achieve rapid economic development. The crux of the difference is the issue of continued association with the former metropolitan power. As such the division comes perilously close to coinciding with the well-known nationalist dichotomy of "imperialist stooges" versus "true nationalists." If we set this issue aside and assume purity of motive on the part of all, there can be little question that

[11] In both the Togoland and Sudanese disputes, there were other factors, such as the Pan-Eweism of the CUT and the Pan-Arabism of the NUP, but the instrumental motive is believed to have been a major consideration. It is pertinent to note that after independence was obtained, and unification was no longer instrumentally relevant, opposition on this issue ceased to exist.

[12] Indeed, the African nationalists of Southern Rhodesia, some of whom at an earlier period welcomed federation (i.e., ur .ication) with Northern Rhodesia and Nyasaland as a potential instrument for their own liberation, now emphatically support the breakup of the Federation so that an independent African-governed Northern Rhodesia can be the instrument for a final frontal assault upon white supremacy in Southern Rhodesia and the Union.

differences in view regarding the most effective strategy for rapid modernization, as well as the relative priority attached to full independence versus economic development, have resulted in party cleavages that up to the present have seriously affected efforts to achieve political unification. This is one of the major points of conflict between the PDG (Guinea), the PFA (Mali), and the RDA (Ivory Coast). This cleavage has meant that parties in the other former French territories have been divided according to the way in which they identify themselves—organizationally and/or spiritually—with the variant positions taken by the three "leader" territories on this issue. At an earlier stage this question was the basis of a division between African pro-federationists and anti-federationists in the Rhodesias and Nyasaland. Although more and more African states are becoming independent, and relations between them becoming more intergovernmental in character, this issue will continue to be a cause of internal party divisions militating against suprastate political unification.

In dwelling upon the problems of political unification created by competitive party systems, we do not mean to suggest that the existence of one-party states would enhance the prospects of unification. Here we are not concerned with the reasons for the emergence of one-party systems except to note that the African leaders concerned regard a single party as a necessary instrument for maintaining internal political discipline and for achieving their broad social and economic objectives. As the problem of national parochialism for Pan-Africanism has its exact parallel in the problem of local parochialism for national leaders, the need for organizational strength and internal discipline is apparent. Whatever the motive or purpose, however, the general *trend* is toward one-partyism in which state and party coincide. Under such circumstances it is not likely that political Pan-Africanism will be achieved through the free association of party groupings from many states. If party and state coincide, then the external operations of a party from one state can be interpreted—as they have been in Niger and Upper Volta—as interferences in the internal affairs of other states, thus raising the issue to the level of interstate relations. If Pan-Africanism is to develop in this context, it must be through the more formal operation of heads of state.

The mere fact that there are divergent political systems—some having only one party and others more than one party—is itself an important barrier to suprastate political unification. In most historical cases of effective integration *by consent,* there have been a set of shared values, and assumptions regarding the character of political institutions. Moreover, a party in a one-party state tends to be built around the personality of one outstanding leader. It could be argued that if the integrative element in a party is a highly personal one based on the unique character and qualities of the leader, then unification, particularly of two one-party states, would present a serious problem.

Once a state has gained its independence, vested interests are quickly built into its economy and social structure and leadership roles. Political activists, as well as the ordinary citizen, perforce are obliged to calculate career opportunities and status not in the abstract but within the concrete confines of the political and social system in which they find themselves. When a class or category of the population has acquired positions of prestige and political power, and constitutes the political and social elite of a state, no matter how small, any change directed toward the formation of a larger unit can constitute a threat to its status. There are, of course, countervailing forces and trends, and in many instances clear prospects of even greater mutual rewards through unification, but we should not minimize the staying power of an organizational unit once it has been created.

The foregoing considerations serve to illuminate the range of problems posed for suprastate political unification as a consequence of the prior development of political communities in Africa's new states. As the number of these new states attaining sovereignty increases, new problems emerge and some old problems remain. In the next section we will deal briefly with some of the implications of international relations for political Pan-Africanism.

IV. International Politics and Pan-Africanism

Once a new African state has formally entered the state system and joined the United Nations, its relations with other African states and its posture on political Pan-Africanism take on a new character. According to the Padmore Dictum, it is at this point that Pan-Africanists are to seek regional unity as the forerunner of a United States of

Africa. Yet an analysis of the actual relations between Africa's new states indicates that here again there are many problems, some of which are transitional, and others that are intrinsic in the situation.

As Africa's new states face outward, they find themselves involved in three types of relationships: (1) relations with areas of residual colonialism and white domination in Africa, (2) relations with each other, and (3) relations with non-African states and the external world in general. Each of these has important implications for the other, as well as for the future of political Pan-Africanism.

African states cannot deal directly with African territories remaining under alien rule. Rather, the liberation of these territories becomes one of the important objectives of their foreign policy. In the competitive effort to liberate other African territories, an amiable rivalry has begun to develop among the new African states—a rivalry moreover which does not preclude the possibility of less friendly relations. The sponsorship of rival Pan-African labor movements as well as the notes of disharmony manifested at the All Africa Peoples Conference provide evidence in point. These minor divisions, however, are more a reflection of the problems involved in their own relationships, rather than of any essential disagreement over the total extinction of alien rule and white domination in Africa. For the African leaders and peoples still under alien rule, there is a general feeling of fraternity and a strong identification with their situation and aspirations.

In turning to the character of the emerging relationships among Africa's independent states, it is clear that the attainment of sovereign statehood leads suddenly to the formalization of relations. The transformation that occurs can best be illustrated by the different styles of conduct and themes expressed at conferences dealing with Pan-African affairs since 1958. The Cairo conference of January, 1958, was a reflection of the wide anticolonialist affiliations of Pan-Africanism developed among the "exiles" abroad during the interwar period. At the time of its origin, Pan-Africanism was only one aspect of a larger anticolonial phenomena. Solidarity among colored, colonial, and proletarian peoples everywhere was an important theme. But the effort at the Cairo Conference to translate anticolonial unity into positive action was not successful. Latent differences between the participants became apparent. The conference demonstrated the difficulties of making anticolonialism a meaningful unified force.

Only a few months after the Cairo conference, in April, 1958, the first Conference of Independent African States was held in Accra. Delegates arrived in the pomp and ceremony that protocol demanded. Formal statements were made. The eight participating states proclaimed April 15 as African Freedom Day, reaffirmed the principles of Bandung, had their delegates photographed in somewhat stiff but fraternal poses, and departed as officially as they had arrived. Although the conference emphasized the need for unity and the freedom of Africa, the presence of so many representatives from the Middle East tended to weaken its Pan-Africanist importance. Implicit in the behavior of the official delegates was a recognition that heads of state needed to act differently on the diplomatic stage than off it. International politics came to Africa with that conference.

Far different was the All Africa Peoples Conference held in Accra in December, 1958. There was no mistaking the spirit of Pan-Africanism. Party officials from all parts of Africa arrived and bitterly attacked the colonial boundaries as hang-overs from imperialism; called for the ending of the colonial system, the abolition of passports for African tourists, visitors, and students to facilitate their free movement through Africa, and the formation of an African Legion composed of volunteer fighters for freedom; and attacked the policies of specific countries such as Portugal and South Africa.

These three conferences illuminated some of the major tendencies that play their part on the contemporary scene. At the Cairo conference some of the ugly realities of world politics introduced a note of caution. Africa and Asia no longer seemed quite so close together. At the Conference of Independent African States there was a note of cautious jubilation, but already international protocol had introduced a reserve and formality in relations. Only at the Accra conference of December, 1958, was the older fraternal spirit and the more characteristic ebullience of both the nationalist movements and the Pan-Africanist traditions very much in evidence.

The realization of the goals of political Pan-Africanism are more and more a matter of external bargaining and negotiation. Pan-Africanist activity has become heavily affected by African power politics. Pan-African allegiances that cut across state lines have become increasingly suspect. They not only threaten the control of a political leader over his own party and state; they also weaken his ability to mobilize the people of his state for national development. Charges of interference or imperialism are the result. Thus, Pan-Africanism can easily become involved in both the internal politics and the external relations of African states in such a way as to confound both. And precisely because their relations are so close, the situation is dangerous. Thus, Ghana's Pan-Africanist impulse regarding the unification of Ghana and Togoland appears to many as an excuse for Ghana's national ambitions. Somewhat similar overtones can be discerned in the relations between Guinea and her neighbors. A union of the French Sudan and Guinea (despite Mali) remains a possibility. In Dakar this appears as the territorial ambition of Guinea to act as the center of a new French-speaking bloc, not as a coöperative partner in the furtherance of Pan-Africanism.

If Pan-Africanism is not to be part of the pattern of interstate relations within Africa, must it develop through Congress-type political groupings which cut across territorial boundaries? For the time being it is useful to use political parties and movements as advance forces of Pan-Africanism because of the uneven development of independence. This makes it possible for political leaders of independent African states, in their capacities as party leaders, to meet the party leaders of countries still under colonialism, as occurred at the Accra conference. Yet when colonialism is finally extinguished throughout Africa, what will prevent such party-to-party activities from being branded as subversive if, in their consequences, they do not happen to suit the purposes of political leaders in power?

Among the many factors affecting the relations between Africa's new states and the prospects for political Pan-Africanism, at least three might be briefly noted. The first concerns the position held by certain territories which leads them to make special claims to leadership in political Pan-Africanism. Here we are concerned with that array of new states in the vast stretch of Africa previously known as British and French West Africa. Elsewhere the situation is still so fluid that it is virtually impossible to isolate key trends and determinants for discussion. In West Africa there are five centers of rival leadership, each with a distinctive claim: (1) Senegal, which has historically occupied the dominant position in French-speaking West Africa and which has always felt a conscious mission of leadership in relation to the rest of that area; (2) Ivory Coast, the richest of the ex-AOF territories and the main base of the RDA; (3) Guinea, the maverick territory representing the militant left-wing tradition of ex-AOF and still the center of attraction for such groups throughout West Africa; (4) Ghana, which through its prime minister has assumed the initiative and presented itself as the vanguard in the liberation of Africa and as the main carrier of the true spirit of Pan-Africanism; and (5) Nigeria, the awakened giant that is not prepared, in the words of the Sardauna of Sokoto, "to sacrifice the leadership which she is bound to play on the continent and in the world as a whole." Each of these five core areas can rightfully claim a special role whether the criterion be historical or militant leadership, wealth, the first on the ground, or size. To date, all other territories of West Africa are in effect appendages to these five or, like Togo, they quietly go their own way. But the main point here is that there is more than one core area around which unity can be developed. This suggests that there will either be competition for leadership, or at least a reluctance on the part of anyone to accept the leadership of one of the other four.

A second relevant factor concerns the variant approaches to political Pan-Africanism which each of these represents. The present Mali leaders, if we interpret Senghor correctly, desire to recreate the "grand design" of the Emperors of Mali and Songhai, with the initial focus on French-speaking areas, and only ultimately to include the former British areas. Both Guinea and Ghana, in their own ways and orbits, are carriers of the original universalism of Pan-Africanism, an orientation that has been tempered by the influence of President Tubman of Liberia. The Ivory Coast has sought to draw within its orbit those territories attracted neither to Mali or Guinea, nor to suprastate political unification, who are willing to maintain close links with her and with France. Nigeria remains cautious and aloof. The diversities of these approaches or attitudes to political unity are understandable, but the fact that there is more than one approach, each backed by the power and influence of different states, aggravates, if indeed it does not engender, competition among those states.

A third, and for the immediate future perhaps the most important, factor is the widely different types of relationships between African states and non-African states. We have already noted the effect this differential external orientation and involvement has had upon competing parties in Africa's states. As the external relations of the new states become more clearly defined and stabilized, we will have a stronger basis for making generalizations. For the present, the union of Mali and Guinea seems most improbable in the light of the new Franco-Malian agreement; the union of Ghana with Guinea will in all probability not move beyond a symbolic link in view of the rather heavy involvement of Guinea with the Eastern bloc and, what in Guinea's eyes must be the equally heavy involvement of Ghana with the Western bloc. The union of Nigeria and Ghana, for reasons known to all, is perhaps the least probable of all. Indeed, even within Nigeria there are considerable differences of view among the regional leaders regarding Nigeria's orientation in world affairs once it becomes independent.

In defining its political relationships with former metropolitan countries, the general trend now is for each state to attain full independence and then negotiate, on the basis of complete equality, the character of the postcolonial ties. Armed with the badge of sovereign equality and with membership in the United Nations, together with a public affirmation of a "nonalignment" policy, the overseas political involvements of the new states do not pose an insuperable obstacle to closer political union in Africa. It is more in the realm of economic and military links —which admittedly have political implications—that problems are bound to arise.

In the economic sphere the differential affiliations of Africa's new states with monetary zones and trading areas, as well as the marked variation in their national directions of trade, are considerations of no little consequence in obstructing the development of closer inter-African relationships, not only economically but politically. An emerging trend, which could possibly become dominant, is for the new African states to avoid single commitments and to diversify their foreign economic involvements.

In view of Africa's profound military weakness and the need to create national armies of varying size and strength, the different overseas defense links of the new states are bound to continue for an indefinite future. Presumably the officer corps will be trained in the military academies of the former metropolitan powers until national military academies can be established in Africa. Similarly, there will be different sources of arms and equipment for Africa's national armies. As national military establishments are developed, there is no immediate reason to believe that Africa's new states will escape what appears to be a universal phenomena, namely, a contagious arms buildup among states closely contiguous who evaluate their power and security in relationship to their neighbor. There is a strong probability that there will be competition among the new states for military aid.[13]

All of the foregoing factors tend to perpetuate and, in some instances, to intensify differentiation. Indeed, it can be stated as a general proposition that any policy or set of circumstances that tends to differentiate one national society from another tends to strengthen a distinctive feeling of national identity, that is, nationalism. This differentiation is the product not only of the colonial period, and of the differences in tempo and manner of attainment of their national independence, but also of the separate and distinctive paths each has selected in the course of postindependence development. The more these paths diverge, either in direction or in the tempo of development, the more complicated will be the process of unification.

To complete our catalogue of problems of political Pan-Africanism, two other points should be made. One concerns the different levels of economic development and wealth of African states. The most obvious consideration here is the disinclination of more developed and wealthier states to unite with less developed and poorer states for the very understandable reason that this would mean a dilution of their wealth and a lowering of the standard of living of their people. Five examples illustrate this point: the territorial separatism of Liberia, the Ivory Coast, and the Gabon; and the regional separatism of the western region of Nigeria and the Katanga province of the Congo. This is not an African phenomenon; Europe, which has pursued unity for centuries, has struggled with the same problem.

The second point is the existence of a variety of ethnic loyalties, both latent and manifest, which if politicized could lead to greater fragmentation of existing states as well as to an aggravation of tensions between states. This potentiality has no doubt been greatly exaggerated by external observers; nevertheless, it would be unrealistic to

[13] Arnold Rivkin has commented: "The situation is ripe for a dozen India-Pakistan situations where military aid to one party in a local dispute will inevitably cause a grievance in a rival country. If, as is likely, the competing country turns elsewhere for military assistance, then an armaments race is set in motion between African states and indirectly between the U.S. and the Communist bloc—or perhaps the United Arab Republic" (*West Africa*, Jan. 16, 1960).

deny its potential effect upon the realization of Pan-African unification.[14]

Finally, in reflecting on the future prospects of political Pan-Africanism from the standpoint of international politics, it is important that we relate the African situation to similar situations elsewhere in the world or in history. Here we are concerned with two points: the question of coercive unification, and the fate of other pan-movements in history.

In his provocative little book *From Many, One* [Harvard, 1948], Clarence Crane Brinton has analyzed the various efforts made throughout history to create larger political unions and concludes that all instances of successful unification have been a mixture of consent and coercion, with coercion predominating and decisive. The ironical situation confronted by political Pan-Africanists is that at this moment in history when they most passionately desire a larger political unity, and are possessed of what may be a fleeting opportunity to achieve it, they are inhibited by a new international ethic of which they have been the foremost proponents. Their struggle for freedom and entry into the world community has been a crucial contribution to the emergence of a new concept of international morality in which colonialism, imperialism, and the use of force or the threat of force are no longer tolerable. The continent of Africa is saturated with a hypersensitivity about a forceful alien domination. The strong reaction to Ghana's suggestion for unification with Togoland is very much evidence in point.

Also, it is most unlikely that any power external to Africa would attempt, in the foreseeable future, any form of forceful domination of Africa. Other forms of penetration and influence may be attempted, but not force. The new international ethic, the alertness of the United Nations, the fact that the Western colonial powers have been chastened, coupled with the extreme competitive deference to African sensitivity on the part of the two superpowers—the United States and Russia—suggests that African states will not be confronted with a

---

[14] There are many well-known situations in which the activation of ethnic loyalties of groups within African states could lead to greater fragmentation. Here we are primarily concerned with those that could and probably will aggravate the relations between states. The list would be very long were we to enumerate all such potential situations. Those that have already become politically relevant include the Sanwi (Ivory Coast) and the Somali (Ethiopia-Somalia).

threat of forceful external domination that could galvanize them into a defensive union. Perhaps the white supremacists of the Rhodesias and the Union of South Africa can constitute the unifying enemy. Only time will tell. The main point we want to suggest is that if it is to occur in Africa, suprastate political unification must be largely the product of voluntary consent. Will this be forthcoming and adequate for the purpose?

Although Pan-Africanism is in certain respects unique, there are important ways in which it resembles other pan-movements that have emerged during the past century. It does not fit neatly into any single category of pan-movement.[15] It is partly pan-national and partly pan-continental in character. To the extent that it is directed toward the political unification of a distinctive racial group (i.e., Negro African peoples) it falls in the pan-national category. It differs from so-called pure pan-national movements—Pan-Germanism and Pan-Arabism, for example—in that the peoples being united do not have an identical language or nationality. Here it resembles more closely such super-national movements as Pan-Slavism and Pan-Turanism (Turkish unification). To the extent that it is directed toward the political emancipation and unification of all of Africa, irrespective of nationality, language, race, or religion, it falls into the category of pan-continentalism. Here it can be related to two types of continental solidarity movements distinguished by principle of unity and motive. Where the basic principle of unity is geographical contiguity and the motivating force is the desire to transcend parochialism and to achieve the power, security, and economic benefits of large-scale political organization, it resembles Pan-Europeanism and Pan-Americanism. Where the principle of unity is common status (i.e., colonialism) and the motivating force is the desire to remove alien rule and all of the indignities and disabilities connected therewith, it resembles Pan-Asianism and Latin-Americanism.

The political development of these other pan-movements are here very much in point. Most of them at one stage or another embraced

---

[15] In his penetrating analysis of pan-movements, written some twenty-seven years ago, Professor Hans Kohn observed that "Pan-Africanism is somewhat difficult to classify." He added, prophetically, that it, "bids fair to become a growing force and to constitute one of the major problems of the twentieth century." See "Pan-Movements," *Encyclopædia of the Social Sciences*, ed. E. R. A. Seligman (New York: Macmillan, 1937—), Vol. II, pp. 544–553.

political objectives. Several had a common political origin. Pan-Slavism derived considerable support from non-Russian Slavs desiring freedom from Turkish and Austrian rule, although it was also used intermittently by Russia as an instrument for expansion. Pan-Germanism was initially supported by liberal and reforming elements, but it later became a tool in German expansion, both under Bismarck and under Hitler. Pan-Turanism, Pan-Arabism, Pan-Asianism, and Latin-Americanism originated among reforming groups seeking national or racial emancipation. With certain exceptions, none of the historical pan-movements have achieved their political objectives without a strong measure of coercion. Most of the Slavs are now embraced within what is in effect one sovereign state (U.S.S.R.), although the fiction of sovereignty of the satellite states is preserved; but, in any event, unification was achieved not through Pan-Slavism—which the Soviet government repudiated—but through Russian military power. Pan-Germanism did help Bismarck and Hitler to unite the German peoples, but Austria remains out and Germany is now indefinitely divided.

In his survey of all pan-movements, Professor Kohn reached the following conclusion:

> . . . when an independent and established state participates in a pan-national movement for the ostensible purpose of assisting weaker co-ethnic groups in the improvement of their position, the intentions of the former are likely to be diverted to imperialistic aggrandizement at the expense of the latter. . . . From the point of view of realistic politics the smaller nations involved in such a movement are likely to waver between distrust of their more powerful neighbors and a desire to participate in the benefits of intercontinental solidarity; while the larger nations, even if innocent of actual expansionist ambitions, are at least tempted to demand the position and perquisites of leadership.[16]

In the contemporary world, the only recent concrete example of a pan-movement being linked with actual political unification and transfer of sovereignty by consent is that of the United Arab Republic and Pan-Arabism. When we turn to sub-Saharan Africa, the Mali Federation suggests itself as the second such example. This union (of Senegal and the French Sudan), however, occurred prior to inde-

[16] *Ibid.*, p. 551–552.

pendence; the real test is whether full sovereignty, once won, will be voluntarily surrendered to a higher government. Again, this is not just an African problem; it is a world problem.

V. CONCLUSIONS

In the foregoing analysis we have endeavored to state as boldly as possible what we believe are the key issues and problems raised by the political aspects of Pan-Africanism. In making our points we may have overstressed certain features, overlooked others, and in general painted a dismal and depressing picture. We believe, however, that the major object of a conference paper is to provoke discussion and debate.

Certain concluding observations are appropriate. One is that it is both imprudent and unrealistic to make generalizations and to suggest probabilities regarding African political developments at this stage when systems and boundaries are still in the process of definition by revolutionary and dynamic forces. Comparisons we have made to experiences elsewhere have involved long-established and relatively stabilized states, which may be totally irrelevant to the unfolding African scene. Who would have predicted, for example, the formation of a Mali Federation by a free act of will of the diverse peoples forming the union? Again, it was not so long ago that several usually well-informed persons predicted the breakup of Nigeria into three or more separate states as an illustration of African "Balkanization." Before Africa finally stabilizes, many unexpected developments are bound to occur.

A second point concerns the implications of the arrival on the political scene of an entire new generation of African youth, more educated in many instances than the practical politicians, and themselves imbued with a passionate belief in the necessity and the realizability of political Pan-Africanism. This new generation is extremely impatient with parochialism and is hypercritical regarding their present leadership. One generation, of course, seldom understands the contribution of the previous one. Just as the older politicians and Pan-Africanists of the interwar generation often feel bypassed by the inheritance that the younger groups of nationalists obtained for themselves, so these leaders, now no longer so young, may find themselves less highly regarded by those pushing to become their successors.

Only recently, members of the All-African Students' Association of North America discussed the need to rid the new African states of their present leadership, which having served the cause of independence, was less suitable for the cause of African unity.

The emergence of this new and more militantly Pan-Africanist generation could be the decisive factor in the success of political Pan-Africanism. In their penetrating historical study of the process of successful voluntary political integration in a number of European countries, Karl W. Deutsch and his associates introduced the concept of "take-off." Here they refer to a period in which

> . . . small, scattered, and powerless movements (directed toward integration) change into larger and more coordinated ones with some significant power behind them. Before take-off, political integration may be a matter for theorists, for writers, for a few statesmen, or a few small pressure groups. After take-off, integration is a matter of broad political movements, of governments . . . often an affair . . . of the organized persuasion of large parts of the political elites or the politically relevant strata of the time.. . . . We may consider take-off to have occurred as soon as at least one major social or political group, or political institution, has become committed to the cause of integration. In most of our cases, the period of take-off was followed, within a period of one to two generations, either by the attainment of integration or by the abandonment of the attempt.[17]

They found, among other things, that the "take-off" was facilitated by "the arrival of a new generation in politics; the younger men were usually more committed to new ways of doing things and more willing to accept the new size of political units than their predecessors had been."

One final point is the special advantage and opportunity possessed by the present African leaders to make crucial decisions regarding unification at this malleable stage in their history. Although democratization tends toward the development of restraints against freedom of action in foreign policy, this has not yet occurred. The idea of unity commands wide acceptance. John Marcum has stated the point most succinctly: "The fluid period of decolonization and common struggle for independence provides a fleeting moment in history during which

[17] Karl W. Deutsch, *op. cit.*, pp. 83–85.

federalists might overcome the opposition of local political, administrative and economic interests before the latter rigidify within the narrower limits of smaller and separate states." [18] Political Pan-Africanists in the Congo, Equatorial Africa, and East Africa might ponder the wisdom of revising George Padmore's dictum, appropriate at the time but now out of date, and adopt the slogan "Unity first, then independence." It will take perseverance and patience if the stage of nationalism in Africa is in fact to serve as the precondition of a wider United States of Africa, and not grind to a halt in unions that have more shadow than substance. Today's leaders not only have a fleeting opportunity; they carry a heavy responsibility for the well-being of African posterity.

[18] John Marcum, "The Challenge of Africa," *The New Leader,* Feb. 8, 1960, p. 17.

SUPPLEMENTARY REMARKS

DAVID E. APTER

In PRESENTING this material on the international politics of Africa, once again let me remind you of our original dilemma, which was to distinguish truly international from internal politics. This is a dilemma because in the context of contemporary Africa the whole problem of Pan-Africanism is simultaneously both national and international. Although the states may act as separate nations on some issues vis-à-vis one another, on others there is a sense of shared appreciation of the common burden of effort and the drive for independence, which in itself relates people in widely diverse parts of Africa. Once a new African state enters the state system and joins the United Nations, it becomes a fully autonomous part of a complicated unity. Pan-Africanism begins to take on a new character. Different ideas of freedom, different methods of mobilizing economic and social reources, different approaches to the burdens resulting from the recent past; are all potentially divisive elements within the African continent and all pose grave dangers in respect to external affairs.

The West African countries have been the first pioneers in independence. It was they who, nationalizing Pan-Africanism, made it possible for independence itself to be realized for all of Africa. Their mission in this respect is not complete. The separate sovereignties of West Africa are handicapped because they cannot deal directly with colonial territories. One of the possible ways in which they can do so is by associating in such Commonwealth and Community ties as may develop and evolve. An example of the use of the Commonwealth in this regard was demonstrated by Ghana and Malaya in their application of extensive pressure against South Africa. This was the first time that the Commonwealth, itself, took a position dealing with the internal affairs of one of its members. Thus the Commonwealth may become more than residually significant in the future affairs of countries that still remain under colonial domination. There is value in the Commonwealth and the Community for such pressures. A more important means by which the free states of Africa deal with those still under colonialism is through political parties, trade unions, various kinds of cultural organizations, and the like. These have the freedom to act in the tradition of Pan-Africanism. They are its main carriers. These groups preserve the vitality, the spirit, and the tradition of Pan-Africanism.

I illustrate these remarks by considering three conferences which took place in 1958, and which in a sense fully illustrate some of the potential approaches and difficulties that may be faced by Pan-African movements in the international sphere. The first conference—the Cairo conference of January, 1958—emphasized the tradition of Afro-Asian solidarity. Here the universal characteristics of anticolonialism and the particular traditions of the Pan-Africanist movement were brought together. At the Cairo conference the symbols of unity were shown. As well, the discomforts of practical politics made themselves felt. There were efforts on the part of certain members to reduce the impact of the Middle Eastern and the Far Eastern representatives. There was fear that the rather large Soviet contingent might spell trouble for the political future of Africa. The meetings were characterized by pride, aspiration, and nervousness. Nervousness took the form of hurried, behind-the-scenes discussions, and tactful efforts to soft-pedal certain ideas. At the same time a more positive aspect was shown in the effort to explore common ground. It also became clear that Pan-Africanism had to look within Africa.

The Conference of Independent African States, which was held in Accra in April, 1958, was the second conference to be held in that year. Here Africans, including those of West African sovereign countries, having for the most part recently achieved independence, were confronted with the search for a practical and immediate program to which they might subscribe. Here, however, the difficulties inherent in committing sovereign states responsible for their action became a significant factor. There was concern that commitments might be made to which a sovereign state would not normally hold itself responsible, given its own electors and its own internal demands. In the clear awareness of internal as well as external responsibilities and the complications that these might impose, the conference of independent states, while it passed extremely useful and interesting resolutions, was formal and protocol-minded.

Far different was the All Africa Peoples Conference held in Accra in December, 1958. The classic spirit of Pan-Africanism prevailed. Here condemned countries were named—for example, Portugal and South Africa. Here demands were made for freedom fighters. Here were party participants, trade union representatives, and people in a voluntary and private capacity carrying on the spirit and traditions of Pan-Africanism in the hope that their own governments would be responsive to the issues raised. The political leaders of Pan-Africanism were not acting as the heads of state.

The lesson is clear. If Pan-Africanism is not to be shipwrecked on the shoals of national expediencies, a new political formula must be found which can avoid the separatist consequences of sovereignty and at the same time identify party and state in a closer and effective relationship. Because of Pan-African demands, relations are possible between members of voluntary associations and political parties, and it becomes possible to find intermediate ground between pure sovereignty and pure Pan-African internationalism in the African continent.

The three conferences illuminate different dangers to Pan-Africanism, but they also illuminate the search for a solution. The spirit of political innovation abounds, although it is hard to achieve a useful innovation unless one knows what one is looking for. This search challenges the notion of sovereignty itself, in its classic sense. Perhaps the Sudan and Senegal will give up a vote in the United Nations by their union, but at the same time they will have found a way of associating in such fashion that they neither lose their internal integrity nor become simply a single national entity. There are other examples of this, of course.

Given these potentialities, what then are some of the potential factors that may preclude their happy solution? One is that Africa is not immune to different points of view. Africa is not immune to different methods and ideas in the resolution of promise. Senegal, Ivory Coast, Guinea, Ghana, Nigeria—five areas that in a very important way represent centers of gravity around which other countries can congregate. Such polarization has not yet done damage because the job of Pan-Africanism—the liberation of other parts of Africa—has not yet been accomplished. This aids unity; but it also intensifies competition between unifiers. In Mali, in Guinea, in Ghana, and in other regions, there is potential friction. Polite tempers begin to fray. Differences appear, not simply because of the power motives of individuals, but because behind these motives there is disagreement about the most effective way of liberating the continent and of developing relationships with one another.

As independence proceeds, Africa is drawn more directly into foreign entanglements. As long as the United Nations can coördinate the activities of African political leaders, there is a framework to which the immediate consequences of unilateral agreements can be deflected. As soon as unilateral relationships begin to occur between African countries and others, not only will the character of African society be reshaped but dangers will appear in the relationships of African countries with each other. An example is the Guinea-Ghana union, which is not an effective union but remains a vague formulation and a hope. Guinea still looks toward the reamalgamation of former French West Africa with itself as the pole. Ghana looks southward to English-speaking territories. The union is an important feature of Pan-Africanism, but it has not brought Ghana into an effective working relationship with Guinea. Indeed, Ghana is frightened of Guinea's relationship with the East, and in many parts of former French West Africa, Ghana is regarded with considerable contempt for her reliance upon the West. As far south as Lusaka, I heard political party leaders saying: "Ghana is the example of what the West can do in propelling countries toward independence and freedom; Guinea is an example of what the East can do." In this case the relationship between these countries and the West and East is dangerous to the hope of African unity.

A word on neutralism is in order here. African political leaders welcome competition between East and West in Africa. I think Americans must recognize that the result of their efforts in Africa will be Soviet intervention. We believe in competition but prefer it only when we think it would be favorable to ourselves. If such competition is to continue, the external relations between Africa· and other countries must be highly diversified, never becoming overly dependent upon a single tie—historic or material. Otherwise, Africans will lose freedom of mobility and be less able to shape their own character. Competition between the East and West must not grind up the new states of Africa.

In making these remarks, we have excluded much. I've only touched upon the role of the United Nations; also, I have passed over the actual external affairs of Africa with Western countries other than the United States.

I would like to emphasize that Pan-Africanism will not develop purely through the political effort of political leaders in political organizations of states. The countervailing forces that work for Pan-Africanism, as distinct from the forces that militate against it, will be matters of spirit and will. What we have emphasized are the structural proclivities of organization—organizations such as political parties or states and the like. What is left out is the determination of people themselves to find a way regardless of the obstacles, regardless of motives and questions of personal or national competition. It will be a matter of determination never to lose sight of the ultimate goals of Pan-Africanism. African traditionalism must be made to serve not as a negative or parochial factor, but as a positive one through placing the emphasis upon coöperation, communalism, and association which are inherent in and characteristic of all aspects of African traditional life. These factors must traditionalize novelty, must make change comfortable, must open the way for social and political expressions above and beyond the narrow limitations of pure politics. There is an internal discipline in African life which must never be allowed to dissipate itself in a welter of external or international affairs. Ideals and ideas are always both powerful and fragile. How they will be able to affect the immediate demands the people may make upon themselves and their political leaders will be far more important than the immediate political aspects of organization in Africa. Functional relationships can emerge in supraterritorial, practical organizations which preserve the spirit and the character of African common-shared values, and which will protect Africa against the forces that may work against her. These are powerful factors in the creation of Pan-Africanism, regardless of the obstacles, regardless of the forces that now seem to divide, regardless of the demands of internal political mobilization and internal political forces, regardless of the conflicts between men, ideals, and personality. Here is one of those rare moments in time when *will*—a very old fashioned word—*belief*, or *spirit* may, in fact, work miracles. I certainly hope so.

COMMENTS

WACHUKU ABENGOWE

*Member, House of Assembly, Eastern Region of Nigeria;
Deputy Chief Whip for the Government*

I AM very sorry that I cannot dwell fully on this paper; within the short time available to me to read it, what struck me most forcefully is contained in table 1 of the document, which deals with the views of political parties on Pan-Africanism.

May I say, with due respect to the authors, that they are not quite correct in all their assumptions as they relate to Nigeria. Pan-Africanism is the ultimate ambition of most African countries. It is racial consciousness stemming from the inferior status in which the people of Africa and of African descent have been placed since their contact in modern times with Western peoples.

I wish to center my comments on table 1. It is not correct that the Northern Peoples' Congress is opposed to West African union and to Pan-Africanism. It is also not correct that the Northern Elements' Progressive Union favors Pan-Africanism under Nigerian leadership. It is correct, however, that the National Council of Nigeria and the Cameroons, of which I am a member, favors Pan-Africanism, and thus favors separate independence for each state.

I do not intend to raise dust in Nigerian politics by discoursing critically on the views of any political party to which I am opposed; I will, however, endeavor to summarize Nigerian opinion on this matter.

Pan-Africanism, or the union of all African states, is the accepted policy of the Nigerian federal government, which is run today by my party, the National Council of Nigeria and the Cameroons, and the Northern Peoples' Congress. During the last budget session of the Nigerian Federal Parliament in March, the Prime Minister—who is also a member of the Northern Peoples' Congress—stated that Nigeria accepted Pan-Africanism as a policy and would participate and send delegates to all conferences dealing with Pan-Africanism. I now declare it to be true that the Action Group is also in favor of Pan-Africanism.

At the last conference held in Accra all the major political parties in Nigeria—including the Action Group, which is in opposition in the House of Representatives—sent delegates. The Nigerian Prime Minister further said that in the future Nigerians would initiate conferences on Pan-Africanism.

May I add this point, to throw light on the Nigerian program on Pan-Africanism: Nigeria believes in Pan-Africanism, but will not bully any of the younger states into joining the Union of All-African States. To our minds, this union will become a reality by removing the artificial boundaries that handicap all the African states. There must be mutual understanding; we must operate like a large family, with the sole aim of combining all the states. Social and economic problems must be dealt with first. One must be able to move around the African continent with a common pass. Communications must be developed. We must not allow ourselves to be isolated culturally. There must be technical coöperation and interchange of professors and teachers in our education. The importance of that common bond, a common currency, cannot be overemphasized.

When these problems have been objectively approached, when the fears of the younger states have been removed, when suspicion no longer exists, then the hope of ultimate political Pan-Africanism will materialize. And the only platform on which these problems can be effectively thrashed out is Pan-Africanism, and that is why we strongly believe in Pan-Africanism.

To us, nationalism is not an end in itself. It is a means to an end. Pan-Africanism is a projection of nationalism in Africa. After the attainment of Pan-Africanism, the ultimate ambition of the world should be world peace, unity, and equality. This will come by one channel and one channel only. What is that channel? It is the channel whereby every race, country, or continent will appreciate the equal existence of the other. It is a channel where each continental personality will be respected. It is a channel where it will be appreciated that each continent has some contribution to make.

RICHARD M. AKWEI
Counsellor, Embassy of Ghana to the United States

It is rather difficult to assess the confusions of the original discussants at this session, because I got the impression that at certain stages they were arguing against each other. I wasn't too satisfied with the definition of Pan-Africanism which was given by the first speaker. I think I got the impression that he was confining, limiting the definition of Pan-Africanism to the political sphere, that is, the creation of what he called "supranational political unification." And then we have this very illustrious, idealistic definition toward the end of Mr. Apter's remarks: Pan-Africanism as the sum of Africa's ideas and ideals, indicating the social complexity and absolute comprehensiveness of the term. Well, of course, academic people always try to make things easier for themselves by citing specific definitions within which they wish to channel their thoughts. I have always, as you probably may surmise by now, adopted a rather flexible approach to this matter of definitions. Pan-Africanism has a political aspect; it has political connotations; but you can't really dissociate the other concepts—the other aspects—of Pan-Africanism from the political aspect. And I would prefer to talk about Pan-Africanism in its total aspect: what has been described in certain parts of Africa as the projection of this thing called "the African personality." And don't ask me to define it precisely because I don't believe in precise definitions. But we know what it means and I'm sure you know what it means too! Take the political aspect, for example, and take a quick look at the geography, the existing political maps of Africa, and you will find that, although the emergence of the independent African territories is under way, large pockets of Africa are still oppressed and suppressed by foreign rulers —in some cases not from foreign rule in the sense of the power being foreign, for you do have places like South Africa which practice the sin of oppression internally.

In the political context, therefore, nationalism is at the forefront of Pan-Africanism.

Now, in the cultural field, although I am told that there was a little difficulty at the Roundtable of Negro and African Artists in trying to define exactly what are African culture and Negro culture and art and that sort of thing, we do appreciate the existence of a core of a way of living just as you, in the same way, refer to what you call the "American way of life." You find this expression in the religion of the peoples of Africa; you find this expression in the ceremonials of parts of Africa; you find this expression in the arts and dances of Africa. And without even going into the controversial question of trying to identify what it is that distinguishes Negro or African art from European art, at least we should be quite satisfied with the knowledge that there is something positive, some great, some noble contribution which is entering into the sum total of world culture and civilization from Africa. Of course, we are not living in isolation and we cannot expect therefore to be unaffected by things in other parts of the world.

In the economic aspect of nationalism and of Pan-Africanism it is quite clear that we are opposed—that is, people who believe in Pan-Africanism are opposed—to the concept of racially segregated trade unions; we are opposed to economic alignments that act as a kind of hangover from the granting of political independence—such artificial alignments as the European Common Market, which sets in opposition one group of African countries against another group of African countries, primarily in the interest of the metropolitan European powers. We are opposed to the concept of economic development that reserves certain economic activities to Europeans and lesser ones to Africans. We are opposed to the investment relationship that condemns Africa merely to the role of a supplier of natural resources for the selfish exploitation by foreign companies. Thus, Pan-Africanism declares its economic essence to be the exploitation of Africa's resources primarily for Africa's development.

And when you consider the racial aspect of Pan-Africanism, we are not restricted in our use of the term. I think it was mentioned somewhere during previous discussions that many of the Eastern and Central African territories, being multiracial, tend to have a much wider breadth of vision in dealing with this kind of problem than perhaps other parts of Africa which are not faced with the same kind of race problem. I submit that that is not so, and there are facts to prove this. You will find, if you will study the preliminaries that led to the convening of the Conference of the Independent African

States, that Ghana did offer, did extend an invitation to South Africa to participate in the proceedings of that conference. But for purposes known only to the South African government, it did not choose to join in our great efforts to establish for the continent of Africa the same noble principles of liberty, fraternity, and equality that it wants only for the white class in South Africa. We have no intention of limiting the concept and principles upon which we conceive Pan-Africanism to any specific racial group or specific class of people in Africa. And I think this is a matter that is important and is worth bearing in mind.

Now, there are certain points to which I should address myself, simply because I think I would be failing in my duty if I did not unburden myself of my own views concerning some of the things that were said about my country, Ghana. I am surprised to hear that Ghana is so frightened of a very brotherly and great associate, Guinea, because of its so-called relations with the East and West, and that we are having second thoughts about our union with Guinea. We also have very close relations with the East and West, and we believe in the policy and principle of positive neutrality; the activities and the policies of the Guinea government have not to my knowledge caused any alarm or fright in Accra. I was in Ghana recently and there was a delegation that had visited Conakry; it was led, I think, by the Minister of Finance, and there was wide agreement on how to further cement and strengthen the very useful political association that we have formed with each other.

As regards what form of political instrument is best suited to the propagation of the concept of Pan-Africanism, I do not think that we will be rendering any service or achieving any useful purpose by saying that one type of political organization or union is to be preferred to another type. Nor do we serve any useful purpose by accusing fellow African states who are pioneering in this field. Of course, in the realm of ideas, ideas should be left alone to find their level. We do have our own ideas as to what is best calculated to propagate and promote this principle of Pan-Africanism. But we are not pushing down the throats of other African countries this particular ideology or concept. We realize there is a wide diversity of views and a wide outlook on the problem of political Pan-Africanism. Are you going to have a unitary Africa, implying a union of African states? Are you going to have a federation of African states? Are you going to have a confederation of African states on the same model as that of the Austro-Hungarian Empire of the last century? These are questions to be discussed. We think, however, that here and now in history, because we achieved our independence from a colonial status and were the first to achieve this independence, an obligation has been enjoined upon us to promote this development of Pan-Africanism, to promote the achievement of freedom by other African peoples, to promote the closer coöperation of African peoples in solving their own problems. And we think that we would be failing in our duty if we did not take these steps.

I'm not quite sure whether a previous speaker's belief that the achievement of independence in India was of great consequence in promoting the independence movement in Africa is a very useful one. We in Ghana have always been very, very much inspired by the existence of the sovereign states of Liberia and Ethiopia, even before the independence of India. And I think most of us will remember the wave of indignation and the rapidity with which people got together all over Africa to support their brothers when Mussolini attacked Ethiopia.

Regarding the categorization of the problems, or of the way in which you want to look at the Pan-Africanism that has been developed— the internal and the external—I am rather disappointed that the analysis didn't go deeper. For instance, in the internal sphere, there was no attempt made to reason out why there tends to be certain one-party or dominant-party systems of government in some of these newly emerged African countries. But the inference is made that political leaders in Africa tend to think they need the one-party system to ensure internal cohesion, to ensure internal discipline. I think this is a fundamental error that many Americans have been prone to make in the past.

On this same analogy, Ghana has sometimes been described as a rather disturbing kind of country, because it has associated with the Western world for so long a time. And we have been told that perhaps certain territorial propositions that we have made have come under the category of political chauvinism. Now we realize there are problems in Africa. And one of these problems, a very important one, is the threat of a Balkanization of Africa. We do not think that the achievement of independence should mean the fragmentation of previously existing territories. You have only to look at the record of some of the colonial powers to see that this can be a very real danger. Our friends the British seem to be the classic example of the believers in the solution of independence problems by the "carving-out" of territories. They carved out India; they carved out Ireland; they wanted to carve out Cyprus; and now we are faced with a very similar possibility and probability in the Belgian Congo, where as a result of certain omissions and commissions on the part of the Belgians, there seems to be some difficulty in arriving at a homogeneous, strong government. Whether you are going to have a unitary type of government within these countries, or whether you are going to have a federal type of government within them, we think, is a purely secondary matter. We think that anything at all that militates against the granting of independence, anything that delays the achievement of independence, is to be condemned. And this playing of one party off against another party which seems to be going on in the Congo, cannot be accepted as being in the best interests of the spreading of Pan-Africanism.

I would go along with my colleague Professor Apter in identifying some of the important internal problems under the headings of traditionalism and tribalism, because both these are factors in the projection of the "African personality," or what you might describe as the "negritude" proposed by Mr. Léopold Senghor. Tribalism, we think, has certain defects. Very broadly, I think that tribalism in a political sphere militates against the full operation of modern democracy. We have had the problem in Ghana. We have had the problem of the chiefs who were not willing to hand over power to democratically elected local councils. We have had the problem of disenchanted politicians who thought they could hide behind the chiefs, and thereby try to carve the country into cumbersome federal units which the country's resources could not sustain. On the other hand, we are not prepared to rule tribalism out of court altogether, or at least some of the ingredients of tribalism. We in Ghana are proud of the institution of chieftaincy, and it is regarded as entrenched and inviolate in the new constitution which we have advanced in Ghana. We believe that music, African music, African arts—some of these things that seem to be dying out as a result of the impact of so-called Western civilization—are important and should be preserved in order to give additional content to the projection of the African personality and the achievement of Pan-Africanism. I wish to suggest that in thinking about Pan-Africanism we should not allow ourselves to fall into the danger of being diverted from our main purpose by critics who perhaps really do not wish to promote the idea we have in mind. This is something that is important to Africans all over and can only be promoted by Africans. We will be told that perhaps the arrangements with former metropolitan powers should persist even after the granting of independence, because there are certain realistic benefits that are to be derived from such an association. Well, what do you make of the association of some of the overseas territories which I tried to mention yesterday, with the new concept of the E.E.C.—which association, I think, and most of us in Ghana think, is a direct limitation on the spreading of this fellow-feeling, this feeling of fraternity between Africans. You are going to have a partial, limited economic development of certain parts of Africa to the disadvantage of certain other parts of Africa. And therefore we consider this panoply of external factors strictly as cold-war ideological manipulation.

A speaker for whom I have great respect, Chief Enahoro, has said in what I regarded as a criticism of the policy of neutrality that we have to make a positive decision on fundamentals. We, as realistic human beings, living in a torn world, know that there are certain variations in the political and social ideologies of the world no matter whether of the West or the East; and we think that we, if we are going to believe in the principle of the sovereignty of nations and help create the peace that only coexistence can give, should allow all peoples to decide which instrument they want to use in ameliorating their condition, and to have the type of government they wish to live under. Therefore, the concept of making a decision on fundamentals regarding the cold war is really not perhaps in the best interest of Pan-Africanism. We need all the friends we can get abroad. Let us not divide the friends that we can win from abroad by making not-very-useful decisions on what are described as fundamentals. Our fundamental is Pan-Africanism, and our international method, the critical examination of problems with a view to solving them.

POLITICS / 129

SABURI OLADENI BIOBAKU

Secretary to the Premier, Western Region, Nigeria

I having nothing but admiration for the two professors of political science and for their lucid and comprehensive papers. Indeed, it is a pleasure for me to comment on the efforts of two friends, especially those of Jim Coleman, whose book *Nigeria: Background to Nationalism* [California, 1958] is undoubtedly among the best of its kind.

But if I may say so, the task of a political scientist is far from easy; he is in constant danger of being out of date even before he puts pen to paper on any given situation. That is one of his occupational risks and that is why historians like myself prefer to leave contemporary events severely alone. Quite seriously, in the ever-changing quicksand of politics there are really no permanent features, and it is a fundamental error to rely on generalizations. I agree that the onlooker sees most of the game, but were I to watch a game of baseball I, unlike the native American, should congratulate myself if I stumbled upon the finer points of the game. Alternatively, I must confess my inability to distinguish between the Republicans and the Democrats in this country, and I may be wrong if I pronounce that the only difference is that one party is at present in office and the other is out. *Ergo,* with all due respect, the political scientist from the outside cannot fully grasp all the nettles, in the African context, of the African situation, and we often wonder why he so deliberately misses the wood for the trees!

I do not propose in the limited time at my disposal to fill in the gaps that are apparent to me in the excellent presentations we have heard. (For example, I think the role of Liberia in promoting the larger African unities has not been sufficiently emphasized. Long in the wilderness along with Ethiopia, the lone star remained a lodestone, in spite of obvious shortcomings; and now that more ebullient sister nations are rampaging, she is doing her best to fix the new stars in the firmament. Nor do I have the time to join issues with Professor Apter on the merits and demerits of a single-party system both in ensuring internal cohesion and in promoting Pan-Africanism.) I shall limit myself to clarifying the position of Nigeria in relation to Pan-Africanism—a position that has been misunderstood in the paper. I shall select just two quotations and refute them:

Nigeria remains cautious and aloof.

Indeed, even with Nigeria there are considerable differences of view among the regional leaders regarding Nigeria's orientation in world affairs once it becomes independent.

First, it must be remembered that Nigeria is not yet independent and her foreign policy cannot as yet be fully formulated or openly ventilated. Biding our time is not the same thing as aloofness.

Second, caution is not necessarily a bad thing, and we in Nigeria are essentially realists who prefer to survey the ground first before taking a leap.

Third, to say our leaders have different views as to our ultimate foreign policy and to take up a position upon that is to illustrate the danger of being hopelessly out-of-date to which I referred earlier. It is true that during the recent election campaign for the Federal House of Representatives the leaders of the major parties expressed some details of their viewpoints, which were necessarily different from one another; but everyone knew that in *essence* there could really be no difference. And if you don't believe me, just glance over the speech made by the leader of the Nigerian delegation to the recent Addis Ababa conference, an NPC federal minister speaking on behalf of a team representing all the major parties. He gave unmistakable proof that despite internal party differences and maneuvers for dominance, which are permanent features of parties in a democracy, the voice of Nigeria abroad is going to be strong, unequivocal, and decisive.

What really is our stand? As my friend Enahoro has already said, we ask basic questions in Nigeria in regard to Pan-Africanism. As an *ideal*, "a consummation devoutly to be wished," we have no doubt whatsoever; it is as much a *sine qua non* of our foreign policy as is our uncompromising opposition to and denunciation of the policies of the present rulers of South Africa.

But we ask the questions: Pan-Africanism at what price? Pan-Africanism for what?

Pan-Africanism at what price? Shall we, or anyone else, be expected to surrender our sovereignty so recently won, without actual proof that in doing so we are ensuring its continual enjoyment for ourselves and our associates? We need assurance that we are pooling sovereignty and not surrendering ours to anyone else in ephemeral union. We want to ensure that the basic freedoms for which we have struggled in achieving nationhood would remain the basis of the larger unity—*freedom for the individual, the rule of law.*

Pan-Africanism for what? Here I think Professor Rostow put our case as well as an economic historian could. We believe in Pan-Africanism not only because thereby we shall be able to project the "African personality" on to the world stage, but also because we want the "African personality" to have a real and meaningful face in world affairs. To us it does not mean merely taking up attitudes, rattling the personality in place of sabres, and securing seats in the Security Council when the basic problems of Africa—poverty, ignorance, and disease—are yet unsolved. We think it a matter of the highest priority to develop our people and our resources, to "modernize" in the phraseology of Professor Rostow; when we can achieve this we shall invest the African personality with a potency that is bound to be respected everywhere, and our influence in the community of nations will be real, not superficial.

So it is a matter of priorities: on the one hand we do not wish to exchange one form of tyranny for another, to exchange King Hog for King Stork or to aid and abet territorial expansionism under the guise of promoting Pan-Africanism; on the other hand, we wish to build the new Jerusalem before proclaiming it from the housetops.

And do not think we have no approaches. As Chief Enahoro has said, our first aim is to hold fast to our own federation, which could be a reassuring minimum in the larger cosmos of African unity. If we succeed in binding together our forty million people in three, four, or nine states under a federal umbrella, others—Cameroons, Niger, Dahomey, Togo, and even Ghana—are welcome to join us: they will have guaranteed to them liberty, equality, and fraternity. A snowballing process can develop and our federation can join others.

In the meantime we believe in promoting joint ventures, establishing regional organizations, pooling our scientific knowledge, and attracting aid from abroad in a manner that will ensure benefit to us. For example, we are prepared to join with Ghana in developing the cocoa trade, with Liberia in respect to rubber, and with Dahomey in exploring the possibilities of the palm produce industries.

We are engaged in tremendous programs of internal development—educational, medical, and economic services. We need to mobilize our resources and attract foreign aid to achieve our objectives. We consider it imprudent to divert our ablest managerial skill from these essential services to the pursuit of ideals for which we do not think others are really ready. Pan-Africanism is no different from Pan-Europeanism or Pan-Americanism, nor is it any more than an aspect of world government. We do not flatter ourselves into thinking we can achieve without difficulties what older independent states have failed to achieve in all these years.

But we are not indifferent to it; we are, however, determined to make it a reality when we do achieve it: real in the sense of ensuring all the freedoms to all people and real in ensuring that the essential problems of Africa—poverty, ignorance and disease—are eliminated throughout the continent.

We too have seen the vision and are persuaded of it, but we refuse "to the fascination of the ideal to surrender judgment, hoodwink'd."

SAIDI MASWANYA

Deputy Organizing Secretary General, Tanganyika National Union

There have been no adverse remarks made about Tanganyika by the other speakers. Consequently, I do not feel obliged to take the offensive approach. There have been serious omissions, however, in the papers presented here by the professors.

For example, it has been stated that American Negroes and West Indians were the first Africans in exile from Africa, and that they were the first to devise the idea of Pan-Africanism. The omission here is the explanation of why and how this idea evolved. I fear that if we don't examine the causes that motivated these persons to come together and initiate this movement, then the underlying forces might again cause these people to go into exile and start something else. The omission of explanation is serious because we cannot find a cure for what we don't understand. I think they had a reason.

The reason can be found in the common sufferings these people endured. All had been the victims of similar treatment. In Africa, they were subjected to being purchased, regarded as merchandise, and taken to other countries as slaves. Those people remaining in Africa were colonized. Both groups had an important factor in common: their dignity as men, from the time of the discovery of Africa by the other nations of the world, was interfered with. The right to govern themselves was taken away from them in Africa. In America and the West Indies this right was also missing. So these people had reason to come together and discuss these abnormal happenings.

What could Africa's freedom mean to these people? Could we suppose that her freedom might give a certain pride to American Negroes? Could her independence give West Indians a certain satisfaction? In all probability it would bring a certain, but not the necessary, amount of satisfaction.

At one time Marcus Garvey initiated a "back-to-Africa" movement here. He and his colleagues were searching for a place to enjoy the dignity and freedom that all human beings should have and which they felt were being denied them here. This movement was unsuccessful. The political experience here teaches us something about the role of the American Negro in the future world. It teaches us that the independence of Africa would not necessarily mean that American Negroes and West Indians will be removed to Africa. This cannot be done because American Negroes are Americans and their role will be as Americans.

Another omission is that of comment on the northern part of Africa. There has been no mention of Tunisia, Algeria, Libya, or Egypt. No mention whatsoever! Do the speakers mean to suggest that these areas aren't part of Africa? Well, I shall tell them that they are a part of Africa. They are African! There are numerous African Tunisians working there and coöperating with us for the same purposes, with the same intentions that we have; we share the same goals. So the speakers should tell us what in their opinions should happen there.

South Africa and South Africans have also been omitted from discussion. This is a very serious omission. In South Africa it is said that South Africa is an independent country—The Independent Country of the White Settlers of South Africa! This may be satisfactory to the white settlers, but experience should make us aware that there is trouble in South Africa. There is trouble because this strong minority of white settlers has taken complete control of the country. It has taken upon itself the right to dictate the lives of the weakened majority. It has assumed the authority to divide the country—the blanket authority to distribute and restrict Africans to areas of its choice. This settler power has denied Africans the necessary opportunities to participate in the affairs—the life—of the country. This is the problem South Africa faces. It is a problem we can't evade. It is there!

Pan-Africanism recognizes this problem. We would have welcomed the advice of the scientifically-minded political thinkers assembled here. We believe that all of South Africa must be made free! The nations of the world should now realize that the situation in South Africa must be changed! And I might well mention here that one of the ends of Pan-Africanism is to seek freedom for the peoples of Africa—wherever they are in Africa!

This doesn't mean that we are being influenced by the origin of the various peoples living in Africa, or that we are being prejudiced by color. No, far from this. We want democracy and democratic institutions established all over Africa. We want all people to have the opportunity to take part in running the governments of their particular countries. This business of qualitative franchise, of choosing from among other "preferred" people to take care of the affairs of the government will not do! It simply will not do!

There is another omission. There has been no mention at all of Portuguese East Africa or the Portuguese peoples. Are they non-existent? Are they not within the area of Africa? And does Pan-Africanism not apply there? Of course, the big bosses there, who are ruling the country against the will of the people, haven't even considered the fact that those people should be governing themselves. You may be sure that there will come a time when Africans there will have the right to participate in the affairs of the country.

It is useless to discuss Africa if we omit the aforementioned areas. They are vital; to omit them is serious.

There is another question. Why did Africans in Africa agree to adopt the theories given birth by Africans in exile, namely, American Negroes and West Indians? What appeal did these theories have to the masses of Africa? Why have Africans taken steps to implement these ideas, to set these theories in practice? The appeal is found in the truth these theories embrace.

Now I shall discuss certain situations existing in East Africa—certain facts that people here aren't familiar with. In regard to them I don't intend to criticize the professors; it's not their mistake. They've done their best. In East Africa we intend to implement the idea of

Pan-Africanism as far as joining various countries is concerned. But what hinders us? We are handcuffed by the existence of colonial governments. They refuse to give independence to large blocs of states. And so the difficulty of forming governmental unities arises. We now have a movement to combat this. We have a Pan-Africa Freedom Movement in Eastern and Central Africa to demand as a body the independence of our countries. On this basis we are reuniting.

But not only in East Africa do we find the aforementioned situation; it exists all over the African continent. The placement of national boundaries by the colonial high caste was unrealistic, improper, and ruthless. Tribes were divided. Take the Masai peoples for example. There are Masai in both Kenya and Tanganyika. If we follow this system of boundaries, we will find that the Masai in Kenya and those in Tanganyika will become alien to each other. This is an unchallengeable fact! It must be changed!

Also in Kenya we find that there are Somalis in the north and none in the south. Yet this is one country as far as colonial boundaries are concerned. These boundaries in the east, to our minds, are unrealistic and necessarily only temporary. We see what happens when the colonial governments give independence to these countries. Consider Somaliland, for example: there was Italian Somaliland, there was British Somaliland, French Somaliland, so-and-so Somaliland [laughter and applause]. But now, after independence has been granted all these areas, we see that they have united.

This is nationalism at work! This is Pan-Africanism! These are the forces that will work not only against the colonizers, but against the "big people," against the big chiefs. They are bound to work against the politicians who want to assume the role of emperors! They have their own way now, but they cannot have it forever!

MAIDA SPRINGER

International Representative, Department of International Affairs, AFL-CIO

When we talk of African self-government, of independence, and of related objectives, as a trade unionist I can see that the accomplishment of these objectives can only be solidified after the trade union movements have taken their rightful place, as they have done, and contributed to the independence of several African countries. Beyond that, in the people's rendezvous with destiny the trade unions must also take their place as responsible units of the new countries; they must concern themselves with the development, the stability, and the viability of the economy, and with furthering the rights of the individual under a democratic and free government. We in the trade union movement accept these moral responsibilities quite seriously.

When we talk of economic aid, I will leave that to the people in government and industry. But the kind of moral and physical aid that the trade union movement is concerned with is the kind of aid that the Africans require and request of us.

To give you a simple example: very recently a trade union center was opened in Kenya—the Kenya Trade Union Centre. The bulk of the money for setting it up came from the American labor movement, with no strings attached. The African citizens of Kenya have this as a monument to our belief in international solidarity and as a symbol in their own drive for independence and democratic institutions.

Of course, you cannot win real independence simply by erecting a building; you cannot win economic advantage by a conversation about solidarity. Thus, there are practical instruments, such as the trade union school in Kampala, which trains Africans to go back to their communities and work for the stabilization and democratization of their communities. The economist at this institution is African. Again, this indicates that what Africans want can be supplied, if and when requested, by the trade union movements in the Western world.

I would like also to raise an independent problem, which I think should be given careful consideration here. It seems to me that before the next conference of AMSAC there will be great steps toward self-government and independence in the entire area of East and Central Africa—comprising roughly twenty-seven million people. This development will pose for the Africans a rather different set of problems than those associated with the independence of West Africa. There is going to be a multiracial society, involving the citizenship of Europeans and Asians as well as Africans. The members of these minorities will have to accept their duties and responsibilities with the exercise of less privilege and greater limitation on the conspicuous consumption that they previously enjoyed. Then, too, the day is not far off when South Africa and Portuguese Africa will join the family; not that they will want to join, but they will have to join. The pressure of international opinion, the force of African responsibility in East, Central, and West Africa will force such a development. Again, I think the new and different kinds of problems that will attend the independence of these areas should receive careful consideration in our discussions here.

IMMANUEL WALLERSTEIN

Department of Sociology, Columbia University

I was interested to hear that Mr. Biobaku cannot distinguish between the Democratic and Republican parties. I was also a bit disappointed, being a member of one of the two parties; I feel that I can distinguish between the two. But I'm not entirely surprised that he cannot make this distinction. I was a bit relieved when he went on to indicate that there really isn't that much difference among his country's Action Group, the NCNC, and the NPC. I suppose that this might be taken to indicate that Mr. Biobaku would be indifferent to whether he votes for one or the other of the parties at the next election. Seriously, this does illustrate a point. On the essentials of some questions, especially that of foreign policy, parties in a country tend to be united. But on the other hand, there tend to be important nuances which some of us can point to even in the foreign policies of our respective parties, whether they be in the United States, Nigeria, or elsewhere.

I was glad that Mr. Maswanya raised the issue of one omission in the previous papers which I think was a rather serious one—the omission of North Africa. I'd like to ask you to do an exercise. Think back to 1954. Think what you might have predicted about the way Pan-Africa would develop in the years between 1954 and 1960. I think you might have predicted most of the things that have occurred. There is one thing, however, that most people in this audience would have been less likely to predict: that North Africa and Black Africa have both been represented at every single Pan-African meeting that has been held in the last three or four years. In fact, the most recent conference on Pan-Africanism was held in a North African country. We are probably one of the few conferences on Pan-Africanism which does not involve North African participation.

I think that if one looks at it from both points of view, one can see that there is very strong feeling on this point. If you look at it from the North African point of view, you can see that there is a tremendous concern taken with the problem of being African. When you hear a Tunisian, a Moroccan, or an Algerian say "We Africans . . . ," one begins to sense the feeling they have of being African. If one reads a newspaper such as *Abou Hajid,* the official organ of the FLN, and if one notices that practically no space is devoted to Iraq, but that in every single issue there is an article on Tanganyika, the Belgian Congo, or some other part of Black Africa, then one senses that they seem to see themselves as Africans first and Arabs second.

Certainly, the effectiveness of the African bloc of the United Nations up to this point can be largely attributed to North Africa. This is owing to the fact that there are so few of the Black African states that have been made independent, whereas North African states comprise at least fifty per cent of this bloc. I only raise this question. I put it before you and ask you to consider it again tomorrow when you approach the question of negritude. Ask yourself what implications Pan-Africanism will have on the whole concept of negritude as it develops on a truly Pan-African basis—that is to say, on a geographical basis—including the whole of Africa.

Another point that to me seems to have been omitted erroneously from the discussion deals with the practical problems accompanying the achievement of large-scale Pan-African unity. I think that the extent of area involved makes an appreciable difference when we consider the question of a state yielding its sovereignty to enter a federation. I'd suggest that a total government might be more willing to make a complete surrender of sovereignty to a full-fledged federation that included all the West African states—British and French, ex-British and ex-French West Africa together—than it would be willing to enter a smaller union. For example, if Nigeria had a choice between a union with, first, only herself and Ghana as members; second, Nigeria and the rest of West Africa; and last, a union that included Nigeria and all of the African continent, then she might be hesitant about the first, slightly less hesitant about the second, and perhaps be immediately ready—even tomorrow—to enter the third. I think it's clear that one of the considerations going into this kind of readiness and union is the degree of impact that the larger union would have upon the internal policies of any given state entering into the union. Hence, the larger the unit to be created, the more likely it will be that Africa will realize the creation of a federation.

Now I should like to refer to a point on the economic issue, one that I think was in a paper originally distributed by Professors Coleman and Apter. This point was made in passing and not mentioned again. However, it is often brought up as an obstacle to unification. The point is that, historically, the richer territories have been most cool about joining larger federations. The Ashanti in Ghana, the Ivory Coast in former French West Africa, and the Western Region in the Federation of Nigeria, along with other rich areas seem to say to themselves, "Well, we might do better economically if we were sort of separated"; and it is the poor states that "sort of" fall for this. To a certain extent this is quite clearly true if one looks at the pattern. However, one might also find economic pressures within the richer states which might push them toward supporting a federation on a larger scale. Let me cite just one example. A French industrialist living in the Ivory Coast recently wrote an article for one of the Ivory Coast magazines in which he says: "Look! I'm an industrialist. I want to build factories—and the Ivory Coast wants to industrialize. Let us face facts. The Ivory Coast has about three million population and this isn't a very big internal market. I'm really interested in a market of thirty or forty million people." It is irrelevant whether the man who makes such a decision is a private capitalist or a socialist "saint." Attempting to establish light industries in any country leads one to consider this issue. For an industry to be viable, to survive, it might need larger markets. So I reëmphasize the suggestion that there may be positive economic factors pushing even these historically reluctant areas toward Pan-Africanism.

Often enough one hears references to divisions in Africa—between North and Black Africa, between French-speaking and English-speaking Africa, and between the areas that have and those that do not have white communities. Of course there are differences. However, I'd like to suggest that certain of these differences form a network that will unite, rather than divide, Africa. For it is precisely the differences that create a network of intertwining ties that may serve as a basis for a real federation. North Africa and French-speaking West Africa have the common heritage of being under the same colonial power. Owing to similar histories and a common vocabulary, Moroccans and Senegalese perhaps see each other with more comprehension than do the Senegalese and Nigerians. On the other hand, Senegalese and Nigerians can in fact be intertwined.

Professor Apter spoke of the Ghana-Guinea union, which has not been a real federation. I really think this is the wrong optic. Think back to two years ago when the two territories were completely separated by language and by the segregation of the colonial systems. The noteworthy feature of this union isn't that it does not constitute a full-fledged federation, but that it exists at all! This seems to me a remarkable achievement. It serves as one of the first bridges uniting French and English-speaking West Africa.

Throughout the African continent I can point to ties such as this. English-speaking West, East, and Central Africa also have the heritage of a common colonial power and consequently, certain problems in common. After the Union of South Africa and Algeria each gets a government of universal suffrage, they will have similar heritages and the mutual problem of what to do with minority and various racial groups. Around the continent of Africa we see that parts of Africa are linked together by a whole series of intertwining ties like those mentioned above.

Considering this in addition to the hypothesis that countries are less willing to yield power to smaller than to larger entities, believing the internal impact in their particular areas to be less in the latter case, then I would suggest that the prospects of Pan-Africanism are reasonably good. Certainly, I don't suggest that it is inevitable. It won't be an easy task. Mr. Biobaku spoke of it as something similar to Pan-Europeanism, Pan-Americanism, and a lot of other "pan" movements. I would suggest that out of all of these movements, the Pan-African seems the most capable of realization as a political possibility at the present time.

ACHKAR MAROF
Press Secretary, Guinean Delegation to the United Nations

Since the question of North Africa has been raised, I must say that we have all been struck by the silence regarding this part of the African continent in the different reports presented. The role that

North Africa has played and is still playing in the struggle for the liberation of Africa and the solidarity of the independent states of Africa in this struggle north of the Sahara constitute essential elements of Pan-Africanism. I am thinking now above all of the heroic struggle of the Algerian people—a struggle surely of great importance to the evolution of Negro Africa and especially of its French-speaking part.

To give you a specific example showing that the colonial powers (or in any case the colonialists themselves) are quite clear about the role played by the Algerian people's struggle in the evolution of Africa, I point out a very eloquent fact, of which some of you are perhaps already aware. I refer to the interest of South Africa in the Algerian war and in its methods. South African army officers have actually been sent to Algeria for a period of macabre "training" by French officers, who have not failed to teach them the barbaric methods of massive repression. To journalists who inquired of them upon their return home the reasons for their "training period," they replied simply: "We were certainly not there to fight a war but simply to gain experience in firing on colored crowds."

This applies equally to the Portuguese colonists whose officers are taking a growing interest in the Algerian war. Thus, you see that all these problems are closely related and that it was a great weakness in the debates that they did not give North Africa its proper place in Africa and in the Pan-African movements.

I must likewise say that the various reports have been somewhat mute on South Africa. I will not dwell on this subject—I know that we have in the room brothers from the Union of South Africa who will certainly not fail to enlighten us on the situation prevailing in that country.

Also, I would like to reply to the orators who spoke of the fear felt by Ghana with regard to Guinea, its partner in the Union. Our friend from Ghana [Richard M. Akwei] has, I think, given a clear answer in this regard. But I would add this: It is a bit of an exaggeration to say that Guinea has a foreign policy directed toward the East or the West, the North or the South. Guinea has a policy directed uniquely toward Africa. We do not think that because Guinea entertains commercial relations with all the countries of the world, including the Eastern countries, that it has thereby contradicted its fundamental option: "Independence and unity for Africa in the framework of positive neutralism." Moreover, given the conditions under which Guinea was led to orient a part of its foreign trade toward the nations of the East, it is impossible to attribute to this act a "political" orientation. The figures giving the percentages of exports and imports by Guinea to and from different countries show clearly that all Guinea has done is to break up the old monopolist system with a view to creating a healthy national economy. Not that we require that the trade of Guinea or of Africa or our economic relations in general be directed toward a given country or a group of given countries—we say simply that Africa is free to orient its trade in the fashion most in harmony with its interests. It is dangerous to interpret the economic relations of Africa with the rest of the world in the tendentious style some have used here.

Guinea's efforts regard the interest and dignity of Africa, and can in no manner whatsoever constitute a basis for dispute between Ghana and herself. Quite the contrary! Moreover, I would like to remind you of three events that constitute a refutation of this tendentious interpretation.

1. Ghana has just signed an economic agreement with the Soviet Union. No one would deny her this right.

2. A delegation of the Ghana government has just been to Guinea. New measures tending to reënforce and consolidate the union of Ghana and Guinea were taken at this time.

3. President Tubman of Liberia has just paid an official visit to the Republic of Guinea. At the conclusion of this visit a most positive and encouraging communiqué was published, which thus constituted a reaffirmation of the desire for union felt by all the Pan-African leaders.

We don't claim that Ghana and Guinea are achieving total integration overnight. As people of pragmatic bent we know that this process requires time and great skill. For the moment, we are attacking concrete problems—we try to resolve them with the means at our disposal. All this proves that Guinea, Ghana, and Liberia are really moving closer to one another. On the other hand, this process will soon be facilitated when Mali and the other West African nations become independent. We are not minimizing the obstacles—we know that as long as one corner of Africa constitutes in any fashion an extension of Europe, to that extent Pan-Africanists' aspirations will remain difficult to realize. But we are convinced that the will of the peoples of Africa, the will of Africa, is directed toward unity. Just how, as a matter of fact, would you determine exactly the boundary between Senegal and Guinea or between Sudan and Guinea? Along these boundaries you will find families cut in two by arbitrary lines of demarcation, while in fact racially these countries are very much alike, and constitute a political, economic, and social unity. Likewise their populations are all animated by the same grand desire for union. But we reject the false preliminary conditions created by certain leaders and repeated even during these debates. For us, the only preliminary condition is our opposition to all interference of the European nations in our family affairs. We find it, moreover, remarkable that in this Pan-African conference no speaker so far has mentioned community or commonwealth. As for us, we want to realize first and foremost an African community that will deal as an equal with any country in the world.

Certain speakers talk of tribalism as if it constituted the most important obstacle on the road to African unity. Let me tell you plainly that Guinea has resolved this false problem. Conscious of the fact that tribalism has always been the essential element of division used by the colonial powers, Guinea's political leaders made a direct attack on its instruments, that is, on the leaders laughingly called *Chefs Coutumiers* ("Regular Leaders"). I must say that this was all the more possible when the people of Guinea had succeeded in forming a united front on the level of political parties on the eve of the referendum of 1958. Thus even the parties with a tribal character chose, under pressure from the people of Guinea, the Guinean nation rather than private interests. Thus was the single party system born in Guinea, and we want to say very plainly here that this route is the only possible way of salvation during this period of African liberation.

Suppression of the *Chefferie* ("Chief System") and of all forms of exploitation of the people, mobilization of everyone—men, women, and children—exemption of no social level from labor—this is the route that Guinea has chosen to conquer misery, ignorance, and underdevelopment. All this is in line with our motto: "Work, Justice, Solidarity." Today in Guinea there are no Foulahs, Soussous, Malinkés, and so forth—but Guineans only, mobilized for the great struggle for liberation and African unity in the National Guinean Movement (PDG).

Today in Guinea no public office is hereditary. All leaders are elected, from the smallest hamlet to the highest level of the nation. There is no longer any monopoly of sovereignty—the only sovereignty is that of the people of Guinea.

Before concluding I would also like to express my surprise at the small amount of emphasis that has been placed on a very concrete manifestation of Pan-Africanism: the Conference of Independent African States, now taking place at Addis Ababa. Likewise I feel obliged to remind the assembly of an omission I consider serious: we have forgotten to mention the African Group in the United Nations, which is the executive body of the Conference of Independent African States. In this regard, returning to the North African question, I would like to say once more that in the African Group at the United Nations, it would never enter our heads to discuss an African problem in the absence of the North Africans. Their dynamism and their faith in the future of Africa have never failed our cause and our commitment. Their action is of decisive importance for the solidarity of the peoples of Negro Africa with their brothers north of the Sahara.

ANTHONY ENAHORO

Nigerian Action Group;
Member, All Africa Peoples Conference Steering Committee

I want to say that I think Professor Coleman's paper has been very competently presented, and not least in the sense that from the very first stage it presents us with some basis for an appropriate definition of Pan-Africanism. I think that we can accept Pan-Africanism defined as the builder of larger African unities. I'd like to omit "political" from that definition—the builder of larger African unities. If we can accept that definition, it does cover considerable ground.

There are one or two points I'd like to make. First, while I don't want to open the question of Nigeria's attitude toward Pan-Africanism, I do want to correct the impression that our attitudes derive from the size of Nigeria, and certain other theories. I suggest instead that our attitude derives from the complexities of the Nigerian situation, which we discussed earlier, and from a phenomenon to which attention has not been paid: a two-tier federation. This is something hitherto unknown; a federation within a federation. I would really have liked to hear the professors on that point. Being preoccupied with these problems, our interest toward Pan-Africanism has not shown the same degree of warmth as is to be found in other African states.

I admit that the great danger in this is that in the process of developing and trying to bridge the gap of centuries, there might be a hardening of our arteries which could prevent a flow of feeling receptive to Pan-African federalism. More important than that, I think, is the fact that two specific matters have not been developed, either in this paper or by previous contributors. The first is the contribution of organized labor to Pan-Africanism. Although touched on briefly in one of the passages here, it hasn't received the treatment it deserves. I think you will find that outside the settler area and other parts of Africa where you have large agricultural communities—which are by nature, as we all know, not very excitable—the nationalist movement has had to depend on organized labor for mass support. Organized labor has acted as a unifying factor in the nationalist movement, not least because there are members who are detribalized.

Finally, I think we ought to consider the effect on Pan-Africanism itself of the development that I call the "continentalization" of Pan-Africanism—the destruction of racial basis in Pan-Africanism by making it a continental movement. The effect, I think, is to exclude the interest of Negroes in the Caribbean and on this continent. I think that we do not realize the tremendous effect that Negro experiences in this country, for example, have on African thinking and therefore on Pan-Africanism; and it seems to me that, for fear of being accused of a new form of racism, all of us in Africa are accepting this new continental basis for Pan-Africanism. This trend has the effect of destroying the racial basis and thus what is possibly the fundamental basis for Pan-Africanism.

RESPONSE

DAVID E. APTER

I was delighted with the comments. I think that many of the issues we omitted in the topic paper have been probed and discussed. This session has been a very straightforward and clear-cut one.

I should like to make several comments about issues that have been raised in passing. First of all, let me say something both about North Africa and about South Africa. Earlier, I spoke of the spiritual enterprise that is essential if Pan-Africanism is to be achieved. I think that South Africa's role is in a sense the role of the suffering giant, which in fact may prove to be one of the most crucial factors in the unity of Africa or the types of associations that will be foremost in the minds of African political leaders, overriding whatever difficulties they may encounter. For one thing, the pure suffering of South Africa immediately develops for other peoples elsewhere a Puritanism of indignation —a Puritanism that burns very clearly among all peoples of sensibility, both inside South Africa and elsewhere. Therefore, the suffering of South Africa is not to no avail. To liberate South Africa means to find and forge links of unity. South Africa, then, is a crucial aspect of African unity. The struggle to free South Africa will provide an immediate focus and objective for all peoples of Africa everywhere.

Second, on the North African side: this is a historical factor which I excluded earlier, and it was rightly put into prominence. I personally believe. that the rapid devolution of authority in former French West Africa would have been almost impossible to conceive of without the Algerian struggle. Algiers showed that there are grave dangers in resisting the tide of independence, so that peaceful devolution of powers in West Africa seemed a far better alternative to the French. Algiers also introduced a kind of Puritanism into the struggle for independence—the Puritanism of potential conflict. The potentiality was itself sufficient. Professor Coleman has pointed out in his remarks that Africans have been primarily concerned with positive, peaceful action, and voluntary ways in which to achieve the kinds of unity that are implicit in the African scene. Professor Wallerstein also pointed out that within conflicts there are also sources of unity. And in the potential sources of conflict and unity, the Puritanism of indignation and the Puritanism of actual conflict both play an important role.

I would like to make just one brief comment about the fear of Ghana with respect to Guinea. This I think was objected to because fear is a very, very exciting word. I certainly did not mean to imply that Ghanaians go around fearful of Guineans. Not at all! They're delighted with Guinea! What they are a bit upset about is not so much Guinea itself; it is the possibility that the superior organization within Guinea, given the great handicaps Guinea faced right at the moment of independence, will in fact make Ghana seem to be less efficient and perhaps less successful in some of its objectives and designs. Guinea's progress along certain lines raises questions within Ghana about the most suitable types of political organizations and associations for bringing about economic growth and the development of social discipline. Fear is a bad word here. Guinea has produced some soul-searching on the part of Ghanaians. They have some hard thinking to do and some inward questions to ask as they go forward on the continent of Africa.

In general, I think Professor Coleman shares with me the feeling that many issues that are raised are, of course, subject to a great deal of interpretation. And on behalf of Professor Coleman and my colleagues, we thank you very much for your observations.

IV ECONOMICS

THERE IS, of course, an artificiality in the division of politics and economics. Any separation of them is bound to cast up glaring examples of overlapping. In our present frame of reference, politics and economics in their interrelationship constitute an inherent and indefeasible "pan" movement. Yet the line must somewhere be drawn for clarity of approach.

The AMSAC conference had, among several noted participants, one whose observations on the economic process have recently been much discussed. Walt Whitman Rostow, of the Massachusetts Institute of Technology, applied to the African continent, in a general way, an analysis of economic development which he had set forth two years earlier, at Moscow, as an alternative to Marx's *Manifesto*. The framework of his observations was his well-known theory of the five stages of economic growth. He finds Africa to be substantially in the second stage—the transitional—a step beyond the completely primitive society but not yet having established the "preconditions" of economic growth necessary to the third phase, the "take-off" period, and the subsequent drive to "economic maturity." The task, then, of the African nations, he advises, is to establish these preconditions: (a) the human element, that is, the training of a corps of Africans competent to establish and maintain an industrialized economy; (b) an agricultural revolution to meet the increased demands for adequate nutrition for the population as a whole, and for a growing class of urban workers in particular; (c) the "social overhead capital" of massively increased transport facilities and sources of energy or power; (d) the creation or increase of foreign trade to bring in the necessary tools for such a transformation, and the capital to pay for it.

It is interesting in this connection to see that Tanganyika's recently revealed ten-year plan announces almost precisely this emphasis on "agriculture, communications, and education."

As to the specific direction industrialization is to take, Rostow suggests to African leaders that, of the various advanced nations, Sweden is the most illuminating example to consider in mapping Africa's industrial drive. Its pertinence lies in the fact that in its rapid rise to technological competence, Sweden did not seek an impossible complete sufficiency but concentrated on her few strong assets: timber, electric power, and iron ore. Duncan Ndegwa, Assistant Secretary of the Treasury in Kenya, and Stanley Sumlin, young American Negro economist with the Federal Reserve Bank of New York, seemed in agreement in acknowledging the clarity of Rostow's basic perceptions, if taken as agenda (Rostow, himself, so couches his remarks) and not as a program of action. Ndegwa states that Kenya, for example, has no particularly strong natural resources and he therefore questions Sweden's applicability. Sumlin remonstrates that Rostow's analysis, while generally accurate, holds little of predictive value in identifying sectors of the economy to be developed or to receive priority. The observations of Ndegwa and Sumlin focus attention on the fact that Africa is not one but many economic areas, and they point up the urgent necessity, which Zinsou of Dahomey probably emphasizes more than any other, of an economic inventory of the African continent, area by area, block by economic block.

Both Sumlin and Akwei of Ghana challenge what they take to be Rostow's extended timetable; they assume that he contemplates for Africa a pace identical with that of the development of most Western nations, although this is nowhere explicit in Rostow's argument. Akwei eschews this "long run" to observe that "in the long run, we shall all be dead." There was a sense of urgency among the Africans; a desire perhaps for a less deliberate approach to modernization, to full industrialization, than they feel is suggested by Rostow's scheme of five stages of growth. Evidence of this sense of urgency is apparent, for example, in Ndegwa's reference to the alarming increase in the Kenyan demand for Western consumer goods—scarcely possible to meet in a society struggling through the first phases of economic growth.

The question of pace, however, impels the argument of method. Rostow's is the not-unfamiliar view that the debate between capitalism and socialism is an old debate—a debate that is passé. Acknowledging the necessity of "government leadership," he urges that certain areas of the economy and of social life be left free. Indirect methods, he maintains, will be adequate for government to discharge its responsibility of guidance and control. The Dahomean speaker, Zinsou, and other African participants, however, reflect that strong intellectual current in Pan-Africanism to which Apter and Coleman refer, which declines to find the issue moot and which opts clearly for socialism. It is a socialism, they remind us, that is not Marxist but is a natural outgrowth of the traditional solidarity of African social organization; it is peculiarly African. It is not impossible to reconcile certain elements in the positions of Rostow and Zinsou. The latter, one may deduce, contemplates a synthesis of certain free sectors of the economy and socialist planning. He firmly rejects, however, a pragmatic muddling-through approach. He warns against the improvidence of improvisation. The impoverished nations of Africa cannot pass through all the steps of the economic history of the United States of America.

It was perhaps unwittingly pertinent for Rostow to point out that industrialization of the United States was largely built, initially, on cotton—an American industry in which Africa's participation is not unknown. The observation recalls the thesis that Western capitalism suckled and grew strong upon slave labor and the riches of the slave trade. What, then, a century later, is Africa's source of capital for industrial growth? One tempting source, the East Africans indicate, is all the industrial wealth piled up by the European through a hundred years of varying degrees of African bondage. Rostow admits the difficulty of the problem posed by what he terms this "enclave" of the European segment enjoying a superior position in the general economy. In answer to the speakers from Kenya and Tanganyika, who have the problem much on their minds, he urges that the crucial issue is not inequality between groups; it is the problem of joining all elements of the society in concerted effort toward economic growth. He suggests that if such coöperation is achieved, the wealthier elements may, like the Indian princes, be permitted to retain their wealth. Here, as with his approach to the basic Marxist concept of the class struggle, Rostow deëmphasizes the divisive nature of factors in the social order which would set one group against another. Implicit in such an accent is (as one finds also in Marx) a perhaps utopian expectation of the nature of man, and a failure to comprehend the intensity of the psychological drives that impel social change, and are explosively present in the African struggle against colonialism.

Relevant also to this question is the paper of the Nigerian research assistant at the Massachusetts Institute of Technology, Lattee Fahm, who develops a comparative picture of the formation of capital in Nigeria and Ghana. He defends what he states to be the contested thesis that the capital "absorptive capacity" of the two countries will support sustained economic growth and is sufficiently great to warrant, at a policy level, the formulation of substantial developmental projects in the transformation of the economy. Such a capacity is obviously crucial to any program of growth and, whether proved or not, would be necessarily a tenet of faith for any nation seriously seeking to enter the industrial twentieth century.

One significant aspect of the economic picture is the increasing emphasis, as discussed by Sumlin and others, on multilateral recruitment of capital from non-African sources. There is an obvious preference on the part of the African nations to have capital funneled through an organization of several states, rather than have it advanced piecemeal from several individual national sources. Conversely, there are advantages for a world bank or an angency of UNESCO or the United Nations to contemplate, in defining Africa's capital requirements, economic areas larger than single African states. As to the related problem of a common African market, or regional African markets, there is again a difference of viewpoint. Sumlin refers to the efforts to develop common markets in Africa as necessary and relatively immediate objectives. His emphasis is the same as that of Zinsou, who, from the state of Dahomey (one of the four small nations of the Conseil de l'Entente), warns against the economic, as contrasted with the political, Balkanization of Africa.

It is interesting that Rostow's position is substantially that of the Nigerians Wachuku and Enahoro: the political energies of the several African nations should be turned to securing the economic growth of the *individual* states rather than exhausted in the "diversionary" question of larger African unities. Rostow's reading of the postwar European experience is contrary to Senghor's. He argues that even the Common Market in Europe did not become significant until the individual European nations had separately recovered their economic strength. The issue is not resolved, of course, but the lines of thinking are placed, at times, in bold relief. It is significant to note that despite the major priority given to the building of the separate states, the subsequent African reaction to the violent, disruptive events of that continent indicates an increasing sense of urgency in achieving closer union among the African nations.

S. W. A.

SOME LESSONS OF HISTORY FOR AFRICA

W. W. ROSTOW

Department of Economics, Massachusetts Institute of Technology

As AN ECONOMIST, I come with some diffidence to talk to a society devoted to the study of culture. But I come without apology. The late Lord Keynes defined the limited but dignified mission of my profession in a toast to the Royal Economic Society in 1945. He said: "I give you the toast of the Royal Economic Society, of economics and economists, who are the trustees not of civilization, but of the possibility of civilization."

This view has a particular relevance for Africans of this generation and for all of us who share the excitement and adventure of their mission. The mission of Africans is not merely to generate economic growth. Their mission is to move on from the legal fact of independence to fashion societies, each of which maintains continuity with its own culture and develops that culture while absorbing and putting to work for the African peoples the tricks modern technology can offer. In the end, the mission of Africa in the second half of this century is essentially human and cultural, not material and statistical.

Economics is a tool; and economic growth is a means to larger human, national, and cultural purposes. But men and women committed to these larger purposes must be respectful of the claims and the imperatives of the economic process; for, although economic growth is not a sufficient objective, the great human, national, and cultural objectives will not be achieved unless economic growth takes place in Africa. Decent modern civilization is not created automatically by economic growth, but it cannot be built without economic growth.

Africa enters the world of modern technology relatively late in the game. This has the advantage of offering to Africans a somewhat greater backlog of unapplied methods than was available to those who came earlier. But, more importantly, it offers to Africans the chance to profit from the successes and failures of the past and to make the transition to modernization a more humane and efficient process than it has been in those parts of the world where this transition has already occurred or is now taking place.

The purpose of my paper is to lay out for you what one economist and historian believes to be the major lessons for Africa derived from the experiences of past economic growth.

Out of my work as an economic historian I have come gradually to the view that it is possible—and for certain purposes it is useful—to divide societies, past and present, into five categories:

First, *traditional* societies, where the attitudes, institutions, and devices that go with modern technology have not taken hold. There are virtually no large areas or nations that are still pure traditional societies, although parts of Africa and Asia are essentially still in the traditional stage.

Second, *transitional* societies. These societies have absorbed some elements of modern economic activity, and they have developed some of the accompanying psychological attitudes and social values; but they have not yet created all the preconditions for sustained growth. Many parts of Asia, the Middle East, Africa, and Latin America are, in different degree, in this transitional stage—for example, Pakistan, Burma, Indonesia, Iran.

Third, there are societies involved in the process that I have called the *take-off* into self-sustained growth. That is the period when the various modern elements, slowly developed, become mutually reinforcing; the modernization process in all its dimensions acquires momentum, centered on a few rapidly growing sectors where modern technology is effectively applied; and the secondary effects spread outward. India, China, Brazil, and the Philippines are among the contemporary nations in this decisive phase of growth.

Fourth, there are societies that, having passed through the take-off, carry forward the growth process over a widening area of the economy—gradually, sector by sector—bringing to bear the advantages of modern technology on virtually all the society's resources. Such societies I would designate as being in the *drive to technological maturity*. The accidents of historical timing afford us relatively few examples of nations now in this stage. But Mexico is, I believe, beginning the drive to technological maturity; Argentina and Turkey are catching their breath after the take-off and should shortly begin the drive to maturity; and Canada and Russia achieved technological maturity in the 1950's.

Finally, there is the stage of *high mass-consumption,* when the resources of a mature industrial machine are turned to provide the consumer with the peculiar devices it can supply, including the variety, privacy, and mobility men apparently seek when their more basic wants are satisfied—typified by the automobile, the suburban house, and the gadgets we know so well. The United States entered this stage in the 1920's, Western Europe in the 1950's.

As you well know, Africa south of the desert and north of the Union, is an area of immense variety. The new African nations differ in resource endowments, degree of literacy, and land-tenure arrangements and level of income—as well as in history, culture, language, and colonial heritage. Nevertheless they all fall in what I would call the transitional category, where their central economic task is to create the preconditions for take-off. None of the African states is wholly without certain modern skills and modern economic activities. But none has yet moved into self-sustained economic growth.

In considering, then, what lessons history might offer contemporary Africans, we can narrow our range to this question: What can history usefully tell us about the preconditions for take-off? What are the essential tasks, the pitfalls, the opportunities, as they apply to Africa?

I shall proceed by outlining first the major economic tasks of the preconditions stage; and I shall then turn to the political and social policies that will determine how soon, how efficiently, and how humanely these tasks are likely to be carried out in Africa.

In the end, sustained economic growth is based on the application of modern science and technology to the economy. The instinct that led Arnold Toynbee (not the one we know, but his earlier kinsman) to create the phrase the Industrial Revolution was in my view a correct instinct. And it is certainly a correct designation if we regard as part of industrialization the application of modern techniques to the production and processing of agricultural and raw material output, as well as to industry, narrowly defined. But the key to successful industrialization—and the key to the preconditions for take-off—lie in four nonindustrial sectors to the economy.

The first and basic precondition for economic growth and industrialization is human. It is the effective training of a minimum corps of modern men and women. Such training must take place at every level, from the most sophisticated natural and social science, from the highest civil service and industrial administrative skill, to the propagation of literacy in the villages. There is no more challenging task for Africans and for those who would help them in the coming decade than the task of training quickly and massively a new, modern generation of African men and women. For at the present time there is an evident gap between the small group of leaders who have pioneered the struggle for independence, and the bulk of African citizens, who lack the basic skills to begin building their version of a modern society.

The prime lesson of economic history is that the first task of economic growth is educational. It is with education in modern skills that the precondition of nations as different as Britain, Russia, and Japan began. I am proud to come from a university—Massachusetts Institute of Technology—that received an important initial impetus from the Morrill Act of 1862, which was designed to accelerate the spread of modern methods in agriculture and industry at a very early stage of American modernization.

In facing this task of producing men and women trained for modern life, Africans have a great opportunity to fashion their educational institutions along their own lines. Specifically, they have the opportunity to avoid the mistake of training men along lines that may have fitted the values and needs of preindustrial Europe, but which were singularly unsuited to nations in the early stage of modernization. In Asia, the Middle East, and Latin America, the universities for some generations mistrained substantial numbers of young men, leaving them incapable of entering into the vital tasks of their own societies and dangerously frustrated by their partial unemployment. I detect among my African friends a common-sense quality which, I hope, will be translated into the new African schools and universities. Whatever the specific skills imparted, the African educational system should inculcate a respect for hard work—including manual work—and a sense that the economic business of a society is serious business, worthy of the highest level of intellectual attention.

The second nonindustrial task of the phase I call the preconditions lies in agriculture. The importance of agricultural development to economic growth cannot be overestimated. Increased agricultural output and productivity are required to feed the expanding population of the preconditions period and the cities that are bound to grow even more rapidly than the population as a whole. (This disproportionate growth of the cities is already taking place in Africa.) Increased agricultural productivity is also required to give the farmer a margin of increased income so that he can both pay taxes and also have a margin of increased consumption, which local industry will need as the market basis for industrial growth. And in many parts of Africa, increased agricultural productivity is the key to earning the foreign exchange needed to import the machinery and industrial raw materials required for the new industrial base Africans must build.

In the broadest sense, a revolution in agricultural productivity is required to ensure that a humane decision—to spread rapidly the modern techniques of public health—does not yield an inhumane result; that is, a population rising so fast it cannot be properly fed. African leaders should note well that the fate of both Communism in China and democracy in India will largely depend, in this decade, on the success or failure of the agricultural programs of the two countries. An industrial revolution without an agricultural revolution is a dead end.

In dealing with its agricultural problems—which vary greatly from place to place—Africans have one great advantage over many other transitional societies. Generally speaking, African agriculture has not been organized on feudal lines. In many areas, communal landholding and communal methods of land cultivation are typical. Each African nation—and each region—will have to decide how best to reorganize its agriculture so as to apply new and more productive methods. But with wisdom among its leaders, Africa should be able to avoid the painful struggles that other nations had to experience before land could be organized on a basis both more equitable and more productive than that in their feudal past. It will not always be easy to transform African land tenure systems to a more productive basis; but it should be possible to achieve these transformations without bitter domestic conflict.

And the lesson of history is that, at best, these conflicts over land ownership proved, in the end, to be merely the prelude to the nation's real task: the raising of agricultural productivity. In Africa that communal task can be approached directly. There is no need to recapitulate in Africa the usually bitter story of agrarian revolution.

The third nonindustrial task of the preconditions phase is the building of what economists call social overhead capital. If industrialization is to take hold, the nation and its resources must be bound together by efficient communications: roads, railroads, and, in our day, airlines. In virtually every country in the past, the building of a new transport net was a major precondition for modernization; and in some countries—the United States, Canada, Germany, and Russia—it was the decisive act that lifted the society into take-off. It is altogether normal —even inevitable—that more than 30 per cent of investment in the First Development Plan in Ghana, for example, should have gone into communications; and that the proportion to be invested in communications in the expanded Second Ghana Plan should be only a little less. There can be no meaningful national market—there can be, in fact, no meaningful nationhood in the new African states—unless vast efforts to improve communications are undertaken and carried through.

Aside from transport, social overhead capital includes another essential foundation for industrialization: the development of new sources for power. Industry requires not merely cheap transport for its raw materials and its products, but increased energy. A high proportion of investment in Africa in the 1960's will have to create these sources of energy. And Africa contains, as we all know, some exceedingly promising natural resources in this respect.

The fourth nonindustrial sector on which industrialization depends is foreign trade. One of the major lessons of history is that economic growth requires expanded imports. An expansion in imports is necessary even if the growing nation gradually comes to produce for itself many items it formerly imported from abroad. Industrialization is an unfolding process: every new stage requires that new kinds of machinery, new kinds of raw materials, be brought in from abroad.

In the past, the early stage of industrialization was often financed by the export of agricultural products or raw materials. Thus, American industrialization was initially built on cotton and wheat; the Japanese, on silk; the Canadian and Russian, on wheat; the Swedish, on timber. Loans and grants from abroad should help Africa meet its import bill during the coming generation; but it is essential that Africa's leaders, in their understandable concern with domestic problems, should not neglect the region's capacity to earn foreign exchange. They should always have before them the memory of Peron's Argentina, which neglected the rich export potential of the nation and confronted his successors with a dangerous and unnecessary foreign-exchange crisis from which Argentina has not yet recovered. The rich mineral and agricultural resources of Africa hold out the opportunity for the new nations to develop in time the capacity to pay their own way, as they move forward through the take-off toward technological maturity.

The preconditions for take-off require, then, the building of a new generation of men and women trained appropriately and motivated to operate a modern society; they require a productivity revolution in agriculture; they require a massive buildup of transport facilities and sources of energy; and they require the development of a capacity to earn more foreign exchange. These are the urgent priority tasks of the 1960's. These are the things that must be done to create commercial national economies to replace the regional subsistence economies that now mainly characterize Africa. These are the things that must be done to break down the dualistic structure that now characterizes most of the area as it emerges from colonialism.

But take-off requires also that industrialization take hold; and it is not too soon for Africans to turn their thoughts to this decisive stage of growth, even if it is some distance off.

What kind of industrialization should we expect in Africa? To which lessons of history should Africans look, if any?

It cannot be said too often that the evolution of each nation, like that of each individual, is unique. We can find similar patterns of development, but no identical patterns. And, once again, Africa itself will offer great variety. Nevertheless, I have a suggestion for African leaders and economists, in this period when their major tasks are those of the preconditions: namely, that they look ahead and study carefully the economic history of the country likely to prove most relevant to their possibilities once the take-off occurs and industrialization is seriously under way. That country is not the United States; nor is it Russia, Germany, France, Japan, or China. It is Sweden.

Despite evident differences in history, culture, scale, and timing, Sweden's history is peculiarly relevant to Africa, for this reason: Sweden has managed to create a rich, mature economy by exploiting to the hilt a few rich natural resources. Sweden had good timber. It did not rest content with the export of timber, but moved up the chain of technological refinement, developing efficient modern pulp and then paper industries. And it did not neglect lesser refinements, from matches to elegant modern furniture. Sweden had good iron ore. It still exports some of that ore on the basis of a highly modernized mining and transport operation, and it is now transferring that know-how to Liberia in one of the most interesting new African developments. But Sweden also developed a small first-class steel industry; and on the basis of that steel industry it developed a first-class engineering industry, including its pioneering effort in ball bearings. Sweden lacked coal, but had ample distant supplies of hydroelectric power. It proceeded to make a virtue of necessity by pioneering the efficient transmission of high-tension power; by building its railways and its steel industry on an electric rather than on a coal basis; and by learning just about all there was to know about the manufacture of electric motors. And as each kind of virtuosity was absorbed, Sweden applied what was learned in processing its raw materials to the production of goods for the home market. It did not hesitate to maintain a large foreign trade. It did not strive for a self-sufficiency its resources made impossible; but it did develop industrial skills over a wide front and increasingly produced for itself what it formerly imported.

In sixty years—from, say, 1870 to 1930—Sweden moved from the status of a poor agricultural society to one that was both technologically mature and rich. The key to its success was the progressively more refined processing of its narrow but rich endowment in a very few raw materials.

As one examines what is known of the raw materials of Africa, it is clear that, like Sweden, Africa is unevenly but richly endowed. There may be no obvious potential Ruhr, Pittsburgh, or Donbas in Africa; but there are extraordinarily rich deposits of chrome, cobalt, copper, tin, and asbestos; and there are sufficient supplies of many other materials on which to build modern industrial activities, if the skills of processing are acquired and efficiently applied. The clue to African industrialization lies, I believe, in the progressively more refined processing of these materials and the exploitation of the skills this experience will develop to build an industrial system capable of supplying an ever-wider range of domestic needs, in substitution for imports.

This is about as far as economic insights, derived from the patterns of economic history, narrowly defined, can take us. They suggest the economic agenda of Africa—no more than that. Only those on the spot can determine the particular forms that the response to that agenda should take.

This approach gets us somewhere; but it is not very far. For it is perfectly evident that the concrete economic jobs of the preconditions period will require a set of psychological, social, and political changes in Africa which transcend the field of economics.

Some of these changes you will be considering in other sessions of this conference, and I shall confine my observations on the non-economic aspects of modernization to one key point. That point is political.

African politics is now undergoing an experience that is quite familiar to the historian. To the extent that unity now exists in the African nations, it is based on a nationalist reaction against colonial rule. Moreover, the leaders who emerge from these colonial struggles are, basically, politicians who have been skillful in mobilizing the anti-colonial sentiments of the people and making those sentiments felt. Now the leaders and the African peoples as a whole confront a searching choice, one that many new nations have confronted before them.

The crucial questions are these: In which direction should these new national sentiments be directed? To what operational purposes should these powerful national sentiments now coursing through the African continent be harnessed?

Should these newly released energies be turned outward, to assert Africa's position on the world scene and to continue the struggle against dying colonialism? Should the political energies of the people be thrown into the domestic political struggle, and notably the struggle of the new central governments to master the regional and tribal prerogatives inherited from the traditional past? Or should the primary drive be towards economic and social modernization?

All of these elements are bound to be present in African political life, as they are present in the politics of the new nations in Asia and the Middle East. The question is: In what proportion should these alternative objectives be pursued? Where shall the primary emphasis be placed?

Both history and the contemporary scene suggest that this is no idle or abstract set of questions. China, for example, passed through a century of domestic torment before making economic growth its central business; and as a result of this long frustrating domestic struggle, China finds itself gripped by a peculiarly compulsive regime. In recent years we have observed Egypt wrestling with these choices, as have

Pakistan and Indonesia. Shall the primary focus of political life in Egypt be the destruction of Israel, or Egyptian development? Shall the primary focus of political life in Pakistan be Kashmir, or Pakistani development? Shall the primary focus of political life in Indonesia be West Irian, or Indonesian economic development?

The lesson of history is quite clear: A new nation is not likely to be an effective force on the world scene nor to develop a serious sense of unity and nationhood unless its nationalism is channeled primarily into the concrete tasks of modernization. This was the perception of the Japanese reformers after 1868 which accounts for the speed of Japan's emergence as an efficient modern state. This is what Ataturk came to perceive in the 1920's in Turkey; and it is the perception that constitutes Nehru's claim to greatness.

It is not easy for men trained for anticolonial politics to make this decision. It is easier to go on doing what is familiar. For politicians, the game of power at home and abroad is more fun than village development projects and all the other homely tasks of modernization. But the most important advice a historian can give the new national leaders in Africa is this: Make modernization the first order of business.

There is a quite technical reason why the priorities of the political leaders in Africa are crucial. Turn your minds back, for a moment, to the economic and technical agenda for the preconditions period which I outlined. It is clear that none of the four major tasks can be executed unless the government plays a role of leadership. Men cannot be trained, new techniques cannot be spread in agriculture, social overhead capital cannot be built, an intelligent foreign-exchange policy cannot be designed—unless the government plays its part.

Does this mean that successful economic development requires socialist governments? Has capitalism no place in economic development? The answer to these questions is that the more we learn about economic development, the less appropriate does the old ideological debate about economic systems appear. In fact, one of the most interesting and important intellectual currents in the modern world is the abandonment of the old debate about capitalism and socialism in its historic terms.

The truth is that no nation has modernized—including highly capitalist United States and Canada—without the government playing an important role of leadership in the four fundamental tasks of the preconditions: education, agricultural policy, social overhead capital, and policy designed to improve the foreign-trade balance.

However, it is also true that nations cannot modernize without excessive human and economic cost unless large areas of economic and social life are left free. In agriculture, for example, the lesson of history is that governments must lead the way in spreading new agricultural methods; but it is also a lesson of history that collectivization is a dead end, and that the incentives and initiatives of the individual farmer or village must be relied upon substantially to produce more. With respect to industry, moreover, the lesson appears to be that there is every advantage for the nation if private industrialists are permitted and encouraged to develop. There are adequate indirect methods for ensuring that the private industrial sector produces the kinds of products the society needs; and there is every reason for the government to conserve its scarce supply of civil servants and administrators for the jobs that only a government can do in the early stages of the development process.

My argument about African politics comes to this: Since the completion of the preconditions for take-off requires that the government lead the society in a number of crucial directions, it follows that these jobs will not be done unless the politicians take them very seriously indeed.

How does this perspective bear on the issue of African unity? Does it mean that Africans must accept as definitive the borders and the groupings that resulted from the quite arbitrary decisions of European colonial rulers? It certainly does not follow from my argument that African unity is to be ruled out. What does follow are these two observations.

First, it is essential that the idea of African unity not serve as a substitute for facing the hard concrete tasks of modernization at the local level. It may turn out that, in the long sweep of history, some of the present African national states survive only as regional governments. But right now they have jobs of modernization to do which will not otherwise be done. There is no point—in fact, there is great danger—in taking the view that the execution of these jobs must await the emergence of larger governmental units.

In this respect there is an important lesson for Africa in the experience of postwar Europe, despite the obvious differences in the circumstances of the two continents. In the immediate postwar years, there was some tendency—notably in France and Italy—to say that effective recovery awaited the achievement of a higher degree of European unity. As things turned out, the Common Market became feasible in Europe only after all the European nations, including France and Italy, had largely mastered their local problems of reconstruction, on a local basis.

I am sure the right of way for Africa is to get on with the tasks of modernization at high priority, while exploring soberly the proper basis and proper forms for larger political or economic units, if they should prove desirable.

My second observation about African unity is that African leaders should give careful thought to the underlying basis and purposes for unity. They should ask themselves in hardheaded federalist terms: What specific jobs could we do better together rather than on a regional basis? What constructive purposes do we wish to achieve in Africa and on the world scene which require and justify higher orders of unity? Although the impulse toward African unity may have—and will have—deep emotional, racial, and cultural roots, its success will depend on a subtle and creative application of the federal principle. If the question of unity is approached in the light of these two observations, we can be reasonably confident that whatever emerges is likely to improve the lot of the African peoples and contribute to world order and prosperity. On the other hand, if African unity becomes a slogan and a competitive plaything of African politics, it will divert men from the real and urgent jobs of modernization; and it will prove a cause of disappointment and frustration to the citizens of Africa.

Now a final word. As some of you may know, I have presented my notion of the Stages of Growth as an alternative to Marxism. The *Communist Manifesto* was, essentially, a theory of how modern history has unfolded down to 1848; and the Stages of Growth are an alternative theory of modern history, coming down to the present.

But the *Communist Manifesto* also contained a famous battle cry: "Workers of the world unite; you have nothing to lose but your chains." And there are those who have asked: "What does the Stages of Growth offer in place of this battle cry?" This question had been raised with particular relevance to the underdeveloped areas of the contemporary world. I am a teacher and student, not a politician; and I am not a maker of slogans. Nevertheless, this is a question I ought to answer.

My answer is that of course conflicts between groups with differing economic interests play a part in the politics of modernization as they play a part in all politics. And to a degree Marx was correct: a part of the modernization process consists in the shift of power away from old groups, or their acceptance of new functions; and the creation of new modern urban groups is an essential feature of modernization. But my assertion, in reply to Marx, is this: The task of modernization is not, at its core, a matter of class struggle. It is a matter of transformation in the minds and hearts of individual men, of local communities and of nations. For modernization to succeed, every group in the society must contribute. In the outcome of modernization every group in the society has a stake. Moreover, that common stake is vastly greater than the special advantages or costs to any one group. The stake is to see emerge a modern version of the old culture which, while absorbing the tricks of modern technology and while affording to the people the benefits these tricks may offer, also yields dignified, constructive societies, which carry forward the best in the old traditions and add richness and variety and decency to the life on this small planet. Modernization—in Africa as elsewhere—takes its start from a communal reaction to the intrusion of more advanced powers—an intrusion with which the traditional society could not deal. The achievement of a modern society must, in the end, be the product of a shared set of goals, to which all elements in the community contribute.

And as one looks around the world, it is evident that the workers of the world and the peasants and the intellectuals have much more to lose than their chains; that is, they have much more to lose than the inhibiting limitations of traditional or colonial life. They can find themselves imprisoned by forms of society that, in the name of modernization, destroy unnecessarily much of the continuity with the past and destroy much of the dignity and human liberty that modernization ought to increase, not diminish. As I said in Moscow, where I was asked last May to talk on peaceful coexistence in the underdeveloped areas: "Hundreds of millions of human beings must live in the world over the next century or so until the age of high mass-consumption becomes universal. They have the right to live their time in civilized settings, marked by a degree of respect for their uniqueness and for their dignity, marked by policies of balance in their societies—not merely an obsession with statistics of production whose technical and philosophic ambiguities you understand quite as well as I do.

"Man is a complex being, as the great artists and writers and thinkers of all countries have long since made clear. And human life is not a numbers racket."

This, then, is my reply to Marx's battle cry: While conflicts of economic and group interest are part of the modernization process, in its largest sense modernization is a communal and human task. It calls, essentially, not for class conflict but for a sense of brotherhood within nations and cultures and between nations and cultures. If this fact is not understood—and acted on—there is much that human beings can lose in the process of modernization. But if they are not to lose, if modernization is to be an essentially humane and constructive communal process respectful of the uniqueness of men and cultures, all of us concerned—both within the new nations and outside—must work together. We must work together not only at the full stretch of our energy and our technical talents, but also at the full stretch of our idealism and sense of human brotherhood.

CAPITAL FORMATION, BALANCE OF PAYMENTS, AND ABSORPTIVE CAPACITY IN GHANA AND NIGERIA

LATTEE A. FAHM

Center for Internal Studies, Massachusetts Institute of Technology

IT IS AN EMPIRICAL FACT that the ability of a country for self-sustained economic growth is determined by the capability to add annually to its productive capacity through ample capital formation.[1] The process of capital formation involves saving and investing certain proportions of gross national product after adjusting for depreciation and other relevant deductions. Besides the problems of local resources and skills, one of the main reasons why the rate of growth in Ghana and Nigeria has not been spectacular is that at the present low level of per capita income, the volume of savings such growth would require cannot be effectively mobilized for investment expenditures from private domestic sources.[2]

Before going into the implications of the available data on national income and capital formation in Ghana and Nigeria, let me clear the deck by summarizing certain general regularities that have been found to exist between capital investment and change in national income. Studies in various underdeveloped countries[3] suggest that in order to increase aggregate output of a backward economy by one unit per annum, capital investment of about three and a half to four times this amount is required. When due allowance is made for population increase of, say, 2 per cent annually, it will require a minimum annual investment of about 8 per cent of the gross domestic product simply

---

[1] See *Employment, Growth, and Price Levels*, Hearings before the Joint Economic Committee, Congress of the United States, Eighty-sixth Congress (Washington, D.C., 1959); E. D. Domar, *Essays in the Theory of Economic Growth* (Oxford, 1957); W. A. Lewis, *The Theory of Economic Growth* (London: Allen & Unwin, 1955).

[2] R. Nurkse, *Problems of Capital Formation in Underdeveloped Countries.* Oxford, 1955.

[3] United Nations, *Measures for the Economic Development of Underdeveloped Countries* (New York, 1951). Also *Foreign Aid Program: Compilation of Studies and Surveys*, Senate Document No. 52, July, 1957.

to *maintain* per capita income.[4] In order to generate sufficient development to permit a significant increase in the standard of living, an annual investment of at least 15 per cent of the gross domestic product would be required. Keeping this simple abstraction in mind, let us now examine the relationship between capital investment and national income in Ghana and Nigeria.

The general observation indicated by the aggregate data and their components is that as a result of the concerted economic development efforts in Ghana and Nigeria, significant increases have taken place in the gross national product and in gross capital formation from 1950 to 1957. The summary data[5] provide a rounded picture of the long-term trend underlying the outcome of development efforts in Ghana and Nigeria. In Ghana, the gross national product (crude and undeflated) increased over the seven-year period by a total of 48.6 per cent, with a cumulative annual rate of growth of 5.8 per cent. Nigeria's record shows a total increase in the gross national product (crude and undeflated) of 39.8 per cent, with a cumulative annual rate of growth of 5.7 per cent. The observed changes in gross capital formation over the same period also indicate a definite upward trend: Ghana, 32.6 per cent, with an annual rate of growth of 4.11 per cent; Nigeria, 114.1 per cent, with an annual rate of growth of 13.5 per cent.

So far I have cited only the crude gross rates of change in the gross national product and in gross capital formation. Let me now take one step further—and a very important step in terms of economic analysis —and extend the discussion to the per capita level of national income and capital formation.

With reference to gross capital formation *per head* between 1950 and 1957, the observed changes indicate a definite upward trend. According to my estimates,[6] the values of gross capital formation per head (adjusted for population changes) for 1950–51, 1953–54, and 1956–57 in Ghana and Nigeria are as follows: Ghana, £5.4, £6.0, and £10.5, respectively; Nigeria, £1.4, £1.8, and £2.9, respectively (all in pounds sterling). These values are incredibly low, but they do show the behavior of gross capital formation per head for selected years.

---

[4] C. P. Kindleberger, *Economic Development* (New York: McGraw-Hill, 1958), pp. 38–39.

[5] See table 5; also tables 1–4.

[6] Calculation based on the values of gross capital formation in *Economic Survey of Africa Since 1950* (New York: United Nations, 1959), pp. 192, 193.

It is clear, of course, that a more meaningful magnitude to estimate in terms of output would be the size of gross capital formation per worker or per laborer. The necessary information for such estimates is not sufficiently documented; hence the presentation of the crude gross capital formation per head.

Now, a brief comment on the behavior of national income per capita over the same period. It does not require deep reflection to realize that the relationship between the rate of growth of income and that of population determines whether the economic progress that has taken place in Ghana and Nigeria can formally be labeled as "developmental" or simply as "rehabilitational." As used here, *economic development* has not taken place if an increase in national income is absorbed by population growth—if it is required in order to maintain the existing standard of life.

As we have seen, the crude percentage increase in the gross national product between 1950 and 1957 was 48.6 per cent in Ghana, and 39.8 per cent in Nigeria. With proper adjustments for population increase and price changes, the rate of increase of per capita income in real terms is about 2.5 per cent annually in Nigeria,[7] and about the same in Ghana. In order to dramatize this important relationship between population and national income, let me introduce the absolute values behind the percentage figures. In 1956–57, the estimated values of national income were £261 million[8] (pounds sterling, or about $731 million) in Ghana, and £812 million[9] (pounds sterling, or $2,274 million) in Nigeria. In absolute terms, the national income of Nigeria is about three times that of Ghana. On a per capita basis, however, the national income for the same years was £56 or $157 in Ghana, and £27 or $76 in Nigeria. The population of Nigeria was estimated at 35 million,[10] and that of Ghana at 4.8 million.[11] Nigeria's population is not only about seven times as large as Ghana, but it also exhibits a higher rate of increase than Ghana's. These differences in size and rate of population growth constitute one of the most important explanations of the marked divergences in national incomes and capital formation per capita observed in the two countries. On the

[7] *Economic Survey of Nigeria, 1959* (Lagos, Federal Government Printer), p. 17.
[8] *United Nations Monthly Bulletin of Statistics*, July, 1959, p. 159.
[9] *Economic Survey of Nigeria, 1959*, p. 18.
[10] *Ibid.*, p. 1.
[11] *U.N. Monthly Bulletin of Statistics*, July, 1959, p. 2.

whole, it appears that official economic development efforts, inasmuch as they have increased national income at a faster rate than the growth of population, have produced some impressive results. Moreover, as this analysis has underlined, because of the differences in relative rates of population growth, the requirements in terms of development effort have been and remain much greater in Nigeria.

BALANCE OF PAYMENTS

In the preceding section, capital formation has been treated as a catalyst of economic growth. Whether or not the positive trend of economic progress indicated in that section of this paper will continue depends on two crucial factors: one internal, the other external. The internal factor, which is largely controllable by governmental policies in Ghana and Nigeria, relates to the capacity of the respective economies for transformation. The second factor depends on external conditions which are virtually beyond the control of countries the size of either Ghana or Nigeria. This factor relates to the availability of complementary foreign resources which are requisite to the implementation of development programs in the two countries. The importance of foreign resources can be fully appreciated when it is realized that the economies of Ghana and Nigeria are still at a stage where, according to my rough estimates,[12] at least one half of their fixed capital requirements are being obtained from overseas. I shall deal here only with the nature of foreign contributions (i.e., skills, machines, factory equipment, etc.), without which subsequent development efforts in Ghana and Nigeria may prove abortive.

The fundamental data for analyzing aggregate foreign-resource contributions are the balance of payments account. My main interest in the balance of payments data is to isolate from them, as far as possible, the net foreign contributions to the resources available to Ghana and Nigeria. I have modified the standard format employed by the International Monetary Fund for reporting balance of payments accounts so as to render it more useful in the context of my analysis.[13] The virtue of the balances on current account so constructed is that it reveals the pattern of the net flow of resources from or into Ghana

[12] Estimates based on varying import contents of major development projects in Ghana and Nigeria.
[13] See "Brief Notes on Data," below, p. 176.

and Nigeria which originate in their respective international transactions.

It is evident from available records that during the first half of the 1950's, the balance of payments of Ghana and Nigeria was characterized by very substantial export surpluses, and the second half was marked by large import surpluses (with the exception of one or two years in Ghana). What factors account for these contrasting trends? First is the price-effect. The export surpluses during the first half of the fifties grew partly because of a substantial rise in the prices of food and raw materials in the world market. The general price increase for these staples began at the end of the forties and, gaining momentum, reached a peak in 1954.[14] Thereafter, the price indices dropped noticeably to a level that initiated a downturn in the terms of trade of Ghana and Nigeria.[15] Thus in a simple way, the increase in prices of export commodities provides a general reason for the growth of export surpluses.

But in the context of Ghana and Nigeria, two compelling facts point up the play of other factors whose combined forces significantly outweigh the price-effect as the prime determinant of the observed export surpluses. The first of these was the price policy of the export marketing board, and the second was the rigid enforcement of exchange controls and various forms of qualitative and quantitative import restrictions. Both policies were postwar survivors of wartime measures designed for diverting resources away from public as well as private investment and consumption in order to satisfy wartime resource requirements in the United Kingdom and the Commonwealth.

The postwar producer (or domestic) price-setting policy was initiated by the West African marketing boards. With only few exceptions, the price paid to the producer has been noticeably lower than the prices reigning in the world market. This policy gave rise to a very substantial increase in the sterling balances abroad, in addition to the wartime blocked-sterling accumulations of the British West African colonies. This forced transfer of the income of producers for future use raises interesting problems of efficiency and equity in resource allocation. These questions, however, must be reserved for treatment at another time.

[14] See *Economic Survey of Africa Since 1950,* p. 181.
[15] See tables 7 and 9.

The second contributing factor to the export surpluses originated in the enforcement of exchange controls and tariff restrictions during the first half of the fifties. These restrictive instruments were relaxed in the second half of the fifties.

It is clear from these facts that the export surpluses stemmed not so much from the price-effect—although that, admittedly, is important —but largely from a combination of domestic policies in Ghana and Nigeria which, on the one hand limited the freedom to import investment goods, and on the other, choked off demand for consumer goods by exchange controls and by the marketing boards' policy. These are the facts of the economic situation. They are, to say the least, antiexpansionary and also have direct bearing on the problems of absorptive capacity.

So much for export surpluses. What about the sharp rise in import surpluses from 1955? With particular reference to Nigeria, the size of exports is closely associated with the movement of the terms of trade until 1954; furthermore, a close study of related data reveals that the turning of export surplus to import surplus, although it is clearly connected with deteriorating terms of trade, stems largely from a sharp rise in the volume of imports—with little change in the volume of exports.

On the whole, there is sufficient evidence that the emergence of import surpluses coincided in Ghana with the beginning of the First Five-Year Plan, and in Nigeria with the start of the Second Five-Year Plan. In both countries, the import surpluses had to be tolerated as long as they represented an inflow of capital equipment and construction materials required for development purposes. Thus, maintaining import surpluses was a practical way of insuring continuity of the projects already underway, even in the face of deteriorating terms of trade.[16]

ABSORPTIVE CAPACITY

The concept of "absorptive capacity"[17] suggests something about the existence of an upper limit to the transformation possible at a

[16] See tables 7 and 9, and notes.
[17] See B. Higgins, *Economic Development* (New York: Norton, 1959), pp. 624 ff.; also M. F. Millikan and W. W. Rostow, *A Proposal: Key to an Effective Foreign Policy* (New York: Harpers, 1957), pp. 56 ff.

given period in a backward economy such as Ghana or Nigeria. Viewed as a boundary condition (i.e., set by unutilized available local resources) upon a society in which urgent economic decisions must be made, its main policy implications are unmistakably clear. It serves as a powerful lever against the formulation and implementation of certain development projects—those merely symbolic of grandiosity and arrogance—for which effective absorption is lacking in the short run. Thus, as a conservative antidote to the sky's-the-limit type of optimism, it makes good policy sense.

Returning now to Ghana and Nigeria, the record of economic development since 1950 indicates that both countries have had a high degree of "absorptive capacity." Let me call your attention again to table 5. With reference to Ghana, the total increase in the gross national product (crude and undeflated) between 1950 and 1957 was, once again, 48.6 per cent. This amounts to an average yearly increase of 6.9 per cent, and a cumulative annual rate of growth of 5.8 per cent. In Nigeria, from 1950 to 1956, the total increase in the gross national product (crude and undeflated) was 39.8 per cent with an average yearly increase of 6.6 per cent and a cumulative annual rate of growth of 5.7 per cent. These rates of growth over a period of about seven years could not have taken place if the "absorptive capacity" was as limited as some observers have suggested to me in private discussions.

After a close reëxamination of statistical evidence on national income, capital formation, and balance of payments from 1955 onward, I submit that the structural impact of certain postwar survivors of the wartime colonial government's policies, rather than limiting "absorptive capacity," prevented a higher level of investment and economic activity in Ghana and Nigeria during the first half of the fifties. As stated earlier, those policies grew primarily out of the war economics of the United Kingdom and the Commonwealth, and were not originally prompted by any serious problems of "absorptive capacity." For the sake of completeness, let me restate the empirical fact that, given both the propensity to import and the ability to import, the process of capital formation in a dependent agricultural economy is largely determined by the availability of certain physical resources in the overseas markets supplying them. Thus, in addition to the governmental policies referred to above, the low level of economic activity in the early fifties may be partly owing to the fact that the Western

European markets, and particularly the United Kingdom market on which Ghana and Nigeria largely depended for complementary resources, were not in a position to supply heavy capital goods as quickly and as regularly as desired.

May I say in conclusion that if the close association between rising gross national product and capital-goods imports, especially since 1954, gives a reliable picture of the pattern of the future industrial situation, it appears that a liberal foreign-trade policy coupled with incentives for capital-goods imports would contribute immeasurably to economic expansion and a better standard of life in Ghana and Nigeria. It hardly seems necessary to stress at this point that any internal governmental policies that might evoke anxiety or erroneous impressions overseas about the ability of Ghana and Nigeria to maintain political stability and a high level of economic activity (i.e., transformation) could prejudice the evaluation and judgment of prospective investors and financial institutions whose funds provide the most feasible means of obtaining the additional foreign resources required for the continuation of economic and social development.

BRIEF NOTES ON DATA

THERE ARE nine selected tables to supplement the text. Sophisticated readers are aware that behind the neat statistical picture are certain unavoidable problems of methodology and conceptions, definitions, and measurement.

CAPITAL FORMATION AND GROSS NATIONAL PRODUCT

GHANA

TABLE 1 shows a summary of the values of gross national product and gross capital formation from 1950 to 1957. By simple arithmetical calculation it will be found that gross capital formation averaged about 12 per cent annually.

TABLE 3   The aggregate figures on capital formation have been decomposed into their major components or types of capital investments for the same period. Note the various intensities of investment allocation.

TABLE 5 shows the changes in national income and gross capital formation. The total increase in gross national product is calculated by taking the difference between the 1950 and 1957 figures. The same method is applied in estimating the total increase in gross capital formation. The figures represent crude and undeflated rates of increase.

NIGERIA

TABLE 2   National income figures for 1950–51, 1952–53 and 1956–57, plus a fairly continuous record of capital formation by year, are all that is available. Consequently, the gross national product figures for Ghana and Nigeria do not permit detailed comparisons between them.

TABLE 4   As in table 3 above, this also summarizes the distribution of investment by major components. The figures in tables 3 and 4 provide very interesting information on resource allocation per period. The proportion of each component to total investment expenditures may be taken as a rough index of the weight of *importance* and *urgency* attached to it in the over-all investment program.

TABLE 5   See table 5 above. The only difference is that the Nigerian record is for 1950 to 1956.

BALANCE OF PAYMENTS
AND TERMS OF TRADE

GENERAL: The method of reporting balances on current account used here modifies the standard format of the International Monetary Fund as follows: the *receipts side* is redefined to include merchandise exports f.o.b., plus receipts for other commercial services effected; the *payments side* includes imports f.o.b., plus freight and insurance charges (both together are the same thing as imports c.i.f.), plus other commercial services used by Ghana and Nigeria in international trade.

GHANA

TABLE 6   The most striking feature of the balance of payments statistics of Ghana is the very large export surplus from 1950 to 1955, with only mild fluctuations. The year 1956 marks a turning point of export surpluses into import surpluses. The size of the recurrent import surplus in 1957, like that of 1956, was about the same as the export surplus recorded for 1953. The importance of nonmonetary gold exports is obvious. Gold shipments were significant enough to change import surpluses in 1949 and 1955 into export surpluses.

TABLE 7   The indices of volume show changes in export and import commodities, with 1953 as the base year. Value indices represent the per unit value of export and import commodities. The terms of trade were calculated from the indices of unit values of imports and exports.

NIGERIA

TABLE 8   In Nigeria, the period from 1950 to 1955 was one of substantial export surpluses. An import surplus has become clearly marked since 1955 (according to available data). A curious feature of Nigeria's (and Ghana's) international account throughout 1950 to 1955 was that sizeable amounts of capital were transferred overseas in the form of sterling balances. The sterling balances were subsequently drawn down to offset some of the import surpluses.

TABLE 9   Same as in table 8 above.

TABLE 1

GOLD COAST—GHANA

GROSS NATIONAL PRODUCT

AND GROSS DOMESTIC CAPITAL FORMATION

1950–1957

(*Million pounds sterling*)

Year	Gross national product	Gross domestic capital formation	Gross domestic capital formation as a % of GNP
1950	197	22	11.4
1951	241	23	9.3
1952	241	27	11.3
1953	262	27	10.4
1954	296	33	11.1
1955	290	44	15.2
1956	277	45	16.0
1957	292	30	10.2

SOURCE: *Economic Survey of Africa Since 1950* (New York: United Nations, 1959), p. 205.

TABLE 2

NIGERIA

GROSS NATIONAL PRODUCT

AND GROSS DOMESTIC CAPITAL FORMATION

1950–1956

(*Million pounds sterling*)

Year	Gross national product	Gross domestic capital formation	Gross domestic capital formation as a % of GNP
1950	609	41	6.7
1951	—	—	—
1952	699	65	9.3
1953	—	67	—
1954	—	52	—
1955	—	80	—
1956	851	87	10.2

SOURCE: *Economic Survey of Africa Since 1950* (New York: United Nations, 1959), p. 206.

TABLE 3

GOLD COAST—GHANA

GROSS CAPITAL FORMATION;

DISTRIBUTION BY TYPE OF INVESTMENT

(SELECTED YEARS)

	1950	1953	1955	1956	1957
Gross capital formation (*millions of £ sterling*)	21	27.5	44.0	44.5	29.7
Fixed capital formation (*millions of £ sterling*)	15.7	29.9	35.8	37.9	36.8
Fixed capital formation (*in percentages*)	74.7	109.5	81.4	85.2	123.9

PERCENTAGE DISTRIBUTIONS OF FIXED CAPITAL FORMATION

BY TYPES OF INVESTMENT

Dwelling and other construction	32.9	68.1	53.6	52.8	79.8
Transport, machinery, etc.	40.8	41.4	27.7	32.4	44.2
Increase in stocks	26.3	−9.5	18.6	14.8	−23.9

SOURCE: *Economic Survey of Africa Since 1950* (New York: United Nations, 1959), p. 192.

TABLE 4

NIGERIA

GROSS CAPITAL FORMATION;

DISTRIBUTION BY TYPE OF INVESTMENT

(SELECTED YEARS)

	1950–51	1953–54	1955–56	1956–57
Gross capital formation (*millions of £ sterling*)	40.5	54.7	78.3	93.3
Gross fixed investment (*millions of £ sterling*)	37.	52.	75.	88.
Gross fixed investment (*in percentages*)	91.2	95.4	95.7	94.3

PERCENTAGE DISTRIBUTIONS OF GROSS FIXED INVESTMENT BY TYPE OF ASSET

Dwellings	23.8	23.9	26.7	20.7
Other construction	37.4	36.2	39.8	43.2
Transport & equipment	24.6	24.1	23.1	24.1
Machines & other equipment	14.2	15.7	10.4	12.0

SOURCE: *Economic Survey of Africa Since 1950* (New York: United Nations, 1959), p. 193.

TABLE 5

GHANA AND NIGERIA

CHANGES IN GROSS NATIONAL PRODUCT

AND GROSS CAPITAL FORMATION

1950–1957

(*In percentages*)

Country; period	Gross national product			Gross capital formation		
	Total increase	*Average yearly increase*	*Cumulative annual rate of growth*	*Total increase*	*Average yearly increase*	*Annual rate of growth*
Ghana, 1950–1957	48.6	6.9	5.82	32.6	4.7	4.11
Nigeria, 1950–1956	39.8	6.6	5.74	114.1	19.0	13.53

SOURCE: *Economic Survey of Africa Since 1950* (New York: United Nations, 1959), p. 208.

TABLE 6
BALANCE OF PAYMENTS
GOLD COAST—GHANA
(*Million pounds sterling*)

Year	Receipts for goods and services (+)	Payments for goods and services (−)	Balance on current account for goods and services	Invest- ment income (net)	Private transfers (net)	Official transfers (net)
1950	90.572	65.410	+25.117	−5.031	−0.047	+0.040
1951	109.099	84.197	+24.902	−5.361	−0.076	−0.164
1952	104.819	89.851	+14.968	−3.144	−0.140	−0.203
1953	111.463	101.478	+9.985	−3.329	−0.275	−1.176
1954	137.432	94.628	+42.804	−1.451	−0.198	+0.585
1955	116.519	113.032	+3.487	−0.908	−0.652	−0.087
1956	106.541	119.031	−12.490	−0.602	−0.838	+0.588
1957	116.461	129.513	−13.052	−0.854	−0.814	+0.287

OF WHICH, CHANGE IN STERLING BALANCES
(*including currency reserves*)

Year	Implied capital movements (net)	Long-term	Short-term	Total	Of which, other
1950	−20.079	+11.921	+18.892	+30.813	+10.8
1951	−19.301	+29.456	−5.593	+23.862	+4.3
1952	−11.482	+8.369	−0.496	+7.873	−3.6
1953	−5.201	−0.741	+15.783	+14.915	−9.7
1954	−40.739	+27.550	+9.648	+37.198	−3.5
1955	−1.840	+22.818	−9.002	+13.816	+12.0
1956	+13.342	+0.635	−15.369	−14.734	−1.4
1957	+14.433	−14.816	+1.007	−13.809	+0.6

SQVRCE: *Economic Survey, 1957* (Accra, June, 1958), p. 35.

TABLE 7

TERMS OF TRADE,

GOLD COAST—GHANA

1948–1958

(Indices of volume and unit values of imports and exports, and of terms of trade [1953 = 100])

Year	Index of volume		Index of unit values		Terms of trade
	Imports	Exports	Imports	Exports	
1948	49	85	87	74	85
1949	75	101	82	55	67
1950	74	105	88	82	93
1951	82	95	105	107	102
1952	81	92	110	104	95
1953	100	100	100	100	100
1954	102	91	95	141	148
1955	129	90	93	121	132
1956	126	101	96	97	101
1957	135	112	97	92	95
1958	120	92	96	128	133

SOURCE: *Yearbook of International Trade Statistics, 1958,* vol. 1 (New York: United Nations, 1959), p. 237.

TABLE 8

BALANCE OF PAYMENTS
NIGERIA

(*Million pounds sterling*)

Year	Exports f.o.b. less imports c.i.f.	Commer- cial services	Invest- ment income	Private donations	Official donations	Private capital
1950	+25.8	−2.6	−3.4	−0.5	+3.1	+2.6
1951	+33.5	−1.6	−3.4	−0.6	+1.3	+8.6
1952	+13.4	−1.8	−3.0	−0.6	+4.6	+7.6
1953	+13.4	+4.0	−3.2	3.3		+5.5
1954	+32.9	−4.2	−1.4	2.4		+10.4
1955	−6.3	−5.7	−0.6	−0.6	+3.9	+9.6
1956	−21.1	−6.9	+0.9	−0.5	+2.6	+19.1

OFFICIAL AND BANKING

Year	Long-term	Short-term	Errors and omissions
1950	−17.9	−7.5	+0.4
1951	−22.2	−14.6	+1.0
1952	−20.0	−5.0	+4.8
1953	−18.4	−4.6	
1954	−19.6	−9.4	
1955	−15.2	+18.6	−3.7
1956	+4.3	+1.7	−0.1

SOURCES: *The Economic Survey of Nigeria* (International Bank for Reconstruction and Development, 1950–1952), p. 143.
Investment in Nigeria (U.S. Department of Commerce, 1953–1954), p. 98.
"The Balance of Payments 1955 and 1956." Mimeo., Federal Department of Statistics, Lagos.

TABLE 9

TERMS OF TRADE,

NIGERIA

1948–1958

(Indices of volume and unit values of imports and exports, and of terms of trade [1953 = 100])

Year	Index of volume		Index of unit values		Terms of trade
	Imports	Exports	Imports	Exports	
1948	46	72	82	70	85
1949	63	87	84	73	87
1950	66	88	86	81	94
1951	73	85	107	111	104
1952	94	88	112	115	103
1953	100	100	100	100	100
1954	118	104	93	111	119
1955	146	103	92	98	107
1956	163	115	93	92	99
1957	158	111	94	92	98
1958	178	109	93	95	102

SOURCE: *Yearbook of International Trade Statistics, 1958*, vol. 1 (New York: United Nations, 1959, p. 393.

COMMENTS

DUNCAN N. NDEGWA

Assistant Secretary, Treasury of Kenya

PROFESSOR ROSTOW is to be congratulated for having managed to capture such a wide compass of economic history in a snapshot of not more than twenty pages. I was, however, a little concerned that his generous generalizations might be taken as prescriptions for action. Nevertheless, he has himself made it clear that his paper should be taken only as an agenda for discussion. I am therefore going to regard it as a basis for a "take-off" to a more serious discussion of the subject at hand. But before I do this, I should like to make one observation. The word "society," for instance, is misleading. We should not forget the wide diversification of the African continent in both its peoples and countries. People who are separated by wide tracks of desert and forests should not be expected to develop a common political or economic sentiment. In the East African territories, we should remember, the society is not by any means homogeneous. Particularly, I should like to point out that in Kenya 3 per cent of the population consists of Europeans and Asians with a high level of both income and skill. This section of the community is able to have standards of living comparable to those of "mass consumption" societies, as Professor Rostow would call them. The other 97 per cent lives in the "pre-take-off" stage, and the problem for this majority of people is to lift their material standards to standards comparable with those of the minority.

I believe that our next lot of economic advisors will have to be more empirical and political in tone while remaining essentially economists in their approach. I say this because my country, like many others in Africa, has no single important natural resource from which to derive the necessary income for transforming its human resources from traditional to modern modes of life. This change is particularly important when we consider the utilization of investing funds. That investment funds have been used by the Asians and Europeans to a greater degree than they have been used by the Africans is simply attributable to the greater availability of these funds to the two immigrant races. The Africans have not been able to step up their agricultural production because in order to do so they must invest in such foreign crops as coffee and tea, which require time to mature. The African who plants such crops must be assured of a living before the maturity date of these crops. To transform the subsistence economy to a positional "take-off" may therefore be a painful process.

Meanwhile, the existence of foreign culture in our midst has so stimulated the human propensity to consume foreign products that it is necessary to restrain the great enthusiasm in this direction. This is a difficult matter, particularly when it affects social services such as education and health. I believe, therefore, that one important role of economic policy in African territories is to formulate an economic plan that indicates priorities of action. The role of the economist in formulating these types of plans will be important in that he will have to use not only the tool of economic analysis but also some political judgment in trying to make such plans acceptable to the community and particularly to the politician. It will be necessary, too, during the early stages of independence not only to plan for current consumption and capital needs but also to find a way of meeting external public and private debts that have been accumulated over the years. The position in Kenya in this respect is that since 1950 the country has invested more than £300 million, much of which was supplied from external sources. Today, the public debt to meet loans borrowed over the years amounts to about £2 million annually. Problems of debt management will therefore have to be taken into account in subsequent years following independence.

Now, what about my attitude toward Pan-Africanism? I believe that during the stage following independence we shall be occupied increasingly by domestic problems of our own respective countries. It will not therefore, I think, be easy for us to develop any political unit beyond the boundaries of the eastern African territories. We shall, more and more, have to consolidate the East African customs union before we can think of Pan-Africanism on lines of political collaboration. But I do look forward to the strengthening of economic coöperation in Africa and to giving such bodies as the Economic Commission for Africa a greater African personality. It is also my hope that West European countries in coöperation with the United States will find it possible to announce a more dramatic economic program for Africa, such as the Marshall Plan. Beyond this, I do not see that political unification of any kind is feasible, and I believe such a possibility will come in sight only if we can develop ideas that transcend questions of bread and butter.

STANLEY SUMLIN

Economist, Federal Reserve Bank of New York

Professor Rostow's paper is perhaps one of the most articulate and thought-provoking statements we have heard on economic development in Africa. Undoubtedly this paper will generate a great deal of discussion and at the same time raise searching questions. In the first instance, Professor Rostow quite properly stresses that economic development is not an end in itself, but only an instrument to achieve the larger human and national objectives. Professor Rostow goes on to set forth a unique theory of economic growth by accounting for economic development in terms of five basic societies. While Professor Rostow maintains that his historical theory of economic development can offer the contemporary African some clues as to his future economic growth, I submit that if you attempt to *analyze* and *project* African economic development within the framework of Professor Rostow's five basic societies, you will find that such an analysis will tell you very little as to Africa's future economic growth.

If it appears that I view this paper too critically, let me say here that I am well aware that the development of an economic theory is complex indeed—to say the least. However, for a variety of reasons, I fail to see the predictive qualities suggested in Professor Rostow's paper. First of all, economic theory involves the analysis of a set of facts that tell us something about the various sectors of the economy and how they relate to each other. Professor Rostow's theory fails to give us new insights into this area. Implicit in his theory is the supposition that the countries have almost identical patterns of development. However, the fact that some countries reach the "take-off" society at different points in history (where technology and applied science spur on real economic development) suggests to me that the experiences of various countries are not almost identical. Although

Professor Rostow recognized the latter point, it appears to me that the experiences of the previously developed countries are not so similar as to give significant guide lines to the new African states. I ask you, will the new African states characterized by a predominantly agricultural economy with low per-capita income develop along the lines followed in France and Germany during the nineteenth century? I think not! Moreover, the fact that we are now in an age of electrification, as compared to the nineteenth century when steam was the source of energy, suggests to me that the pattern and, perhaps what is more important, the *pace* of economic development will be different. In addition, since consumer demand and international trade have changed over the last century and a half, it stands to reason that economic development may be steered along other lines.

Another point that puzzles me with respect to Professor Rostow's "take-off" of society is that, while he points out that modernization should focus upon growing sectors in the economy, his theory fails to lend itself to practical application. To illustrate, while we can in broad terms say, for example, that Nigeria is moving from the "take-off stage" to the drive-toward-maturity stage, economic theory should tell us how to identify the leading sectors of the economy, which in turn tell us something about how to accelerate expansion in the secondary sectors. For example, one would think one could always count on transportation facilities, notably railroads, as a key sector of the economy to spur on economic development; yet while railroads in the nineteenth century quickened the pace of economic growth in the United States, they did not promote growth in India.

I totally agree with Professor Rostow that education is the basic prerequisite for sustained economic growth. Despite the public declaration of universal acceptance of educational development, there is a tendency even for a country such as the United States not to give meaningful support to educational development. I think there is a need to emphasize perhaps more than Professor Rostow does that human development is one of the greatest assets that any nation can possess. Moreover, in developing the human factor, undoubtedly it will be useful to analyze the African educator and find out the manner in which he develops and becomes important to society. Such an analysis in all likelihood will suggest ways to speed on economic development at a faster clip.

There is no doubt in my mind that, as Professor Rostow observes, there is an ever-present need to increase the productivity of the agricultural sector of the African economy; it is crucial to African development. Moreover, it is perhaps needless to say that the establishment of basic facilities in the African states, the adoption of an intelligent foreign-exchange policy, and above all, direction by imaginative, capable leadership are necessary prerequisites for economic, social, and cultural progress.

Professor Rostow spells out the developments in Sweden and gives a good example to the newly emerging African states; however, since economic development in Africa will represent, in my judgment, a culmination of a variety of ever-changing forces, I am not yet quite sure whether Africans will or indeed want to pattern their developments after those in Sweden. Perhaps our African friends can shed some light on this.

Turning to the problem of African unity, which as you probably know is now being debated in Addis Ababa, Professor Rostow implies that the concept of African unity may operate to stave off economic development at the local level. I suspect that the majority of African leaders are well aware that their position to negotiate for some kind of African unity is strengthened by the very fact that they can demonstate some economic progress on the local level. Therefore, it appears to me that in the first instance, leaders in the new independent states will move to foster economic progress on the local level and at the same time press for unification along broader lines. To illustrate the latter point, at this very moment, in Kenya, Tanganyika, and Uganda there is being formulated a trade organization which may well be the forerunner of an East African Common Market. Moreover, as you probably know, there have been a number of proposals relating to West African coöperation which would deal primarily in expanding and stabilizing West African exports, fostering intra-African trade, and at the same time promoting regional industrialization.

Just a few remarks about Mr. Fahm's paper. I might say at the outset that Mr. Fahm has presented a meaningful paper regarding capital formation, balance of payments, and the absorptive capacity of Ghana and Nigeria. I think we will all agree that Nigeria and especially Ghana have shown impressive results in the last few years. Since Mr. Fahm has observed quite appropriately that rapid economic development in Ghana and Nigeria will be determined to a substantial extent by external aid, perhaps the question should be raised about the probable outlook for external aid to these new African states. As pointed out by Mr. Fahm, certainly both Ghana and Nigeria can absorb more capital. It is perfectly logical to ask where this capital is coming from. In terms of the East-West struggle (which, incidentally, appears to be the most important issue in this country) this question looms ahead as being most significant. I trust that this question will be discussed from the floor—for it is a crucial problem.

I should like to say in passing that there appears to be an increasing and wider recognition of multilateral approach in aiding African countries. This is owing partly to the apparent reluctance of most African states to be tied to any particular power bloc and partly to the increasing significance of the new African states in the East-West struggle. It is hoped that this shift in viewpoint will deepen to the point where it is actually reflected in the government policies of economically developed countries.

What does this mean as it relates to African unity and Pan-Africanism? For one thing, as I intimated before, within the concept of African unity and Pan-Africanism, economic coöperation would indeed pave the way for the creation of an African Common Market, which I think is vitally necessary to expand and stabilize African trade. Success in this area may well provide the setting for gradual coöperation for all common problems facing Africa—whether they be educational, cultural, or perhaps political. All of these things will not only be feasible, but also, needless to say, a step in the right direction.

Perhaps the best way to sum up is to say that if Ghana, Guinea, Nigeria, and all of the other newly emerging African states promote economic development with as much dogged determination as they showed in successfully gaining their independence, they will undoubtedly move ahead with dignity and understanding to take their proper place in world affairs.

EMILE ZINSOU

Secretary, African Federation Party, Dahomey

We have heard two brilliant talks, and my intention is to be as succinct as possible, but practical.

To speak of African economy, to examine the trends of this economy, to define the paths of its development, is to depart from our present situation and to envisage our future.

We are colonized or formerly-colonized peoples; the objectives of our development, up to this very day, have been defined and elaborated in relation to the needs of the metropolitan countries. We colonial countries were expected to complement their economies with raw materials required by their industry and within the framework of a capitalistic economy. By the same token, the inevitable and indispensable preface to all economic development—the period of analysis and research—has been dominated in our countries by the colonizers in this same spirit and with this same end in mind. Actually, the true inventory has still to be made in many areas.

We young nations who are entering independence are confronted with the economic currents of a capitalistic world. The analysis of our economic situation should involve analysis of such data as the condition of the soil and the subsoil, demography, the needs of the internal and external market, the means and methods of financing, the supply of specialized labor, the problem of management, development programs. All this, which I merely mention in passing, requires special study, which would take us too long; but all this must be based, fundamentally and in all truth, on a basic choice. For, we must ask, economic development in what direction, to what end, in the service of what system? Thus the need at the outset is to define this choice both from the point of view of the colonized or ex-colonized peoples of an underdeveloped country like ours and from the historical point of view—and, I would say, from the philosophical point of view of Africa. It can only be a choice for socialism. I mean (and the soldier-poet Senghor developed this magnificently in a report to the Constitutive Assembly) a reconsidered socialism—into which we can integrate African values; that is, spiritual values—but socialism just the same. If this choice is made at the outset (and if we are in agreement), then, although I do not say that everything will become easy, the battle lines of our economic activity will be distinguished a little more easily, or at least with a little more clarity.

If we have felt the need to call it African socialism, it is because in our eyes it represents not an import thrust onto our situation from stem to stern, but an original search, fertilized by the facts of our lands. Our socialism, though it accepts all the contributions and all the research that went into the development of socialist thought in the world, and though it does not repudiate the contributions of Karl Marx, is nevertheless not Marxism. We recognize the analytic method of Marx; we consider it as methodology and not active philosophy, since if Karl Marx were alive today I am not sure he would write *Das Kapital* without changes or modifications. Thus, we do not propose to renounce the use of a method of social analysis that has been proved; rather, on the basis of this analysis—on the basis of fundamental considerations which this research will reveal—we should undertake to create, to achieve a synthesis where the African element will be determinant and creative. Thus, we make the choice for a socialist system—and hence for a certain directivism, for at this stage of underdevelopment we cannot afford the luxury of complete liberalism, which would only be anarchy for us. Consequently, rational planning, directivism, as to the large choices and the broad direction of our economic policy—such seem to me to be the key words that must preface all research on economic activity in Africa.

How contrary is this aim to what is happening in Western Europe or in America? How much state intervention should be involved in the elaboration of plans and their implementation? In countries of the West (when I speak of the West, I mean Western Europe and America), economic development is primarily aimed at achieving a surplus of well-being, since the minimum has been attained; it is aimed above all at getting more and more of the world market each day; it is aimed at achieving that excess that permits leisure. But as far as we are concerned, we are even lacking the minimum; it is not uncommon in African countries for men to get only two meals a day, meals that are ridiculously low in calories.

It is an error to think that at our stage we must inevitably go through all the levels of economic development, or at least that we must wait many decades and undergo many stages. We are integrating ourselves into the modern world with the resolution—I might even say the obligation—to enter into the *present*. The moral proposition is to immediately apply to our situation all the results of our own experience and the experience of others without having to relive those experiences in order to profit from them. Moreover, the example of Russia and the example of China are there to serve as witness. I am dealing mainly with a fundamental choice on which it is essential that we agree. We have already discussed how dangerous political Balkanization is, and how we must struggle against it; I would add that there is another Balkanization still more dangerous—economic Balkanization. As well as our nations themselves, our various regions could evolve in different, sometimes opposed directions. We must realize that we would encounter with this Balkanization of our economic system not only conflicts of interest, not only conflicts of understanding, but ideological conflicts also.

Hence it is evident that Africa's economy as well as its history and its interests must not remain in doubt; it is already written out, for anyone who knows African society, as socialist in tendency. It can be proved that the micro-nations that we run the risk of constituting cannot validly be inserted into great economic wholes. We must think well, or we shall face certain difficulties that will arise from the geographic location of certain of these micro-nations, for the laws of economy by extension are the same everywhere. One state will want to touch on the coast; another will need its neighbor's nearby region in order to make effective economic planning possible. Who does not see, for example, that Gambia and Senegal form a crescent, which, if integrated, would facilitate the development plans of Casamos? Who does not see that the Central African Republic needs an exit to the sea, a window on the ocean? It only requires a look at the map—and one must always look at a map when one is developing an economy.

To consider seriously our economic problem, we always reach the same conclusion, for in our situation—of course, I have just said we require rational analysis—we cannot, in our economic planning, rely on pragmatism and give a free rein to improvisation. We must analyze our sociological situation, our geographical situation; we must consider the world economic situation and insert ourselves into that situation, with the African no longer merely as a complement, but as an active partner. It has often been objected that the difficulty of Africa, of the economic development of Africa, arises from the lack of a source of energy; and yet it is now established that we are the continent with the most important resources of energy in the world. And finally, putting to work financial means presupposes at the outset that we find in ourselves a minimum of resources; it presupposes that we reconsider the notion of an African economy of savings, and presupposes also that the wealthier nations extend their aid, because, as we hear it phrased, it is their duty and to their interest at one and the same time.

I think that I have indicated how much these problems, which often appear to be the specialty of a few men, lending themselves for solution only to a few oracles, must be the problem of all thinking and responsible Africans, and how urgent it is that the developed countries should support this growth, either for reasons that we know, or as an expression of intelligent and liberal capitalism that has an interest in fostering economic development and an abundant life. These countries must understand that as far as we are concerned, we make a choice for the present that must necessarily be different from theirs—at least in the matter of development—but which is not opposed to theirs. We must make a harmonious mixture of the capitalistic contribution and socialist planning, and may it be given to us, even in this domain, to make an original contribution to universal civilization. If we did otherwise, we could make exhaustive analyses of the production of such-and-such a country—accounts, commercial balances—we could present balance-sheets of all kinds. But we would not have made any progress toward the economic development of Africa; we would not be integrated into the modern current as a complete partner. We would simply have become an adjunct of Paris, of Wall Street, of the city, where a man in some office by the mere scratch of a pen disturbs not only our economy but also our politics.

Independence, certainly; political independence above all. For, you see, we are returning here to problems that, however old they may be, are still political problems. Independence, certainly. However, we shall have raised our new flags, sung our national anthems, seated ourselves in the chair of honor in vain if we are not economically viable countries. If, above all and in every contingency, we are not economically independent, we shall merely have nurtured a great illusion.

In conclusion to this brief survey, I should like to say that for the present, the developed countries of America or elsewhere who have the good fortune to have a more advanced economic formation than ours, have an immediately useful task, a useful contribution to make to us: as the first favor, analysis and research. They can greatly aid us by furnishing all sorts of cadres: geologists, statisticians, geneticists, engineers—experts in all fields in which we must make rapid progress.

But the outcome, we must remember, will depend not only on their specialist knowledge but also on our unity.

VINCENT C. IKEOTUONYE

M.P., Federal Parliament, Nigeria;
Headmaster, Zixton Grammar School, Onitsha, Nigeria

I have just two brief points to make. First, I cannot look kindly on any statement that attributes wealth to any of the African states. It was said here that Western Nigeria is a rich country. How can it be rich when its annual budget is less than sixty million dollars? This would not even be enough for a big corporation's advertising budget! Yet it is the national budget of a "rich" country!

Second, a combination of warning and appeal to my friends from the other African states: I remember that Toynbee, in *A Study of History,* said that the development of a civilization depends on the ability of the people to answer the various social or economic or geographical challenges that face them. I am appalled at the thought that we Africans are getting a little bit complacent after having achieved our so-called independence. I don't know what independence or what independent sovereignty we Africans can have when our continent has already been Balkanized. I think that, much as we have fought for our independence, now that it is won we are faced with a more important problem: the federation of the African states. I think that if we do not form a federation now that a historical cycle has been completed, we shall again find Africa colonized, in one form or another. This is my message to my friends, especially to the youth, from other parts of Africa.

DISCUSSION

SAIDI MASWANYA [*speaking from the floor*]: As Mr. Ndegwa has already remarked, there are some areas in Africa where the national wealth is concentrated among certain groups of people. For example, in East Africa the national wealth is among European or Asian communities. Up to now, you see, the distribution of such wealth among the people has not been attempted. The colonial powers have encouraged this approach. On the other hand, I am sure you understand that in some other places, such as West Africa, a similar situation exists, although it cannot be identified by color or racial lines.

So, I would like to hear Professor Rostow's explanation of what the scientific approach should be for the distribution of such wealth.

W. W. ROSTOW: This very good question is also, in a way, at the heart of the contention that Mr. Ndegwa made when he raised the question of where these societies fit in the stages of growth. My feeling, in response to Mr. Ndegwa's remarks, is that he is absolutely right. In a situation where a colonial history produces an enclave of modern life in a setting of traditional society at a moment of independence and responsibility, and in a situation where incomes range from eight to thirty-three hundred pounds a year, the essential task of the society— if it is to be a society, a homogeneous one—is going to be political at the very highest level of human statesmanship; otherwise, you are going to have, in effect, brutal civil wars.

I have no ready answers for this very searching human and historical problem. I have a few observations. Kenya is not the only society that is faced with what I call the "enclave problem." There are many parts of the world where quite rich sectors, linked to the outside world, grew up in a setting in which the rest of the society was mainly traditional and of low-income status. Where you have had a successful resolution of the problem, it has been accomplished by an agreement, a consensus, an operating consensus, that the first responsibility of everyone—rich and poor—is to get on with the job of developing a society. This means that the art of statesmanship, the political job that Mr. Ndegwa referred to, is the job of linking modern life with the traditional part of Kenya; this is the agreed, central, overriding task.

As we know, the distribution of income from the rich to the poor will not in itself solve this task in Kenya. It may or may not be possible as an act of statesmanship, politics, and psychology, in order to obtain the necessary concensus. But if there is one thing we know from other cases, it is that the first goal is that the number-one job of the rich in Kenya is to gear their lives and their fortunes to a national program, the objective of which is the modernization of all Kenya. In other words, the "double life"—which, as I say, is quite familiar to a historian or to an observer of the modern scene—must end. There may be no need to seize the wealth of the rich, their capital. The terms they must meet are that their creative, economic, and other activities must be part of a national program.

This is not saying very much; but it is saying something, because you realize that you are dealing with a special and unusually difficult version of what has happened in many societies moving from a feudal agricultural past into modernization. This is a version of what the Indian princes have had to face in India as that country became independent and began to develop. There was also a range of income far greater there than in Kenya. The clue to overcoming this kind of income spread does not lie in civil war—unless you wish to have it, and unless human beings are capable of no other responses. But the Indian princes must say: "Yes, what we have we will be permitted to keep, but only if this ceases to be an enclave and becomes a constructive part of a living operation."

Hence, I would say to Mr. Ndegwa, with very great humility, that the agenda I outlined is the most generalized that any science can make in this biological field of growth. The agenda around which the white, the Indian, the Negro in Kenya must concentrate is not unlike my programmatic agenda. These are the jobs, these are the criteria, to which they will all have to subject their lives and their fortunes. The key, as he indicated, is a political and creative act that would, in fact, end the enclave. It would lay down the overriding criterion for Kenya as a working country—the criterion that the common job for all three elements is the modernization of the whole society.

V EDUCATION

THE DISCUSSION OF EDUCATION ranged around three or four provocative issues. Must the high standards of the present European-sponsored African universities yield to the necessity for rapid training of huge numbers of administrative and technical personnel? Must academic freedom be maintained at all cost, or should the university be responsive to community pressures? More particularly, to what degree should the universities of Africa be "Africanized"?

The remarks of Karl Bigelow, Professor of Education at Columbia, and of Abdoulaye Fofana, Minister of Education of the ill-fated Mali Federation, developed into a kind of dialogue on the subject of academic freedom. Fofana's remarks are graphic illustration of the drive toward "Africanization" in the continent; except for certain scientific disciplines, he feels the university should be "Africanized" from personnel to curriculum. Blind devotion to French standards in education does not commend itself to him. Africa, particularly the then Mali Federation, is faced with certain pressing educational needs. The production not of a few elite but of large numbers of competent personnel is especially important. Adherence to a system designed essentially for the cultivation of a handful of members of a favored upper class is ill suited, he argues, to Africa's needs. Bigelow wisely refuses to provide a perfect counterpoint to this position; in a large measure, he agrees. He urges, however, in the best academic sense, the timeless importance of the concept of the university, by its name universal, inspired by the spirit of free inquiry. Emphasizing the necessity of academic freedom, he expresses alarm at the attitude underlying Nkrumah's remarks that University College at Accra, Ghana, has become "a breeding ground for unpatriotic and anti-government elements."

The subsequent discussion of the various panelists centers on the tremendous job of devising and developing an educational system adequate to meet the problem, which has arisen almost overnight, of training leadership for nothing less than a continent. Horace Mann Bond urges a Pan-African approach, that is, the development of major regional universities to serve students of several nations. He cites Alabama Polytechnic and other regional institutions as illustrations in the United States. It is significant that as to this specific suggestion of a functional Pan-Africanism, Hagan of Ghana appears convinced that the climate of intense nationalism would not permit such a solution. The Ibadan experience, he says, confirms his point.

Easton and Bond suggest the partial abandonment of the English university system, with its rigorous screening, in order to meet the huge demands of a young dynamic society. Bigelow commends examination of the American land-grant system. (Rostow had previously referred to the Morrill Act of the 1860's.) Jones of California urges the Africans to adopt a daring, creative approach in the effort to solve their educational problems. Ikeotuonye, schoolmaster and Member of the Nigerian Parliament, was at Lincoln University, a former student of AMSAC's President Horace Mann Bond and of the Executive Director, John A. Davis. He tells the story of the presumptuous porter, who, after helping him and his countrymen with their bags upon their arrival at Lincoln, invited them to lunch. Recovering from their sense of outrage, they learned that the porter was, of course, a dean of the university. Ikeotuonye finds the liberal, egalitarian spirit of American education essential for Africa in preparing the student to be useful to himself and to society. He adds that the British were baffled by the drive and energy in the independence movement of those Africans educated in the United States.

In the informative picture Hagan gives of higher education in Africa, complementing Bigelow's description, it is notable that again we find reference to Belgian miscalculation: the Belgians created a university in the Congo, but all the graduates, Hagan observes, were Belgians. At the time of his remarks, at the prelude of independence, the Belgians were finally turning to the Congolese, making them "public administrators" in a ninety-day course at the university. "Mass production, indeed," he says.

S. W. A.

HIGHER EDUCATION IN TROPICAL AFRICA

KARL W. BIGELOW

Department of Higher Education, Teachers College, Columbia University

HIGHER EDUCATION IN TROPICAL AFRICA is fundamentally a postwar development. The only real exception is that of Fourah Bay College—now become the University College of Sierra Leone—which as early as 1876 was affiliated with the University of Durham, thus being enabled to prepare students for the Durham degree in arts and sciences and the Diploma in Theology. Gordon College, in the Sudan, and Makerere College, in Uganda, were also in existence before the last war but did not achieve status as institutions of higher education until after it had ended. At the same time the University College of Ghana and that at Ibadan, in Western Nigeria, were established. That of Rhodesia and Nyasaland is even younger.

Also of relatively recent origin are the three universities in French West Africa and the Belgian Congo. But here I should say that I know little of these institutions. My remarks in this paper will, indeed, relate all but exclusively to higher education in those African territories that are, or until recently were, related to Great Britain.

The postwar developments in British-related territories were based on the recommendations of a Royal Commission on Higher Education in the Colonies and of its ancillary committees. Those developments were facilitated in three important ways. In the first place, money was provided from the Colonial Development and Welfare Fund. Next, advisory services were made available through a newly created Inter-University Council for Higher Education in the Colonies. Finally, the young university colleges were given a so-called "special relationship" to the University of London whereby special tutelage was provided. Something more should be said about each of these provisions.

Let me take up the connection with the University of London first. This was, as an arrangement, nothing new. London's charter (of 1836) had required that examinations be offered not only to resident, but also to "external" students, who might never have attended the university or, indeed, seen the city of London. This provision was taken advantage of, not only by individuals, but also by institutions seeking to achieve university status. The latter could, as "university colleges," prepare their students for London examinations and degrees. The institutions in question were often British. So the postwar application of the scheme to Africa (and to Asia and the Caribbean as well) had nothing patronizing about it.

Under the special relationship it was intended that courses of study and examinations in the new university colleges should receive the joint approval of local and University of London authorities, with local conditions being taken into account. Students whom London was satisfied had properly completed the work leading to a degree were granted that degree—by London.

The particular advantages considered to inhere in this arrangement were that during the early years of a new institution of higher education the quality of its program was guaranteed and its young staff was provided with access to advice and assistance from an established source. It was understood that the umbilical cord would be severed once the university college had had adequate experience of work of a university standard, once it had been demonstrated that research activities on the part of staff members were possible and under way, and once enough students had demonstrated their capacity to earn London degrees of the types for which they had been prepared. At this point the university college would become a university and take on the responsibility of degree-granting itself, though continuing, of course, the standard British practice of involving representatives of other universities in examination procedures.

This step, in Africa, has already been taken by the University of Khartoum and is not likely to be long delayed elsewhere. The period of tutelage is proving to be somewhat shorter perhaps, than was originally expected. This seems partly owing to the fact that with political independence came increased desire for university independence. But recognition must also, surely, be given to the generally successful way in which the scheme has worked out.

The Inter-University Council for Higher Education in the Colonies was something new. Made up of representatives of the English universities, it was created to provide advice, both to the new university colleges and to the United Kingdom government, insofar as such advice was sought, with respect both to policy issues and to the selection and appointment of staff. The council's services, like those provided by the University of London, were designed to ensure the maintenance of high quality in the new institutions. Both ensured to local administrators and teaching staff members ready access to established sources of ideas regarding higher education.

The original financing of the new university colleges—with the exception of that in Ghana—came from the British Treasury via the Colonial Development and Welfare Fund. But for several reasons this did not imply political control. To begin with, the special relationship to the University of London and the connections with the Inter-University Council guaranteed a dominant influence to representatives of higher education. Moreover, the British government was already accustomed to providing support for the home universities by a method calculated to make certain of their autonomy. The device in question is the University Grants Committee, constituted of senior university teachers and former teachers, whose recommendations to the Treasury as to grants to be made to the several universities in England are invariably accepted. Although this body has had no direct responsibility as respects the African university colleges, the principle that it represents has been influential, not least because of overlapping membership between it and the Inter-University Council.

Let me now attempt some appraisal of the entire system as it has worked out in practice.

In the first place it can scarcely be denied that the British have earnestly attempted to develop, in Africa, institutions of higher education of real quality according to their standards. While local governments have shared—increasingly, of course, and in Ghana predominantly—in the expense, the British investment has been heavy. And no one who has visited the University College at Ibadan, for example, can have suspected any cheeseparing.

But more significant has been the insistence on academic quality. The Africans have never had cause to doubt that anything second-rate, by British standards, was being fobbed off on them.

Now there is, of course, room for genuine argument as to whether the British model of higher education is wholly suited to African needs. To be fair, it should be said that the British themselves recognized this from the outset. Thus the University of London agreed to consider proposals for adaptation of syllabuses and methods to local circumstances. That there have been relatively few adaptations of this sort is not really surprising. The staffs of the university colleges were, of necessity, largely imported, chiefly from Britain; and such Africans as were available for staff appointment had, with rare exceptions, received their own university training in the United Kingdom. University people—even in the United States!—tend to teach what and as they have been taught. Moreover, the staff members of the new African institutions had many difficulties to contend with and often did not expect to occupy their new positions for more than a few years. It is probably unrealistic to be very critical of any failure on their part to gain rapid understanding of their unfamiliar situations and to invent new and more functional courses of study and methods of instruction. (Parenthetically, I may say that only the other day I read a letter from an American teacher just concluding two years of service with an ICA project in Africa. "After a few months," she wrote ruefully, "one feels one understands Africa; after a few years, one doubts one ever will.")

We should also recognize that not only the relatively few university-trained Africans but also the African public generally (to the degree that it was concerned with the issue) would have been deeply suspicious had the British introduced practices in the new university colleges that deviated more than a little from those of institutions in the United Kingdom. To understand this, we have only to recall the higher education for women in this country which was originally modeled slavishly on that for men, and the feelings roused by higher education for Negroes that deviated from the same standard model.

Nothing that I have said, of course, has been intended to imply that I myself consider the pattern of British university education to be ideally suited to African needs. There is a great deal in American higher education—especially in the land-grant college tradition—which seems to me to be more suitable. But that statement does not mean that I think Africa should be encouraged to shift to the American model. Certainly what is to be sought for, and ultimately expected, is the emergence of African universities that are genuinely African.

But while they should be African, they should also be universities. And the university, in concept, is supranational. Thus, in their start under British tutelage, the young African institutions have been most fortunately imbued with those elements of the university tradition that are of universal validity.

Of these elements, devotion to high standards of scholarship and academic achievement, and to the maintenance of institutional autonomy and academic freedom, may especially be noted. It may not be too easy, in future, to maintain these essentials, but it will be easier because of the good start.

The pressure on standards will, I suggest, be twofold. First, there will be—indeed there is—an insistent demand for expansion of higher educational opportunity. Young Africans, partly from a desire to serve their countries but partly, too, from personal ambition (not necessarily related to ability), are clamoring for places in the university colleges. And governments are harassed by the terrible need for highly trained manpower. Second, there is the pressure for Africanization of university staffs. In principle, of course, this is eminently sound. But the supply of properly trained Africans available for university appointments is small and must for some time remain so, especially in view of the existence of important and attractive alternative opportunities for national service.

There is, then, a very real possibility that the quality both of student bodies and of teaching staffs may decline—or, perhaps, be established at a lower level in institutions yet to be created. Within limits, some such adjustment may not prove too disadvantageous. The United States has had—indeed, still has—colleges that have varied appreciably in quality, and the consequences have not all been bad. Even poorer institutions have bred some distinguished persons; and the training received by young people of less than the first quality has benefited them and society. Such arguments, however, must be advanced with caution, not enthusiasm. And it is important in Africa, as it has been here, that high and rigorous standards should be maintained somewhere and recognized for what they are.

The point at issue becomes especially significant as American influence on higher education in Africa increases. It is well known that in British university circles, and also among highly educated Africans, there is a tendency to think of American higher education as inferior. This is partly owing to the propensity we all have to measure everything with the yardstick of that with which we are familiar. This custom all but automatically results in difference being equated with weakness. A *summa cum laude* graduate of Harvard, turning up in Africa to teach history in a secondary school, would lack some of the equipment of a pass graduate of the least of the British universities. This would properly be attributable to the difference in undergraduate curricula. But it would be easy for those familiar with the results of British training to conclude that Harvard had done a poor job. Of course, informed and sympathetic people in both the United Kingdom and Africa know better—but even they have to recognize that the American has special problems of fitting into a system of education modeled on that of the British.

It is especially important, then, that Americans who become involved in higher education in Africa should be both of the highest quality by American university standards and flexible and personable enough to be able to adapt successfully to unfamiliar situations. Good intentions will not be enough. And Anglophobia will be a positive handicap—more, after independence, than before.

It is therefore gratifying to note an increasing number of coöperative efforts, ·involving Africans, Britons, and Americans, concerned with problems of African higher education. Through the American Council on Education, leading representatives of American universities and colleges have in the past year or two been conferring with their opposite numbers in the United Kingdom—specifically with members of the Inter-University Council. Now approaching conclusion is the work of a joint commission to study the future of postsecondary education in Nigeria, the members of which represent that country, the United Kingdom, and the United States. Further, I may be permitted to mention a coöperative program for the strengthening of teacher education in Africa, with which I myself am to be associated and in which Teachers College, Columbia University, will be joined with the Institute of Education of the University of London and six institutes and departments of education at African university colleges and colleges.

Of special interest, in this connection, is the way in which the new university, to be opened in Eastern Nigeria in October of this year, is being developed. The moving spirit in this enterprise, Dr. Azikiwe —erstwhile Prime Minister of the Eastern Region and now President of the Federal Nigerian Senate—has all along been eager to make use of American ideas and practices. The Provisional Council of the new institution accordingly includes Americans as well as Nigerians and Britons. And it has now been agreed that while the university will, from the outset, grant its own degrees, it is to enjoy the cosponsorship of Michigan State University and the University of London. Thus, regular channels will be provided for the provision of advice and guidance from representative institutions of higher education in both the United Kingdom and the United States, though with fewer powers of temporary control than have been present in the case of existing university colleges. It is hoped that two-week seminars may be held in the late summer, attended by Nigerian, American, and British experts, at which plans for the conduct of each of the major divisions of the university may be hammered out. This effort, if successful (as I am confident it will be), may well establish a pattern for further expansion of higher education in Africa.

Let me now turn to the issue of university autonomy and, more specifically, that of academic freedom. The idea that scholars should be preserved from subservience to the influence of the supporting community (particularly as represented by political forces) is a relatively modern one, and it is not easy for the man in the street to grasp. It rests on a conviction that free and untrammeled inquiry, while its outcomes may often be disturbing to conservative souls, will in the long run prove advantageous to a progressive society. It presumes that what is today considered to be truth is always subject to correction in the light of new discoveries, that those discoveries will be jealously checked by competent scholars (perhaps in far-distant countries), and that if they succeed in running the scholars' gantlet they should be accepted.

Unfortunately, as Walter Bagehot put it, there is no pain like the pain of a new idea. So, novel propositions are likely to disturb many people, whose normal reaction will be to demand that they be suppressed. It is a remarkable society in which the threat of such effort at suppression is not present. Certainly scholars in this country are aware of its existence: at the moment, for example, the expression by university professors of scholarly conclusions favorable to educational desegregation risks reprisal in certain parts of the United States.

By and large, university autonomy and academic freedom are most secure in firmly established institutions in highly educated societies —or, at least, in societies in which political power is in the hands of highly educated persons. Neither of these characteristics is clearly present in African nations. The "idea of a university" has never even occurred to the vast majority of the African peoples. And the politicians, first driven by the cause of independence, and later by the necessity of maintaining control, may well find it difficult to suffer the arrogance of scholars, determined to declare the truth as they see it no matter how unpopular it may be.

Thus an ominous note was struck by Dr. Nkrumah last August, when, speaking at a meeting of his Convention People's Party, he attacked the University College of Ghana as "a breeding ground for unpatriotic and anti-Government elements." An "anti-Government attitude" he identified with "an anti-Convention People's Party attitude, for our Party," he declared, "forms the Government and will continue to do so for many a long year to come." And Dr. Nkrumah warned the University College: "If reforms do not come from within, we intend to impose them from outside and no resort to the cry of academic freedom (for academic freedom does not mean academic irresponsibility) is going to restrain us from seeing that our University is a healthy, Ghanian University devoted to Ghanaian interests" [quoted from *Evening News* (Accra), Aug. 5, 1959]. I am told that Dr. Nkrumah subsequently assured the Principal of the University College that his remarks were not to be taken too seriously, but the fact that they were made at all is disturbing. Concern is also being expressed over current efforts to establish a Convention People's Party unit among Ghana undergraduates.

What is really at issue, I suggest, is a conflict between the universal idea of a university and the local idea. It is good that higher education should be directly related to the needs of the given community it serves. What was suitable for nineteenth-century America no longer fits our situation. What is best for the United Kingdom and the United States today is, we may be certain, less than perfect for contemporary Sierra Leone or Uganda.

But if higher education should relate to needs, the needs recognized should not be merely local ones nor merely those of immediate pressing importance. They should not be narrowly national, nor narrowly racial, nor narrowly anything else. The very name "university" implies universality. And the great glory of the scholar is that he is a citizen of an international, interracial, intercontinental, potentially interplanetary world.

I can appreciate that the Africans now achieving independence must also struggle to achieve an essential nationhood. I can appreciate their impulse, even though it would appear to conflict somewhat with the nationalistic drive, to join together in a spirit—somewhat mystical, perhaps—of Pan-Africanism. But nationalism and Pan-Africanism (however understandable and however serviceable in many ways) still remain limited ambitions.

The true university, at the very center, knows neither Jew nor Gentile, African nor European, white nor black. We must hope that those Africans to whom, increasingly, responsibility for higher education in that continent is entrusted will understand this and act upon that understanding. We must all strive, as we seek to promote higher education in Africa, to ensure that we serve the cause, not of Africans merely as Africans, but of Africans also as Men.

The expanding universities of Africa must produce doctors and lawyers, teachers and spiritual leaders, engineers and scientists, scholars and skilled civil servants. They must produce good citizens for their nations and good neighbors for their continent. But this is not enough. If they fail to serve the cause of truth that knows no boundaries, of humanity that knows no limits, they will fail as universities. Let us in America resolve that every act of ours will support the universities of Africa in their essential mission.

THE UNIVERSITY OF MALI

ABDOULAYE FOFANA

Minister of Education, Mali Federation (now Senegal)

THE UNIVERSITY OF DAKAR has become a public institution of the Mali Federation, and its administration has been confided to the Republic of France.

When we are concerned with the formation of an elite, we must remember that if "to govern is to foresee," this seeing into the future is of capital importance. In the light of experience, we are able to judge the disadvantages of higher intellectual formation when it is cut off from the normal environment. In France during colonial days, such studies were often deplored, even when successful, as "manufacturing" Africans unsuited to African life. The students were encumbered with European concepts, and their dearest wish was to live like Frenchmen, not to say in France itself. If they failed, readaptation was an agonizing procedure.

If it appears that studies in Dakar were less "destructive," it would seem that the reason for this could be attributed to a certain anti-colonialist sentiment that, animating the students, prevented them from "adhering" to Western concepts that were thrust at them in large doses. Whatever the reason, this defense was only a kind of negativism, progressively disappearing, which rendered them indifferent to any culture that did not offer them any personal or collective emotional experience outside the pure pleasure of learning.

The danger is still present. Is the University of Dakar at the present time the ideal instrument for the formation of these young people who will be the elite of the Mali Federation? What disadvantages does its system represent? What can be done to better the situation?

Positive

The University of Dakar, profiting from the great experience of the French university system, and at the same time from the generosity of the former Overseas Department and the Department of National

NOTE: Subsequent to the presentation of this paper, the Mali Federation split into Senegal and Mali (the French Soudan), and Mali joined Ghana and Guinea in the Union of African States, a loose league involving no transfer of sovereignty.

Education, has been able to equip itself better than have most metropolitan universities. It is not under the handicap of being in old buildings; it has the room and the potential for extensive modern and future development. And, thanks to qualified professors from France, it offers a true higher education on the metropolitan level. In the present condition of our nation, it would be impossible to assume the financial burden of such an establishment. It is thus apparent that the majority of the agreements on the economic and national level have been of a constructive nature.

However, it is worth considering the negative side; not for the sake of criticizing or returning to things as they were, but in order to emphasize in all frankness and reality, the future evolution of the University of Mali. In this regard, the reserved attitude of the Mali authorities, who have wisely considered the future, must be stressed.

Negative

What is this university we have been offered? From its very creation it has been defined as a French university implanted in Africa. For many years it had to staunchly defend its position against the Colonial Administration, in order to preserve its traditions and its independence. This struggle is thus to its honor.

However, this spirit of resistance to the surrounding political environment now runs the risk of perpetuating an unfavorable attitude. The rector has seen his authority progressively lessened. His system has been to give way little by little, not abdicating his powers until the last possible moment and as seldom as possible, and to scrutinize all possible avenues in order to preserve certain areas of independence.

Step by step he has found himself confined in his university. How then, under these conditions, is one not to consider this establishment as a refuge—like a fortress where the remaining troops take a last stand against assault to save their honor—as a basis for operations in the cultural reconquest? It is one of the most difficult things for a man to abandon, of his own free will, that for which he has lived and struggled for many years. The better he has proved himself at his task, the more stubborn he is in the defense of his work. The historical reconversion of a work, and above all of a mentality, is always a serious problem.

There is no doubt that this sense of being the "last bastion of French culture" continues to characterize a part of the university. It is sufficient to recall its formal inauguration to understand the spirit in which it defines itself. While historical events rush along, and almost simultaneously with the famous trip of President de Gaulle, "the French university in the service of Africa" wants to remain pure and protected from any pollution. Guardian of an almost fiercely French culture, it is unwilling to accept even the slightest stretching of its programs or its traditions. On the platform, raised even a little higher than usual, one could admire the multicolored robes of the teaching body; below were the most elevated persons of Mali, permitted to receive the good news.

The speeches hailed this "mission" of France, this "French culture transplanted into Africa," dedicated to shine out and form the elite of Mali who will eventually take over the job. If Africa is admitted, it is with the status of a guest. No one on the dais has any lesson to learn. Africa has only to let herself be led; the cultural machine is at her service; everything will go all right if the Africans don't interfere.

In a more recent address, when the transfer agreements had already been signed, an elevated personage emphasized the "wisdom" of the governors who had left the "responsibility" of university education to France. Now, Mali had no choice. Most insistently it was made clear that nothing was to be changed; traditions were to remain intact—any modification being fatal to the unity of the system; any adaptation being a sign of weakness.

Does this mean that the university has taken a racist position? Certainly not. In reality, to offer Africa what one considers the acme of French culture and civilization is not to scorn her; it is more simply not taking her into account. The university considers itself a pioneer on a virgin land devoid of all culture.

Certainly the French want to occupy themselves with Africa, but as an object of study. And in such a way they can and will render real service to the country, particularly in the scientific and medical fields —but always with the aim of giving to French research a new element of honor which she alone is capable of pursuing efficiently.

In this order of thought, the creation of an Institute of Black Africa is a real gauge. Indeed, that there is in the University of Mali an institute dealing with African questions is symptomatic. It would, to be sure, seem more logical that each department deal with African problems. Is not the Department of Science qualified for botanical and zoölogical studies? Is not the Department of Arts and Letters fitted to study ethnology, sociology, history?

It seems, rather, that sequels to the old system are bearing down heavily on the present shape of the university. This will to "have faith" in culture shows itself in its secondary but symbolic aspects. Thus, the museums and libraries administered by the former IFAN, which are undeniably national property, have been absorbed by the Institute of Black Africa and the university. These bodies have gone so far as to have decrees issued by the Minister of the French Republic, creating or organizing the museums.

The council of the university must thus be "converted" in its entirety and made to understand that henceforth the university is a public national institution of Mali. If its administration is left to France, it is a result of the present difficult circumstances and not from political choice. Thus, *the dearest wish of the Government of Mali is the complete Africanization of the university and the elaboration of a modern African culture—and this is what Mali expects from the highly qualified specialists to whom it has confided the university.* It is essential to repeat this in all solemnity to avoid any misunderstanding, which becomes more dangerous day by day.

Indeed, ever since the university, territorially speaking, has been isolated, it is undeniable that a "de-Africanization" on the minor level has occurred. The salaries and degrees are all aligned with those of the metropolitan area—which in itself has some disadvantages, since the break with the civil service of Mali has provoked claims of homologous personnel.

One might assert that the present teaching staff, if it now pridefully defends the worth of its diplomas and degrees, has not always been so severe with itself. And, without quibbling about circumstances, it would be well to keep in mind the fact that the university has carried out its functions and even grown, because the norms that are now being emphasized as so necessary have not always been respected.

Among the other elements unfavorable to a "pro-Mali" university spirit, I might also mention that the Schools and Faculties are the only institutions of learning in Mali that have a solely French staff. On the secondary school level, the existence of African teachers has already created an important atmosphere of change.

The presence of numerous European students also does not render any easier the adopting of an "African" spirit. Similarly, the fiercely defended spirit of Pan-Africanism is not favorable for Mali. Mali students, who feel at home in their own country, are more easily irritated and demanding. Those of other states are often more docile, because they somehow feel themselves "aliens." There is a tendency to oppose ethnic groupings and to establish student hierarchies—and on the emotional level, the Maliens are often relegated to an "unloved" position.

When an African student is brilliant, he is taken in hand, brooded over, pushed, and protected from all "undesirable" influences. They invest him and make him a prisoner of the system. A sublime product of French culture, he is inculcated with the idea that since he is homologous with the French university system, he belongs to a superior cultural species outside of which there is no salvation. It is thus not surprising that as soon as they leave the university these young people aspire to superior positions and are unwilling to accept any advice; they often approach their African chiefs, and even cabinet ministers, telling them what to do and how to do it, completely forgetting that any culture not acquired through personal experience is pretentious, unrealistic, and dangerous.

A purely French educational system in the university can be more easily defended in the field of science or medicine, in the sense that the "basic material" is necessarily African—or universal. African sick are treated, or the biological environment is studied, or one learns a universal mathematics.

But when one thinks of the arts, history, law, psychology, or philosophy, it is evident that the absence of African cultural elements on a superior level is disadvantageous to the cultural formation of the students, who see their personal preoccupations cut off from their studies and the facts of their civilization veiled over as their education increases.

Is it possible to alleviate the disadvantages of the present system? That is the aim of the following suggestions.

Suggestions for a Tentative Africanization of the University

As a preamble I stress that there is no intention of devaluating the teaching or the degree. However, we must avoid a trap: using the pretext of preserving the integrity of these high qualifications to oppose any variation, any accommodation, any arrangement, especially since qualifications are often less severe in France. Don't forget that some people even refuse to mention certain provincial universities and ironically hold reservations about the value of certain metropolitan French faculties and schools. The University of Dakar wants to be a child of the Sorbonne. Is there not therein a danger? Would it not be injurious to align ourselves with institutes, schools, or faculties of the provinces, of other states, or other countries?

But, under the pretext of not lowering its standards, is the University of Mali forced to espouse certain recognized weaknesses of the French system? Could she not have some highly qualified French specialists study certain structural reforms along the lines of some valuable foreign experiments? In a word, is the University of Mali sworn to imitate without ever having its own personality? I believe that at least the principle of such reforms could be officially recognized.

Let us return to realistic and practical points. The problem here and now is to deliver the students from this "extraterritorial university" —to maintain for them a sane perspective of their civilization and their culture, and to help them to live in an African environment.

A first easy reform is the Africanization of the lower levels: the office workers, clerks, secretaries, and stenographers. Thus, students would have fraternal relationships within the university. Certain middle-level positions, among them secretaries of departments, could valuably be held by African administrative secretaries, as is done in the departments of education, administration, and supervision. European M.D.'s could doubtless be replaced by Africans. I believe it would be worthwhile to specify Mali employees for a Mali public institution.

Similarly, the ceremonies, celebrations, and other cultural manifestations could be Africanized by the presence of African-inspired insignia, coats of arms, decorations, costumes, and music.

The students must be carefully mixed in with the life of the nation: visits to youth camps, participation in ceremonies, invitations to the Assembly and Congress, talks with politicians, the use of an information center in the university. Cultural organisms must be multiplied with the aid of governments: artistic groups, discussion groups, and meetings with local artists and responsible Africans speaking the local tongue.

At the university level itself, a larger place could be devoted to Arab and Negro-African civilizations, to sociological and philosophical research, to local or Islamic law, carefully avoiding, however, the reefs of ethnology or ethnography in their more exotic aspects. As for history, literature, and poetry, research could make up for the lack of texts. The recording of historical legends, chants, and poems, and their translation and exegesis could be an excellent subject for study.

Professors should be obliged to devote a part of their work to African problems, and more particularly to increasing the knowledge of black-African civilizations and their plastic and vocal expressions.

Finally, it would be desirable for each professor to make it his duty to personally aid some of the thousands of students by accelerating every means of preparing assistants, *always selected from among the Africans,* in order to permit them to rise rapidly to professorial positions. I do not believe it is too much to ask of men of such elevated conscience that they themselves prepare those who will succeed them.

In conclusion, the problem of the University of Mali is a problem of substance. The Mali nation has the right and the duty to see that its elite is not deprived of its African soul in the name of an undeniably high intellectual formation. This "Africanization" of the university is perhaps more urgent than that of the secondary level. To be sure, high schools and junior colleges can be content with education purely about diverse techniques, if the very Africanized primary school leaves its imprint on their young years and if higher education does not put an interdiction on the soul, the people, and the Mali nation.

To do this, we must affirm these principles:

The University of Mali is a French-language African university.

The Government has confidence that the French administration will accelerate the preparation of African personnel, will consider reforms permissive of a reasonable adaptation of curricula and structure, and will broaden African elements in all levels of education by a constant search for the African cultural patrimony.

Concrete reforms must be made, illustrating the will of the university for an African spirit, and using the people and the resources of the country on every level.

Finally, the students must be integrated into the life of the nation, its people, its joys, its arts, its struggles, and its achievements.

This is the cost of having the Mali colors, on which the students' eyes should be constantly fixed, validly flying over the university.

COMMENTS

KWA OWUNA HAGAN

National Secretary, People's Educational Association, Ghana

In the discussion concerning American Negro contributions to African education the name Aggrey was mentioned. Aggrey came here to Livingston College and returned to his continent imbued with the idea that he was not just a Gold Coast man, but an African—"Aggrey of Africa." And when he went on the first Coast Commission and traveled through the various states of Africa, his continual message was: "I am Aggrey of Africa; I do not come from just the Gold Coast." "There is a new age to come," he said—"the youth of Africa are going to rise." Further: "Africa is a question mark; we will tell the other continents of the world, 'We have a new hope for you in all the problems that face you.'" So it seems to me that American Negro colleges here, right from the beginning, imbued our African students with the idea of nationalism, or Pan-Africanism. Aggrey came back and gave us heart; Dr. Nkrumah and Mr. Daniel Chapman, who was here as our ambassador, were among the men who were inspired by Aggrey. So I want to pay tribute to the American Negro colleges for the spirit of Pan-Africanism that they instilled in us.

Now I should make a few remarks about institutions of higher education in Africa. We have been told that before World War II the only higher institute of learning in Africa that enjoyed a status comparable to that of a university was Fourah Bay College, affiliated with Durham University and therefore able to confer Durham degrees. But in regard to this we should note the omission of two institutions in Sudan: Kitchener Memorial College and Gordon College, which later grew into the University College of Khartoum, and which in 1956 became the University of Khartoum. I happened to be in Khartoum in March and April of 1957 when this institution had just achieved university status. I make this comment because, according to Dr. Bigelow's paper, political pressure was brought to bear on higher institutions in Africa, especially the university colleges affiliated with London University, to become autonomous institutions. There was no such pressure brought upon the University of Khartoum. The authorities of the university told me themselves that Gordon College and Kitchener Memorial College had existed for so long a time that, by the time the country became independent, the institutions were ready for independence too. A compliment is due to the politicians of Sudan who did not assert any pressure upon the authorities of the university.

We have also been told about Makerere College, but I did not hear any mention of Achimota College in my own country of Ghana. Achimota College certainly was not an institute of higher learning in the strict sense. It developed as a sort of educational mixture—from kindergarten right up to the intermediate grades. Children who went there were able to go through the kindergarten, primary school, and then the secondary school. From that point they could take intermediate courses of London University. As a result, our few engineers and administrators, some of whom are now in the higher levels of government, got their opportunity for higher education at Achimota College. Therefore I certainly feel that Achimota ought to be mentioned when we discuss African institutions of higher learning that existed before World War II.

Our friend from the Mali Federation [Abdoulaye Fofana] has told us about the two institutions of learning in the French sphere of influence. There is also the one in the Belgian Congo, about which we have very scant information—Louviennes University in Leopoldville. In 1952 I had the good fortune to meet the secretary, that is, the registrar, of this university, which then was just a few months old. The university had about twenty undergraduates at that time, and they were all white Belgians; there were no Congolese Africans whatsoever. I wonder if there are any now. But independence is to be thrust on the Belgian Congo on the twenty-eighth of this very month, just a few days from now. Our good friend and nationalist leader there, Mr. Lumumba, is faced with the great problem of creating a new policy for higher education; suffering from the serious disadvantage of having no men to run his administration, he must take urgent action. In fact, I was told just this morning that a ninety-day course in public administration is now being given at the university in Leopoldville to produce by the quickest possible means (this is, indeed, mass production) administrators to take over the reins of government.

I do not want to go much into the question of university finances, but I feel one point should be made. In Europe and, I think, in the United States, universities often have their own sources of revenue. But our new universities on the continent of Africa are fully dependent on the governments for money with which to operate. Now we have the rulers saying, "*We* give you the money, and therefore *we* must have the whole hand in running this institution." It seems to me that sooner or later our politicians will have to learn the great lesson of simply giving the money to the university and letting the university men administrate as they wish. But we must remember that the institutions of higher learning in Africa have to satisfy needs peculiar to Africa. A good university must belong to the community, and the community to the university; each will derive much from the other. For that reason there should be all possible liaison between the politicians who give the money and the university men, so that they will try to understand each other and, from time to time, meet informally to discuss their common problems.

If we are to develop universities in Africa, we must have universities of our own brand; we must produce *African* universities. When our own university started in Ghana there was a Department of African Studies. But soon the question arose: What are you doing with a separate department for African studies? The university belongs to the country, and it should concern itself with the life of the country in *all* phases of study. You want a philosophy department that will emphasize African philosophy in its research. You want a sociology department that will study the new African societies. You want a history department that is not going to concern itself strictly with the histories of Europe and America, but more with the history of Africa, the history of the great empires of equatorial Africa. We now call ourselves the nation of Ghana; and there is the Mali Federation; and perhaps someday there will be federation along the lines of the great empires of the past. How do you relate this new nation to the old? This must be the realm of study of the department of history.

We want to set up *good* universities in Africa. There are so many universities in the world—some of them very good, others very bad, and the bad ones are indeed sometimes horrid. Those that we establish in Africa must be of the best kind. I remember an address of a former president of the university, in which he said: "The idea here is not to set up an Oxford University, or a Cambridge University, or a continental university, or an American university on the soil of Ghana. The idea is to set up a university that comes in direct succession to that university Plato founded to be the instrument of civilization and citizenship." It seems to me that this is exactly what we want in Africa. Here are newborn nations. Our task, in our universities, is to train young men to take their places effectively as civilized people wherever they move around the world and as citizens in their own nation. This is the challenge to the new universities of Africa.

There is one further aspect of university education that we have not yet discussed here. This is the field of adult education, which is my special area. After all, in any society—whether an undeveloped one such as ours, or a highly developed one such as Europe's—there are very few people indeed who attend university. I am told that in West Germany, for instance, the estimate is one out of every five hundred persons. In Africa, where the whole idea of a university is so new, perhaps one out of five thousand attend a university. What, then, do you do with the great mass of people who have not had the opportunity to do so? Through the processes of learning, through the processes of discussion, they must be brought to face the issues of their nation, and to become effective citizens. I feel, therefore, that the various universities that are developing in Africa must have departments of extramural studies, or departments of adult education. These would go out of the walls of the universities and into the community; they would establish the opportunity for all young men and women to come together in evening classes, and to take courses in philosophy and economics and politics and international affairs, so that they may be able, as new citizens of new nations, to understand the issues of the day.

VINCENT C. IKEOTUONYE

M.P., Federal Parliament, Nigeria;
Headmaster, Zixton Grammar School, Onitsha, Nigeria

I want to present just a rough picture of the educational set-up in Nigeria. It is a historic experiment, a federal experiment involving the governments, the local councils, the missionaries, communities, and individual proprietors. Each of these can and do own and operate primary schools and colleges with general direction, inspection, and financial help from the governments. I own and operate two such schools.

Imagine a child of five in shirt and shorts, hair cropped close, bare feet digging into the muddy earth during the rains or skipping on the burning sand during the hot season. It takes him four years to go through the Junior Primary, and another four years through the Senior Primary.

Better clad, comfortably shod, and wearing colorful cap and blazer, the budding gentleman or lady walks into a secondary school, that is, grammar school or your high school. Here he grapples with mathematics, science, literature, and history for five to seven years, and emerges as the sheet-anchor of democracy and civilization. But his fellow graduates are few—less than 4 per cent of the secondary school age group.

From this minority, only six hundred in a population of forty million enter the universities. There is presently only one university in Nigeria, when Nigeria could do with at least fifteen universities and many more university colleges.

By these figures, statements, and descriptions, I imply mordant and basic criticism of the British education policy, which is colonial, and a mild and sympathetic disagreement with Dr. Karl W. Bigelow's paper.

The governments of the Federation of Nigeria have all introduced free and universal primary education and are now pushing secondary school education into new frontiers and horizons undreamed of by the British. Rather, the British dreamed and knew of them; they just refused to introduce them—education is the bloodstream of freedom.

One of the governments of the Federation is now building a university, the University of Nigeria at Naukka; it does so at the cost of great hardship. It is spending more than a quarter of its annual budget on this project. But this university is not being patterned on the classical traditions of the European universities. It is dedicated to the service of man and his societies, in the belief that the activities of man in his quest for life, liberty, and the pursuit of goodness should be the subject of university inquiry—the principle animating the institution of the American land-grant system.

At this point there are certain things I would like to point out about the influence of American education and of American Negroes on the rise of Nigerian nationalism. The British are very much baffled by the drive, the initiative, of some of us who have been educated in America. They sometimes want to know the origin of the drive. I must admit that a good part of it is the result of native characteristics. But we have also gained much from our experiences in America. I say these things for the edification of those persons who helped us to achieve this drive.

American education is unquestionably liberal and egalitarian. And when we Africans arrive here, coming from an area where higher education is an aristocratic attribute, we receive the shock of our lives. As an example: When some other students and I arrived at Lincoln University in 1946, our suitcases were brought out and we stood around with our hands in our pockets waiting for someone to carry them. Then a short fellow, elderly, came over to us and picked up the suitcases; we followed him to our rooms and he helped us to get settled; all the while we addressed him as we would any other porter. Eventually he said, "Gentlemen, let's go over to my place for something to eat." We were bewildered, feeling that perhaps this porter was being too impertinent. However, we were very hungry, so we went with him. To our permanent humiliation, we soon discovered that the gentleman was the dean of the faculty of education. This and many other similar experiences taught us a permanent lesson: The purpose of education is to make us useful to our society and to ourselves. This is one of the major lessons we acquired with our education in America.

There is something magical in the statement that life, liberty, and the pursuit of happiness should be self-evident truths, and that for these things governments are instituted. As soon as we come here, we begin to learn this liberal philosophy. Rather, we don't actually learn it; we absorb it—by going to Philadelphia, to Washington, by seeing what really lies behind that old song we learned when we were children, "John Brown's body lies a-moulderin' in the grave." And after we absorb these things, we go back to Africa determined that it shall be our duty to see that we are free. The quest for freedom has a way in which it redeems a person, in which it relieves a person of his own past. This is another lesson that we take from our American education.

We have also learned much from the lives of the Negroes in America. We have learned to be determined in the pursuit of an end without being embittered, and without being inclined toward the use of dynamite. Observe that in our political struggle in West Africa we have evolved a nonviolent method. My belief is that we have not, as many people claim, taken our nonviolent and constitutional methods from Ghana; no, we have learned these from the example of the American Negro in American society.

There are two other points I would like to mention; it would grieve my soul not to do so. Every society, every stage in the social development of societies, has its own apparatus of cultural and educational diffusion. To apply the university standards and requirements of highly and technically specialized and economically differentiated societies like Britain and the United States to the schools of an emergent and pioneer society like Nigeria, would be to confound the purpose of education and to arrest the flight of creative thought. The specialization and scholasticism of your country are not the pressing needs of mine. The nuclear physicists are vital to the progress of your societies. We would not know what to do with them in Nigeria, because our social problems are different. We want pioneers, not specialists.

My final point is one raised by Professor Bigelow in his paper. It is the issue of university autonomy and the nature of academic freedom. I want to tell you, good friends, that we do not like the control of our universities by British universities under the so-called special relationship. It is the projection of imperialism into the intellectual life of Nigeria. As soon as Nigeria is free, our universities will be strong, good, and efficient enough to be free and independent. This point needs no elaboration. The University of Nigeria, itself the intellectual and academic manifestation of free Nigeria, will prove this point.

It is good and democratic that universities should grow and act with freedom and that governments and parties in power should not dictate policy to universities. But no government should allow itself to be hampered, endangered, or driven into unpopularity by the active or partisan propaganda of the university professors. University men can hold political opinions; it is their right as citizens, and this is confirmed by their superior knowledge. Whether or not they can propagate those opinions with freedom and impunity depends on the extremeness of the opinions, the stresses of the society, and the security of the state. Only the duly elected government of the people can be the judge in these respects.

But no citizen should take political action and then shrink from the consequences of his action or the reactions of those against whom he has acted in the name of academic freedom. In politics we fight battles; we sustain injuries, there are casualties, and we gain or lose our good names and sometimes our jobs. The battle is free for all. But democratic politics has a rigid rule: Don't shoot or blow from an ivory tower; come down and out and tumble freely with all.

WENDELL P. JONES

Department of Education, University of California, Los Angeles

I am not so kindly disposed as some people might be toward a few of the ideas expressed concerning the imposition of one's educational program on the African nations. Some person distinguished in history has written that to the degree a profession controls admission to the profession, in the same degree that profession tends to become a conspiracy against society. Sometimes, when I think of the American Medical Association, which has permitted the number of doctors per ten thousand of our population to be reduced year by year, and when I consider the control that this association has over who gets admitted to the profession, I am inclined to believe this statement might be true.

Likewise, when I look at the status of the expansion of higher education's facilities and of staffing so far as Africans in certain African universities and colleges are concerned, I think that one might be a little cautious about inviting too much relationship between these institutions and external universities, such as the University of London, the University of Michigan, and Columbia University. It was amazing to me as I traveled in Africa to note that in the institutes of education, for example, I found not a single African who held a post of senior lecturer; and in many of these institutes I found no African on the staff whatsoever. I pondered this; I asked questions about it. And I inevitably got the answer: "They are not qualified."

I actually shuddered when I read of the award, the grant, that Carnegie has so generously made for the improvement of African education. Of course, I'm glad to learn that the *New York Times* can be wrong; because it said that the program would enable senior lecturers in these institutes to move about, that is, there could be exchanges, and they could engage in further study. But it said nothing about junior members of staff; it said nothing about training Africans to assume positions as staff members. (But you [Dr. Bigelow] tell me that there will be, after a year or so, some junior members; and I hope it will be Africans who get this training.) At the time I read this article, I said, "But there are no Africans in these posts, so they won't get this opportunity." Yet I did have to smile, for I am not quite so critical of the little things that happen from day to day in the African setting as some of the people are, nor as worried about them. As I read the last part of Dr. Bigelow's paper, in which he set some pretty fine standards for African institutions to meet and maintain, I thought of the American institutions and wondered just which ones really met those standards.

While we are dealing with factual information, I think we might add to this list of African institutions of higher learning some other post-secondary schools, such as the Nigerian colleges of arts, sciences, and technology; the University of Liberia in Monrovia; and the University College of Addis Ababa in Ethiopia. Each of these is making significant contributions to the advancement of education in Africa. I think, too, we should mention the coming development in East Africa—the promise of new institutions in Kenya of university college grade, and in Tanganyika, and with them the development of original plans that will lead away from this matter of external ties which sometimes hinder progress.

There are many, many things that could be discussed here—technical education, trade education, vocational education, more about teachers' training, and so forth—but you highly educated people seem to be more concerned with "higher learning," so we'll stick with that.

The question is often raised about the contribution of the United States. I have a funny notion here, too. I think that the greatest contribution that we can make is not, really, the adding of somebody to a university over there to teach, but in having somebody learn what he needs to know if he is going to teach. I would like to see about two-thirds of the money that we expend used to bring Africans here to be given the education essential if they are going to assume worthwhile roles in their own educational institutions.

On my African travels I constantly heard complaints about the cost of expatriate teachers: "We've got to bring them in and keep bringing them in, and they cost three times as much as the African who teaches here." Now let's cut out that type of talk; let's train the *African* to take the role. When the American foundations and the American government choose to embark on educational programs, let an important part of that program be the training of the *African* to do the work, rather than the use of some expatriate to do a survey. Then, the Africans in the future will be able to do the necessary surveys themselves and to put the things they discover into practice.

I really feel there is need, so far as the whole theme of African education is concerned, for creativity, for daring new projects, for new looks at things. Try something! If it works, keep it. If not, cast it aside and try something else! Actually, many of the Africans with whom I have talked are, deep down, a little afraid to try what the English, in the English-related territories, have not succeeded with; they are a little afraid to venture out in this field. They will venture out in the matter of politics, government, and so forth; perhaps the other things will come later. But ask yourselves—since you [African delegates] say you cannot take in many students, since you have just limited enrollment in your higher institutions—ask yourselves: "Why don't we try to have *two* students sleeping in one room?"—"Why don't we double the number of students a teacher has?"—"Is it really necessary to have 175 teachers for 575 students?" *Is* it? If not, try something else.

Be creative! Experiment! If, as you say, everything is too expensive, is it *necessary* to pay someone to sweep the floor of a student's room? Really? Can you not cut down at that point by letting the student do it? Ask yourselves, then try it. You might be surprised at some of the results. I was talking just a few moments ago with a distinguished American whose son is still in college; and one of the things that this man is determined about is that the son will do some *work* while he is in school.

I'm a firm believer in comparative education. But at this point there is no country or territory in Africa that does not have many Africans who have studied in America, in England, in India, and elsewhere, and who are therefore, in a sense, comparative educationists. If these people could get together and forge some new, daring plans for new projects and get the coöperation of their people, then some tremendous results might develop in this matter of African education. I urge upon you *creativity* and *experimentation*—the development of something totally *new*. If you think well of America, remember that she did it, too. We are not English. I could tell you about a lot of little relevant incidents, such as the fellow who failed to get his honors at secondary school graduation because he could not speak English the way the English professor spoke it, although he did make honors in seven other courses. Well, we have American teachers of English who would never meet the approval of . . . [*laughter and applause*].

DISCUSSION

(EDITOR'S NOTE: Following the presentation of the preceding papers and commentaries, Messrs. Fofana, Bigelow, Hagan, and Jones joined others in a panel discussion on education in Africa. William O. Brown, professor of sociology and director of the African Research and Studies Program of Boston University, was chairman of the panel, which also included Horace Mann Bond, president of AMSAC and dean of the School of Education, Atlanta University; and Stewart C. Easton, of City College of New York. A summary of the discussion follows.)

After opening remarks by Dr. Bond on the ignorance of American students concerning Africa, especially their tendency to view Africa without geographic and other distinctions, Dr. Brown turned the panel's attention to an issue common to the earlier presentations of Messrs. Hagan, Fofana, and Jones; the problem of adjusting educational institutions, objectives, curricula, and so forth, to Africa's new societies.

Dr. Bigelow stated the problem in terms of polarities. "For instance," he said—"higher education's relationship to the *immediate* needs of the community, on one hand, and its relationship to the *infinite* needs of humanity, on the other. Such a polarity is extremely difficult to deal with; certainly it does not allow an either/or resolution." Another polarity, Bigelow noted, involves the function of the professor. "There is always the professor who can say but not act. Of course, politicians understand the need to conform; nevertheless, in the long run the welfare of the society is advanced by the institution authorized to have 'wrong' thoughts." Bigelow cited Mr. Fofana's earlier contentions as an eloquent statement of the opposite view in this polarity.

How will these polarities work out in Africa? How *should* they be worked out? In answer to Bigelow's questions, Dr. Easton stated that although one cannot be certain how such problems will or should be resolved, "it is at least evident that large investments in higher education for a very small segment of a society is not in the interest of the country." He noted that a great many more students are needed than those currently being educated in Africa, particularly in the English-speaking areas. He called attention to the Belgian experience in Elisabethville, and quoted the university rector there to the effect that the Belgians did not have a university but a "social experiment"—a necessary one in developing social cohesion.

"Perhaps the Belgian experiment in dealing with the pre-university years is also valuable," Easton said. "They were aware that they could not provide students for the university in large numbers; so they took the best students for the pre-university years. Perhaps this kind of operation is an answer to bridging the gap between secondary and higher education. The high schools are presently not doing a full job of preparing students for university work. In Rhodesia, for example, no students were available for the university, and it was necessary to bring in students from the Union. The University of Rangoon, after independence, changed from the strict English system and increased the number of students from six hundred to ten thousand; during the transition period they used the course method."

Bond added that the English system is inappropriate to any new, dynamic frontier country. "In such a country they need a great number of trained men quickly. The English system trains an elite. One of the problems of the Prime Minister of Ghana is that students think they are an elite; and the Director of Education of Ghana said that that is just what they are training—an elite. A study should be made of the Scottish system, which concentrates on training everyone—especially the poor. The effect of this system has been considerable."

Mr. Hagan then observed that there has been some divergence of views in Ghana concerning the ideal educational system. Some officials, he stated, desire educational standards on a par with Oxford and Cambridge, complete with rigid tests in English language, literature, etcetera. Others would prefer "something on a different level." Hagan also said that the American system has been considered, "but Ghana wants international standing for its university."

In Bigelow's view, Hagan had stated the heart of the problem: Do you take people of the highest potential only, or do you take people of particular stages of development and give them training? "America," said Bigelow, "is fortunate in having all types of approaches through decentralization and many private colleges and universities."

Hagan's frank response: "In Ghana, some American educational standards are considered low. We wish to avoid any low standards in order that our university might achieve international standing. You see our dilemma, in West Africa, of trying to maintain very high standards and at the same time trying to produce large numbers of trained personnel for our ambitious development programs."

Bigelow suggested that a solution might be found in the example set by the new university in Eastern Nigeria: "University of London, not Oxford, and Michigan State University, not Harvard, are coöperating in its establishment." But Hagan commented that the new university would also create problems. "There will be debate over whether it or Ibadan is better suited to meet the needs of a new society."

Yet, "the debate should be over the *purpose* of a university, after all," said Easton. "Perhaps this debate cannot be afforded from the human point of view. Americans believe it is not degrading for graduates to go into business, even if the particular person happens to be a member of the social elite. Apparently, the problem involves both what you want and what you can get away with."

Fofana, bringing Mali's problems into the discussion, was more kindly disposed toward the American system than was Hagan. "American universities may not be of the first order, but technologically they certainly appear to have been successful. An old country such as France can afford to produce a highly cultivated individual and to concentrate on maximum research and formal theses. Countries of this kind can produce elites in natural economic and social upper classes."

Fofana did not regard his country as obliged to continue the French system. "Our preoccupations are modest for the moment. Our problem is that we have a certain number of people at the top and at the bottom of the educational structure, and a great vacuum in between. This makes for a special educational problem: we have grammar schools and the university, but nothing intermediate. We have no technical schools for engineers, teachers, etc. Under the present system, second-

ary school teachers must pass from five to six years of graduate requirements. We cannot wait that long. By one means or another we
must accelerate the production of instructors for the secondary
schools. We want the University of Mali to be able to include disciplines not found in French universities—applied arts, technology,
etc."

To Hagan's question as to whether or not Mali planned to develop
both a French university and a college in the same sector, Fofana contended that the best solution would be to have one institution. He
noted, however, that since funds and instructors for the university
came primarily from France, an institution separate from the university might be necessary. "French professors at the University of Mali
are dominated by the notion of making students over into their own
image." Fofana wished that French professors would "step outside
themselves and consider what, if they were African students, their
needs would be. They must modify their teaching by assuming the
role of the other."

Here Easton made a suggestion, which Fofana received appre-
ciatively: "Perhaps this problem could be solved by hiring French
Canadians from the University of Montreal who teach in French.
French Canadians speak bad French but are taught it well."

Bigelow remarked that "the French and the French Canadians are
as different as the English and the Americans"; and Hagan added his
measure of humor to the exchange by demanding of Fofana: "Can
Mali do this? Are you not satisfied to be within the French Community? Do you want to lose French *culture?*"

Chairman Brown felt that the discussion had gained enough focus
to allow formulation of certain generalities regarding the problems of
adjustment of educational institutions. "What kind of educational systems, techniques, etc., are necessary to meet the needs of the newly
developing societies? What are the requirements of the societies?"

Bigelow answered the questions with another: "What is *practical?*
—and this means more than financial practicality. What is possible,
given the many vested interests—the French, British, French-trained,
British-trained, and so forth? Where do you want to go? How do you
get there?"

Easton observed that "the Indian could forgive England for everything except the fact that he was trained to think of himself as in-

ferior," but Hagan felt this was an independent problem. "The major
need," said Hagan, "is for trained men at the earliest possible moment.
Should we use the British or the American system, or a combination
of both in an entirely new situation?"

Bond, however, advised an approach more suited to the special
problems of Africa. "It is quite important for countries such as Ghana,
Mali, etc., to produce their own systems of national education and not
to duplicate the French, English, and American systems in relatively
poor and small nations. Do not let politics entirely control the situation. Educate from the standpoint of pan-Africanism. Create *international* institutions, within the existing language framework, to serve
special sciences in order to have high standards. Use one university
for those fields, another for technical educations. With this method the
governments would be able to use funds for secondary education."

It was on Bond's suggestion that much of the subsequent discussion
turned. Bigelow supported it with the remark that the type of education offered at the new university in Eastern Nigeria will be respected
in twenty years, "when its graduates are making more money than the
others." Easton also predicted this university would be "a pilot institution." But, Brown cautioned: "There is a fallacy in replacing one
educational model with another model. The problem is one of institutional transfer—that is, of getting concepts of what you want from
wherever you can get them. Inventiveness is called for. The approach
should be pragmatic, not idealistic."

Bond then illustrated his point with examples from the United
States. "Some states are too poor to maintain many true universities.
They have developed regional contract systems. For example, Alabama
Polytechnic offers veterinary training for its entire region; the University of Virginia and Meharry Medical College offer medicine. In Africa
there must be available schools of medicine and veterinary medicine;
one big school could do the job. Regional coöperation could be of
great help."

Here Hagan intervened with the theme that, in varied form, had
been debated throughout the conference: "Coöperation in education,"
he argued, "will happen only after federation."

Bigelow, Brown, and Bond were quick to draw the opposition lines
clearly. "Educational coöperation should precede political," Bigelow
stated flatly.

Hagan called this "unlikely" in view of historical precedent, and noted that while Ibadan was to have served all of West Africa, Ghana nevertheless established its own university.

"All states can have their own universities," Bigelow rejoined, "but they do not have to have their own professional schools."

When Hagan urged that the experiences of the United States seemed to support his claim, Brown suggested that it would be possible for expensive facilities to share faculties. Bond introduced the example of Kumasi: "Consider the huge investment in just the heat laboratory. Very expensive, and only a handful of students are using it. Sierra Leone would welcome an opportunity to have its students share it and pay part of the cost of investment. Why should Forah Bay duplicate the lab? Gambia might jump at the chance of using the same facility."

Hagan professed to remain unconvinced, and Easton diverted, suggesting a bilingual university for Africa modeled on the universities in Ottawa and Puerto Rico. "One pilot university that was bilingual might overcome the cultural imperialism." Again, Fofana received the suggestion appreciatively.

Bigelow began the summary: "We have identified a series of dilemmas. We have tried to favor a median point, not extremes. Extreme positions would not help us in coming to an agreement; they would only precipitate violent disagreements. At any rate, the decisions rest with the African countries. Our discussion, perhaps, will be useful to those who must act."

"The decision-making has passed to the African countries," Brown added, "but we must not forget the influences from metropolitan areas and even ourselves."

Bond referred again to the problem of an elite: "How to prevent education for just an elite—this is the most difficult educational problem of any culture or economic system. In Soviet Russia this is a great problem. An analysis was made of the Heroes of Science, who numbered thirty-two, after Sputnik. They were found to be the children of professors; this was a heritage of the German system, which was Russia's model. The dictum of compulsory nonacademic work after secondary schooling is not a corrective. One simply cannot abolish the inheritance of literacy and status."

Bond found that the American system has at least one great advantage: "The tradition that it is decent for university students to work. In Africa some provision must be made in the educational system for work and for association with the masses by the elite. Something like sweeping one's room would, of course, be too artificial. But let the genius of students be constructive. Quaker work camps are good examples."

Easton took up the same theme, speculating that "such an idea could be part of the ethos of a university—you could introduce the idea in philosophy courses that the purpose of education is service."

"This is the purpose of Negro universities," Bond added. "They even built their own buildings."

Bigelow recalled that when the Minister of Education from Sudan visited the United States in 1959 he was quite impressed with Berea College students, whom he saw working with their hands.

"Teachers who really understand this problem," said Easton, "could express the idea through both their teaching and their lives. Students should have the notion that the community and the state provide their education through great sacrifice. This idea would appeal to the younger people."

Bond concluded by expressing the hope that African countries will broaden their education base and utilize their fullest intellectual potential.

VI SOCIAL THOUGHT

THE CONFERENCE PANEL on African Social Thought opened with two illuminating papers dealing with the philosophical basis of African social organization. William Fontaine, professor of philosophy at the University of Pennsylvania, traces the lines of African thought, both traditional and modern, and considers their implications for the current renewal of Africa's independent development. AMSAC's George Carter, a product of Harvard's graduate school in philosophy, presents in a seminal paper a consideration of the religious beliefs of the Fon of Dahomey and the Dogon of western Sudan. He develops the philosophical basis in African religious beliefs for the solidarity in African social organization, using the graphic example of the billiard balls striking each other on the table to illustrate the discrete individualistic situation of man in Western liberal thought.

The paper that aroused probably the greatest interest of the panel was that of Joseph Ki-Zerbo, Secretary General of the African Movement for National Liberation, Voltaic Republic. His unified, coherent statement is incisive in its perceptions, and the substantial body of material is pertinent to the area of African social thought and organization. We shall not digest his remarks here, but it is worthwhile to refer to some of his observations. We gain, perhaps, a new insight into the motivation of those men in the forefront of the struggle for independence (Sékou Touré, grandson of a fierce old nemesis of the French; Kenyatta, son of the sorcerer; Nkrumah of the Blood Oath) in Ki-Zerbo's emphasis upon the role that ancestors still play in the lives of even those who have abandoned the metaphysic. (In the matter of cultural survival, it is interesting to contemplate the origin of the prayer heard in some American Negro churches beginning, and continuing indefinitely, "My *Father*, My *Father's* Father, My Father's *Father's* Father . . . ," etc.).

Ki-Zerbo does not shrink from the more unfortunate aspects of African life: for example, the intense solidarity of the African social order included, sometimes with tragic consequences, even the sick; there was no isolation.

In Ki-Zerbo's remarks regarding the French policy of cultural assimilation, we see perhaps one reason for the greater emphasis on a return to African origins among Africans of French rather than English influence. It was, as we have observed, a French-African, Blaise Diagne, who said, "I am a Frenchman first." Ki-Zerbo feels this "cultural oppression" was not necessarily calculated, differing thereby from Aimé Césaire, who finds it to be the planned cornerstone of the entire colonial structure.

Ki-Zerbo devotes considerable time to an examination of the elements to emerge in the new Africa, the shape of which, he emphasizes, is the option of the African people. He feels, however, that the new Africa should be built upon the foundations of traditional Africa, shorn of its less useful aspects. He points to the historic chance that permits an economic transformation to begin without an a priori economic class structure. He laments the fact, however, that there is an increasing political class differentiation; for example, a bureaucratic elite receives a disproportionate share of the national budget in some of the small emergent African states. His criticism of Senghor's theory of African socialism is perhaps not completely warranted. There is evidently general agreement that African culture, with its emphasis on communal living, contains certain basic conditions of a socialist order. The value of what could become an acrimonious debate to establish whether this developing socialism should or should not be characterized as Marxist appears doubtful. Ki-Zerbo does point out that if African tradition is not Marxist, it is even less capitalistic, having no emphasis on profit and individualism.

His solution to the dilemma of tribalism is to overcome or break it politically, but to encourage its survival otherwise as a source of cultural and artistic riches. It is necessary, he feels, to rehabilitate the African history and the African cultural heritage. There are those who challenge this as a treacherous base on which Africa is to build. Ki-Zerbo remarks, however, "One cannot live with the memory of others." Here he is strikingly close to Du Bois (as quoted by Fontaine), who warned against looking at one's self "through the eyes of another." It would seem that the sober conclusion here is not that the right to build a future is preconditioned upon the discovery and exploration of lost African civilization, but that whatever that heritage proves to be— and, as Nehru writes in regard to India, this is not likely to be learned from the West—it should be known and properly assessed.

Finally, after first warning of the catastrophe that may threaten Africa again if she does not become technically and economically strong, Ki-Zerbo states that nonetheless the important contribution that Africa can make is in the realm of relationships between people. Suggesting that ultimately the role of technology and industrial development is only instrumental, Ki-Zerbo's remarks recall the description in *Présence Africaine* of the visit of the European engineer in Africa, who said that despite all of his infinitely superior technical knowledge, the camaraderie and *joie de vivre* of the Africans made him feel like a "white-smith," who, having finished a job, should then pick up his tools and go home. Ki-Zerbo's ideas here, though cast differently, are strongly similar to those developed by Senghor, as discussed in the panel on negritude. In contrast to the Western proclivity toward domination, the African tradition is characterized by a "personalism," by a social order of solidarity, which, as Dr. Jean Price-Mars states in his introductory remarks to the conference, is the real message of the African—one of "love and a sense of brotherhood."

S. W. A.

PHILOSOPHICAL ASPECTS OF CONTEMPORARY AFRICAN SOCIAL THOUGHT

WILLIAM T. FONTAINE

Department of Philosophy, University of Pennsylvania;
Secretary, American Society of African Culture

INTRODUCTION

It is an accepted fact that the many varieties of Pan-Africanism and African nationalism agree in their attitude of strong disapproval of colonization. This anticolonialism includes, among others, two major objectives: (1) a return of Africans to indigenous forms of cultural expression; (2) a return of the control of Africa to Africans. These objectives bring to mind the persistent questions raised by both critics and sympathizers of African nationalism: Is the return to indigenous forms of cultural expression a return to a primitive way of life? Does it mean a return to tribal customs and conflicts? What is the relation of African nationalism to Communism? Are the methods of African nationalist leaders undemocratic? Is African nationalism a new brand of racism?

THE RETURN TO INDIGENOUS AFRICAN CULTURE

"Primitivism" is one of those persistent words whose meaning changes radically every century. One century considers primitive man a "noble savage"; the next considers him a lesser breed outside the law—a kind of subhuman or "prelogical" mentality who thinks in a way qualitatively different from that of his more highly developed successor and civilized relative. For more than a generation now, scholars have agreed that there is no qualitative difference between the thought of primitive man and that of his civilized successor. Primitive peoples do not think on a prelogical level and civilized peoples on a logical, qualitatively different level. Both gather facts, employ the principle of causation, and make use of various kinds of logical inference. The major difference is that primitive man does not seek general laws as a self-conscious project. And yet primitive peoples have fashioned more or less incisive cosmologies containing closely articulated schemes of social and political organization. Consider briefly, for example, Dr. K. A. Busia's analysis of the cosmology of the Ashanti of the Gold Coast.[1]

The Ashanti world is a world of spirits. There is the Supreme Spirit, God or the Wise One, who created the universe; a lesser pantheon of deities, who are His intermediaries; a group below these who animate rivers, trees, and charms; dead ancestors of the chiefs who watch over the tribes as a whole; and ancestors of particular individuals who are worshiped by them. Two principles—the mother principle and the father principle—link the individual, his society, and the political order to the world of spirits. The link between one generation and another is the blood of the mother. All of either sex who can trace their genealogy through the female line to a common ancestress are said to belong to a lineage. The lineage constitutes a residence unit, since, as kin, they live near one another. It is also a political unit, since the head of the lineage represents it on the chiefs' council and is elected by the male and female adult members. The mother principle thus determines citizenship status. Inheritance of property is likewise determined by this principle. From it also arises the communal organization of labor.

The father-child bond is the second link of the spirit world to the human. The father transmits to the son his *Ntoro* or *sunsum;* that is, his personality or traits of character that distinguish him as a human being. This spiritual principle derives its power from a river god, who is the intermediary of the Supreme Being. The sunsum is not immortal; at death it perishes. On the other hand, the *kra,* a second spiritual principle, which comes directly from the Supreme Being and is part of the divine life-force, is immortal and returns at death to its source. The kra that a man receives when about to be born contains his destiny. This does not mean that a man's life is fixed, that there are no alternatives of action, or that he cannot express himself as an individual apart from an all-enveloping destiny. Further explanation of the relation of Ntoro to sunsum makes this clear. Ntoro and sunsum differ only in that the latter is a specific instance of the more general personality type. This close spiritual relation between father and child has great moral significance. It is believed that a child cannot prosper if his

[1] Daryll Forde, ed., *African Worlds.* Oxford, 1954.

sunsum is alienated from the father. He must respect his father and obey his precepts. On the other hand, if the child commits a wrong such as adultery, the father may be held responsible. The social significance of the father-child bond, centered as it is in the spiritual principle of the Ntoro, extends even beyond the family. There are Ntoro groups or spirit-cleansing groups consisting of all those who presumably possess similar personality types. The names of these groups, and, therefore, of the personality types, are most significant, for they point up the fact that the Ashanti places a high value upon individuality. Thus the close watch of the ancestral spirits and the fact that at birth a man receives his kra and with it his destiny does not mean that his sense of individuality is crushed by supernatural sanctions of conformity. Of the twelve Ntoro groups listed in Busia's work, the names of eight indicate personality types of a very strong and spirited nature: the distinguished, the tough, the audacious, the eccentric, the fanatic, the truculent, the virtuoso, the fastidious. The remaining four are more disciplined, suggesting self-control: the human, the chaste, the liberal, and the chivalrous.

The high value that the primitive African places upon human life is reflected in certain attitudes toward the various deities. The higher gods are remote from human life. Lesser deities, such as those animating charms, are condemned if they fail to aid the individual and the group. Prayers ask both for rewarding of the good in this life and for punishment of evil. Busia denies the allegation that Ashanti religion is lacking in ethical content. The worship of ancestors points up the normative significance of those virtues that make both for individual distinction and for a responsibility for the well-being of the group.

This brief analysis of Ashanti cosmology discloses three principles of great significance for the thought of contemporary Africans: (1) humanism—a concern for this life and for the spirit world, mainly as it has a bearing upon this earthly life; (2) collectivism—a concern for the family, extended family, and tribe: an idea involving a concern for each individual as a member of the tribe, for example, sharing of labor in common, or adoption of common mannerisms by all of a particular Ntoro group; (3) individuality—an outflowing, exuberant, Dionysian sense of personality, as distinguished from selfless, passive conformity.

The name Aimé Césaire is known to only a few in the intellectual circles of the United States. And yet, Sartre has spoken of Césaire's poems as entities that burst and turn upon themselves like a fuse, or as "bursting suns which turn and explode in new suns, in a perpetual surpassing." Césaire is also a social philosopher, as foxy and incisive in argument as he is brilliant in his poetry. In the concluding sections of a paper, "Culture et colonisation," delivered before the Congrès International des Écrivains et Artistes Noirs in 1956, Césaire discusses the problem of returning to primitive African forms of expression. In his prior analysis of colonization he borrows heavily from the functionalism of Malinowski. But the more intimate friends of Césaire are Hegel, the dialectical idealist, Marx and Engels, the dialectical materialists, and Nietzsche, the voluntarist. Césaire recognizes the charge that the indigenous African civilization is puerile, inadequate, and *dépassée par l'histoire*. But he contends that the alternatives do not lie narrowly between the indigenous civilization and the Europeans. The return points beyond itself to a synthesis that will be something new. It will be a new emergent level. The attempt, however, of the colonizers to impose their alien forms upon the indigenous African resulted in a mechanical and spurious juxtaposition of parts—a false synthesis. The real synthesis requires as one of its conditions the freedom of those who are to be its bearers. Such was the synthesis effected by the Japanese people. They were a free people, and from their own native base they conjoined in their own way forms adopted from the alien West. Nor is such a synthesis as extraordinary as it sounds. Within every culture each generation must make a synthesis of the new and the old. The synthesis to be effected by black men will contain African and European elements. When asked what those elements would be, Césaire answered that there is no a priori determination of them: "Notre rôle n'est pas de bâtir a priori le plan de la future culture noire." The role of the black men of his time is to announce the coming and to prepare the way for those who will actually make the response.

DEMOCRACY AND THE ONE-PARTY STATE, AFRICAN SOCIALISM

Césaire spoke in 1956. Since that time Ghana and Guinea have become independent. The Mali Federation has been formed. Nigeria is about to obtain independence. Inspired by this march of freedom, African youth, meeting at Addis Ababa in 1960, began to evaluate and give substance to the future ideals that Césaire projected in a general way. Their recommendations concerning the compatibility of democratic principles with one-party states tended to justify the policies of nationalist theoreticians as well as those of rulers of independent nations.

> The number of political parties should, as much as possible, be determined by the need for an effective government within the context of a functioning democracy and the implementation of the United Nations Declaration of Human Rights, as well as the need to avoid the weakness of government by the presence of too many parties which can conflict at the expense of the nation.

This recommendation is broad enough and realistic enough to comprehend such policies as those of Prime Minister Nkrumah, which encourage opposition within the party and not outside of it. Similarly, it accords with the views of Julius K. Nyerere of Tanganyika, who contends that in the early stages of the existence of the state, parties and viewpoints of such a factional nature that they endanger the very existence of the state are inadmissible. Nyerere's analysis of this problem[2] is the most complete and incisive analysis I have seen. It consists of three major arguments: (1) A nationalist movement fights for and wins independence; it forms the first government and one could not expect it to conform to a particular expression of democracy which happens to be seen in terms of a government and opposition party, or expect it to do this in mid-stream when the struggle calls for unity of all the people. (2) the presence of an organized opposition as a visible symbol of democracy is not universal. The two basic essentials to democracy are freedom of the individual and insurance that the government of a country is freely chosen by the people. (3) "In traditional African society, the African never was—nor thought himself to be— a cog in a machine. He was a free individual in his own society and his conception of government was personal, not institutional." Colonialism did little to change this. Why expect institutional government to replace *personal* government immediately after the change from colonial to independent status?

When the above-mentioned political recommendation is coupled with the further observation of the above-mentioned students that African societies have lost their original "spirit of generosity and fel-

[2] Julius Nyerere, *Africa Special Report.* Washington, D.C.: African-American Institute, Feb., 1960.

lowship," there arises the crucial question: Just what kind of society should be the aim of the independent African nations? Prime Minister Nkrumah on occasion has declared himself to be a Marxian socialist; but recent opponents contend that the prime minister has sold out to the capitalists. Sékou Touré has been criticized for the economic transactions with the Soviet and the presence in Guinea of Czech technicians. Perhaps the most enlightening statement of what the future African society should be has been given by the distinguished poet, scholar, and statesman Léopold Senghor. Senghor advocates an African type of socialism, a communal society or, better, "a communion of souls" rather than an "aggregate of individuals." He is not a Communist, but he will not practice anti-Communism. He opposes Communism on theoretical grounds because Lenin's definition of matter proceeds from a one-sided concept, from a purely materialistic and deterministic postulate. He opposes it on practical grounds because its principle, the "dictatorship of the proletariat," destroys the freedom of man and the freedom of collectivities. He retains the dialectical method as a necessary supplement to traditional logic, but condemns the use of it as a ruse for justifying "cowardice, betrayals, and thoroughly reprehensible electoral tactics." He opposes liberal capitalism and free enterprise[3] because of its ethics of material success, machinism, and racial segregation. Beyond Communism and capitalism there is taking place before our eyes a third revolution, which will integrate moral and religious values with the political and economic. Senghor calls his objective a *dynamic symbiosis*: "a cultural blending which, like all blending or grafting, produces a more succulent fruit." More specifically, this turns out to be a strong federal democracy. It begins with the primacy of politics, a phrase that means that the black man must be advanced in all respects and become not only a consumer but above all a *producer* of culture. Federalism will allow for local diversities with their complementary qualities, thus to enrich the whole. Federalism does not mean a weakened democracy. However, two dangers will be avoided: fascist dictatorship, which one observes in the antifederalist states, and the governmental instability common in France during the Third and Fourth Republics. The electoral law will be impartial. There will be freedom of opinion, speech, press, assembly, and association. Free

[3] Léopold Senghor, *African Socialism* (New York: American Society of African Culture, 1959), p. 29.

settlement of the citizens will be the rule whether born in Mali or not. Minorities "will find their natural and legal limits in the rights of the majority, the popular will, which is sovereign." Majorities will similarly respect minorities. Criticism means critical spirit, not systematc carping. It must be constructive and serve the general, not factional interests. The masses of people will be led by elites. Among these will be political leaders, students, and labor leaders. Having already abandoned the class-struggle theory, these last-named should not seek to replace the politicians, but, conscious of their responsibilities to the people, they should help the political leaders to carry out their program. From the production standpoint, this program consists of three sectors: a socialized sector—agriculture; a mixed sector—public utilities and societies with mixed economy; and a free sector—banks, commerce, and industry. Private capital will be welcomed, but with the proviso that no political strings be attached. The problem of nationalization will not arise, mainly because of underdevelopment, meager capital, and lack of the necessary cadres. Senghor gives the following summary statement of his more significant objectives:

> The ultimate aim of the Party of African Federation is the construction of a *Negro African Nation* in West Africa, which would correspond to a Central African Nation. For *Nation* is the first reality of the twentieth century. These nations will consist of the former French colonies in Black Africa. They will be inspired by the ideal of socialism, but it will be an "open socialism." Within this perspective, they will be groups in federal States. As their objective, these States will select the progress of Man by raising his standard of living and culture. The ways and means will be a strong democracy and a planned economy.[4]

TRIBALISM AND RACISM

There are many who do not share Senghor's sanguine hopes concerning the establishment of an African federalist democracy. The history of African societies, they say, consists almost solely of uninterrupted warfare between fanatical tribes. Tribal organization and conflict are so deeply rooted in the African mind that neither nationalistic fervor nor even the future centuries can uproot it. Though he does not share

[4] *Ibid.*, p. 45.

this view, Professor Coleman in his book *Nigeria: Background to Nationalism*[5] confirms the existence of the widespread belief that the African is behaviorally predispositioned to the best and to the worst of tribal life. Professor David Apter in his *The Gold Coast in Transition*[6] does not share the view either, but he is quite aware of the tremendous effect of tribalism upon the African. Sometimes he suggests that a possible source of the charisma of Nkrumah is the fact that he symbolizes chieftancy on a national scale. He observes too, and rightly so, that public behavior of certain upper-class individuals might be in accord with Western etiquette, but once in the home, tribal behavior takes over. Professor St. Clair Drake in *Africa Seen by American Negroes*[7] answers this criticism in part. Professor Drake makes judicious and sparing usage of the radical ethical relativism espoused by Melville Herskovits and Ruth Benedict, of the functionalism of Redcliff Brown, and, with a side glance at Karl Mannheim's "situationally incongruous" idea, combines all into an eclectic philosophy. He shows that many of the traits surviving from traditional African cultures are highly disapproved of by the educated elites. Among these are gustatory and ritual cannibalism, human sacrifice, sorcery, witchcraft, pawning and slavery, inefficient technology, and intertribal warfare. Among the moderately disapproved are ornamental scarification, curing disease by magic, and polygyny. Those approved, if not hampering progress, are excessive discussion of problems by elders, ancestor cults, matrilineality, extended family ties, and communal land tenure. Among the new traits approved by the elites are paid employment for urban women, voluntary associations, Christianity, and Islam. Ndabaningi Sithole believes that urbanization, industrialization, and greatly disrupted tribal structure weakened tribal customs. Mr. Sithole believes the dominant trend is toward a new nontribal African. He estimates that over forty million Africans have left the tribal regime and have been caught up in the industrial system.

With the coming of mines, towns, and cities the different tribes of Africa found themselves thrown together. Tribesmen who had never had anything to do with one another found themselves

[5] James S. Coleman, *Nigeria: Background to Nationalism* (Berkeley and Los Angeles: University of California Press, 1958), pp. 395–396.
[6] David E. Apter, *The Gold Coast in Transition*. Princeton: Princeton University Press, 1955.
[7] St. Clair Drake, in *Africa Seen by American Negroes*. Présence Africaine, 1958.

living together in one area, working side by side with one another, and the need to get along well with one another became imperative. For instance, in the Johannesburg gold-mines tribes from British East Africa, Portuguese Africa, British Central Africa, South West Africa, Basutoland, Swaziland, Natal, the Cape Province, and the Orange Free State are to be found in big numbers. Southern Rhodesia is full of native labourers from Northern Rhodesia, Nyasaland, Tanganyika, and other neighbouring territories. Briefly, colonialism introduced African tribes to one another. With the coming together of these tribes the horizons of many Africans have been greatly extended. While the U.S.A. is popularly regarded as the melting-pot of the nations, it is equally true that every mine, town, and city in Africa is a melting-pot of the tribes.[8]

Professor Drake points out the criticisms of traditional tribal behavior made by the ever-growing African elite. Sithole focuses attention on the mass migration of Africans to the centers of industry and the resultant changes in behavior. It is imperative, however, that we view tribalism and chieftaincy in the actual struggle with the new political forces. Such a problem is difficult enough for the social scientist when a social order is undergoing normal change. But when the rate of change is accelerated and uneven as in the case of the aspiration of African nationalists, difficulties are increased a hundredfold. This is the reason for Professor Coleman's informative, though necessarily imprecise characterizations of such terms as "tribe," "tribal union," "extended tribe," "incipient nation," and "nationality."[9] A tribe is a ". . . relatively small group of people who share a common culture and who are descended from a common ancestor." It is a group intermediate between a clan and a nationality. A nationality is "the largest traditional African group above a tribe which can be distinguished from other groups by one or more objective criteria (normally language)." Besides language, a shared historical tradition, a common mythology as to origin, and similar customs are criteria. Although in several passages[10] Professor Coleman stresses tribalism and kinship as the most significant factors in the Nigerian political struggle between the Hausa, the Yoruba, and the Ibo, it is in his comparison to the

---

[8] Ndabaningi Sithole, *African Nationalism* (Oxford, 1959), pp. 68–69.
[9] Coleman, *op. cit.*, pp. 422–424.
[10] *Ibid.*, pp. 330, 350.

traditional nationalism of Burke and Jacobin nationalism that his position is disclosed. "Nigerian nationalists seeking the rapid transformation of Nigeria into a modern state would incline more to a Jacobin nationalism, which would extinguish all obstructive intermediate groups." [11]

The issue was settled in a more definitive way in Ghana. In 1954, members of Nkrumah's Convention Peoples' Party attacked the validity of belief in the Golden Stool because the ruler had invoked the time-honored power of the stool against the party.

The African students assembled at Addis Ababa, Ethiopia, in February, 1960, also made the following additional recommendations:

> Pan-Africanism must not introduce black imperialism in place of white imperialism, that is, it must not be a mere object of ambition.

> Pan-Africanism must not give way to a new kind of racial discrimination.

Pan-Africanism is indeed liable both to negative prejudice against other ethnic groups and to positive prejudice in favor of its own. But no universal racial myth has been used to counter the myth of white supremacy. It is sometimes said that Ghana and South Africa stand as contrary symbols. But Nkrumah and Padmore stand for a trans-racial conception of man. Orizu,[12] who synthesized the elements of Zikhism in the 1940's made mention of a myth, but pointed out that Azikiwe's philosophy was humanistic and not racist. African leaders, almost without exception, are interested ultimately in man. However, the interim is one of uncertainty, as the students suggest. If the nationalist would remove the effects of colonization from his mind, then he must always be on guard against using the detested techniques of the colonizer. He may reconstruct history according to the truth, but not by arbitrary contrivance. He may elect his own African language, but he must be aware of the intentions and purposes of human beings which lie beyond all linguistic expression. Socially and politically, he must be aware of counter-"Bantustans" and spurious race-tainted ballots. Since in the independent lands the labels of segregation are

---

[11] *Ibid.*, pp. 322.
[12] A. A. Nwafor Orizu, *Without Bitterness: Western Nations in Post-War Africa.* New York: Creative Age, 1944.

down, they must remain down. There must be no malignant racial epithets, no causal explanations by blood type, no theories of African supremacy. If there is negritude in art, then the black artist must be aware that only in so far as he transcends his racial position and *projects* his images will it be possible for him to prevent their malformation and consumption within their own flames. From this point of view, Pan-Africanism may be race-centered without being centered in race prejudice.

TRADITIONAL AFRICAN SOCIAL THOUGHT

GEORGE E. CARTER

Director of Information Program,
American Society of African Culture

IT WOULD BE more convenient than accurate to speak of the idea of a
correspondence between social organization and cosmological order as
characteristic of traditional African social thought. For to speak thus
would be to imply that African thought distinguishes two such orders
and in turn sees them as systematically related. The distinction is
Western. Yet, traditional African thought has much to say about what
in the West would be called social and cosmic phenomena and the
relationships between them. Can it not be assumed that some statements about social phenomena are descriptions of a social order and
some statements about cosmic phenomena *pari passu* of a cosmic
order? If we are permitted such an assumption, then it can be said
about African thought that one can meaningfully speak of two such
orders and of a relation of correspondence between them—the one
both reflects and is contingent upon the other. An analysis of this
notion of correspondence with respect to various aspects of the social
order will provide us with an outline of the major features of traditional
African social thought.

Before proceeding to this analysis, however, I should like to make
two points explicit. First, I shall concentrate upon those relevant common features within a wide variety of societies in sub-Saharan Africa.
Second, I shall assume that for various reasons some African societies
have achieved a greater degree of precision and elaboration of the
nature of the correspondence and its implications, and I shall therefore focus attention upon those societies. Further, I shall assume that
the greater degree of precision in these societies results in large measure from those conditions within them that gave rise to a priestly leisure
class that could achieve and maintain that critical distance that is a
sine qua non of systematic thought. I believe it follows from these
assumptions that a similar development in other African societies
would have issued in a parallel, if not similar, precision.

One of the most sophisticated expressions of the idea of a correspondence between the two orders is to be found in the writings of the French anthropologists who have done field work among the Dogon in the southern part of French Sudan. They have found that underlying the world-view of the Dogon is the conception that a sign or symbol or image or any form of the representation of an object is isomorphic with that object. In great detail the Dogon have worked out a table of signs or symbols on the assumption that a given symbol, when interpreted by the initiated, provides a key for understanding that which it symbolizes. It would follow from this, for example, that the social order can be described in a system of representations. The myths of the Dogon can in turn reproduce this system of representations in a system of symbols. Hence, Dogon mythology is, in effect, a system in terms of which the Dogon can achieve an understanding of the social order.

> Among the Dogon exoteric myths correspond to a superficial knowledge common to the greater part of the population; . . . esoteric myths, parallel to these, present other identifications and much wider connexions. Finally, within and beyond this totality of beliefs appears a logical scheme of symbols expressing a system of thought which cannot be described simply as myth. For this conceptual structure, when studied, reveals an internal coherence, a secret wisdom, and an apprehension of ultimate realities equal to that which we Europeans conceive ourselves to have attained.[1]

Given the terms of the Dogon theory of symbolism, one can conclude that a series of representations can be identified, each set of which is analogous to every other. And so it is in the Dogon's world-view. As in a series of concentric circles, one level reflects the order found on another. Man as an individual reflects the order of his family structure, which in turn reflects the order of his clan of his society, and finally, of the universe. Man is a microcosm of the world order.

In great detail the spokesman for the Dogon explains that man is the seed of the universe. His adumbrated form was the pattern, the order, within the original "World-Egg." As the "World-Egg" broke forth from its envelope, impulsed by the inner rhythm and vibration of

---

[1] M. Grizule and G. Dieterlen, "The Dogon," in *African Worlds*, ed. Daryll Forde (Oxford, 1954), p. 83.

matter and following a predetermined course, it developed into the universe. At each stage and with respect to every element the primordial shape of man served as the pattern. Hence, all things in the universe: the stars, the earth, society, and the universe itself reflect this primordial form. (Even today among the Dogon the family household and all the accouterments of family living are laid out in accordance with a plan that follows the shape of a man.)

Thus, through their theory of symbolism the Dogon achieve an understanding of the universe and man's place within it which leads to the fundamental premise controlling their behavior and informing their social outlook. For them it follows that if man at one level and society at another are structural analogues of each other and both of these are analogues of the universe, then a disorder on one level is causally related to disorder on another.

> Disorder among the seeds, which for an individual results especially from the breaking of the rules of life, prefigures the universal disorder which spreads by stages from the individual to his close kinsmen, his family, his clan, his people. . . . Thus the individual through his family and the society in which he lives, is linked in his structure and in his evolution with the universe; and this connexion operates in both directions.[2]

This view is by no means peculiar to the Dogon. It can, in fact, be found in varying degrees of explicitness in many parts of sub-Saharan Africa. Among the Southern Bantu hunting societies, for example, good hunting is considered the best sign that all is well within the village. If the results of the hunt are bad, the villagers know that someone somehow has committed an offence—broken the harmony of the village.

Among the Abaluyia in Kenya again we find the view that God created and ordered the world in a way such that man might live in it. Yet the intermediaries of God can and do disrupt the order of the world as a punishment for wrongdoings in the social order. Such a disruption can bring about death, famine, pestilence, and so forth. The only way to avoid such disruptions is to maintain harmony within the clan, which is to say, to avoid wrongdoing. This notion gives rise to an important conception among the Abaluyia—that of "neutral ritual status." A neutral ritual status describes a person or clan whose life

2 *Ibid.*, p. 88.

is normally happy, normally in harmony with others, and normally successful in undertakings. As long as one has "neutral ritual status," one knows that all is well. When adversity strikes, the person knows that his "neutral ritual status" has become negative. He must take action to restore it. Such action involves a complicated system of magical and religious rites. These rites are directed at ancestors who as the intermediaries of God are the guardians of order and the causal agents of the disruptive forces.

Among the Lovedu in the South African Transvaal the Rain Queen, who is divine, is the focus for the well-being of society. She as the embodiment of the universal order shares control of the good forces with the ancestors. It is around her that the society focuses its ritual. It is she who must be propitiated. If at any point she lacks the efficacy to produce the rain and its consequent good for society, it is assumed that her failure is related to a disorder—a lack of harmony—in society.

The Shilluk, a Nilotic group in north-central Africa, worship a divine king who is thought to be a direct descendant of the eponymous hero Nyikang. Nyikang, a vaguely human historical personage now a god in the minds of the Shilluk, is the link between the historical Shilluk peoples and the creator god Juok. The well-being of the divine king is directly and causally related to the well-being of society in the Shilluk's world-view. And at one time in their history, as with many ancient peoples in all parts of the world, the divine king was never allowed to die from natural causes, since only when he was in the best of health could society enjoy its greatest good. If he were permitted to become ill, this condition would be reflected in society.

Among the Fon of Dahomey, where again one finds a high degree of sophistication and comprehensiveness, the interdependence of the social and cosmic order become very explicit. However, for a clearer understanding of this interdependence we might look, in some detail, at the Fon conception of man. Two purposes can be served in this way. First, the Fon idea of man comprehends in one coherent and fairly explicit system a number of ideas and elements implicit in and scattered through many bodies of African thought. Second, the nature of man is an excellent point of departure for the understanding of any corpus of social thought, particularly African social thought.

The Fon conception of man can be understood when analyzed in terms of the four aspects that constitute the unity of the human soul.

The first aspect is the *Se*, which is that part of the human soul that partakes of God. The second is the *Joto*, which is the aspect of the soul inherited from an ancestor. The third is called *Ye*, which is the Joto incarnate; immortal, it is that part of a man that is best understood as what is remembered about him. The fourth, the *Selido*, is the aspect that is and informs a man's uniqueness—his personality. Let us in turn see what each of these aspects has to say about the conception of man in African thought.

When a man dies, his Ye leaves his body and becomes a wandering disembodied Joto. The Joto is sent in search of the object of its reincarnation. The object sought is the body of one about-to-be-born. Unerringly the Joto finds as the object of its reincarnation a member of its own clan; it remains the guardian of the fate of the new member throughout the latter's mortal life.

In this role the Joto provides the basis for the relation between the past and present, the dead and the living. Further, this perpetual replenishment of the clan is the foundation upon which the ancestor cult is structured and it therefore becomes crucially important in understanding the attitudes and values that regulate Fon society.

In its search for the object of its reincarnation, the Joto is directed by its *Tohwiyo*, who is the eponymous hero of the Joto's clan. Each clan of the Fon has its Tohwiyo—one who founded the clan, informed its members of right action, and the laws and organization of the clan. The Tohwiyo governs the clan members, living and dead, in accordance with laws that he has given.

It is interesting to note parallels to this view to be found among other African peoples. The Lovedu, for example, believe that ancestors can influence the fortunes only of their direct descendants. No misfortune can come to a Lovedu if his ancestors are considerate. Hence, ancestors are propitiated in times of trouble and thanked for gifts of fortune.

In the Dogon world-view there is the belief that the entire race is descended from one group of four pairs of twins that gave rise to four clans, and these clans share the universe among them.

For the Mende of Sierra Leone there is a significant relation between the living and their ancestors. For it is believed that at death a Mende's soul goes to live in a city that occupies a position in the scheme of things much closer to God than the living can achieve. The ancestors thus become the intermediary between God and the living, and as such they participate in governing the fortunes of the living.

The Banyarwanda of Ruanda-Urundi believe that the souls of the dead retreat to the underworld, and as such, except for those who are the direct ancestors of a given individual, become evil agents. The Banyarwanda is protected from the evil agents by his direct ancestors if he shows them proper respect.

The Ashanti of Ghana, along with the Akan people as a whole, who have also developed a complicated theory of the human soul, are at every point aware of the influence of their ancestors in their daily lives.[3] They give food and drink to their ancestors, clothe them, and pray to them. For again it is their ancestors upon whom the Ashanti depend for good fortune. Each family is protected by its ancestors, and the ancestors of the chief protect the tribe; hence, a justification for the position of the chief. The governance of the ancestors is a beneficent one as long as the living keep the customs and fulfill their obligations.

The relation between the living and the dead and the influence of the dead over the well-being of the living as expressed in ancestor cults is one of the most universal characteristics of African cosmology, and perhaps the most distinctive.

The social implications of the African's view of his ancestors are not difficult to understand. In each view alluded to above it is abundantly clear how one's ancestors can exercise a determining control over one's comportment in the social order. Ancestors are the givers of law, and by their influence they compel obedience to it, for the wrath of one's ancestors is greatly to be avoided. We can see further how the conception of the nature of the role of ancestors has direct implications for the structure and function of social institutions, patterns of behavior, moral attitudes, and values.

There is, I believe, yet another set of social implications of this aspect of the soul. Classical Western liberal thought is, in part, predicated upon a notion of man as a discrete entity—an individual. Socially significant discussion and description of the individual in Western liberal thought is limited to the analysis of those relations between men—and groups of men as collections of discrete entities—that are

---

[3] The Akan theory provides an interesting contrast to the Homeric and pre-Socratic Greek conception of the human soul.

external. A mechanical analogue of this condition can be found among a group of billiard balls at rest, in motion, and striking one another on a table.[4] The mechanist's description of the relations between the balls at rest and in motion with respect to one another exhausts the class of mechanically significant statements that can be made about conditions on the table. If we substitute the word "social" for "mechanical," it becomes clear that Man in this view is a closed universe. The relations between men are never internal; that is, are never an integral part of the entities related.

The African view of man admits of the possibility of socially significant statements about internal relations between men. Man is not a closed universe. Those frontiers of being that mark off Western man as a discrete entity are in the African view blurred and vague. Men become integral parts of one other. The group, no longer a collection of entities, is substantively interrelated.

Nietzsche's distinction between the Apollonian and Dionysian components of Greek culture begins to adumbrate the spirit of the difference between the two views. The Apollonian component, which corresponds to the Western liberal notion, sharply opposes man and the forces that rule the universe, and holds that laws are precise, ethics is normative and discursive, theology is rational, and God is unapproachable. The Dionysian is in touch with the forces that govern his destiny. He is or can become a part of God. Laws are the rules of ritual and ethics qua system is of little concern.

The *Se* is that aspect of each man's soul that is God—Mawu-Lisa. It is the principle of life and motion. Through it each man partakes of the vital force, the inner rhythm that is the source, or better, the precondition of being and the order of the universe.

When Mawu-Lisa created—fashioned—the world, he was aided by *Da*, who played, and continues to play, a decisive role. Da is the life force with which Mawu-Lisa makes man complete. Da, not a god, is force, motion, the inner rhythm that is the *sine qua non* of order in the universe. He is symbolized by the Fon as the great serpent that when coiled about the earth holds it together in its proper form. Da is in all things, above all things, the necessary condition of all things. Da is the Fon conception of the category that P. Tempels describes as the most

---

[4] This analogy, incidentally, is historically not unrelated to the development of the western liberal conception of Man.

fundamental in African metaphysics—the vital force of the universe. M. Roland Colin, in speaking of the vital force in African metaphysics, makes the interesting point that "rhythm is to force what consciousness is to the idea," [5] and thus suggests a major reason for the preëminence of concern with rhythm in the life and culture and art of the African. Rhythm provides the medium by which the African realizes the immediacy of the vital force in his being. M. Colin at another point says, "Rhythm is the medium by which one achieves a consonance with the inner mystique of being, for it is in rapport with the inner rhythm of the forces which sleep, which live in being." [6]

Hence, the Da of the Fon becomes far more important and immediate in the daily life of the African than Mawa-Lisa.

This last point, we believe, suggests a generalization that can be made concerning most traditional African thought. African theology is monotheistic. Most views imply the notion of one creator god, yet God in most views, is a deistic god. God created the world and informed it with order, then moved to a distant point. So far removed is He from the currents of daily life that in most African societies little or no ritual is directed at Him, and practically no interference, good or bad, is expected. The result of this is that despite the presence of theological conceptions, traditional African thought is humanistic.

Man is the center. God, though not dead, is indifferent. Man plunged into the center of the social order is perforce "engagé." He is the center of an order for which he and he alone is responsible. He must find, which means create, and fulfill his destiny.[7] The mention of Man's destiny brings us to a discussion of the last aspect of the African conception of the soul—one which from the point of view of social thought is most important.

We now come to the Selido, that which makes a man what he is as distinct from all other men—his intellectual powers, his personality, his identity, his fate. At Death, the Joto seeks a reincarnation, the Se is reabsorbed into Mawu-Lisa, the Ye becomes the Joto, but the Selido dies with the man.

[5] Roland Colin, Les Contes noirs de l'Ouest Africain (Paris: Présence Africaine, 1957), p. 184.

[6] Ibid., p. 185.

[7] The objectives of the movement out of which the society sponsoring this conference grew are sustained by this kind of humanism. For most assuredly it can be said that the intellectual renaissance that accompanies Africa's reawakening is in many respects a reaffirmation of traditional African humanism.

For our purposes the most important function of this aspect of the soul is the fact that it determines a man's fate, his *Fa*. According to Maupoil:

Fa is an actual communication from the supreme deity Mawu. It is an abstract indirect and deductive mode of interpreting or revealing the past or future, whereby an enquirer receives, through the medium of a specialist, an answer to the problem which is exercising his mind. Above all, it offers to everyone the possibility of learning the fate which Mawu had appointed for his soul before giving it its earthly incarnation, and enables him to practise the cult of that soul.[8]

Human fate is fixed by predetermination. Each man has his place in the scheme of things, the way in which his life is to unfold is set. It is set within a larger pattern of destiny, which is the destiny of his family, his clan, and the universe itself. Man is determined. Hence, in African philosophy we thus find posed one of the classical quandaries of Western thinking—Free Will and Determinism.

For the Fon, one of the most interesting and colorful characters in all literature (in this case, oral literature) appears to solve this problem —Legba. (Legba in Fon literature, and Eshu his parallel among the Yoruba, is sometimes thought of as the crown prince of trickery and mischief, and in many places is pictured as an evil spirit—so much so that in many instances Christian missionaries in their attempts to teach the principles of Christianity identified Satan as Legba. The identification is hardly an apt one.)

Legba is one of the sons of the male-female god Mawu-Lisa, and by special privilege the envoy of God and intermediary among gods. His role as mediator obtains also among the *Tohwiyo*, the clan founders. Through mediation between the gods, which often involves tricks and malefactions against both gods and men, Legba is capable of introducing chance and accident into the affairs of men and thus is able to break the iron law of fate. Legba, in this role, is the object of divination so important in Fon religious conceptions. If a man seeks to know his destiny, he beseeches Legba. If he is unhappy about his destiny, he urges Legba to intervene and thus to break the law that directs him toward his doom. By virtue of Legba's role and man's ability to reach

---

[8] B. Maupoil, *La Géomancie à l'Ancienne Côte des Esclaves*. Travaux et Mémoires de l'Institut d'Ethnologie, Vol. LXII (Paris, 1943), p. 17.

and persuade Legba, a man's destiny becomes a tendency—an orientation or disposition. Without Legba, man is like Oedipus inextricably caught in his fate. With Legba, man can be free.

So, according to the Fon, as a man can know and change his destiny, he can also change that of the family, the clan, and the universe. Herein lies the profound optimism of African humanism and the crux of African social thought. We have already seen how this kind of optimism permeates the social views of the Lovedu, the Ashanti, the Dogon —in fact, the majority of African world-views. Herein lies the real significance of my initial statement about the correspondence between social organization and cosmological order—the idea that one both reflects and is contingent upon the other. For though God is indifferent and man responsible is the center, he is not without a tool with which to forge his destiny.

These in brief and summary form are the philosophical foundations of African social thought. What issues from them in the social order? What is to be their significance in Africa's wakening future?

Antisocial behavior among Africans is not censored by superhuman entities whose moral standards and ideals are difficult for man to achieve, but rather by former men who understand the difficulties and limitations of being human on this earth. The ancestors do not ask the impossible of man. They do not treat man as though he were conceived in evil and oriented toward an otherworldly goal. The ancestors lived as men and therefore know what man must do to live well with his fellowmen.

If man fails to live up to the requirements imposed by the ideal of harmony in the social order, the ancestors cause them great misfortune. A West African proverb says, "The ancestors do not play; they do not forgive; they kill you." The ancestors do not forgive because they do not ask the impossible of man. Had they set the goals at ideal behavior above man's heads, they would, if just, have to forgive the constant failure to achieve the ideal. The social ideals of the African are based upon the social realities of their lives. The African does not sin against God or his ancestors; his sin is against man, and this the ancestors censure.

As one reflects upon the features of traditional African social thought in the face of the enormous and pervasive change that sweeps the continent, two questions pose themselves: What will persist? What ought to persist? Any attempted answer to the first will be highly problematic; any answer to the second, highly speculative, highly controversial.

Yet, let us be bold. To whatever extent the past is a measure of the future we can say that much of traditional African social thought will probably survive the fundamental changes now in process. Further, if the past is any indication, the inherent flexibility and genius for accommodation of the African peoples argue well for the possibility that traditional African forms will not only survive but, wedded to the new, will issue in concepts, institutions, and values that the rest of the world might do well to regard.

It is profound testimony to the strength and vigor of African thought that wherever African people go, much that is characteristically African in thought and culture goes with them and survives centuries of alienation from the source. Peoples of African descent in Brazil, and throughout South America, the Caribbean Islands, and the United States in varying degrees still carry as part of the inner rhythm of their being the marks of their former African cultures. The survivals range from that which is hardly distinguishable from the source to that which is the wedded mother of what is, in fact, a new culture—American culture.

One detects the increasing currency of the view that affirms that once a society chooses, as many African societies will, a course that leads to industrialization and urbanization, a certain kind of inevitability and predictability sets in. In this view, whatever have been the nature of the social structure, the traditional culture, and underlying philosophy of the area involved, industrialization produces a set of social consequences that destroys the traditional base and gives rise to a culture that in essence is similar to that of every other industrial society. This view cuts across the great ideological debate of our times. For in different ways and with different aims in mind, adherents to both sides of the great debate hold this view.

I would deny the validity of this notion. I maintain that there is a significant distinction to be made between industrialization and Westernization; the former is not a function of the latter. Industrialization, though it first occurred in the West, is not Western in essence. It has yet to be demonstrated that the process of industrialization necessitates total and slavish Westernization for its achievement. It is possible, and highly desirable, for a non-Western society using its own cultural assumptions and social values to reorganize its modes of production and consumption, to create the necessary infrastructure and to raise standards of living without the headlong rush to absorb those nonessential aspects of Western culture that have been consequent to the peculiar history of the industrialization of the West.[9] To believe that non-Western societies must Westernize in order to industrialize or to believe that industrialization inevitably leads to Westernization is to see cultural history in the terms of an all-too-narrow determinism.

A society changes as it fashions the ideas and institutions by which it deals with the problems and satisfies the needs it deems significant. A group of people become aware of and define their problems and needs in terms of a frame of reference that is rooted in the assumptions and ideas and values of their culture. The root assumptions and values of African societies are fundamentally different from those in terms of which Western man understood his needs, defined and dealt with his problems. It follows from this that an important part of the task of the contemporary African leader is to fashion a social and political philosophy incorporating a set of goals and the instruments of their achievement that are appropriate to the unique character of the African scene; a scene that remains unique, however much it has been influenced and stimulated by the impact of the West. For it would be indeed a tragic irony if the notion of destiny and of man's ability to fashion his destiny and therefore his history, which underlies the optimism of traditional African humanism, were cast overboard in the urgency and enthusiasm to enter in full bloom into the twentieth century.

[9] It should be noted here that the history of the Soviet Union is considered as an integral part of the history of the West.

AFRICAN PERSONALITY AND THE
NEW AFRICAN SOCIETY

JOSEPH KI-ZERBO

*Secretary General, African Movement
for National Liberation, Voltaic Republic*

I, WHO AM neither a philosopher nor a sociologist, but a historian and geographer, propose to make a few observations about African society. And it is first of all essential to underline the importance of this problem within the context of the theme chosen for this conference.

What is Africa? What ought Africa to be? Such are the basic questions to which the conscientious African or Africanist must find a reply. Africa must be defined. Now what is a country if not, above all, the human beings who live in it, are part of it, and transform it? For example, when we have returned home after this conference, people will ask us: "What is America? What is it like?" We shall speak of the people we have met here, their appearance, their gestures, their opinions, and so forth. And so it is with Africa; she is not merely the iron ore or the aluminum with which her soil is rich; she is not only her forests of ebony and mahogany and other precious woods. Africa is above all the African people—insofar as man creates his own history—and the Africa of tomorrow, the African personality of which the whole world is speaking, will be what the African people make it. The development of that personality is the ultimate aim of all our efforts, both in the political struggle and in the economic field. And in spite of the difficulty of the subject, it is therefore important to examine this final aim of our efforts, this African personality, this goal of all the efforts and the sacrifices of African nationalists, many of whose blood was spilled and who died for the development of this personality.

As we are speaking now, there are still thousands of Africans, especially in North Africa, who are continuing to give their all in order that this same African personality may evolve. It is thus most important to examine the emergence of this new African society whose positive characteristics will represent our contribution to the great meeting of civilizations. And may I, at the outset, make an observation: we would be wrong to treat this problem from a purely academic viewpoint. Too many anthropologists and sociologists have wielded the scalpel on this subject, giving us analyses and descriptions of the past that are already outmoded and fossilized by the rapid evolution that is taking place. Certain sociologists for example, giving way to the convenient, are content to interpret the feelings of the present-day African toward his leaders as a mere transposition of the attitudes of tribalism into 1960. As if the African mind had not been touched by the new way of life! Africa is no longer the Africa of the Dogons; Africa is not a museum! It is a dough in full ferment. And the dialectic method is still the best method of approach to the sociological reality of Africa. In my opinion this approach could be made from the three following directions.

First, what are the main features of the social organization and conception of the traditional African society? Next, what are the principal elements of the present crisis? And finally, what prospects and what transcendant structure will emerge to create the new African society for her to attain a higher sociological level?

What are the main features of the traditional social organization and conception? Contrary to the colonial image, which presents precolonial Africa as a collection of tiny groups torn by internal strife and tribal warfare, sociologically frozen at the stage of a protozoan or an amoeba, African society was highly organized. Its principal features, in my opinion, were the following: first, the authority of the old people. You are all aware that in Africa the hierarchy of power, of consideration and of prestige, was in direct rapport with the hierarchy of age. When I was a shepherd, for instance, and we tended our goats, our little community was rigorously governed by the law of the hierarchy of age; I mean to say that it was the eldest who was the undisputed head, who assigned the day's work, and who, for example, designated the one among us who was to return to the village for provisions for all the other shepherds. Often enough, even today, one hears on the lips of Africans: "Don't talk to me in that tone of voice! I'm older than you." The council of elders in traditional Africa was the supreme political master of the city or the tribe. It was often this autocracy of the old that evolved into a veritable cult of ancestor worship. This cult closely identified ancestors with the main acts of the living—who were nothing but a tiny link in the giant chain of generations. The living were but a microcosm restricted to certain narrow duties in comparison with the tremendous cohort of those whose shades still peopled the ancestral home or the patriarchal or tribal territory. The African, even when emancipated of his metaphysical beliefs, still gives a large place to his ancestors. For him more than for any other, the famous statement of Renan holds true: "The nation is made up of more dead than living." It is for this reason that, for the African, patriotism has a distinctive dimension. The word *fasso*, which means "ancestral home" in Bambara, evokes for the African not only territorial or ethnic overtones, but cosmic and metaphysical ones as well. The oath at the tomb of one's ancestors is the most binding in existence. Certain nationalist parties have taken advantage of this, and by drawing from their followers such an oath, have bound them ever closer. Some people have contended that this respect for one's ancestors and for the past has made of the Africans a people forever mired in the stereotyped repetition of the same ceremonies and congenitally unable to invent anything new. But such arguments, supported by the colonialists, are easily controverted by the many contemporary or historical examples of African creativity that we can all advance.

Another important characteristic of the traditional society is solidarity, and this point is too obvious to require any lengthy examination. I would, however, like to say that this solidarity is not just a phenomenon of the superstructure, a trembling of the spirit, or a tenderness of heart toward others. This solidarity is imprinted on the very basic structure of African culture, and especially in its economic organization. You know that in the traditional African society the notion of property was defined in terms of the family community or the village and not in terms of the individual. The concept of personal property in terms of the individual is generally alien to African social concepts. Fields are often common property and work is most often collective. Another social manifestation of this solidarity is hospitality, which, it is true, is obviously not an African monopoly but which nevertheless is particularly strong there; and here I am pleased to associate North Africa with the rest of the continent. How many times when I was a child did my mother prepare a hot meal for us; but strangers, travelers who stopped in to stay with us, arrived suddenly, and we had to content ourselves with a cold meal, while the hot meal that had just been prepared for us and which we were already enjoying in anticipation, was served to the guests. Even the white conquerors, when they arrived in Africa, were the recipients of this hospitality, of this African openness of heart, of this predisposition to kindness toward all new arrivals. Many conquerors who entertained unhappy thoughts for Africa in the back of their heads, were received with extraordinary friendliness, housed with the chiefs, fed, and generally surrounded with consideration and respect up to the very moment when they left this collectivity and considered themselves free of any obligations in this regard. In traditional Africa, there were no orphans—but, it must unfortunately be added, there was also no quarantine or segregation of even the contagious sick. In the African mind it was unthinkable that because one of the members of the family or the tribal group was ill, he should have been separated and isolated. We are dealing, therefore, with a solidarity with unlimited mutual responsibility.

Another important feature is the equalitarian character of African society. Naturally, I do not intend in any way to idealize or to present traditional Africa as the best of all possible or imaginary worlds. Africa has had its tyrants, as have other nations throughout history. But it must be stressed also that the traditional African society often included classes based solely on functional differentiation. There was, for instance, the mason class, the blacksmith class, the warrior class. But the fact that in Africa property was common, the fact that there was no class that accumulated the capital property and reduced others to the state of mere tenancy—mere peasants or farmers whose toil was used to amass profit—well, that fact proves that the exploitation of man by man never achieved the status of a system in the traditional society of Africa. And, moreover, by reason of the unlimited solidarity of which I have just spoken, the true principle of such a society was "To each according to his needs," to the extent of the complete utilization of common revenues, in which case, of course, everyone also participated in a common famine. And even in the political field, where it has become the custom to depict Africa as swarming with uncontrolled and bloody petty tyrants, power was in fact limited by custom. For example, the supreme chief of the Mossi tribe, the Moronaba, was invested with extraordinary power, even divine power, and was compared to the sun. At the Moronaba's death, the Griot (medicine man), who had to announce it to the people, merely said: "The fire has gone out" or "The sun has set." Well, even in that Mossi society, the Moronaba was not an absolute monarch; his power was restrained by a council of chiefs as provided by custom, that is, by a sort of unwritten constitution—and any Englishmen who are present will understand that concept. This council of chiefs was endowed with great power to brake, hinder, oppose or even to effectively veto the desires of the Moronaba. One could mention many other characteristics of the traditional African society. One could, for example, speak of its ideological tolerance. It is a constant in the history of traditional Africa that there were practically no wars of religion. There is a tolerance toward others which may perhaps be explained by the fact that African religion did not develop through a structural elaboration of a dogma but through the elaboration of a special social cadre of priests consecrated to the cult, the celebration of ritual, and liaison with the supernatural world. You are aware that in traditional African culture the king generally was the political leader and also the head of the society.

What are the principal elements of the present crisis? The historical origin of this crisis was the gigantic trauma inflicted on the African personality by colonialism. Colonialism has not only been a tremendous embezzlement of material wealth, but also a tragic sidetracking of the African personality toward ideals and roles that have adulterated it. Thus the African personality has become a sort of shipwreck towed along by the thread of a history made and written by the European conquerors. This is, moreover, especially true of the African of French culture, where assimilation was one of the categorical imperatives, one of the canons of colonization—the final aim of the colonizers being to completely annex the mentality and concepts of the colonized people. Education has thus become one of the main points, one of the most important methods of colonization. And I believe that one could almost make mention here, speaking of colonialist education, of a colonial pact of minds. Now the origin of this trauma, of this cultural oppression, is the singleminded European conception of civilization: There is only one Civilization with a capital C.

I should like here to tell a little story to help you understand how far this mentality extends, even to children. When I was in Paris, I was often received in French homes, and once, after dinner in the living room, a little girl seemed uncommonly interested in my appearance. She began walking around and around me, felt my hair, and finally took my hand. She turned it over and over to study it, and then holding up this part of my hand, said to those present: "It's clean here." You will see that already in that little head there existed a conception with regard to color. For her, that which was clean was white. Obviously, from the African point of view and the black point of view, you could also say that what is clean is black. This attitude is going to drag out the crisis in the African personality—and it does not necessarily arise from a calculated colonial point of view.

Each time we have the contact of two civilizations, mutual perturbations arise *ipso facto* and of necessity. A few examples: first, the introduction of money. In traditional society, money existed but its use was restricted by reason of a closed economy—an economy based on barter. Well, the very presence of money in the capitalistic sense of the word—that is, as a general equivalent, property that can be equated with any other kind of property, merchandise with an extremely rapid turnover and (according to the expression used by Aristotle and, I believe, taken up again by Karl Marx) capable of begetting children —money in that sense could not help but occasion profound upsets in the traditional society. Accumulation becomes possible. For example, farms develop into individual landed estates; the worker, too, earns his salary on an individual basis; and new social cleavages, new social classes, are tending to develop in Africa today, as they did in Europe in the seventeenth and eighteenth centuries. In traditional Africa money did not afford the right to everything, as it does in the capitalistic system. For example, titles were not bought and sold. As in Europe in the Middle Ages, there was no artificial nobility; the only nobility was of the blood.

Similarly, another disturbing element is that of a city considered as a gigantic laboratory for a new humanity, where the West is on hand with its goods—which are, moreover, not always particularly useful for Africa. I am thinking of the immense quantity of alcohol that has been imported into black Africa. Well, the West is on hand with its goods, its services, its publicity, its multitude of solicitations, and slowly and surely it penetrates the traditional civilization. It is said that when the Upper Volta was being colonized, a military column under Vonlay and Chauvine met an old African near Gonvadonjon. This old man had just left his village, along with a little child who was leading a goat; the old man himself was carrying a chicken, and was on his way to a funeral where the goat and the chicken were to be sacrificed. Brenton tells us that this old man did not lose his head. He went up to Vonlay and said: "I heard that you were supposed to come this way; everyone else has fled, but I decided to come and meet you and I have brought you this chicken and this goat."

It is certain that that was a meeting of two civilizations; the old man, pondering the traditional ceremonies he must perform and the formulas he must pronounce to ensure peace for the soul of his dead relative, is brusquely confronted by European civilization, as represented by material military power. Now, imagine an old man who leaves his village and goes to the city. This trip is not just a trip in space; it is also, and perhaps primarily a trip in time, across many centuries of evolution, which leads him from the sociological context of the Middle Ages, so to speak, to a completely different context: the context of the material, moral, psychological, and mental civilization of Western Europe.

Similarly, setting up a factory in Africa has sociological implications. Such was the case with the creation of Fria in Guinea; there were not just engineers, geologists, and geographers who set to work; there was also a team of sociologists to determine the possible social repercussions of this installation. Likewise, with the development of unions and parties, which create new solidarities, sometimes stronger than the old. It has been determined, for instance, that after 1946, there were often quarrels among family relatives, and the subject of these quarrels was political struggle and divergencies. The result, you all know—it was well expressed by Frantz Fannon in his book *Black Skins, White Masks*—is imitation become a system; it is the uprooting, the disembodiment, and the calculated withering of a civilization; it is cultural genocide. I have seen people taking great pains to learn the French dictionary by heart, as if culture were a matter of pure accumulation of knowledge and not one of comprehension and communion. I have seen Africans wearing sunglasses in the middle of the night. I have seen colonized peoples don the colonial helmet as the sign and the test of social advancement. And since one's basic nature is always just under the surface and impossible to subdue completely, the end result is the drawing and quartering of conscience and the formation of serious psychological complexes. We have the rifleman, for instance: that very African soldier who struggles in the African armies for a policy external to Africa. And here I shall make a brief digression. With regard to Pan-Africanism and African unity, it is difficult to conceive that those black African soldiers who are now fighting in the colonial army against the emancipation of Algeria will not be retired from the front after the attainment of independence by their states; it is difficult to believe that those independent countries will not withdraw their soldiers so that their Algerian brothers, who are of the same continent, who often shared the same history, may free themselves and attain their political aspirations. Well, very often the soldier who tries to speak French as it is spoken in Paris will show you the talisman he wore in the fight for the liberation of France. Similarly, during electoral rollcalls, I have often seen candidates call upon both the voice of the people and the intervention of witch doctors.

But we must determine whether or not the present crisis is a fatal illness or if it is just a phase of disequilibrium in the coming blossoming—a sort of puberty. It depends mainly on the Africans themselves—and this brings us to the examination of the third and last point of this study: *What prospects and transcendent structures will emerge?*

What are the principles? What do we want? What sort of Africa do we desire? The African people themselves must answer these questions. There is no culture but that which is fixed in space. On his little island, Robinson Crusoe was perhaps educated, but it cannot be said that he was cultured. Cultured with regard to whom? Culture is a social idea. And the great inventor, the creator, the genius, is the people. Thus, the first duty of the social revolution is to free the people, to liberate man. This was well expressed in the slogan of the Accra Congress of 1958: "Hands off Africa!" And I think it was Alioune Diop who pointed out that after the independence of Guinea the very fact of political freedom gave rise to extremely interesting lyric and epic poetry, especially in the Fonta area.

Of course, it is not up to an areopagus of sages or leaders to pre-organize or to prefabricate the future African personality. But the people often do need to be guided, especially after such a deep and fundamental trauma as the colonial era. You Americans are familiar with this experience, because immediately after the abolition of slavery —which was in itself a positive factor from the point of view of historical evolution—there was for a certain time an equivalent to the present total confusion among the black Africans; that is, certain deviations and aberrations occurred in the Negro society of America which was not accustomed to the breath of freedom or the free condition into which it found itself so brutally thrust.

So, the role of the leaders is to know what basic choices must be presented for the evolution of African culture and civilization—and here it is obvious that each has complete freedom of self-determination on the condition that he does not enter into flagrant contradiction with the recognized values of the original civilization. Within this framework of respect for traditional African civilization, there is still room for a great variety of choice. Hence the necessity of frequent meetings among political, union, and cultural African leaders, in order to localize and to illuminate the points of friction and opposition and to clearly present ideological problems. Failing this, we run the risk, after the precolonial clannishness and the colonial cloistering, of a sort of ideological tribalism in the independent nations, which would obviously be to the detriment of Africa as a whole. They tell the story of two African students in Paris—relatives, who did not get along and who did not even speak to each other because one considered the other a Trotskyite.

The possibility of opposition to Pan-Africanism does exist, as other speakers here before me have pointed out. The battle formation to counter such action, to direct the new African society, would, in my opinion be the following: first, decolonization of social values; next, self-examination leading to the suppression of certain customs and social factors in present-day African society, and, on the other hand, the invention of new social forms better adapted to our situation in the twentieth century—thus arriving at the progressive formation of a new Africa, sociologically and culturally speaking.

To be sure, a civilization is not a museum; it is a living organism—like a tree, which harbors positive and negative elements, young shoots and dead branches, blossoms and fruit. It is the role of the political and cultural leaders to make this new tree of African culture, of African personality, grow straight, by pruning the deadwood and the new shoots also. To begin with, one could start with the decolonization of social values, and specifically and above all the education of the masses. In the African tradition, education is not something apart from society but is intimately connected to the people. You are aware that in traditional Africa, different age groups acceded progressively to civic responsibilities, passing successively through the initiation stages, which were generally quite long. For instance, in Guerdé, the initiation stages for men generally lasted up to seven years—seven years of separation, during which the youths underwent very vigorous exercises, civic training and formation, and moral instruction—true education in the etymological sense of the word, that is, in the passing from an inferior state to a superior one. This education was aimed at making them into men completely a part of the city. Such education is not a superstructure; it is not an epiphenomenon in the social weave; it is, on the contrary, minutely integrated into the social body. There is thus in it the functional character of education to which our friend, Fofana, the Education Minister of Mali, has referred and which seems to us quite valid: the university, within the cadre of the traditional African society, cannot be an alien body in regard to the society, the state, or the government.

The same observation, in my opinion, could be made with regard to African art. It has often been said that African art has never been "art for art's sake." It was, for the most part, functional art—an art that was part of the principal acts and works of a society that had as its aim and its objective the augmentation of the vitality and the potential strength of the social body. It has, for example, been stated that African art is often utilitarian. It may serve as a weapon; and it can always serve as a weight, as can be seen in the art of Benin (Dahomey) on the Ivory Coast. There are small-scale weights that are fashioned according to a lost technique, and which are both useful and esthetically pleasing. It is thus necessary to restore African art to its traditional significance.

There is also another means—the transformation of society on an economic basis. You are aware that there is a process of classification in present-day Africa. In certain wealthy countries, especially those rich in export commodities, such as the Ivory Coast, a class system is obviously developing. This problem of the existence of classes in the traditional African society has long been debated, and I believe it is a basic problem, for on its solution depends to some extent the ideological choice that must be made. Is there segregation of classes in traditional African society? I personally believe not. As I have already mentioned, there was no class that exploited another through the accumulation of capital under a capitalistic system of economy; it might be said that there were social categories. There were not, in my opinion, social classes, and I believe this is the opinion expressed on many occasions by President Sékou Touré. It is also the opinion of a good many other African leaders, who believe that Africa reaps from this historical good fortune the benefits of a very rapid evolution, allowing us to become the masters of our destiny at a time when social classification has not yet crystalized and when, in spite of acceleration of the process in regions such as the Ivory Coast, we can still apply the brakes to this classification and avert in Africa the tragic experiences of the class struggle as it existed in Western societies. There are also developing, besides these classes based on economics, certain classes based on politics. Certain governments in power profit from the national revenue or the national budget to such an extent that they are little by little cutting themselves off from the masses through their special comforts, way of life, and income, and are becoming a sort of class. In certain countries of French West Africa, for instance, 120 people, who constitute only 1/30,000 of the population, are benefiting from 1/20 of the national budget.

The role of money and the problem of a fundamental economic choice should also be noted here. It is the problem of socialism. It is obvious that the choice of socialism is almost naturally and inevitably the end of African evolution. But, in my opinion, it is not the socialism elaborated by Marx on the basis of an analysis of a society fundamentally different from the traditional African society; for the society that Marx had before his eyes in nineteenth-century England was a class society. I think it would be a basic methodological error to transpose Marxism to Africa as the general philosophy of society. It would be an error of method because, as has been often said, if Marx were to reappear now he would probably not be a Marxist. So, it would be a basic error of method and also an error of principle. Some say that scientific Marxist socialism is valid as such everywhere and at all times. In my opinion, it is not sufficient to transplant socialism into the tropical latitudes of Abidjan, Conakry, or Dakar in order to have African socialism in Africa. African socialism must not be distinguishable only by the climate and the temperature of Africa. This socialism, if it is to be truly African, must be based on more solid foundations. If we purely and simply transplanted scientific socialism, it would constitute a new spiritual colonization, which, moreover, would not be justified by effectiveness. To be sure, there is a positive contribution in Marxism; no one can deny that Marxism, as a method of analysis of social factors, as an analysis of social dynamism, as a method of social and political action and organization as well, has contributed new things from which we can and should profit. But, in my opinion, it would be a lack of intellectual integrity to pretend, as Léopold Sedar Senghor did, that atheism is not essential to Marxism. It is apparent that atheism, the most fundamental materialism, is one of the essential characteristics of Marxism. One cannot declare oneself a Marxist and a spiritualist at the same time, taking away from Marx everything that concerns social analysis pure and simple. I believe that the person who would go that far could not be a true Marxist.

The best approach, in my opinion, would be to begin from the concrete socioeconomic structures of Africa itself. It is obvious that 80–90 per cent of Africans are peasants who still live and work under the system of collective property. Thus, we see that African society presents an embryo, a form, perhaps primitive, of socialism. In this society, the revolutionary class is not the working class, for the good reason that it hardly exists in terms of numbers; it is very small, which does not mean that in the process of African emancipation the organized unions were not among the better elements, the better tools, and the better instruments of the political liberation. But as for the question of independence and the organization of the social revolution, it is obvious that the class upon which the transformation must be worked is the peasantry. The African peasant enjoys extraordinary enthusiasm for work, contrary to colonial depictions. You all know the role of the Negro in toil through the course of world history. One might almost say that the Negro has been the proletarian among nations. He was used for the accumulation of capital, not only here in America by the transportation of many tens of millions of the best Africans to American soil, but also in Europe, where the work of the Negro race made possible the amassing of capital and the industrial revolution, of which we are now seeing and admiring the effects. The Europeans, coming to Africa, pretended to be struck by the so-called laziness of Africans, and they suggested forced labor as the cure for this disease. In short, we must stress the role of the state in recapturing the traditional coöperative forms of labor, in modernizing them, by adding new elements—for example, use of the concept of planned production, preliminary studies, and so forth. It is a question of stopping the evolution toward a capitalistic society, for individualism and the systematic search for profit are not in the African tradition either.

There is another question it would be interesting to debate—chieftaincy. In any event, as far as the countries of French West Africa are concerned, chieftaincy seems to have terminated its role and should not be considered from a formalist point of view, but rather from a functional one. The chiefs who are useful as individuals must be rehabilitated—the institution itself being impossible to integrate into the new society. Besides, the sinister role often played by the chiefs during the colonial period must also be underlined. From the political standpoint, let us emphasize the role of the party as the transcendental structure; the old role of the council of elders, that is, the dream of the integration of all the living forces of the country, in order to realize a common program and common ideals. The question of the unity of the party should be resolved in that direction. The unity of the party ought not to be a system but should have a value of method, of utilization during a given phase, and thus a circumstantial value, in order that the centrifugal forces, which are numerous in a new country, may be restrained and braked, thanks to the existence of this powerful nerve center, which serves as a catalyst for all the values of integration. Thus, it is a question of breaking down tribalism, not as such, but as the political basis for possible parceling. The tribe as such can be the center of an artistic blossoming, for political unification does not mean the complete destruction of the tribe in its artistic, folkloric, esthetic, and cultural manifestations. For instance, in the long run, the French Revolution and the political and administrative integration brought about by Napoleon did not hinder an esthetic, folkloric, and artistic blooming in France, in Britain, and in the Netherlands. The same in Soviet Russia. But there is obviously a danger of institutionalization on the part of a single party. This danger is not fatal, as has had to be stressed; even in the political history of the United States there was a phase when the regime of the single party was in power for a long period.

The principal agents of this sociological revolution are, above all, the young, for the old are often incapable of incorporating new elements. Speak to an old polygamist and tell him to send away his other wives. He won't understand you; and he would be right to tell you that you are a bit late. There is in that an important factor; the disappearance, each day, each week, each month, of the old. There are many old people to whom, in the African tradition, we owe every respect and to whom we should address ourselves to learn the most about African tradition; but this does not alter the fact that the numerical decline of these old people renders it impossible for them to be leaders in the sociological transformation. What is tragic is that the young are often more impressed by the new than by the old traditions. For example, they are more sensitive to the cha-cha-cha than to normal African tradition. This is a great problem for sociological evolution. Other highly important agents of society are women. Women will be, I believe, among the best representatives of the sociological and cultural renewal. Why? Because they are very sensitive. This sensitivity allowed them to be mobilized during the struggle for political freedom. You know the role played by women's associations in Ghana, in Guinea, and so on. This sensitivity is also an important element as concerns attachment to the past. A man can more easily throw off the past than can a woman. Consequently, the role of women will be fundamental. Concretely speaking, this has already been translated, in French Africa, for instance, into practical innovations; in clothing styles, there have been inventions that have captured both the African and the Western style. Finally, the general philosophy of all this, as I have said, will not, in my opinion, be Marxism, except for certain aspects that I have already mentioned. Nor will it be capitalistic individualism, which is even less in the African tradition; the best approach will be to constitute a general philosophy of African society—personalism.

There is in Africa a particular conception of the human being as a member of a community with all its rights and privileges—remember the unlimited mutual solidarity of which I spoke—but also with very strict duties extending even to the sacrifice of one's life. For example, many youths have died in the initiation ceremonies of which I spoke. But the tribal framework of the personalism, which is the foundation of traditional patriotism, is too narrow; the frame will break. We must transcend this traditional framework of the microcommunities of the tribe to reach a higher level; hence, the utility of Pan-Africanism as a material basis for an economic substratum sufficiently strong to substantiate and sustain the new culture. But I must stress here a very great technical weakness: Africa could become a cultural disaster and microstates could only damage the formation of a new African personality. So, there is a foundation to this personalism; there is in Africa a common history through a common experience of oppression, particularly in the colonial period. And here, as a professor of history, I could not but stress the role of history in the edification of this conscience and this personalism. History, as it has been said, is the memory of nations, and one cannot live with another's memory or another's history. Consequently, we must rehabilitate our own history.

There are also common customs and attitudes—a common conception of the world. While the West adopts a position of separation from nature, a position of logical and technical analysis of nature in order to dominate her, the African has rather an attitude of participation in nature and thus an attitude of participation in the whole social body. Dancing, for instance, is merely a technique of participation; there has thus developed in Africa an extraordinary blossoming of social relations. Africa tends rather more toward social relations than toward the exploitation of the world. When one travels in Europe or in America, one notices the presence of human intelligence; everywhere the landscape has been transformed and humanized; in this there is the expression of universal civilization, to the extent that man is called to dominate and organize nature. But one of the other important aspects of human civilization, in my opinion, is the organization of social relations, interpersonal and international rapport. And it seems to me that, in this domain, Africans are capable of making a contribution that no one else can make. The greatest asset to be saved, in my opinion, is the functionalism of African personalism. It is a great economic asset, which can, for example, be translated through human investment; it is a great political asset, consisting of a readiness to share the joys and sorrows of the entire world, to accept others, be they of the same race or not, be they of the same tribe or not. And, this, in my opinion, would be a great contribution to a world where aggression, still far from being eliminated, has become incalculably more dangerous owing to the technical means of destruction.

To conclude, I would say that negritude has been sufficiently sung and celebrated in story; it is time for a transformation—not for a new or so-called new, culture, consisting of a cloudy veneer over merchandise coming from the West or from the socialist countries. This new culture must stem from an African basis; it must resemble the great African trees, whose heads are thrust up into the civilization of the Universal but whose roots, on the other hand, plunge deeply into African soil.

DISCUSSION

Question:

I am Hubert Ross, an anthropologist from Lincoln University. I don't wish to quarrel with the presentations, which I think have been most interesting and excellent and stimulating. But I would like to add a few observations. I think that the study of social thought of Africa, both traditional and contemporary, is still in its infancy, and that most commentators still have to refer to a relatively limited number of source materials, such as those found in the Daryll Forde studies, and so forth. Now, these analyses may be essentially correct, but they will not be quite acceptable as definitive for cross-cultural generalization until there has been accumulation of more sample studies and sufficient replication of the original studies. I would suspect that the Africans themselves, as Mr. Ki-Zerbo has suggested, will have to do most of this work, because of the language barriers and the difficulties in the interpretation of symbolism. It occurred to me that in the field, for example, of linguistics, a young scholar who was aware of the implications of the Sapir-Wolk hypothesis; who commanded knowledge, say, of one of the language stocks as developed by the analysis of Greenberg in his linguistic classification; who commanded the methodology of historical linguistics, which would make possible the reconstruction of the proto-language of that stock; and who also had control of the methodology that leads to generalizations on modes of personality— this scholar would be presented with an extremely formidable and interesting challenge.

As a teacher, I've been somewhat disappointed that most of my students from Africa tend to be so preoccupied with their current social problems that they don't seem to be interested, at least as much as I would like, in challenges of scholarship, per se.

CHAIRMAN HILL: Who would like to comment on the reasons why students coming to this country might not appear to be so involved in scholarship as Mr. Ross would like them to be? Would you care to comment on that, Dr. Ki-Zerbo?

JOSEPH KI-ZERBO: I think the question might be answered briefly. It is apparent that in the present phase, Africans are almost all mobilized for objectives that seem to them to be necessary prerequisites for the discussion and resolution of other problems. The problem for Africa at the moment is not to develop lawmakers; that is not the main problem. For one to act effectively, things must be done one at a time. We must face problems in the order in which they have arisen historically. Now, many of us who would be interested in studies of a purely scientific nature—not only in the field of linguistics, but also in many other fields; history, philosophy, and so on—are prevented from shutting ourselves up in a museum or a library to study, because there are more urgent tasks requiring our attention. I believe this is the explanation—perhaps a simple one, but one that seems to us valid—for the present kind of indifference, which is not, I might say, a structural indifference but a conjunctural one.

CHAIRMAN: May I ask members of the panel to indicate for me actual areas of compromise, areas of conflict, areas of alignment, between Christian social thinking and indigenous social thinking?

GEORGE CARTER: I cannot answer your question; but I would like to make a comment. For it seems to me that there is a significant middle ground where compromise is possible between traditional African social thought and some, at least, of those ideals and values that have emerged within the Western tradition. An example of such compromise might develop out of the efforts of the Ghanain government to introduce some aspects of the British system of Social Services into Ghanain society. The Ghanain government relates itself to a given beneficiary as government to individual. This is, of course, the kind of relationship obtaining in the U.K. What, I wonder, would result if instead of distributing benefits to individuals, the government agency distributed through the family nexus? Such a relationship would be more harmonious with the indigenous social order. I am not suggesting that the Ghanain government should try such an experiment; I know far too little about Ghana, past or present, to be able to anticipate the kinds of problems that such an arrangement would precipitate. I am suggesting, however, that it would be profitable to consider a pattern of modernization that as far as possible is based upon indigenous traditional structures. Such consideration, I believe, would produce some important and useful compromises between African and Western social ideas.

WILLIAM T. FONTAINE: Fools enter where angels fear to tread. But I might take a look at the question. We might take Protestant Christianity—there may be, within Protestant Christianity, much more freedom apart from the clear-cut conception of human rights than we might find in the Catholic conception—and relate it, let us say, to the conception of individuality or the distinctive personality of the individual as found in the Ashanti religion, that is, the old primitive religion. Then we might say there is definitely a difference between the distinctive personality traits of the individual in the Ashanti religion. In the old Ashanti religions (the source of this is Daryll Forde's *African Worlds*) the father gives the individual his distinctive personality traits. And in these religions the individual would form in Ntoro groups, so that you have much more of an emphasis upon collectivism in primitive African social life, since the religion and the social organization are connected, than we might find in Protestant religion. Now, if it is a matter of the Catholic "world-view" and conception, there might be a difference of interpretation. We might start a dispute about that right here, as to how we are going to interpret the Catholic religion and also the Protestant religion. But I think I'll run out on the dispute by using the old army method of "I'll give you a referral." Professor Northrup, in *Biological Functions and Humanities*, analyzes the distinct views of the world held by Roman Catholicism and then the Protestant religion, and differentiates between the two.

JOSEPH KI-ZERBO: I should like to reply in part to this question, but from a historical standpoint rather than from the standpoint of anthropological and theological analysis. It is certain that Western religion, in the form of either Catholicism or Protestantism, has often appeared in Africa as the ally of colonialism. Some have even claimed that missionaries are the quartermasters of colonialism, who prepare the way for colonization. And it is certain also that, with regard to traditional African structures, missionaries have used a strong dose of incomprehension, not to say aggression, in order to implant the new religions.

In this, I believe, there is an important factor of cultural transformation, for someone who goes from traditional confession to Catholicism or Protestantism, for instance, literally goes from one world to another —which implies a radical transformation of his attitude toward society, toward his duties and his rights in society, as Mr. Enahoro has pointed out. This is a factor in the upset of African society, and missionaries have often played a quite negative role in the sense that they could have brought religion in its essentials—dogma and morality— without such brutal transformation and destruction in the sociological edifice. Catholicism, for instance, in its ceremonies and its rites, could have incorporated certain values, certain rituals, certain institutions from African religion which were not in violent contradiction with Catholic dogma and morals. It is certain that many Catholic rituals that we see now were rituals from Gaul, Armenia, Greece, or Rome at the time when they were converted to Catholicism and integrated into the theological body of the religion. I believe that certain practices— for instance, African funeral ceremonies—certain rituals that have great moral and spiritual significance, could be integrated into Catholicism without that religion being destroyed. But more and more, missionaries have seen the evolution that is taking place and have tried to adapt themselves, not through dogma or morals, but through exterior forms, by adopting, for example, rituals and ceremonial dances, and integrating them into the general context of the religions imported into Africa. In this sense, we could say that religion now is following the general pattern of trying to understand Africa and to assimilate certain European values into the African context.

ANTHONY ENAHORO: Of course, it is a very broad question, but I think one can at least indicate certain areas of conflict between Christian and indigenous social thought. I can think here of three instances.

One involves moral standards, particularly in reference to the place of women in society, and marriage, adultery, etc. Concerning the concept of adultery, it would appear that in certain respects Christianity allows for the existence of the "uncatered-for woman," if I may put it that way, or the woman who is uncatered for; at the same time Christianity tries to apply sanctions, in certain respects, if one tries to cater for women. On the other hand, in the indigenous system there is no such being as the "uncatered-for woman"; therefore, the concept of adultery is completely different, and this difference runs through the whole field of moral standards.

Second, I think you will find in indigenous African thinking that the Hereafter is a final place of rest after man has returned to the world to expiate his misdeeds in past life. It is said in parts of Africa that man returns to earth several times—in fact, according to some tribes, fourteen times—until he has expiated his misdeeds through these various comings and goings. However, Christianity holds that we are here once, and that we then go somewhere to be either rewarded or punished for our present life. I think, generally speaking, that because of this new Christian concept it may be said that people are less prone to take liberties than they were in the past, when they thought that there was always the second or fourth time when one could make up for one's misdeeds and have that final opportunity of becoming clean before going up to heaven.

Third, I think there is also the question of man's approach to God. It appears to me that Christianity believes that the one God, the Great Being, plays a more direct part in ordering our lives than is thought in an indigenous society. We believe, in the indigenous society, that there are various beings, spirits, and so forth, between us and God, and that God is not really concerned from day to day with what happens here on earth.

I think that perhaps these are some areas of conflict.

SPEAKER FROM THE FLOOR: Professor Fontaine, in view of Dr. Franklin E. Frazier's observations in his *Black Bourgeoisie* that the American Negro suffers from a sense of "nothingness," I wonder if you would comment for a moment upon the prevailing spirit of "Africanism," which I think we will all agree has any effect but one of "nothingness." I wonder if the American Negro can be caught up in this spirit that prevails now in Africa, and even here in this conference. It is very obvious that the Africans feel worthy, and that they do not suffer from a sense of "nothingness." Would you comment upon this, please, as it affects the American Negro? Will it have an effect upon the American Negro?

WILLIAM T. FONTAINE: There is not much comment I can make. I might say, to begin with, that I do not agree with Dr. Frazier. For example, you might raise a question of this sort: "Is Dr. Frazier an American Negro? And does he suffer from a want of 'nothing'?" What I mean is that there are many other American Negroes. Would you say, for example, that those youngsters who are so nobly engaging in the "sit-down strikes" are motivated by a "want for nothing"? Would you say that the noble white youth who are collaborating with them and doing the same thing are also motivated by a "want for nothing"? Would you say that the Negroes who are attending this conference, for example, are motivated by a "want for nothing"? It is very easy to say, with Schopenhauer and some others: "There is a hungry will to live that preys upon itself, and everything is vanity!" But even a pessimist like Schopenhauer seeks a way out to stabilize artistic types, and I suspect that Dr. Frazier himself has his own sort of "virile escapism." So it seems to me that within the *bourgeoisie noire* of America we are motivated and have been motivated by a will to equality and freedom. I think this could be traced all the way from Booker T. Washington (my good friend, J. Saunders Redding, notwithstanding). It is possible to trace in Negro literature something like Manheim's dominant wish to equality and freedom. And I suspect that Dr. Frazier, himself a member of the *bourgeoisie noire*, is motivated in the same way.

SPEAKER FROM THE FLOOR: I would like to direct this question to Dr. Joseph Ki-Zerbo. We have been listening much, and we find that there is a division here. First, we hear of the colonial culture: that is, the colonial bosses bring a certain culture to Africa; then a line is drawn, and we hear that there is an African culture, all of its own, which may break away from this colonial "something." Dr. Ki-Zerbo said: "We cannot live with the memories of others. We must live our own memories!" In the lectures on negritude we might find out what these memories are. But could you give us a little idea as to whether this "memory" you are talking about, this culture that was once in Africa, is strong enough to tie entire Africa together? (By entire Africa, of course, I mean *black* Africa.) Is there not a certain amount of cultural division between French Africa, the former German Africa, British Africa, and Portuguese Africa? What is that "something" that is going to tie Africa together?

JOSEPH KI-ZERBO: I think this question poses the problem of the cultural or emotional base of Pan-Africanism. I have said that the common history—the common experience lived by Africans, whatever the colonial region where the hazards of the partition of Africa had thrown them—this common experience can serve as a base. I do not say that now, in 1960, it is possible to make all Africans of a French or English cultural influence aware of this necessity. I pose this as a necessity and I say that this can serve as a means of integrating and unifying, to give an emotional or psychological base to the national conscience. We have only to see how, for example, in Guinea tribalism was very often surpassed by the development of this idea of a common history. There developed the sense of a single people who had certain common customs, certain common attitudes toward life, and who, in any case, had followed the same course during several centuries.

I think that this is the only way to surpass tribalism. The microscopic history or, if you wish, the micropolitical history of precolonial Africa could otherwise lead to dissension because, before colonialism, there were tribal wars. Thus, we ought to refer to that which unites us, and not to the small local antagonisms that could obstruct African unification.

And I shall stress that one must not, when speaking of Africa, schematize things and present them in a bad light by saying "Africa of English culture" and "Africa of French culture." How many Africans are there in French West Africa who have a French culture? It is a negligible minority. And likewise, from the English side, you know the small degree of literacy in English. Consequently, one must not give a false idea of Africa by referring to French Africa or to English Africa. From 60 to 80 per cent of the people benefit only from an African culture. Moreover, these Africans are often situated from one end of the colonial horizon to the other. For example, to the north of Ghana, you have the Mossi, the Lobis, the Gabarils, the Jiliters, who are as at home in the French as in the English language. You cannot tell them that because of a parallel selected by a round table of English and French colonists, they are therefore divided. They enjoy a unity of culture. The same is true of the Sanouffas, who are divided among the present republic of the Ivory Coast, the Upper Volta, and the Sudan. I believe you would get a false idea of Africa by speaking of Africa of an English or a French culture. It is up to us, however, to profit from the factual situation that the Europeans have left us. Certain elements of unification such as the French and English languages can serve as a vehicle and an instrument for unification, but they are the official languages only; they are not the national languages. Our national languages are those which are still spoken by eighty to ninety per cent of the Africans, and which constitute the excellent bases of the national culture.

VII   ART

THE AMERICAN NEGRO ARTIST
LOOKS AT AFRICA

JAMES A. PORTER

Art Department, Howard University

THE COURSE OF ART throughout the Western hemisphere until our century has been marked by the endless struggle of the artists for understanding, patronage, and independence. To the tyro in the affairs of art this struggle may seem to have been curiously formless or lacking in consistency in its successive organizational aims and drives; to the sophisticated, it may seem to have been burdened with a provinciality of artistic pretense at variance with those principles of liberty that first inspired the American colonists. The briefest but by no means most adequate explanation of such disparity between the spiritual and material aspects of American culture is probably to be found in the rapid, gangling, and irregular growth of the young nations of this hemisphere, which only now, in this century, are entering upon a period of cultural maturity which promises to effect a working balance of means and values. Understanding this, however, we cannot but note further that change of this type has liberated both American art and the gifted Negro from bondage to religious or folk stereotypes, allowing the free creative energies of both white and black America to turn to tasks of a more constructive as well as more altruistic order.

It goes without saying that one could not read the history of art in this or any other country of the West through the historical experience of the Negro alone without running the risk of grave distortions of fact or perspective. Nevertheless, one finds that the course of art among the American Negro people, until recent decades of this century, has been understandably similar to artistic progress among the Caucasic or Latin majorities. Similar, too, have been the controls—even stringent or binding—and the promotional stimuli—both vigorous and callous—that were applied to the profession of art until the reformatory periods of our own century brought significant change.

In the course of time, tough experiences have developed in the Negro artist both a brittle tenaciousness of spirit and a mellow warmth of temperament. He has experienced or known only grudging acceptance by the white public until recent years, while his own people have not appreciated the importance of seeking him out for patronage and encouragement. He has survived in spite of public, or official, or critical indifference. Still, as one who has studied the Negro artist and his production both long and earnestly, I can testify that it is sweetness of temper and optimism of faith instead of the expected bitter reaction of rejection or disappointment that dominate his expression today. Something in his experience has induced—as I have said—an altruism of feeling, not to say character. I should like to express the hope that this is a healthful and promising condition, rather than one of decline. However the case may be, there is little doubt that experience has predisposed him to sympathy for the problems of other artists, as well as to an active interest in the march of artistic events both here and abroad.

Without sanction of popular statistics behind me, I venture to say that there are signs as well that the American Negro people are awakening to a sense of responsibility toward the work and progress of the world and its new integrations of communities and powers. Certainly, it is within this context that the Negro artist can be said to be riding upon a new wave of sympathetic kinship with progressive artistic and intellectual groups of Europe, Asia, and Africa.

Therefore, it is by no means a digression to call your attention to the fact that this was not true of the Negro artist of the nineteenth century, however gifted. In arriving at his present position in contemporary life, the Negro artist has passed through four stages of development. In the nineteenth century, when hardly more than artisan, he was seldom responsive to the implications of social, moral, and cultural obligation in the role of the artist; but, in the later years of that century and during the first twenty years of the present, he came to recognize and consciously cultivate advantages issuing from a balanced pursuit of art and education together. Still later, in the 1920's, when the New Negro Movement emerged and in the following years of the New Deal, the Negro artist found himself upon the highroad to maturity and artistic enterprise which federal planning assisted him to follow —at least individually—even to the higher altitudes of regional and national expression. I have already accounted for his viewpoint and role today, except to say that while he is still not free, he has become more alive than ever before to the international currents of art and culture which are bound to have their effect upon America and Africa alike.

In appraising his own position, the American Negro artist has taken note of his cultural involvement with many other sources of tradition and inspiration, but most especially those of Africa. It is to African tradition—even of the most ancient vintage—that he owes the deepest obligation, if not the most venerable attachments. This fact has been certified most strikingly, of course, with reference to the origin and development of American Negro music, the dance, and even certain literary forms. Through the most assiduously attentive research, the persistence of African traditions has finally been revealed in the content and form of much American Negro painting and sculpture. Many an apostrophe to olden Egypt, as well as to modern Africa, can be found in the writings—especially the poetry—of Negroes; and many a pictorial or plastic allusion has been devised by such artists as Meta Warrick Fuller, Aaron Douglas, and Sargent Johnson.

Yet, it was not the American Negro artist—as we all very well know —who first discerned the high artistic values of African Negro art through having seen it in the museums (although Negro missionaries in Africa, before 1900, sometimes showed their appreciation for African art by making collections of it). Rather, it was through the eyes of white Europeans that we first learned to look at it admiringly and finally to study it to the point of saturation. I, for one, am not ashamed of knowledge thus acquired; but must aver that long ago, at the knees of my father, I learned about the black peoples of Africa, and in that way, acquired an abiding interest in them as a people and as representatives of a complex and richly endowed civilization.

In view of the healthy effect of African Negro art on European art and other breeding centers of modern art, perhaps it may not seem too unreasonable to suppose that modern Western art will, in turn, exert some salutary influence on African art. Whatever happens, we cannot shield the African artist from the experiences of exciting discovery. We can but hope that he will take whatever he finds and wants, and will use it, not imitatively but creatively, in the best interest of Africa.

As we look toward Africa, we see many new aspects of the arts emerging and many new idioms of form or expression being shaped and promulgated. Appraisal and criticism can scarcely keep pace with the rapid rise and expansion of this incipient renaissance; while educational and institutional programs falter and despair of being able to harness these eruptive energies through satisfactory channels. With many misgivings we in America observe the painful struggle for survival of African art of the collective type, while its modern counterpart—marked for good or ill by brash experimentation or naïve regionalism —flourishes in the light of rising nationalism. African artists are responsive to the winds of taste but they have not yet flung off the steadying hand of tradition.

But in many formerly fertile oases of creative art in Africa, the less favorable winds of change have brought the withering effects of colonialism or, as now, materialism. Besides this, the blight of commercialism—a by-product of reckless industrialization from which African artists must at all costs be saved—is competing with and gradually finishing off the old arts and handicrafts.

So great and virile an artistic tradition as that of Africa must not be allowed to die; for it would be as if the soul of a people had died. It is not the duty only of the American Negro, but that of the whole civilized world, to give advice as well as practical help toward the recovery or revival and, ultimately, the assured continuity of the living traditions of Africa.

An incalculable amount of printer's ink has been spilled to detail the wonderful blessings bestowed by African art on modern art and culture. However, the American Negro knows what he has inherited through the parentage of the African arts.

The question now is what further can be learned from the arts and the artists of Africa? Can this continent in transition reveal further mysteries or provide other sensations equally as vital and challenging as those already advanced? What, indeed, can she learn from us through close contact, or through direct exchange of visits, studies, and exhibits? What more can we do than we are now doing to bring about a more fruitful relationship between her artists and intellectuals and our own? To these questions, this round table of artists must and will address itself. This is the purpose of this meeting: to deal with these questions. Therefore, I now turn to our several panelists and invite them to speak freely, though not too long, on these questions that are so fraught with meaning and so imperative for us all.

DISCUSSION

Professor Porter's remarks keynoted a discussion on the meaning of Africa and African art for the American Negro artist. Two African and several American Negro artists participated. Upon the unrestricted terrain over which the discussion was projected, the remarks of the artists ranged far and wide, contradicted each other, and served at times to confuse rather than clarify the subject matter—which is, of course, the modern artist's license. Most of the participants, being artists and not art critics, produced no sophisticated aesthetic statements on the African artistic experience; but they did express with honesty and insight the unfolding of their aesthetic awarenesses, particularly as concerns the impact of African art.

The American artists indicated, among other things, how they had learned to appreciate African art for its great contributions to the formal aspects of modern Western art, as revealed in the work of Braque, Picasso, Modigliani, and others. Selma Burke (sculptress), for example, indicated that she had copied from African antiques when she was only six years old; many years later while attending art school she was so unconscious of an "African influence" in her work that she was surprised when it was pointed out to her.

The panelists stressed, however, that the influence of African art ranges far beyond the purely formal. Some said their appreciation of it was especially enhanced because they saw themselves in it; African sculpture, the magnificent Benin bronzes, and so forth, had taught them to find beauty in things African, in things black. In a society poisoned by a slanderous Hollywood, by "Steppin' Fetchit," by huge, humorous and feeble-minded Negro maids, the magnificence and beauty of the bronzes of Ife, of the Bambara masks, has come as a welcome antidote. Ernest Crichlow (painter) of New York City spoke for many of the American panelists when he said: "I have come to my concern and interest in Africa by searching and trying to understand myself." (The Negro's search for himself was the point of Crichlow's story about his small son's resistance to the father's desire to expunge television's "Amos 'n' Andy" from the living room; for the small boy, there on the screen appeared someone who looked like himself.)

Margaret Burroughs (painter) of Chicago saw a parallel to her own feelings in the reactions of some of her American Negro pupils to African sculpture: "At first they looked at it and laughed, as if it were just a curiosity. But after a while it began to grow on them, and the children began to see something in it that was akin to them, and was positive. It began to have an effect upon their own image of themselves as being beautiful, as being black, and having the so-called Negro characteristics. They saw that it is beautiful to be black, to have a broad nose, to have full lips, to have beautiful oval eyes, to have a rich dark color."

John Biggers (painter), head of the art department at Texas Southern University, took a different tack in exploring beyond the formal values. He had learned, he said, to appreciate the formal aspects of African art, but it was only when he arrived in Africa a few years ago that the real sense of Africa and her art came upon him. In a moving statement, which communicated to his audience the warmth and exuberance of which he spoke, he told of the impact of Africa upon him when he first arrived there. He found, in contrast to what he termed the "mournful grandeur" in Rivera, Orozco, and the other great painters of Mexico, a "spontaneous and exuberant grandeur" in Africa and African art. (Ben Enwonwu, the Nigerian sculptor and painter, had been struck the day before by Biggers' African paintings which hung in AMSAC's art exhibit for the conference. He expressed appreciation for the compelling manner in which these paintings, although tending in some instances toward the pictorial, had so brilliantly captured the virility and the intensity characteristic of the African, particularly the West Africa, scene.) Biggers said he placed the formal aspects of African art second to its role in the total drama of African life. He noted its similarity in this respect to early Christian art, the representative and symbolic significance of the art of the church. Africa and African art had, for him, the meaning of a return to his artistic and cultural roots.

Hughie Lee-Smith (painter) of New York also stressed the significance of African art in its full social and cultural context. He noted that the social function of African art has many implications for both American art in general ("in view of the growing deterioration of official American art to the level of simple decoration or visual entertainment") and Negro artists in particular. Lee-Smith expressed the hope that the high social esteem and relative economic security enjoyed by the African artist would be a source of inspiration to the American Negro artist, who presently "is in a position of being at once a part of, and apart from, his society." Further, he envisioned an increased social significance for African art of the future: "At a time when we in the West hear predictions from some quarters that art will soon cease to exist, we greet the emergence of the new African nations as the saviors and extenders of the best that has come out of Western culture. The merging of the best of Africa with the best of the West will, we hope, give rise to a new and vigorous life-oriented art. Perhaps a new African art will take on, among other things, some of the exuberance and sense of color of the American Negro. It is also reasonable to expect the continuation of the tradition of social art which will reflect the social and moral aspirations of these new nations. Above all, I expect this new art of Africa to be a fresh reaffirmation of the human will to survive, and an inspiration to humanists throughout the world."

In dealing with this broad realm of social and cultural goals, some panelists made it evident that the "meaning" of Africa for American Negro artists is not necessarily confined to African art. Elton C. Fax (illustrator) of New York expressed the belief that African art, per se, contains certain mysteries that Americans of African ancestry cannot penetrate. "But there is one thing," he said, "that is no mystery to me": "I, as an American Negro, find it completely impossible to be withdrawn and objective in viewing any people, anywhere, in the world, who are faced with a special struggle to be full men." He could summarize his own regard for Africa in the greeting given to him by total strangers in Nigeria: "Welcome, brother, it's good to have you here."

The "mystery" of African art mentioned by Fax was the object of considerable discussion by other panelists. Eugene Grigsby (painter, art teacher), who taught art in the U.S. Pavilion at the Brussels Exposition in 1959, challenged the oft-repeated opinion that African art is purely functional; there is a definite aesthetic sense in much of African art, even exclusively so, he insisted, in areas where there is no conceivable functional purpose to be served. And Grigsby felt that there is an inexplicable something, "something of the soul" of African art, that the non-African artist cannot hope to comprehend. "The way of producing involves not only the technique, but that which is behind it—much of which we don't know and which I feel we can never know, because we can never project ourselves into the kind of society in which these people live and in which the artists work. We can never really get the understanding and feeling of what it meant to be an artist working in a particular African community."

Ben Enwonwu, art advisor to the Nigerian government, agreed: in African art there is a mystery, and this mystery resists both the aesthetic and the anthropological analyses of the West. In fact, he implied, the analytical approach merely compounds the mystery.[1] "I have experienced this mystery because I was born into it . . . because it is part of the pattern of life in Africa. It is inexplicable, in a way, but at the same time it is part of the fabric of society and tradition."

In a similar vein, Selvy Mvusi (painter) of South Africa cautioned against attempts at simple transpositions of African art into non-African contexts. Yet if the full measure of African art is not to be taken through mere copying of form, and if the real significance of African art is indeed an inpenetrable mystery to observers outside the African social and cultural fabric, what can the American Negro gain from the African art experience? Mvusi's answer: Inspiration. "If there is just one contribution that the African artist today is lucky to make, it is perhaps the assertion of an intersubjectivity, a new sense of worth of a human being—not because the artist has a particular artistic awareness in this regard, but because he is in a context where he must give this, because his social environment and his role in history now call on him to give expression to this. I might therefore say that the artist in Africa, as I see him, is an artist of the *now* before he is an artist of history. He is an artist mixed up with all the political, economic, and social turmoil of our time. And this is what he expresses, whether he likes it or not. You are what you know."

The moderator, Professor Porter, finally questioned whether, whatever the merits or the impact of the African idiom, it can be continued; whether the African tradition can be maintained and renewed in contemporary expression, either in Africa or in the United States, by the Negro artist. There was, of course, no definite answer to the question; several participants expressed optimistic views, referring to a snythesis of the old with the new influences. In this regard, the view of Jan-heinz Jahn, the German literary critic, is interesting: a cultural renais-

---

[1] See also Enwonwu's comments in the next section.

sance occurs not in the same medium of the ancients, for that would permit little more than a slavish copying, but rather in another art form in which the idiom may serve simply as an inspiration for the unrestricted play of the creative imagination. Praxiteles inspires the Sistine Ceiling, not "David."

The question of what precisely constitutes the African idiom which has had such an impact in modern Western art was left to the panel on African culture for more detailed consideration.

VIII AFRICAN CULTURE AND NEGRITUDE

THE PACKED AUDITORIUM in Houston Hall reflected the interest with which the last panel was awaited. The discussions centered upon the most provocative subject of the conference. Much has been written and more has been said regarding negritude. It has been assailed as racism; it has been patronized as an African version of the French chief of state, in his cloudier moments, invoking *nos ancêtres Gaulois;* it has been dismissed as "signifying"—signifying nothing. In the heat of the controversy, the main theme of the conference, Pan-Africanism, threatened to pass unremarked; the chairman, Mercer Cook, found it necessary to ask, pointedly, that someone discuss the relationship of negritude and Pan-Africanism. The manner in which the discussion developed reveals that, as far as Negroes from the United States and South Africa are concerned, negritude, because of its racial overtones, is perhaps as divisive as otherwise. For the other Africans, however, including the two Nigerians who spoke on the subject, negritude is an object of enthusiasm. Ezekiel Mphahlele of South Africa was in dissent. After an eloquent statement of the agonizing experience of the black writer in South Africa, he carried the implication of the concept of negritude to what he felt is its absurd conclusion. Sterling Brown was, among his colleagues, perhaps the most sensitive to the entire development of renewed African interest and its implication for the American Negro artist; but he also expressed reservations about the concept of negritude.

The two prepared papers constitute a dialogue in emphasis, though one is principally concerned with art, the other with literature. Probably none of the papers delivered during the conference received so sustained an ovation as that of J. Newton Hill of the art department at Lincoln University. In his characteristically apt phrasing, Hill weaves the pattern of the African idiom. Through all of African sculpture, he observes, runs a basic generic quality, "an escape from naturalism." He defines related aspects of this idiom: a preoccupation with a spirit world; a "primitive abstractionism"; an emphasis, as with Henry Moore, on negative light areas rather than on positive mass (The African, in a reversal of the Western approach, Hill maintains, carves out space or "apertures" rather than mass.); and, lastly, a rhythmic order. These tendencies and their synthesis in the skill of the American carver have produced, says Hill, one of the "finest sculptured expressions of the unconscious."

He warns the contemporary artist, however, against undue emphasis upon this idiom and upon negritude, and states that his goal should be, rather, excellence in producing a universal art.

Allen assays the various elements that have been ascribed to negritude, and traces the reaction to it among writers of differing national and cultural origins, finding the English-speaking Africans and American Negroes generally less responsive than those of French influence. He considers evidence, however, of the existence in the American Negro of characteristics—emotion, participation through intuition—delineated by Senghor as part of the prototype Negro-African personality. Contrary to some other speakers, he feels this is an epoch in which more, not less, emphasis should be placed upon African values. He believes also that a great deal of the American unresponsiveness to a concept such as negritude stems from emotional and intellectual patterns formed by the American Negro over generations of effort to gain complete integration into American life. To achieve his goal more quickly, the American Negro feels it wise to minimize, not to accent his differences. Allen observes, however, that the melting pot remains an unrealized dream, and calls attention to Oscar Handlin's suggestion that a cultural pluralism, as ideal and reality, may gradually be taking the place of the earlier myth.

The Nigerian commentators resist the attempt to analyze and define the term. Negritude for them is a synthesis of the life style of the African and, for Oruwariye, a fighting faith with which to meet the tremendous challenge of the future of newly liberated Africa. They sense a danger in the Western proclivity to analyze as part and parcel of the will to tame and to control—a danger elaborated by Senghor, to whom they both referred. Their feeling appears to be—and they are of an English formation which would not have predisposed them favorably to this "French" phenomenon—that here is a rallying force in African life, and that any analytical approach is peculiarly Western, covertly hostile, and potentially subversive. We recall again Akwei's refusal to define the "African personality."

The discussion indicates, however, that if a definition is insisted

upon, even in the face of a denial that negritude exists, it could meaningfully be said to be a literary phenomenon; it is a word, a French
word. It is a word that originated in French-African poetry and
represents or, more simply, *is* the poet's reaction to his estrangement
in the Western world. If we recall the words of Aimé Césaire, "the
poet of negritude,"

> The words surpass themselves. It is indeed toward a sky and a
> land whose height and depth cannot be troubled. It is made of
> the old geography. Yet there now emerges at a certain level an
> area curiously breathable. At the gaseous level of the solid and
> liquid organism, white and black, night and day.

we find them to be a metaphorical distillation of the remarks of
Ezekiel Mphahlele, who is strongly critical of the term. Mphahlele,
in his tour de force at the conference, brilliantly described the process
of the emergence of the black South African writer into creative
maturity, into a realization that he is "the personification of a paradox
which is a meeting point between acceptance and rejection." We find
here a striking similarity in the creative stance of these two artists.
The difficulties that Mphahlele, Hill, and others have with the term
appear to stem largely from the implications of the existence of psychic
traits or dispositions on a hereditary racial basis. There has, however,
been no such assertion by those who have been decisive in its
development. Senghor, whose theories were frequently referred to in
the panel, has explicitly stated that he makes no assumption of biologically hereditary characteristics. There is a legitimate area of meaning for the term which has no greater implication of hereditary traits
or of a mystique than, for example, the terms "democracy" or "nationalism" or "patriotism" or, more immediately, the "American profile."

We turn to other aspects that appear to inspire disagreement. First,
the term is French; it is French with a flair. A pragmatic mentality
formed by Anglo-Saxon influences is immediately alert. Second, inasmuch as a racial nomenclature is embedded in the word itself, it inevitably takes on a racial flavor and carries with it the pejorative associations of the race it designates—a circumstance that is scarcely ac-
cidental. We recognize the not unfamiliar tactic of plunging, in an
area of tension, to the heart of the sensitivity, to extract some flagrant
symbol of its essence and thus exorcise the particular unclean spirit.
The term Negro has, over the course of his Western experience, taken

on and embodied the derogatory overtones of his role in the society. Rather than avoid these associations by avoiding the word that carries them, the French-African poet picks up the very term, uttered as epithet, to throw it back in the teeth of a hostile world as defiance and, at the same time, as assertion of his fundamental dignity.

A phenomenon such as this, though it is the pulse of the private emotional world of the poet, may nonetheless have a universal significance. It is less certain that it can serve in a widespread manner, with unform effectiveness, as a rallying slogan in a multicultural struggle toward the regeneration of a people.

There is willingness enough, it appears, to accept the alternative term of the "African personality" (despite the recent assertion by a South African professor that this term is without "scientific" validity). The term negritude, with its more patent racial implications, finds, as we have seen, a mixed reception among American Negroes and evidently among some South Africans. P. O. Oruwariye of Ibadan, Nigeria, upon observing this reaction, stated that American and South African Negroes could undoubtedly be of considerable help to Africa in technical and administrative areas, but that they would be completely dispensable in the task of producing a dynamic faith. He called upon Senghor to appear at the next conference to defend his intellectual offspring, negritude.

Ben Enwonwu illustrated the sharp difference in attitude of some Africans and the evident majority of American Negroes in his flat statement comparing the white man and the Negro African: "We are different people; there is no question"—a statement with which the average educated American Negro might find himself obliged in certain respects to agree, but which he would in all likelihood never, in the same gratuitous manner, volunteer. Enwonwu denied that the Africans feel a superiority to the American Negroes; he assured the American Negroes he does not consider them inferior. (He did not assure them, however, that some of his best friends are among them.) Oruwariye explained that the evident assurance of the Africans stems from the fact that they are in full possession of their culture. The link Africa may well make with the New World, he says, is with the West Indies and Brazil, where the impact of the white populations has not been so severe in influencing the attitudes of persons of African descent.

Alioune Diop, Secretary General of the Société Africaine de Culture, and one of the founding fathers of the cultural movement that gave rise to negritude, astutely does not seek to resolve the issue in his eloquent remarks that concluded the last panel of the conference. In his characteristically statesmanlike manner he undertakes to draw together those threads of the discussion upon which agreement had been or could possibly be reached and which might serve as an integrating factor in a cultural Pan-Africanism. Each cultural area, he observes, has produced its own terminology—French-speaking Africans, negritude; those of English influence, Pan-Africanism; and both had come upon the African personality." All the terms stemmed from substantially the same impluse to achieve the common goal—the regeneration of Africa and the African people.

S. W. A.

NEGRITUDE: AGREEMENT AND DISAGREEMENT

SAMUEL W. ALLEN

Law Department, Texas Southern University

THE TREATMENT OF THIS SUBJECT is more speculative and less systematic than that indicated by the topic originally suggested by AMSAC: "Negritude, Its Origin, Nature, and Impact on African Unity and Pan-Africanism." Negritude as a phenomenon is not readily defined. It may be considered narrowly as a recent literary development, an aspect of the creative imagination of Negro African poets of French expression; or it may be considered broadly in a manner that would discover its influence in every manifestation of Negro life. As it is a relatively new phenomenon, as it is an intangible resistant to compression within a neat outline, it will probably suffice to indicate simply that my consideration of the subject will fall somewhere between the two indicated points of view.

In an article in AMSAC's volume *Africa As Seen by American Negroes,* I attempted to describe the development of the concept, finding it first denominated as such in the work of French African poets, principally Aimé Césaire of Martinique and Léopold Senghor of Senegal. The term represents in a functional sense the effort of the Negro African to recover for himself and for his race scattered throughout the Western world a normal self-pride, a confidence shattered for centuries by the advent of the colonizer and the resulting political and cultural subjection. It is his effort to recover a world in which he may have a sense of unashamed identity and an unsubordinate role. Its origin has been in the arts, and it may be termed in its original sense an aesthetic, formed by the characteristic manner, style, and traits that may be considered more markedly Negro African than white or European. The extent to which its scope has widened, however, is suggested by the statement of Alioune Diop at the Rome congress, which appears to contemplate negritude as the complete ensemble of values of African culture and the vindication of the dignity of persons of African descent.

Insofar as negritude is considered in this broad manner to include common psychic tensions, common political disabilities and aspirations in the struggle toward freedom, it may be said to serve with little disagreement as a unifying force. There are two aspects of this concept, however, in which there is less than general accord—one being the importance for Negro nationalism of the African cultural heritage, and the other, the postulation of negritude as a composite of psychic and cultural traits as characteristically Negro African. Let us consider them in turn.

The pragmatic emphasis among Negro writers formed under an English or American influence tends to be upon the political, economic, and industrial problems involved in the development of the new Africa. Nkrumah's injunction: build ye first the political kingdom, is their first and great commandment; and the others are not unlike it: mobilize as swiftly as possible the commercial and technological resources of the country; promote vigorously a program of industrialization which alone can lead to a higher material standard of living; and jettison as quickly as may be expedient the traditional customs of African life, which, backward (from this point of view) as they are, can serve only to obstruct entry into the twentieth century. The Accra conference of 1958 condemned without qualification "tribalism" as an impediment to the building of the modern state. Richard Wright, in his address to the Paris conference of 1956, referring to the shattering of the traditional and highly religious African way of life, said, with a certain irony, but sincerely, "Thank you, Mr. White Man, for freeing me from the rot of my irrational traditions and customs," and again, "Bravo for that clumsy and cruel deed." Peter Abraham, the South African poet and novelist, joined him in emphasizing the inadequacy of Africa's age-old "superstitions" to meet the demands of an industrial and scientifically oriented modern world. They are representative of a considerable body of thought in rejecting the African past to accept the cultural heritage of the West and identification with the West, qualified by an effort to select from Western civilization only those desirable aspects applicable to the African situation.

The more dominant attitude, however, toward the African cultural tradition, at least as it appears to exist among French-speaking Africans, is rather to accept it as a unique and worthy heritage, to build upon it as the source of psychic energies and of a cohesive morale for a people newly entered upon the stage of history. Alioune Diop expressed this view in his remarks to the Rome Congress, when after declaring that European values have hitherto been held to be the *only* cultural values and the yardstick for measuring all else, he urged a new orientation, stating it was for the purpose of affirming the values of African culture and to find a basis for unity in that culture that the congress had been called.

This quest for a cultural patrimony is felt to be a necessary stage in the liberation of the African people. There is not only, as Césaire, Diop, Senghor and others have emphasized, a political and economic colonialism, but worse, more deadly in its impact, is a cultural colonialism that subjugates the minds of men. Césaire remarks that an industrial West finds it curious: "they need technicians and they produce artists." However, the cultural renaissance is, he urges, the liberator of unsuspected psychic forces. Rather than thank the West for its shattering of African traditions, Césaire tells the story of the Hawaiian prince Kamehameha II, who after Cook's discovery of the islands, was converted to European ideas and in a dramatic ceremony destroyed the ancestral totems, at one stroke abolishing the indigenous religion. There shall be, Césaire affirmed, no Kamehameha II in Africa. Reciting Africa's contribution to world culture: "the art of Negro sculpture, original communal institutions, as for example, the village democracy or the age-group fraternities, family ownership, that negation of capitalism, and so many institutions marked by the spirit of solidarity, and on another plane, an original philosophy based upon respect for life and its integration in the cosmos"—reciting these contributions, Césaire refuses the clean slate proposed by Wright and others as a prerequisite to entry into the race of nations.

His, however, is not an indiscriminate embrace of Africa's past. His position in this regard is similar to that of St. Clair Drake. At the Paris conference, he urged what Drake has since (in AMSAC's edition of *Présence Africaine*) systematically set forth and denominated "pragmatic pluralism," that is, a selective retention or rejection of the varying elements in the traditional cultural pattern. It is interesting that Césaire's proposal, at least in the rhetoric of its delivery, is more democratic in cast than Drake's—the selective abandonment of nonviable aspects of the cultural ensemble he confides to the "people," to the pragmatic test of their experience in the new orientation of independence; whereas Drake would relieve the European of this task to assign it to the "African political elite" (which may or may not be simply a recognition of a present reality). His work is notable in its attempt toward a comprehensive evaluation of the various elements of the traditional African pattern, which through the instrumentality of his estimate of probable attitudes of an "educated African elite," condemns as well as approves. This appears to be a type of critical undertaking from which some African scholars have refrained, either as a matter of emphasis in a period of historic redress or on the grounds that such a critique would be a usurpation of the pragmatic role of experience. It is interesting also that Drake's extensive list can scarcely be considered to include those positive contributions of African culture described by Senghor, Cheik Anta Diop, and such earlier Africanists as Frobenius, Delafosse, and Tempels. In any event, we see the debate over the significance of the African past tending to resolve itself, in part, in a selective and progressive abandonment of its less positive elements. Negritude, as cohesive ethic, interpreted in the light of the attitudes of those among whom it originated, would insist, however, upon the African past as a cultural frame of reference while admitting a necessary abandonment of elements no longer serviceable in a transformed world.

We find further differences in our effort to establish, in Diop's terms, that ensemble of values that are essentially African. Sartre, in *Orphée Noir*, in speaking of negritude, observed that such a central concept necessarily subsumes a framework of supporting values and characteristics notable principally, he remarked, by their absence. Senghor, in the two seminal papers prepared for the Paris and Rome conferences, has emerged as the chief theoretician of this enterprise (as well as the head of one of the principal newly self-governing African nations). Let us, then, examine his position relative to the characteristics of the Negro African personality. Senghor finds that the psychic traits of the Negro African are his heightened sensibility and his strong emotional quality. He locates the origin of the psychic profile of the Negro African essentially in two sources: the milleniums of his tropical experience and, second, in the agricultural nature of his existence. In the heat and humidity of Africa's tropical zones, in his pastoral life traditionally close to the earth, constantly sensing its pulse, and in uninterrupted communion with the rhythms of its seasons, the Negro African developed an extreme sensibility, a nature almost feminine in its responsiveness to its environment and in its consequent adaptability. Senghor points out how French army officials were surprised to discover the dread Senegalese warriors, supposedly simply brutes, had practically a woman's sensitivity to change of both physical and psychological environment. From this sensibility, developed over thousands of years until finally hereditary (Senghor's is evidently the Lamarckian view of the hereditary nature of acquired characteristics), came the strong emotional quality of the Negro African temperament.

Senghor finds emotion to be at the heart of negritude; more precisely, he asserts "emotion is Negro," for which equation, he remarks, he has been criticized. Wrongly so, he says, and he insists upon it, citing Count Keyserling, who speaks of the stormy vitality and of the "great emotional warmth of black blood." It is this type of reference to racial traits transmitted presumably by blood heredity, through the racial genes, that appears thus far to have found a substantial body of Negroes within the cultural spectrum of the English language unresponsive. In the area of the creative arts where these characteristics would lend themselves more readily to inspection, we see marked differences of opinion. Senghor, in his discussion at the Paris conference developing the aesthetic profile of the Negro, cited a poem of Richard Wright as an illustration of the fact that Wright, without realizing it, wrote in a style in its imagery, its intensity, and in its rhythm characteristically Negro African. Wright himself, in an essay on American Negro poetry (in that startling volume of trenchant observation of various aspects of race, vigorously entitled White Man, Listen!), ascribes the common characteristics of this poetry, its rebelliousness, its intensity, its despair, to a common social environment of oppression, projecting a direct correlation between these characteristics and a rising or receding racism in American life. With its disappearance, those elements that seem to be characteristics of Negro poets will also disappear. G. Lamming, whose In the Castle of My Skin has been called the outstanding novel yet produced by the Caribbean, is of essentially the same view when, in discussing the "Negro Writer and His World," he states that politics is the only ground for a universal Negro sympathy. Peter Abraham, the South African poet and novelist, appears, also, to attribute any singular characteristics of the Negro's creative art to the social fact of his rejection by the West. Returning to Wright, we see that his compatriot, novelist and critic Saunders Redding finds that they are American totems which beat like a tide through the former's work.

In view of this impressive array of opinion, it is interesting to observe that what has been termed the first major, full-length study by an American critic of the novel of the American Negro finds in the work of Wright the same quality remarked by Sartre and elaborated upon by Senghor. Observes Sartre, he writes, "not objectively, in the manner of the realists, but passionately and in a manner to compromise his reader." Richard A. Bone in his critical volume *The Negro Novel in America* remarks that *Native Son* is written in a style that he is compelled to recognize as a new thing under the literary sun, a style that he can only call "visceral." He refers to the fierce narrative drive with which the novel moves and which becomes no more simply an intellectual adventure for the reader but which in its passion and intensity evokes in him a literally visceral reaction—an observation that is even more applicable to *Uncle Tom's Children,* which after a quarter of a century has remained too intense for the general American reading public.

The same stylistic intensity, though perhaps finding its chief apostle in Wright, is not unique with him. Chester Himes also comes to mind, principally in his *If He Hollers,* and also, in rarer instances, Baldwin (the graphic characterization of the father of the protagonist in *Go Tell It On the Mountain*) and Ellison (Ras in the apocalyptic scene of the night street fight in *Invisible Man*).

The rebuttal offered to this position is, of course, that stated by Wright to the effect that the intensity, the dramatic power of these writers is owing to the compressed force of their thwarted drives and their resentment against a proscriptive American society. Such an explanation appears easy and incomplete, however, when we observe through Senghor and others the same characteristics in the aesthetic impulse of the African in pre-European times.

Senghor continues the task of the elaboration of the values of negritude. He opposes the Negro African's intuitive assimilation of the perceived object by emotion, by intuition, to the European's analytical dissection and reduction of the object to serve his ends. Through the rhythmic dialectic of the word or of musical sound, or other media, the Negro African seeks not to dissect and overpower the other, but rather to accede to a state of emotional grace in which he intuitively installs himself in the other. The English writer Geoffrey Gorer, in *Africa Dances,* and the American dancer Pearl Primus, among others, have described this process in its most dramatic form in African life—in the form that has been the most pervasive in determining the idiom of an entire culture—in the dance.

Césaire's oft-quoted lines are particularly apropos:

Hail the royal Kailcedrat!
Hail those who have invented nothing!
Who have explored nothing!
Who have tamed nothing!
But they abandon themselves, possessed, to the essence of all
  things,
Ignoring surfaces, but possessed by the movement of all things,
Heedless of taming, but playing the game of the world.
Truly the elder sons of the world,
Porous to every breath of the world,
Flesh of the flesh of the world,
Throbbing with the very movement of the world! [1]

The Negro African, Césaire thus says, does not seek to master the object, to analyze, to explore, to reduce by his analytical reason and by his power; he weds himself, rather, to the rhythm of the object. As Senghor writes, he does not see the object—he feels it, going in a centrifugal movement, from the subject to the object on the waves of the other. He adds that herein is not a simple metaphor inasmuch as contemporary physics has discovered energy within matter, in wave and radiation. And Sartre has, in turn, put it succinctly: negritude is comprehension through sympathy.

In 1959 at the Rome conference, Ignazio Silone, in extending greetings in the name of the writers of Italy, expressed the thought that often a civilization, exhausted and weary, finds renewal precisely in those elements the most oppressed and condemned. Although this statement, generous as it is, is an interpretation of the significance of an African renaissance from a European viewpoint, it is particularly pertinent here when we consider the curious similarity between Senghor's hypothesis of the intuitive Negro African personality and the argument of that remarkable essay by Norman Mailer, "The White Negro." From the traditionally rejected, the outcast, the pariah in American society comes a creed, a way of life, adequate to sustain

[1] Aimé Césaire, *Cahier d'un retour au pays natal*. Gallimard, 1956.

that victim of the robot world of the squares, the "philosophic psycho-path" who refuses to choose as the scene of his healing the secure premises of the couch but prefers rather some dark heroic alley and its desperate creative deed, if he dare. He lives on the forbidden fringe of society, condemning and condemned, and it is not by hazard that Mailer's explanation of the psychopath's need for violence reads almost like a quote from *Native Son* as Bigger explains to his lawyer, Max, why he murdered. But more relevant here is Mailer's description of the Negro and the psychic qualities he brings as "cultural dowry" to his marriage with the white hipster.

Father Tempels, in his classic study *Bantu Philosophy*, has indicated how the key concept in the Negro African ontology is vital force. The value of any phenomenon, any physical thing, any act, any relationship, is measured by its influence upon the vital force of the individual. That which enhances it is good; that which diminishes it is bad. And rhythm, that hallmark of the Negro African aesthetic—"it is the archi-tecture of being, the internal dynamism which gives it form. The system of waves which it emits to the attention of others, the *pure expression of the vital force!* Rhythm, it is the vibratory shock, the force which through the senses, seizes us at the root of being." Here is a set of values that, developed in a precolonial African society, cannot conceivably be attributed to the pressures and frustrations of existence in an alien culture. It is therefore doubly interesting to ob-serve a discovery of certain of these values, these same psychic traits in some American Negroes who from their origins in time and space are considerably removed.

Mailer states that the hipster, or the hip, who turns to the Negro as forerunner and mentor in this dangerous arena, seeks, above all, *energy*. His concern is how to find it, how to acquire and conserve it. He seeks to grow nearer and nearer to his God, "that trapped, mutilated and nonetheless megalomaniacal God who is It, who is energy, life, sex, force, the Yoga's *prana*, the Reichian's orgone, Lawrence's 'blood,' Hemingway's 'good,' the Shavian life-force, 'It'; God. . . ." To which a cool cat might reply, "Crazy, man!" Mailer continues his thesis ex-plaining that the "cool cat" achieves his ends through means that are principally the maintenance of a state of movement, of motion, from whence the words in his vocabulary such as "go" and "make it" and "swing." In motion he has a chance to dispose of greater energy, to find more people with whom he can swing. "For to swing is to communicate, is to convey the rhythms of one's own being to a lover, a friend or an audience, and—equally necessary—be able to feel the rhythms of their response." [2]

Here Mailer's and Senghor's theses bear striking resemblances. We cite a concrete example by each, given to suggest the actual operation of the process. Mailer continues:

To swing with the rhythms of another is to enrich oneself—the conception of the learning process as dug by Hip is that one cannot really learn until one contains within oneself the implicit rhythm of the subject or the person. As an example, I remember once hearing a Negro friend have an intellectual discussion at a party for half an hour with a white girl who was a few years out of college. The Negro literally could not read or write, but he had an extraordinary ear and a fine sense of mimicry. So as the girl spoke, he would detect the particular formal uncertainties in her argument, and in a pleasant (if slightly Southern) English accent, he would respond to one or another facet of her doubts. When she would finish what she felt was a particularly well-articulated idea, he would smile privately and say, "Other-direction. . . . do you really believe in that?"

"Well . . . No," the girl would stammer, "now that you get down to it, there is something disgusting about it to me," and she would be off again for five more minutes.

Of course the Negro was not learning anything about the merits and demerits of the argument, but he was learning a great deal about a type of girl he had never met before, and that was what he wanted. Being unable to read or write, he could hardly be interested in ideas nearly as much as in lifemanship, and so he eschewed any attempt to obey the precision or lack of precision in the girl's language, and instead sensed her character (and the values of her social type) by swinging with the nuances of her voice.[3]

Consider another setting recounted by Senghor, in which both parties, rather than one alone, are active participants in a rhythmic

[2] Norman Mailer, "The White Negro," in his *Advertisements for Myself* (New York: Putnam, 1959), pp. 337–358.
[3] *Ibid.*

intuitive interchange, and in which the word and idea are merely the instrumentality of matter in the accession to an emotional state of grace.

"Here is a scene from daily (African) life. Two relatives—or two friends—meet. They have not seen each other for a long time. The litany of greetings begins on a banal rhythm:

> As-tu la paix?
> La paix seulement.
> Ton père a-t-il la paix?
> La paix seulement.
> Ta mère a-t-elle la paix?
> La paix seulement.
> Les gens de maison ont-ils la paix?
> La paix seulement.

And they continue asking about certain ones and others: relatives, allies, friends, fields, herds. Then they recall memories of other times. At the recollection of certain events, at the evocation of persons dear, emotion overcomes them, they embrace and fervently grip each other's hand. And they recommence the greetings, but this time on a more sharply accented rhythm, on the rhythm of the poem which tightens the breast and chokes the throat, evokes emotion.[4]

Here, then, we see a concern not with an exchange of ideas nor simply of information. The word, after focusing attention and providing a certain basic informational content, serves, in its rhythmic utterance to achieve an emotional rapport between the speakers; it releases the imagination and leads thus to a deeply felt, mutually shared affective experience impossible at the essentially rationalistic level of an exchange of information or of ideas. Again Senghor: "Such is the Negro African who sympathizes and identifies himself with the other, who dies of himself to be reborn in the Other. He does not assimilate the other, he assimilates himself. He lives with the Other in a symbolic rapport."[5]

There is a difference here. In Senghor's illustration we have the

[4] L. S. Senghor, "Eléments constructifs d'une civilisation d'inspiration Négro-Africaine," *Présence Africaine*, special number, first vol. (Second Congress of Negro Writers and Artists, Rome, March 26-April 1, 1959.)
[5] *Ibid.*

beginning of the actual rhythmic interchange between two speakers with both participants at the intuitive and emotional level; whereas in Mailer's illustration one of the parties projects herself upon a purely intellectual plane and it is left to the other to learn from her by installing himself in her speech rhythms, by intuitively feeling for the strengths and uncertainties of her experience. Senghor employs his illustration in emphasis upon the manner of accession to emotion and its deeper level of communication. Mailer avoids the term emotion, but emphasizes Hip's drive to increase his energy, his force, life, sex, etcetera, and his reliance upon movement, upon motion to achieve it. Senghor points to the etymology and the generic sense of the word "emotion"—*e movere*, to move out, to move from one to the other, which process, in the symbiotic rapport he describes, terminates as a "commotion." There is in both an emphasis upon comprehension, intuitively through sympathy, through the installation of the one in the life rhythms of the other rather than through the rational use of that abstract symbol, the word.

There appears to be, however, a profound difference in spirit in the incidence of this phenomenon in the Negro African and in Mailer's "cool cat." The latter's search for the life force for which he borrows the rhythms and the intuitive manner of the Negro appears to be overcast with a hostile competitive quality, with a latent violence to which at any moment he may feel it necessary to repair. Hip, the psychopath, has been wounded in a society whose *Weltanschauung* is profoundly shaped by a will to power, and from that fierce, mechanized competitive world that has crippled him, Hip stands in the shadows, mobilizing his courage to redress the wrong and become again whole by striking out in an act of violence. One senses that Hip avails himself even of this intuitive manner that is essentially a way of love, to employ it as the West has employed the analytic and rational faculty to tame and to control. We are reminded here of Cheik Anta Diop's speculation that Western man's well-known "will-to-power" had its origin in his reaction to his unease in a hostile environment—the desolate Eurasian steppes where European man first emerged.

The purpose here is not to establish a hierarchy of racial values, to be judgmental in any chauvinistic sense. An awareness of the differing traits composing the human cosmography should serve to enrich mankind, and not to serve as fodder for a "creeping Eastlandism" or a last-stand apartheid. There is little question, however, that the cultural image that the backwash of colonialism has left upon the world is one that attributes universality to the values of Europe and the West, and which tends to recognize as legitimate only those non-Western traits that may be fitted into its scale. There appear to be two lines of attack upon such cultural imperialism. One is inspired by the fundamental assertion that there is but one basic humanity motivated by the same fundamental needs, desires, and fears, and given identical circumstances, capable of the same brilliant achievement, the same wretched stupidities. (Sartre's speculation is interesting here when he attributes the motivating force behind the imposing superstructure of psychoanalytic theory and of Marxist ideology to the basic desire to establish, in lieu of the separateness of Europe's traditional outcast, the lowest common denominator of economic and psychological man.)

The other basic reaction to the occlusive tendencies of the West has been to reject not Western culture but its cultural narcissism and its imposition upon other societies as absolutes, the values of the West. This has been, as we have seen, the more positive form of seeking to discover the contextually valid and viable elements in the particular non-Western society, and those psychic and cultural intangibles that create the style and the spirit of a people and are the source of its internal cohesion and morale. It is the first attitude that has dominated for almost half a century the approach of American social scientists to the study of the Negro and his status in Western civilization. Klineberg and Herskovits, among others, have been part of a considerable scholarly enterprise in the United States rebutting alleged proofs of inherent racial differences. This approach, which has served well the drive to end segregation in American life, has left the American academic world and the American Negro as a group unresponsive to the effort to associate psychic or cultural traits with a particular racial group. The tendency among American Negroes, and it appears also among Africans who have experienced a British tutelage, is to consider themselves men among men, with an undoubtedly maligned historical past in need of restoration, but part of a group differing in no respect from other members of the human hegemony in psychic or cultural proclivities. It is noteworthy that even Eric Williams, Prime Minister of the West Indian Federation and one of the most sympathetic in the English-speaking community to the emphasis upon the unique cultural development of the African, finds little surviving in the African heritage upon which the Indies can build, in contrast to the infinitely richer cultural situation of Ghana and, going far afield, of India.

It is not, however, to return to the arrant racism of the apologists for the slave trade, for the inhumanity of the colonial era, of *Mein Kampf*, to attempt an assessment of the psychic and cultural traits of a people on a scale for the first time other than the xenophobic measuring-stick of the West. As to the aspirations of some toward complete absorption in American life, it would be well to remark Oscar Handlin's observations regarding a cultural pluralism which may be displacing the aged dream of the American melting pot. As to Senghor's position considered in this paper, it should be noted that he poses no biologic postulates, observing (without adhering throughout to the limitations of his awareness) that too little is known relative to the transmission of biological traits to establish sound theories of hereditary psychic patterns. It would be, however, a denial of that spirit of free inquiry that since the Enlightenment of Diderot and his contemporaries has been a cardinal tenet of the Western creed itself, to refuse in the name of democratic or other ideal to consider the coincidences of cultural or psychic phenomena and their implications.

The *appel* of the Society of African Culture to Rome observed that the Negro African had been scattered by the slave traders to the corners of the earth, that from his, and Asia's, long subjection, Bandung had marked a power shift. And although, as Alioune Diop remarks, it is a sad thing in one sense to be compelled to espouse the cause of one's race, it becomes a necessary task. The world has been taught that there is no culture other than the West's, no universal values that are not hers. The effort to determine the common elements of Negro African culture is but one phase of an historic renaissance that has only begun to reshape the image of man upon the earth. As Professor Dresch of the Sorbonne in his greetings to the congress noted, the statement of the unity of Negro culture is as yet theoretical; as Jacques Rabemanjara, the poet, said, it is an act of faith. It is not, however, an aggressive or chauvinistic movement it announces. Its end is the redemption of a people, and, more generously, to create new dimensions in a pluralistic world culture. From the West that has "died of machines and cannon," Africa is looked to by many for a new humanism, for new psychic ways, for a vital force—which may sustain such a venture in man's self-organization where the new humanism of the Orient, or of Settembrini's Europe have not yet found fertile soil.

THE IDIOM IN AFRICAN ART
WITH SPECIAL EMPHASIS ON
AFRICAN SCULPTURE

J. NEWTON HILL

Department of English and Arts, Lincoln University

IT IS PROBABLY WELL for us to admit at the very beginning of this study that an artist may express, and frequently with remarkable ability, the sentiments of the race to which he belongs. This is not subscribing to any philosophy regarding environmental influences on the artist, nor is this an admission that the artist is inescapably controlled by ethnological factors. What we mean is rather that an artist, by virtue of the simple relationship that he bears to the persons and things all about him, can seldom speak absolutely for himself—as if a being in isolation. John Donne's observation "No man is an Island" applies to the artist as well as to persons in other walks of life.

Our chief concern here is not so much that of the individual, but his work, and it is our task to search through the mazes of art products of persons south of the Sahara in an effort to determine the nature of the idiom that marks their artistic efforts. I propose to attempt the identification only of the basic idiom as observed in African sculpture. Thence I hope to apply the principle involved to the music and dance of western and west-central Africa.

This procedure, first, must be as objective as possible. And I caution you to make an early reservation regarding the possibility of being particularly objective about African art. It is just possible that this art may be one of the most subjective arts known to man.

What, then, is this idiom we seek? How should we search for it? How shall we recognize it when we find it? These are not simple questions. They pose a most difficult series of problems involving anthropological, psychological, and aesthetic analyses. African art is still a relatively new subject—one that awaits further documentation. Candidly and sometimes cautiously, I may take my stand with the aesthetes. Frequently, however, when I need concrete data I must seek out the company of historians and ethnologists.

The geographical area of our immediate concern comprises the nations and peoples of west Africa from the Senegal River east and southward to the Congo River. From this point we move eastward and take in the Belgian Congo. You will note that I have skirted the Sahara and have omitted most of eastern Africa. The areas chosen have produced the most striking examples of sculpture, house paintings, grilled ironwork, bronzes, music, and the dance.

But it is the idiom with which we are to wrestle, and I suggest a working definition. The word "idiom" may be defined as designating a peculiar property: "that which makes a product one's own" or "a thing separate from all others" or "a peculiar form or variation." These dictionary definitions are typicaly terse, academic, and confusing. Permit me to submit a more generalized definition, but one more adapted to our purposes: The African Negro idiom is found in those indigenous qualities of his art which, because of their unique style rather than their subject matter, distinguish it from the art of all other peoples. This definition focuses our attention on certain indigenous qualities which, of course, must be identified. It also suggests that there must be some outstanding characteristics that partake of the nature—in African sculpture—of artistic traditions. It may seem preposterous to speak of traditions in African sculpture when our knowledge of the subject is so new. But Leo Frobenius,[1] Olbrechts,[2] and Fagg[3] have all indicated, quite clearly, that the art of the African Negro has definite and longstanding traditions. We are prone to emphasize the historical aspects and the motifs observed, however, rather than the idiom per se when we follow the ethnographic rather than the aesthetic evaluations. This is understandable. The ethnologist pursues scientific data and hesitates to venture beyond his hypotheses. The aesthete, on the other hand, is willing to risk judgments on sensuous images, intangible surmises which often speak more eloquently than logical deductions—eloquently and sometimes more convincingly.

There is a basic generic likeness in the vast body of African Negro sculpture. I call it the art of escape from naturalism. This is so fundamental to their art that we are forced by it to move into a realm of

[1] A. L. Frobenius, *The Voice of Africa* (trans. from German). London, 1913. 2 vols.

[2] Frans M. Olbrechts, *Plastiek van Kongo*. Antwerp, 1946.

[3] William Fagg, "The Study of African Art," *Allen Memorial; Art Museum Bulletin,* Vol. XIII (Oberlin, Ohio, 1956), p. 7102.

unfamiliar aesthetic values. We find a world of strength and simplicity, suggesting, at times, what may seem naïve and childish. Yet on closer scrutiny, African art represents a directness, a patterning evolved over the centuries. It therefore can be neither naïve nor childish.

Enter upon this mission with me, but tread softly, for you enter upon a dream world and I would not have you disturb or tread on these dreams.

The first manifestation of a quality allied to the African art idiom, I have identified as an escape from naturalism. By such avoidance, the African introduces us to a world of rare plastic organization and of striking rhythmic order. The unusual proportions given the human body impress us as being complete distortions and we stand amazed at the grotesqueness. We have to learn that the African sculptor seldom seeks the real, for that has already been supplied by nature and is obvious. He reserves his art realm for a system of communicating with the universe. And that universe is peopled by spirits, demons, ancestors and verifiable life forces. His world is an unseen world, unless observed through fetishes and masks; it is populous and pregnant with subtle meaning such as only a pagan could conjure up.

One reaches into the poetry of Wordsworth and snatches a few lines that might be appropriate here:

. . . Great God! I'd rather be
A Pagan, suckled in a creed outworn;
So might I, standing on this pleasant lea,
Have glimpses that would make me less forlorn.
["The World"]

The African primitive sculptor echoed a pagan world and felt close to its intimate spirits. His was a vibrant world—incredible to us but completely credulous to him, for the spirits hovered all around him:

As thick and numberless
As the gay motes that people the Sun Beams.[4]

This, then, is our first desideratum regarding the world of the African Negro sculptor. It is a zone in which he records his escape from naturalism and seeks, in turn, a spirit world. Here is, I believe, one aspect of the sculptor's idiom—a figment of unrealities to us, but a

⁴ John Milton, "Il Penseroso."

vital and moving realm to him. It is invisible to his physical eye until his imaginative concepts have gained reality in the form of animated fetishes.

This different world, with its discernible idiom, does not make the African artist either inferior or superior. Extraordinary psychic or psychological powers characterize some people in nearly all lands. Ralph Linton, late professor of anthropology at Yale, has said: "No scientist has been able to demonstrate the existence of innate psychological differences in persons of different racial groups." [5] One should be wary about implications suggesting racial differences when it may be highly probable that these so-called differences may be attributed to environmental factors, stages of cultural development, or to beliefs in the supernatural. The only significant truth regarding this uncanny ability observed in primitive sculpture is the fact that "in all of them, the individual tends to be more involved with the supernatural than the average member of our own society." [6] This first aspect of the idiom may be defined, succinctly, as an awareness of a supernatural world—always about them, always close to them, always inculcated in the exotic and mystical flair of their sculpture.

A second approach to the idiom in African sculpture may be observed in the reflection of a quality known as animism. Here we are dealing with something that is a logical development of the African's soul-filled world. It is the belief that practically all things—especially animals, the earth, fire, and water—have indwelling souls which, in turn, have their autonomous thought and will.

This is not strange in a primitive culture. American Indians, Eskimos, and tribal groups (many of Negro ancestry) in the South Pacific have demonstrated this same concept. It is strikingly reflected in African sculpture because the soul is all-important and therefore sculpturally justifies a large and distorted head as the seat of this life-force. Reliques and funeraries are accepted illustrations of this idiom.

Interestingly, this manifestation remains unaffected by other religions, not excepting Christianity itself. The African thus represents his subject as he and his society think of it, not as he sees it. He is capable of seeing with his mind's eye many things that we prefer to leave to

[5] Ralph Linton, "Primitive Art," Kenyon Review, III (Winter, 1941), 34–51.
[6] Ibid.

our world of dreams—unseen, unheralded, and often denied. He does not know the psuedo-sophistication of the Western world. He is a man of great faith and sometimes of a fearful faith, where we are less credulous. He is intensely subjective where we are boldly objective. He is willing to abide with the spirit world, whereas we eagerly scorn it. Perhaps a highly significant digression is not impertinent here: Is man any wiser or better if his scientific genius and predatory powers of annihilation have destroyed his respect for that which is not accepted simply because it cannot be demonstrated? Is it not still true, as Coleridge pointed out, that the clearest evidence of man's creative powers is found in his imagination?

To me this whole idea leads us to a sort of early primitive abstractionism, unintelligible to us, at times, but not at all unrelated to our concept of intellectual abstractionism. As a matter of fact, I believe that careful documentation will eventually reveal that African sculpture has unveiled several idioms—longstanding in that art world— which have subsequently blossomed into a controversial newness since "Les Fauves" and "Die Brucke," or the wave of "Der Blaue Reiter" and the later "Neue Sachlichkeit."

We need to be reminded of the ever-present risk of limiting art movements to individual races.

Plastic systems and styles are not isolated things. They have a formal correspondence to a more comprehensive system of relationships in which man of a given period is involved, and into which is tightly woven his attitude to the world and to himself. They are based, therefore, upon a broad human foundation. But this foundation is affected by his surroundings and his origins, by tradition and national peculiarities. We can only understand the interaction of national and international factors in the formation of modern styles if we recognize that modern art is essentially a composite pictorial system to which individuals and regionally determined forces have contributed. Jean Jaurès once expressed poetically a wish which promises to become a reality today: that the peoples of the earth should be like a bouquet of flowers, in which each flower has its own perfume and color, and yet is essential to the effect of the whole bouquet.[7]

[7] Werner Haftmann, German Art of the 20th Century (New York: Museum of Modern Art, 1957), p. 15.

Permit another quotation from Ralph Linton:

Many of our best and most productive artists seem to be equally incoherent about these matters [how they created abstract effects] and one suspects that the main difference between primitive and civilized art—at this point—is that the primitive has never felt the need for rationalization after the fact, which has been responsible for our own intellectual involvement with aesthetic problems.[8]

The African sculptor achieved the art of his invisible world, of his abstract world, with ease, since he believed in that world. His abstractionism was real—ours is unreal. His spirits were concrete and irrevocable, whereas ours are looked upon as the vague figments of a groping mind. Some few comparisons have been made, quite inexcusably, between African art and modern expressionism on the one hand and the art of children or of the mentally weak on the other. This is absolutely untenable and hardly warrants refutation.

The African sculptor established this idiom as a plastic procedure through which the expressive inner world of man was made visible without having to resort metaphorically to the images of the outer world.

If perchance Kandinsky discovered this fact in Germany about 1910, and if Larionoff reached the same conclusion in Moscow about 1912, and if Delaunay and Kupka did the same thing in Paris in 1912, then permit us to say, with all possible racial modesty, that the black man in Africa many centuries before this, was practicing his own "emotiointellectual" abstractionism.

Another feature of the African idiom may be inherent in its dynamism. This is the quality of power or force projected in emphatic patterns, exaggerations, and distortions in keeping with their remarkable conceptions of virility and of increase. This concept applies not only to mankind but to the earth and to the entire natural world. We see it in their ritualistic sculpture in the round and in their flattened masks as well. The "Nok" sculptures of the ancient Benue Valley of Nigeria are good illustrations of dynamism, and these have been dated at approximately 100 B.C.[9] The dance and ritualistic masks of most tribes are also representative of dynamism. Such works, marked

[8] Ralph Linton, "Primitive Art," *Kenyon Review*, 1941.
[9] Margaret Plass, "Special Comments on African Sculpture." 1960.

by infinite crosshatchings and with extraordinary adornments, including vivid pigments, are not only indicative of a distinctive form but of inseparable elements of design. They might well pave the way toward a synthesis of African art.

One can trace dynamism quite objectively in spatulate noses. Nigerian cubism, in the massive monumentality of some sculpture and in the push-and-pull thrusts of accentuated rhythmic portions, is especially noted in Gabon pieces. Such conceptions, I have little doubt, inspired Stravinsky in composing his *Sacre du Printemps* or even Milhaud's calmer yet strident symphonies.

And still the end of the idiom is not in sight; for one cannot escape its startling bizarreness. At times it is traced through the delicate scarifications of the Bena Lulua tribes. Again, one finds it in the Senufo helmet dance masks or in the fragile Bambara antelope headdress. Stridency is sometimes relieved by undulating curves, by the adroit intermixing of dynamic, excited and often of static lines, and by magnificent interspatial carvings as noted in some Yoruba sculptures. This attenuated aspect of their carving is one of the most overlooked features of their sculpture, for this aspect of the idiom is often lost in the maze of Africa's more monumental works or in the attention given to the tiny gold-weights.

Judging from the manner in which the African sculptor handles his tools, especially his adze, I am inclined to believe that his technique is at times a strange reversal of that followed by artists of the Western world in that his negatives and his positives strike us as being reversed; hence his ability to literally carve out negative light-areas rather than positive volumes. He evinces his own concept of a space theory wherein apertures may become more important than masses. Here, too, is something that Henry Moore incorporates in his sculpture.

The bizarreness of this art-product probably reaches its height in patterns of geometricity seen in dance helmets of the Senufo tribes and particularly in Bakota funeraries. Here we find an expression of the idiom which gave rise to Picasso's three-dimensional planes. I do not claim that this motif originated with the Africans. Cézanne, when interested in the simple problem of trying to paint a movement from realistic, rounded objects to flat, decorative areas, did so in terms of color and modeling, whereas the African sculptor did very much the same thing in terms of planes. Skill and geometrically counterbalanced planes mark this as one of the most pertinent aspects of our idiom and as one of the most striking concepts applicable to the entire field of architectonic sculpture.

We must not overlook the pleasing bulbous figures of Fang and Baluba sculpture. Those of us who have been nurtured on Greek sculpture will have little difficulty in accepting these smooth surfaces, which almost eliminate striations and sharp lines of force. Perhaps this work reflects influences of other lands in its approximation to certain classic proportions and with a patina at once welcome to a foreigner's eye. It is astounding to find out how readily factors presumed to be indigenous to one national group have their parallels among other peoples for whom history and anthropology claim no previous contact. Of course, this supports some theories about the universality of art. Yet the idiom here seems clearly African, though it stands in contrast to the violent drama discernible in other African Negro sculpture. There is compactness here and satisfaction, too, in the realization that African sculpture, with only one basic generic quality so far—that of an escape from naturalism—affords so wide a range of sculptural types.

Their artists, unmoved by any doctrine of "mimesis," carved out a world of expressive works, which, in turn, amounted to their unique expressionism. Masters of plastic organization and of a rhythmic order, they evolved one of the finest sculptured expressions of the unconscious—and this they accomplished with comparatively few basic and original manifestations of their ephemeral art. I say ephemeral, simply because so much of it was in wood; not merely because wood was immediately available, but because a tree represented the finest concept of life itself—ever-growing, strong, ever-increasing.

Even the ability to see concepts of divination all about them was made to serve the purpose of art—and all this from a people whom we unwittingly regarded as hopelessly lost when measured by the aesthetic principles of Western civilization. Divination is the discovery of that which is obscure or the ability to foretell future events—a sort of augury or even a prophecy. Here the African relied on his fetishes, for the fetish was the habitation of a deity although it was definitely not an object of worship. Rattray makes this point clear in his studies of the Ashantis.[10]

[10] R. S. Rattray, *Religion and Art of the Ashantis*. Oxford, 1923, 1927.

I have considered these several aspects of the African idiom, based primarily on sculpture, from what appears to be an objective point of view. You will recall, however, that I stated earlier my doubts about the possibility of considering this sculpture from such a perspective. There is something decidedly *intime* about African sculpture, and he who attempts to consider it apart from this personal slant of subjective attachment may lose much of its major significance.

Roland Colin, writing on the "Situation de l'Art Nègre," has given what I consider to be brilliant support of this contention in a graphic description with all of its drama—of the going forth of the *Tyiwara*. Permit me to repeat the picturization in translation:

Let us confront this analysis with the testimony of a concrete artistic manifestation: the going forth of the Tyiwara. The similarity is simple, the outline perfectly followed, without a break. From the hut the men wearing masks leap, stirred by the force of fecundity of the Tyiwara. The Tyiwara, caught in the field of this force, submits to its law of emotion and stimulates the beholder with its rhythmic impulses. The passage from the stimulating force into the dance becomes a reality. The men of the village in their turn enter into the game of forces. One can perceive the extraordinary cohesion of this fraternity penetrated by a single rhythm with which it vibrates completely.

Thus the plastic arts are indissociable from the context of the life-force dance, and it appears evident that the sculptor of the mask sculpts it in the same style of emotion. He impregnates the wood that he fashions with the rhythm and with a feeling of the intensity of the life-force which will come to be inserted in it. I have observed this very directly in many sculptors. I know a Samago sculptor on the border of the Senufo Country of Sikasso. His name is Coulibaly, which means that he was born after the death of his father. He sculpts admirable statuettes and masks whose svelte and elongated lines show a strange similarity to the drawings of Modigliani. This is especially true of his carvings. Fako carves only at night in a soft wood. His name signifies the burden of the old woman, and he integrates the blow of his adze on the wood with the songs or chants which one must not interrupt. In this way, he explained to me, the singing and the rhythm are incorporated in the wood which becomes an art object. To contravene this rite would be tantamount to ruining the whole work.[11]

There is, then, a synchronizing and correlating of these several factors that Colin has mentioned. More than a synchronizing, he says, there is a kinship between rhythm, emotion, and the life-force. It is in man's muscular energy as well as in his blood, and it surges through his being into his art product with pulsations as regular and as dynamic as the beat of the human heart. The sculptor of Africa does not merely carve or chisel; he gives birth, and if in the process of delivery anything should be misconceived, a gasp of anguish or of disdain may be heard emanating from the spectators standing by, communally participating in the delivery, feeling his labor pains, and joying in the ultimate arrival of a new work of sculpture.

This scene and my interpretation may help to emphasize my conviction that African sculpture, so far as the African is concerned, can never be appraised with complete objectivity. The finished work must bear an intimate relationship to the life-force. And although there are clearly discernible evidences of a particular artist's technique, those evidences are unmistakably *his*. They are like the "accents" that Malraux holds as distinguishable and distinctive elements of the individual artist. These accents, he warns us, are not mere accents as we conceive highlights in a painting, but actual marks of the artist's own genius—not mere touches.[12]

I would like to offer a synthesis of the manifestations of the idiom in African art, but the African himself has already done this in his full ceremonial or ritualistic exercise. In these, he incorporates all aspects of his idiom. The qualities I have outlined pertain to his dance and to his music as well. Though the music of Negro Africa is pre-eminently a social manifestation, so, too, is the dance, the sculpture. Where in sculpture we find distortion and grotesqueness, in music we find irregular canonical form with intricate polyrhythmic accompaniment—not only from drums but from a wide variety of unusual in-

[11] Roland Colin, "Situation de l'Art Nègre," *Présence Africaine*, XXVI (Juin-Juillet, 1959). Trans. L. C. Hill.
[12] André Malraux, *The Voices of Silence*, trans. Stuart Gilbert. New York: Doubleday, 1953.

struments, including "idiophones, gongs, woodblocks and stamping tubes." [13]

The pentatonic scale and the heptatonic as well are commonly established. But African music has its complexities in spite of its simple, single-note melodic lines. No doubt the complexities are caused by our ignorance of the communal multi-synchronization of the whole African art world. We have probably grasped only one significant factor in this music: the off-beat phrasing. That one matter we have learned so well that we are apt to beget a generation of "beatniks."

The idiom in African art is a collective manifestation of the several indigenous factors outlined here. They are in a state of balance and harmony. When imbalance strikes our ear or eye, it serves only to emphasize and heighten the fundamental qualities, by enriched contrast, of the major theme within the major work.

But the idiom in art is very much like the idiom in language. The moment·we lift it out of its original context or linguistic form, it ceases to be a true idiom. How can the young African or the American Negro today be true to this idiom? My immediate answer is that he cannot; though he may attempt it with the questionable valor of a Don Quixote, his success will probably be in the same proportion.

Here the disciples of negritude must be challenged. Their respect and admiration for African art must be conceded and defended. But it is a hazardous procedure to apply Garveyism to art. I accept Carlyle's statement of a century ago [from his essay on Burns]: "Given a poet, let him be when he may be, or where he may be, and true poetry will not be lacking." Anything more than this tends toward regimentation, or at worst, by an inordinate emphasis on the superlative features of a Negro's roots when he himself cannot be certain of those roots, becomes a tacit admission of inferiority.

The young artist of Negro descent may impart African Negro "accents" to his work, but these must not be pseudo, they must not be imposed. Eliot Elisofon reminds us that the great variety of sculptural types in African art still leaves us wondering, "why one tribe's mask is cubistic and another's animal-like." [14]

[13] J. H. Kwabena Nkitia, "Drums, Dance, and Song," *Atlantic Monthly*, April, 1959.
[14] Eliot Elisofon, "African Sculpture," *Atlantic Monthly*, April, 1959.

Then, lest we assume a false premise of originality regarding so-called African idioms, may I remind you of what William Fagg has said on this subject:

African thought is conditioned by their ontology, that is, their theory of the nature of being; for them being is a process and not a mere state, and the nature of things is thought of in terms of force or energy rather than matter; the forces of the spirit, human, animal, vegetable and mineral worlds are constantly influencing each other, and by a proper knowledge of use of them a man may influence his own life and that of others.

He continues:

Of course . . . foolish and naïve superstitions, developed ad hoc to plug gaps in the primitives' understanding of natural phenomena, are in fact part of a coherent and logically ordered system which . . . has some affinity, for example, with the world of Democritus and even of modern sub-atomic physics.[15]

I doubt seriously that the most ardent proponents of negritude accept this philosophy of increase and expect to find it genuinely reflected in modern art. Yet it is basic to African art.

An African poem, mask, or fetish carved today, because of the impact of our modern industrial and scientific economy, would be necessarily "de-consecrated." [16] It would therefore lose much that negritude should like to claim for it. It is my suspicion that negritude carried to its ultimate end could result in "Kibanguism." [17]

Forrester B. Washington lists approximately fifty contemporary sculptors and painters in all of Africa, and only a few schools that give serious attention to the subject. This quantitative judgment is not a promising one.[18]

What can be claimed for the future of African Art? That question is difficult to answer. I suspect, however, that it will survive in the

[15] William Fagg, "African Sculpture," *Atlantic Monthly*, April, 1959.

[16] Leon Underwood, *Masques de l'Afrique Occidental*. London: Alec Tiranti, 1952.

[17] A term designating a xenophobic dogma founded about forty years ago in the lower Congo by Simon Kibangu. Advocates believed in the coming of a black Messiah.

[18] Forrester B. Washington, *Contemporary Artists of Africa*. New York: Division of Social Research, Harmon Foundation, 1960.

evolution of world art and that it can do nothing better than lend its finest expression to the sum total of the art of mankind. This, I know, portends a sort of absorption, but I do not stand in awe of that. Such has been the march of man since the beginning of time; such it will be to the end of time.

All that the Negro artist needs do is achieve excellence. That will always endure; though its recognition may not be timely, it is finally the recognition of enduring excellence that really matters. For then, by some standard of judgment, from Plotinus to Hegel to the concept of synaesthesis as espoused by Ogden, Richards, and Wood, African art will not only survive but will be rated on its own merits in terms that both the African and we of the Western world can fully appreciate.

REMARKS ON AFRICAN
PERSONALITY AND NEGRITUDE

ALIOUNE DIOP

Director, Société Africaine de Culture

I SHALL SPEAK in the name of the Société Africaine de Culture, not so much in an attempt to define the African personality as to indicate the interest that the members of that society naturally have in the Pan-African movement. But first, may I be permitted to clear up some misunderstandings.

We understand the anxiety of our friends—about the absence here of representatives of North Africa.[1] It is certain, or at least may I tell those who do not know it, that our friendship for North Africa is deep and indisputable. Not only because throughout the course of history ties between Africa south of the Sahara and white Africa have been established, not only because we have had common experiences in the past, not only because it was Arab historians who helped us most to know our precolonial past, but also because we have shared with them and other Easterners the same colonial experience. Victims of the characteristic phenomenon of the twentieth century—colonialism —we feel ourselves very closely allied with all the peoples of North Africa and their aspirations, and perhaps at this moment more especially with those fighting in Algeria in the name of their liberty and the liberty of all Africans.

We are grateful to the FLN for having manifested a great part of our pride. It is well know that there are Africans mobilized to fight against the FLN, but it is less well known that there are black Africans in the ranks of the FLN fighting for the liberty of the Algerian homeland. We know the active inclination of African youth toward the FLN and the various occasions on which these young students, or simply these young Africans, have loudly and passionately demonstrated their sympathy for all victims of colonialism, especially the Algerians. Let there thus be no misunderstanding; if our association was originally an association having its view on the black world, it is

[1] Professor Diop was referring to criticisms raised in the previous panel sessions on Economics and Politics.

purely by accident. We Negroes do not consider that history has spoiled us. We were not the only ones to suffer certain kinds of experience and misery. I mean to say, we have known racism, as have other peoples of course—the Jews, for instance—but racism against Negroes, as we are all aware, is of a specific nature.

We, the inhabitants, the black peoples of these countries, have been the victims of slavery; the inhabitants of the Antilles also suffered grievously from it. And we know that movements such as Pan-Africanism, at least on the intellectual level, were born from the struggle carried on by America against racism, and emanated from there, by a sort of gesture of solidarity, to Africa. And we know that the Negro personality, its context and contents, was launched by the Africans in Paris and the Antilles and incarnated by African writers—especially by the people of the Antilles. They are twice-uprooted people, because, unlike the Africans, they have not had the advantage of retaining their roots in African soil and because, unlike the Americans, they have not had the advantage of living in a modern and developed society. Consequently, we had reasons to limit ourselves initially to the history, the art, and the various creations of the Negro world, for the Negro has been the most scoffed at by history; but for many years now—and you can verify this by leafing through certain issues of *Présence Africaine*—North Africans have been collaborating with us. I might mention a few: Lacheraf, who is now in prison in France, was, right up to the time of his arrest with Beau Bella, a regular contributor to *Présence Africaine*; Cafediatine, a well-known young writer, Jean Amrouche, Labdavid, and many others contributed and still contribute periodically to *Présence Africaine*. There is thus no desire on our part to eliminate the North Africans.

They know—and the ties that we have with some of them leave us in no doubt of the confidence they place in us—that we are for an Africa *completely* free, from North to South, from East to West.

Having said this, I must associate myself with the homage rendered insufficiently in my view, to the victims of racism in South Africa. We have not effectively or sufficiently spoken of the particularly dramatic situation of that part of Africa, which is a part of our common fatherland. South Africa is a sort of concentrate of different dramatic situations which the colonized peoples of all countries, and particularly of Africa, know only too well.

It is possible that this situation, if it continues over a period of time, will lead us into a real war, as in Algeria. If we emphasize our sympathy and our solidarity with North Africa, it is proper also that we render homage to the victims of South Africa and that we reaffirm here our complete solidarity with that part of our common homeland, since upon the solution reached in South Africa will depend the future destiny of Africa as a whole. Having made these remarks and reservations, I now come to our subject proper.

Pan-Africanism was launched here and was of an essentially intellectual nature. Many years after its birth, the African peoples and their leaders—some of their leaders—took hold of Pan-Africanism and made an elaborate doctrine of it, adapted to our aspirations and our situation. Each country or each cultural region has its terminology; in France, we invented *négritude* (negro-ness); in the Anglo-Saxon countries, they invented Pan-Africanism; and together, we launched another expression with the same perspective, the African personality.

Well, as to this African personality, we are often asked what does it mean, where does it come from, where does it lead to? I should like simply to recall the moving eyewitness account that our friend from South Africa [Ezekiel Mphahlele] has given us, describing to you the particularly alarming and anxious feelings of those who find themselves in a sort of ghetto.[2] Africans, especially black Africans, have lived for centuries in a kind of ghetto—a political ghetto, a cultural ghetto, and a sort of economic ghetto.

We are reaching a period in history when it would seem that, on a theoretical plane, the problem of independence finds its solution in political independence. But we must not forget that political independence is only one step, it is only a means, and that independence will never be total until the moment when it is assured on both the economic and the cultural levels.

The struggle is far from being over; even on the political level, it is far from over. It is probable that on the economic level we shall encounter still greater difficulties. And, what can be said about cultural independence? For we have finally understood the anxiety of those among our Western friends who mistrust the constant evocation of our originality and who repeat to us that men are alike. They are perfectly right—men *are* alike—we have always thought so, and we cried it

[2] See following comments by Ezekiel Mphahlele.

aloud. At that time, we were reminded, however, of differences between us; now we are on the threshold of independence, and we see the emphasis shift to the similarities of humanity in all races.

They are right, but they would be wrong to want to prohibit us from underlining our characteristics, because it is in the name of these very characteristics that we can incorporate ourselves into a general movement; the peoples of the world are creating a fraternal justice and coexistence. We are particularly fragile people, who have decided on our own behalf, either in the United Nations or elsewhere, that all Africa will ultimately be politically independent. But I believe that the struggle will not be ended thus; for Africa to be politically, formally, independent in a world built along Western lines and Western philosophical and economic options, that world must be remodeled, reconstructed, so that the interests of diverse communities are in equilibrium—and when I say interests, I mean cultural interests; for history, official history, the only one that is widely known, the only one that is heeded and read, is Western and largely influenced and even dominated by the perspectives or problems, if you wish, of the Western hegemony.

History must be remodeled from top to bottom, and I believe that whatever reservations one might harbor toward such a task, toward its hypotheses, we must render homage to the initiative of men such as Cheik Anta Diop who were the first to put their finger on the falsifications of history throughout the centuries, to the advantage of a minority—the white minority—and the disadvantage of the colored peoples.

History must be the history of all peoples or it is not history. Similarly with other studies. It is certain that in the field of poetry, as in the arts in general, we come face to face with reality—which should be accessible to all temperaments. It has often been said that art knows no homeland; our hearts must be prepared to love all forms of art. We Africans have taken a great stride toward the West as far as integrating ourselves more or less into that culture: we have come to love the great Western musicians, the great sculptors, the great artists, the great writers; and as to the love we bear these writers and artists, it is to be desired that the West might display an equal love for the arts that please us, for the arts that enchant our people, and in such a way would communion be possible.

But if one operates as the leaders of the French Communist Party seem to want to operate, it is probable that this communion will be difficult. You will recall that some years ago the leader of the intellectuals of the French Communist Party, Louis Aragon, a great poet and novelist, began to rule on rights and mete out duties. The French Communist poets were to write only in the sonnet form, which is the product of French emotion. The reaction of certain Negro poets—who believed that other forms, another style, other vocables, were better suited to translate fully and authentically the message they had to give —is understandable. This cultural imperialism which men like Aimé Césaire encountered in the Communist Party to such a degree that they left it, is not confined to the Communist Party, but exists in many milieux and many men of the Western cultural world.

You will remember that on many occasions the leaders of the Western cultural world peremptorily affirmed that the experience of the Universal had been attained and exhausted by the West, that the Negro world had nothing to do but docilely insert itself into the Western cultural current, and that it was not only childish but dangerous to speak of other cultures than that of the West. This tendency, which lasted over many years, is today breached; we know that from all parts of the Negro world voices are being raised up to remind us of what the West had forgotten: that the Universal is only a goal and that the Universalist world will only be achieved by all peoples and their geniuses. This will perhaps be more clearly illustrated if we refer to the Christian world. Christianity, as has been remarked, is often considered by militant African nationalists as the quartermaster of colonialism—and simply because Christianity developed in the West and borrowed from Western culture its music, its arts, its philosophy, the shape of its dogmatism, and from Western mentality its dogma, or rather its theology, and its institutions. Well, Christian Africans and even priests and pastors, have long been raising their voices to point out that if the Christian message is universal, Western forms are simply the means that the churches employ to transmit the Christian message. It is not indispensable to sing Gregorian chants, to use certain forms of expression in rites and ceremonies; it is not necessary to refer to Aristotelian philosophy to express what Christ expressed simply: "Love thy neighbor."

It is undeniable that from the resources of our cultural traditions of animism and with the necessary prudence of the true believer, Christianity can legitimately be enriched by legitimate contributions to the music, the liturgy, and the philosophy of the Christian world. What is true of Christianity and history is true in other areas such as economy and sociology. Indeed, I am speaking of a veritable revolution, which Negro poets and all colored men, the cultured men of the non-Western countries, will undertake, not only on the level of their national life (of which I shall speak in a moment), where they will be recruited to affirm their destiny, but also on international levels.

They desire that, on the level of world events, in all studies and all institutions, the initiatives and the responsibilities be mutual. We are not children, we are adults; and it might even be said that we have nothing to learn from the Western culture for which we could not find an equivalent in our own cultures. The only misfortune is that these cultures are based on institutions, on an economy, and on a political freedom which are shaken and frustrated by colonialism. But we are convinced that our cultures are as organic, as deserving of respect and as rich as Western culture—and we have the advantage over Westerners here, for we have for the most part experienced that culture in all its dimensions.

The African personality is manifested in various disciplines and also in the political field. Dr. Ki-Zerbo said that the thinking African should not accept the pure and simple transference of the teachings of Marxist Communism into Africa, for the very simple reason that Karl Marx lived in and belonged to another era and environment, and that his concepts, whatever his genius, can apply only to the society he knew—and at the present no one could contend that the economic situation of Africa is the same as that of nineteenth-century Europe.

It is certain that if we cannot go backward, that is, return to primitivism, we can, with confidence in our personal genius, elaborate a political way of life that is our own and which will assure us more security and dynamism and will permit an easier collaboration with other countries. I am thinking now of certain experiments that are at present being made in Africa, particularly West Africa. I am thinking of that tendency which is more and more clearly emerging among political leaders, to let the people speak—those people who have so often been ridiculed and considered less mature and less responsible than children. The political leaders are manifesting their confidence in these people, and more and more it is not just national problems, but international ones as well they feel it their duty to explain, provided the people are organized. We have on many occasions witnessed their reflection, their deliberation, and their formulation of solutions adapted to their aspirations—solutions that add to the dignity of their community.

There is no problem of an economic, a political, or a cultural nature that the African peoples, organized in a certain way, cannot deliberate upon and for which they are not capable of finding an appropriate solution. Hence, this African personality of which we just spoke and which is troubling certain Western quarters, particularly Communist quarters on the one hand and Christian quarters on the other—that is, those who live by a universalist doctrine or have a tendency toward an elaborate universalist doctrine—this African personality of which we have been speaking is manifesting itself in many areas; it is manifesting itself in political life. I wish that those of you who could or would might have the opportunity to visit certain regions of this new Africa which are being born of themselves to international responsibilities. I wish you could visit not the cities or the capitals, but that you could go to the grass roots and see at close hand how the various sections are working in political parties and with what lucidity and seriousness political responsibility is assumed even in the smallest villages. And I would hope that in the West, in France for instance, where I lived for a long time, one might encounter the same conscience, the same seriousness of political reflection and exercise of political responsibility in the various provincial societies.

We are not, therefore, anxious about tomorrow, at least as far as the elaboration of our cultures and the construction of our political future is concerned. The only thing that troubles us is, perhaps, lack of comprehension, the tendency to annex us, to assimilate us in one sense or another, and the tendency to scoff at our maturity to the degree of wishing to exercise certain responsibilities in our stead. What is troublesome is to see that the Occident (be it the Occident of East or West, because for many of us Moscow is a part of the West—and I am not the only one to think so; I believe that General de Gaulle is not far from so thinking thus) has a tendency, probably an unconscious one, to profit from our present lack of responsibility, our present immobility, in order to orient our future and our destiny in one direction or the other. What troubles us is this mentality of the power-ful—that all who do not think like them think against them—it is this will to divide the world in two: those who are with the West and those who are with the East. We maintain that there is one-third of the world that is neither of the East nor the West. And this one-third of the world wants, claims, demands the tools necessary for the exercise of its responsibilities in a world ever more gravely threatened—threat-ened because the armaments race is continuing at an accelerated pace, because those responsible for this situation are at present particularly tense, and because those in power constitute only a small minority on our planet.

We are worried to see them exercise such responsibilities without consulting us, when it is a question of reconstructing a world where two-thirds of the inhabitants are underdeveloped. And the African per-sonality must not be considered as a racist tendency. On the contrary, I believe that to the degree that the African writers and artists and the African people themselves become aware of what characterizes them in the present world and become aware at the same time of their an-cient. patrimony and the possibilities of their future—to the degree that they affirm themselves different and original—to that degree they will integrate themselves much more easily into a new family, because they do not come with empty hands. What is embarrassing to us and a threat to the world is precisely that the very rich West persists in always wanting to give and not to take anything. We want to come into the world, our hands full of gifts so that all—mutually profitting from the particular geniuses of each other, wedding our thoughts, and taking into account the necessary equilibrium—so that all may rebuild a new world where the problems, from the moment we make the sole choice for international peace, will be others than those posed by the East or the West.

Consequently, I shall not define the African personality in our sense; it has already been defined in various ways. But our color does not isolate us; we do not withdraw into ourselves. The African per-sonality, on the contrary, is an effort to permit us to join others on the universal level and to truly build—taking into account all condi-tions, necessary ideas, concepts—institutions necessary for the defini-tion of a new justice, which this time will be a justice for all, for all cultures and all peoples. Until such time as technology and science may put us in contact with other interplanetary humanity—which is spoken so much of recently—at least we can organize our little planet on the condition that we do not forget that when one is burdened with riches one is less disposed to reflect upon the value of justice; and that the poorest, above all if they are numerous, are in a better position to correctly reflect upon the new values that will bring about the new construction of future society.

EZEKIEL MPHAHLELE

Extra-Mural Department, University College of Ibadan, Nigeria

MIRIAM MAKEBA's performance[1] was symbolic of South Africa. There we saw American forms infused with the African idiom. The film *Come Back Africa,* which was originally a musical in which Miriam Makeba starred in Johannesburg, shows the sordid conditions of life for the vast majority of South Africans.

Let me take you on a brief spiritual journey, and as we progress on this journey may I ask you to ask yourselves, where is negritude? You are born in a ghetto. You have a number. All your life you have your place and you must stay there. The white man is strong and you are made to realize this at every moment.

As you grow up, everything that you do is separate from the white man. You have a separate school, a separate curriculum, etcetera, from the white boy with whom you are in competition. You go to the university, if you are lucky. You feel a constant kick in the back. You are not accepted. The Boer tells you this is not your place. Minute by minute you receive one insult after another. You want to write. Your reaction is protest, protest, protest—till you are sick of it. You find that it is shriveling. You have a real artistic problem. It is as though you are fed too much on candy. Sometimes, then, you will turn to the romantic cliché; you will write crime-does-not-pay stories; you will model your work on the tripe of Hollywood.

Then you turn back to protest. One day you wake up. You're one of four million Africans in the white man's cities. There are three million more on the farms, and only three million left in their original tribal moorings. These seven million must produce some kind of culture. I remind you: where is negritude? It's still a problem. Still we have no negritude.

The African—at least the South African—does not feel superior to the American Negro. We identify with the American Negro. Why?

[1] Dancer Miriam Makeba performed in a special program of entertainment, "The Development of Negro Music," at the AMSAC conference.

He is of a slave origin, and we ourselves are slaves. And we hold the American Negro as a symbol of some kind of freedom that we're longing for. There may be some kind of estrangement in other parts of Africa, but the American Negro has been an inspiration for many of us in South Africa. We have seen the developments of the picture of the Negro in America, through Hollywood and other media of communication. First we saw the buffoon, the frightened Negro, the fat "mammy." The picture has changed. We read of Robeson's rejection of this portrayal of the Negro on the screen. There is a new type of film, and there has evolved a new stereotype: the Negro of the big heart, accepting the white man in his arms without question—beautiful, sweet, harmonious [Laughter]. This development itself has served as an identification with you. We too have undergone a change. Tribalism as such has disappeared and we are fashioning something new.

Continuing our journey: All the time, we're trying to come to terms. We're growing up, looking at ourselves, feeling the development of our creative personality, which is subjected to these cross-cultural impacts and enclosed in this ghetto that shuts you up. We find a mutual impact of the white world and the African. You realize you are the personification of a paradox, a paradox that is a meeting point between acceptance and rejection. You reject certain things, and you accept certain things that seem to express your longing. Finally, when you realize this, you have a real feeling that you have grown up; you feel that you are a man and what you are going to express is that paradox, that irony which is the meeting point between rejection and acceptance. You have a glorious feeling of emancipation. You may be forty already—or thirty. You feel yourself in control at last. You have that excruciating feeling of being the meeting point of two streams of consciousness, black and white, a feeling that is at the same time exciting. After all, you still have a spur in the back, though it is often paralyzed. You are very much excited by reading [J. Newton] Hill —you first recognize that the artist may express frequently with remarkable ability a sentiment of the race to which he belongs, but that this is not to subscribe to a philosophy regarding environmental influences on the artist, nor is this an admonition that the artist is inescapably controlled by ethnological factors. What we mean is that the artist, by the simple relationship that he bears to persons and things all about him, can seldom speak absolutely for himself as though he were a being in isolation. And there you are creating something. Still, where is negritude?

The other day I was making a reassessment of a South African writer of the 1930's who had written a purely romantic novel, and I caught myself having written: "This is the fatalism of Africa which enables the African to endure tragedy, to negotiate the tragic moment." I asked myself—I wasn't satisfied—I asked myself: was I saying something that is very true? I am saying this in reference to what [Samuel] Allen said when he quoted somebody who talks about this feeling, these psychic traits that are said to make up the African. I say I was not satisfied because, you see, it is a changing personality. We keep looking for it all the time and it is the creative artist who keeps looking for it. It is elusive. We must not cheat ourselves into believing we have now caught the African personality which we can describe in any tangible terms. We can only look for it, and that search for it is the very thing that makes the artist. The very conflict we're in the midst of makes the content of our art.

Mr. Ki-Zerbo said that because of our common experience, in effect, Africans in Africa feel they are one.[2] Yes, all right; so far, so good. What, then, when the colonial master has gone? What have you left? It is a different story in West Africa, where you're left alone. But in South Africa, where you're still left in the presence of the white man, where is negritude? If you are an artist at all, of course you will bring out all these cross-impacts. If you are a real artist, you will bring out this African pulse in you, which will always be a compromise within you. We don't feel ashamed of it at all.

I have not said anything at all about the white writer in Africa. He is in a predicament. The white writer is at the mercy of the white politician who tells him he can't come to terms with the African and form a nonracial society where you will have a common stream of culture, and he thus refuses the competence or the human reality that the African offers. And so he remains an outsider.

This question of negritude is bound up with the question of roots. I was very much disturbed the other day when we were talking about art and there seemed to be some Negro artists who felt very much

[2] See "African Personality and the New African Society," in the section on Social Thought.

disturbed that they hadn't been to Africa. I don't see why they should be. Why should you go to Africa as a duty—as if you are going to some shrine, as a cult? I should say, go to China, go to India, go to Pakistan, go to Hungary, go get a broader vision of human reality—go anywhere.

There are two ways in which you can identify with Africa—one, through humanitarian sympathy. (And John Biggers can go to absorb the spirit of the country, to feed his creative inspiration.) Another way to identify yourself would be, of course, to go to Africa as a lotus-eater, stroll around stripped to the waist under the blazing tropical sun and feel negritude and Africanism ooze out of yourself [laughter and applause]. If you do that, of course, you know that you are as good as dead and your art is going to be as sterile and as ridiculous and as embarrassing to your audience as it is embarrassing, basically, to yourself.

BEN ENWONWU

Art Advisor, Federal Government, Nigeria

Time will not permit me to dwell upon Professor Hill's views of theoretical synthesis, or what you might call *aesthetic materialism*. It is very interesting; it recalls many phrases, many clichés, and many comments upon the influence of Negro art on the Western esthetic position. It recalls much of the domestic-science idea of African art. I find the language most exciting, because some of the terms are the very ones that most of us who begin to learn English commit to memory, more or less with exactitude.

I cannot pretend to speak on art, on African art, in the same academic sense in which Professor Hill understands African art; nor would I consent to look upon African art in the same way that the European or American collector of Negro sculpture treasures it. To me it is my bona fide property. I venerate it through what Senghor has analyzed as the Negro knowledge, which he calls "intuitive participation." As long as a person is an African, and as long as the penetration of colonialism has not completely "de-Africanized" him, he continues to create with the same vehemence and the same vitality. Whether it is the art of dance, painting, or sculpture, it retains that same mystique which will always remain a mystery.

Of course, what we call "mystique" is inherent in every civilization. It has been transmitted either biologically or psychologically to certain races or inhabitants of certain geographical locations, where you find either pigmentation or customs and tradition differentiating the people from others. We are different people; there is no question.

Anthropology and theology have afforded many theories which, I think, have helped me to an understanding, or at least an appreciation, of the qualities of African art. The characteristic features of African art, I agree with Professor Hill, are the visible signs that one sees in any art work; that is, the quality of color, of form, etcetera. The difference between the quality of African sculpture and that of other sculpture—as he said in this thesis—is that it has geometric shape, symbolical form, and the quality of what you call "sculpture-in-the-round." These three—at least to name a few—are characteristics of the art of the peoples of Africa generally, and are the common qualities in all African sculpture. The reason, of course, is that while you have the unselfconscious approach by the artist, we have the basis of religion, of what anthropologists call animism.

We have already gone into these religious backgrounds sufficiently; it would probably take a long time for me to go into them again. My view of animism is completely different from the Christian one, which reduces it, more or less, to an anthropological term. This term animism is a nebulous one. It does not apply and will not apply in a free African continent, because it does not conjure up religious aspirations, the fears and hopes of the people. Animism is a limited term. It connotes fear. The African god, or the keeper of the sanctuary, was not afraid of the spirit. He was not afraid of his ancestor.

My father was a carver. He was not afraid of his ancestors, nor did he worship what he carved. The images that were symbols of his ancestors were not even used in the same way that the Roman Catholics, generally speaking, use the figurines of the Virgin Mary, regarding them with adoration and sanctimonious reverence. Our ancestors, our fathers, and their fathers did not revere the images that they created to the same degree that is revealed in the mystique of African carving.

This mystery, this wonderful spirit, has baffled the Western superstitious; it has mystified them. The search for the practical or logical explanation of this mystique will never be possible with the Western analytical approach, because it is an approach that seeks to exploit rather than to give. Having studied anthropology myself, I am one of the few Africans who wouldn't mind assisting a European intellectual colleague to conduct a further study in African sculpture; but I would view with great suspicion any white man who came to collect or. learn by feigning friendship in order to get to the root of this mystique. Those of our people who study here will always respect you; they will never fail to give you hospitality or to remember what you've done for them. That is the characteristic hospitable spirit of the African. But when it comes to a question of analyzing us, it's a different matter.

After all, this mystique that we've been talking about is quite simple to understand, quite simple to accept. It is there without all the analysis. The spiritual realm of African art, the hierarchy of the gods, the psychic significance and the veneration, the way we carve images in order to express our hopes and personify our desires in terms of sculpture, the mystical awareness of the carver, the spiritual world of the trees and animals, and the belief in the existence of a soul in inanimate objects—I have experienced it all. I cannot express it; I cannot explain it in words. But I used to be absolutely overpowered by my own imagination. Even now, as an adult, I still fear darkness. It is my imagination, and the imagination of every African person—because of environmental influence, possibly, and because of the nature of Africa itself. The physical appearance of an African village has to do with the mystique. The shadows of trees in the darkness of Africa—this is beautiful to an artist. It is beautiful because it is pure. Christianity came and influenced it, distorted it. The real primitive came; what I call the "primitive" is the Christian influence, the mercantile, the commercial enterprises, the colonial era in all its facets.

The effect of Christianity has not been deep on the African mind. The rhythm, which is inherent, is still there because of our religious beliefs. The African retains that which is characteristic of his own society, because the society is not completely disorganized; it's in the process of evolution.

Now, in my simple explanation, negritude is an attempt, either conscious or unconscious, to express or to assert our personality. It is the "Africanness" of being an African. The African students who have come here have not yet begun to experience this "Africanness" because they are in the process of change. In the process, they are passing through a special aspect of the evolution of the African mind.

Psychologically speaking, they are just coming out of the impact of colonialism, if I may put it simply. They are coming out of that yoke, and they are now going through the academic period. They venerate you, they respect you, they think that you are wonderful gods because you are teaching them something written in books. But later, in the period when they will be ready to write about you and about themselves, they will regard themselves as superior.[1]

I am talking about the relationship between the American Negro and the African Negro. There will always be that air of superiority in the African Negro. It was there even when colonialism was at its height. I've always been a rebel because I come from a small village in Onisha, and my father had accepted the position as father of our people. My name has a meaning. I prefer my little home to anywhere else. Even when you talk about improving the standard of living, we laugh, because when we started eating your Western food we started getting your disease of ulceration; in a world of panic, a restless world, everybody gets this kind of thing. I realized this, and I had to go home and eat fufu and pepper. That cured me. I prefer fufu and pepper to European food. I wear this clothing because I have met some European people. But I wear my own native gown whenever I want to wear it.

In short, there are things that the African—especially the African artist—can select, and there are things that he rejects. There will always be certain elements in African art that are characteristically African. If I paint a picture and an American Negro artist paints a picture, the difference will show—except that some people paint pictures when they're not artists! [Laughter]

If any artist, in any country, has a message, and that message is deep in his mind—and he is prepared to suffer because of that message—then the character, the mystique, of his country, nation, or race comes out in the work of art, if it is a work of art.

[1] Many people at the conference were shocked by what they regarded as a statement by Enwonwu that Africans regarded themselves as superior to American Negroes. Enwonwu explained that he was only talking about the African's feeling of security in his own culture. An American Negro admires the American white man and learns his skills as rapidly as possible, but he does not want to be a white man. He enjoys his own culture and in this sense believes it superior. Any group that feels it would rather be some other group is suffering from cultural insecurity—something comparable to lack of ego formation of the individual.

T. O. ORUWARIYE

Oke-Ado Hospital, Ibadan, Nigeria

Just a few minutes ago I was teasing Mr. Mphahlele by whispering into his ear: "You South African Negroes and American Negroes will only be useful to us in the future as vehicles of technical and administrative knowledge, and so forth. You will be of no use to us in producing a dynamic faith."

Next time someone will have to bring Mr. Senghor himself to answer these American Negroes and South Africans, because I'm sure we can't deal with their notions. He's the author of the idea; I can imagine him conjuring up such an idea as cultural resonance to explain that there is always some connection between West Africans and other black men, regardless of how separated they might be in time or space.

There are many West Africans here to bemoan the fact that we never had a pre-independence effort at producing a general philosophical framework, such as India had. Indian speculation was mostly of a Marxist type. Marxism was applied to the reinterpretation of Indian history and Indian struggle, and there was a certain amount of philosophical writing before the actual change of administration. Probably the writers were thinking of a change in perhaps a thousand years, but the change came too soon. They also wrote theoretically about African life, about Negro administration; such speculation had a short life. Then educators, missionary educators, also tried to speculate a bit. They wrote such books as *Changing a Nation of Men in Africa.* They thought the African man was not good enough. Something had to be done about him. They speculated mostly from Christian motives, but again, their speculation was very shortlived. Well, we in West Africa are very thankful to be French-speaking West Africans and to be working out what appears to be a promising new fate with which we will be able to organize our efforts in the future. I suggest that, if it is possible, the next meeting of AMSAC be held in Nigeria, the real center of population.

Concerning negritude, I think you are trying to be profound about the obvious. If you were African it would all seem so easy. What happens? The music goes, you dance to it, and you sing. The foreigner complains that our music is monotonous. Usually he is a European; he has abstracted a little bit of it, and he sits down to listen to that. But if he were an African, he would not only listen to it; he would dance, he would improvise his steps, and it might become syncopation. In other words, it's the whole complex that is important.

The tendency of Europeans is toward abstraction, and I think this is their primary difficulty in understanding African culture. Negritude is no more than a reminder that there is such a thing as experiencing life as a whole, a synthetic whole, without the necessity of splitting it up. If you understand this and apply it to various aspects of culture, you do not waste your time splitting hairs. I think it is very simple.

Many people talk about the African cosmology. I'll give you an idea of it, because it is so important in understanding African life and African culture. In Europe you consider man as a part of nature; but I think the essential thing about African culture is that we consider nature as part of human society. You believe that human society obeys the same laws that govern the universe, the plants, the stones, and so on; but we turn it around. Our world consists of ancestors, animate objects, and inanimate objects. These inanimate objects are not just neutral. They share our hopes, our fears, and they have influence on us. The essence of our culture, really, lies in the interpretation of this statement. We believe that it is possible to alter the course of history, to get the gods to do this or that for you. I think that is a very essential part of our cosmology.

Think of a house falling on someone who is passing by. From the European point of view the explanation is simple: the house is old; maybe there is an earthquake, or a breeze blows, and the house falls. the African doesn't leave it at that. He wants to know why that man, why that day, why that particular hour, and why that particular house, out of so many possible houses, is involved. For practical purposes, for engineering, the European would reduce all the unknowns to a few, which would help him to make a prediction. All he has done is to simplify things. The African views the whole situation as a compact system; hence you will not be able to understand his activities, his cultural activities, unless you take his way of thinking into account.

However, I think I'd better leave the matter in much abler hands, to people who are professional artists and so on. I think that negritude is quite a reality, and I seem to feel that West Africa, or Negro Africa, is very likely to bypass the American Negro. As independence comes to West Africa we are more likely to find ties with the Negro in Brazil, the Negro in other parts of South America, where the impact of the Anglo-Saxon peoples has been less severe, where synthesis is easier, and where a connecting link is more permanent. I don't quite agree that we look down on anybody, especially not on the American Negro. Nonetheless, we're usually very self-confident, and we're full of self-assurance. This is because we are in full possession of our culture. After all, negritude is a matter of daily life to us. It is not a matter of speculation.

DISCUSSION

(Persons participating in the panel were Samuel W. Allen, chairman; J. Newton Hill, Professor, Department of English and Arts, Lincoln University; Sterling Brown, poet, Professor of English, Howard University; Ben Enwonwu, Art Advisor, Federal Government, Nigeria; Ezekiel Mphahlele, Extra-Mural Department, University College of Ibadan, Nigeria; T. O. Oruwariye, Oke-Ado Hospital, Ibadan, Nigeria.)

Mr. Allen opened the session by stating as its obectives a greater clarification of the concept of negritude and its relative value for emerging Africa, or its relationship to Pan-Africanism. In response to a question, he further stated that negritude originated as a literary phenomenon among the French African poets, particularly Aimé Césaire of Martinique and Léopold Senghor of Senegal.

Professor Hill, who had delivered the paper "The Idiom in African Art," commented that the idiom in African art cannot be precisely defined because it encompasses too much—it is too comprehensive. He discussed it in general terms first, and then aesthetically, observing that the Western world has regarded African art as a series of curios and sentimentalities. *Unless negritude is modified or redirected, it might destroy the seminal quality in African art.*

The question arose, "What is the reaction of the masses to negritude?" Hill answered by saying that negritude is emotional to the masses and intellectual to more sophisticated Africans.

Mr. Enwonwu confirmed certain theses in Hill's paper and declared further that the symbolism and the contemporary expression of African art is not inferior to that of previous generations, despite Western influence; modern African art is equal to any other art. The colonizer did not destroy its vigor. Enwonwu added that the African does at times feel a superiority to his colonizer, but that he does not have such a feeling toward the American Negro. The universality of the music of the American Negro, he continued, in its spirituality, conquers colonialism and every oppressive force. The Negro spiritual, he finds, is the result of the African heritage, whereas jazz is Negro but also strongly American. The spiritual asserts more profoundly the African personality. Negritude, he continued, is inevitably expressed despite condition or circumstance; it is the essential intrinsic nature of the Negro and is thus inescapable.

Mr. Oruwariye said that negritude is for him a kind of fighting faith of a superior quality with a high mission to perform; it is the sustaining spirit in a historical fight; its influence is in the culture and will naturally assert itself. He remarked, however, that there is the artist's conception and the more general, more comprehensive layman's conception of it. The two are not synonymous.

There was considerable disagreement with these understandings of negritude, and several participants attempted to explain their conceptions: whereupon Allen alluded to Sartre's statement that negritude is a rebel to analysis; it is the living expression of the creative impulse of the artist.

Professor Brown found a "fighting faith" more necessary than an analysis. He firmly believed that negritude can be defined, explained, or significantly discussed only through direct experience. The Negro alone, therefore, to the exclusion of all others, is qualified to do so. The meaning of negritude for the French African poet is different from that for the American Negro. And Sartre is "beyond the pale"; not having had the experience, he is not able to define it, and the same inability is true of Norman Mailer.

Negritude, continued Brown, helps one to become better, to lead a better life in his circumstance. *Présence Africaine*, in projecting a new profile of the African, renders an invaluable service. It negates the idea that everything African is bad and distasteful; it abolishes the stereotype of the Negro-African.

We must have desegregation but not assimilation, said Brown; we don't want to disappear.

Negritude is a concept that, for those far away from Africa, has great soundness. According to Alioune Diop, Brown continued, it is a kind of nostalgia and thus it began in the Caribbean. Considered in this light, it is not necessary for the Africans, for they are at home. Contact with other civilizations has destroyed some of the traits of African culture for those who are scattered throughout the Western world, but negritude has remained.

Allen observed that the aspect of negritude that evokes the greatest dissension appears to be the suggestion that it is a hereditary quality. He stated, however, that of those who have written seriously upon the subject, only Professor Guberina of the University of Zagreb in his study on Negro poetry has ascribed, explicitly, a hereditary character to the Negro aesthetic impulse. Senghor specifically states that not enough is known in biology to sustain a theory of hereditary traits. Although the issue is not resolved, Allen continued, it need not be a subject of disagreement undermining the sense of cultural identity negritude might inspire.

Brown observed that the biological argument is not new—it was rife, in the bad sense, over a century ago among the apologists for slavery in the South.

Mr. Mphahlele of South Africa entertained considerable doubt as to the meaning of negritude. He said he could not conceive of it as a "fighting faith" as Oruwariye of Nigeria expressed it, because of the limitations thus implied. If it is "negro-ness," it expresses itself in art; abstract it and it becomes an ambiguous philosophical concept, too ambiguous for him to have a clear idea, he concluded.

Brown drew an analogy to the Irish writers; he pointed out that the preoccupation with things Irish, with the Irish past and its mythology, was not for William Butler Yeats and John Synge a "fighting faith"; it was a sort of regionalism among the Irish writers, with James Joyce carrying it further. American Negro writers are kicking over the traces of negritude, said Brown. He referred to several American Negro writers and their varying attitudes toward Africa.

The discussion ended with the group agreeing only that negritude is a reality, but by virtue of its intrinsic nature it cannot be defined precisely.

IX CLOSING ADDRESS

THE RELATION OF AMSAC AND THE AMERICAN NEGRO TO AFRICA AND PAN-AFRICANISM

JAJA A. WACHUKU

Speaker, Nigerian House of Assembly

I WANT TO SAY first how grateful I am to be called upon to deliver the last address of this conference. It is of extraordinary coincidence that when we had the Pan-African conference in Manchester in 1945— attended by Dr. Du Bois, Kenyatta, Nkrumah, and the late Dr. Millard of British Guinea—it fell to my lot to deliver the last address. My subject then was "Where to Begin." I suggested to the conference that the two starting points of our Pan-African activities would be the Gold Coast and Nigeria. I remark on this now to point out that you can have your high ideals and philosophical speculations, but, really, they are nothing unless action is contemplated.

The year 1945 was the turning point from a period of speculative thinking to an era of practical action. Following the meeting of that year, we started what was then called the West African Secretariat in London. I went back to Dublin to manage the affairs of African students, and we left Nkrumah in London as editor of our paper, *The New African*. Of course, in some places when you begin to collect money to publish a paper and write seditious articles, the authorities clamp down on you. But in London we had freedom of expression; we said anything we pleased about imperialism and imperialists.

You will recall that this was not quite so easy in the case of Dr. Azikiwe when he was editor of the *African Morning Post* in the Gold Coast. The aim of his paper was independence in all things and neutrality in nothing that affected the destiny of Africa. Hence, when Wallace Johnson wrote an article, "The African and God," for the paper, Azikiwe landed in the warm embrace of the law. We who were then youngsters in Nigerian schools and colleges lapped up everything that was put in that paper, particularly the column "My Odyssey." We could recite the whole thing from memory. In 1937 those whom Azikiwe served conspired to get him into difficulties, and he had to leave the Gold Coast and return to Nigeria; there he started the *West African Pilot,* which still retains the maxim it had in that year: "Show the light and the people find the way." There were other leaders before him, but from 1934 to 1937 he was the moving spirit of African nationalism.

Therefore, when you are writing of Pan-Africanism or nationalism in Africa, if you have no page for Dr. Nnamdi Azikiwe, editor of the *African Morning Post,* your work is very incomplete. I mention this because in the papers presented at this conference there have been only passing references to him. Even persons who were inspired by him and who were encouraged by him to come to the United States did not give him the credit he deserves. I think that a lot of us who are younger people are here as a result of the fire he set in us. Some of us went to jail; some were restricted in other ways. (I can see here a good friend of mine who, as the result of youthful impetuosity and the challenging of established authority, landed himself in jail; but that did not stop him from being a nationalist. I refer to Anthony Enahoro.)

We all went through the mill, but we did not mind, because we believed that mere thinking—mere speculating, writing, living on a cloud—would do nothing until we actually planted the seed on African soil. Water the seed, the seed grows, and then—then the collective will of our people challenges the established authority, the imperial powers. And today we see what has happened on the continent of Africa. If in 1945 anybody had foretold what would happen, he wouldn't have been believed. How would you do it? Would you fight against the soldiers with bayonets and rifles and the like? What could you possibly fight them with? Well, our experiences in West Africa have shown that whatever the critics might say, the pen, the brain, human intelligence, human ingenuity are mightier than any soldier, mightier than any atom bomb. We have been able to do it by skillfully outmaneuvering the imperialist powers.

So you see, speculation is not enough. At this conference our subject has been African Unities and Pan-Africanism. AMSAC's executive director, Dr. Davis, has told us in his paper when speaking of the purposes of AMSAC: "Our aim has been to provide an understanding of the validity of African and Negro cultural contributions in order to provide a basis for mutual respect between Americans and Africans, and, indeed, between Africans and other citizens of the world." I must say that after listening to all that has been said, I don't think this conference got down to the objectives of the organization given in Dr. Davis' statement.

Now, I would like to begin the main part of my discussion of African unities by asking you to make a choice between the viewpoints expressed in two quotations I am about to read concerning the American Negro.

I refer to an article written by one Leslie A. Fiedler, entitled "Negro and Jew Encounter in America." I think this was published in *Midstream* in the summer or autumn of 1956. To me, as an African, it seems that the article states the antithesis of the values of this organization and particularly of those Africans and descendants of Africans in the United States. If you have not already done so, I urge you to read it carefully. It says: "Whatever the shape of his own life, the Jew comes to America with a history, the memory of a world he cannot afford and does not want to deny. But the Negro arrives without a past, out of nowhere; that is to say, out of a world he is afraid to remember, perhaps could not even formulate to himself in the language he has been forced to learn. Before America there is for him simply nothing, and America itself—white America—scarcely exists until he is present." Further: "It is fashionable to forget this now, but salutary to remember that the Jew is the boast of the United States, as the Negroes are its shame. And it is across the barrier of this discrepancy that our two people comfort each other."

The same article continues: "The Jew is the father of Europe—irksome as that relationship may sometimes seem on both sides; the Negro, only an adopted child. If Christendom denies us [Jews], it diminishes itself; but if we reject the West, we reject not our legend, only a historical interpretation of it. We are what we always were—ourselves."

I have decided to cite this because, as I am sure my fellow Africans here will agree, it presents a challenge. That's how we are. We get these things, we read them, we let others know about them; we make up our minds about them. I am not embittered by this article; I say it is a challenge, that's all. My question is this: Sons and daughters of Africa, now nationals of the United States, what are your views on this matter? Do you accept these statements?

The circumstances of those earlier people who came here are known to us. Africa was not a barren place. Africa was a continent where kings were still building empires, a continent—like any other—where wars were going on. When one kingdom conquered another the tendency was to seize those who were conquered, those whom the victors feared would be detrimental to their vital interests. In those days it became very serious if one challenged the authority of the conquerors. They either finished him then and there, or they sold him into slavery. Sometimes youngsters were captured and sold; just children of circumstance. Also, women were often seized, their males segregated and rendered harmless. In short, slavery did not start in West Africa just for the fun of it. It started with the taking of prisoners of war—just as in the Roman Empire, whenever there was a triumphal return from battle, prisoners were taken along.

After the discovery of the Americas, the freebooters came over here and found themselves in a position—while extirpating the indigenous Indians—of being unable to cultivate the soil. They found the ubiquitous Negro was the only person capable of handling the environmental situation. He was brought here by force of circumstance. He arrived here and by his wit, toil, and tears he cultivated the soil and created the wealth that has made the Americas what they are today.

Now I ask you: Should such a history make the American Negro ashamed of his past? After all, even the descendants of criminals who were sent to Botany Bay, Australia, are proud of their ancestors; they pridefully trace them back to Europe—the same Europe that convicted those ancestors, deported them, threw them on alien shores. Today there are prime ministers and big businessmen who are proud of such despicable ancestry. Why, then, should the American Negro not be proud of his?

We can go to remotest antiquity to trace the deeds of the blacks. I am not a theologian, but surely American scholars know this. You must have read *The Dawn of Conscience* by Dr. Breasted. Almost certainly a lot of the writing of the Holy Writ came from the Africans. Some of the phraseology used in the Bible today was not of Hebraic origin at all; as Breasted has said, the Jews were only the conduit through which those things were transmitted to the Western world. The Phoenicians, in the graves of their kings, recorded that their civilization came to them from Egypt. We know, also, that circumcision was a universal practice among the blacks in Africa and had great significance for them in their religious traditions.

Moreover, the slave played an important role in the early development of Christianity. It was to the slave that Christianity was preached. It was through the slave that Christianity gained roots in Rome. Today the center of Christianity is in Rome, but don't forget the reason for that. Your scholars know these things. Do the masses of Negroes in the United States know them? Has any effort been made to bring this knowledge to them? Do they know that Western Europe owes its civilization to their ancestors? Is it not extraordinary that Pliny could have written, "Ex Africa semper aliquid novi"—"From Africa there is always something new"?

Yet we are told that we have no history, we have no past. Obviously, this is not true. From remotest antiquity we were there, and to the end of the world we shall be there. This century is *our* century, as we shall see in the next quotation.

It was during the second [AMSAC] conference that the Honorable Charles C. Diggs, Jr., U.S. Representative from Michigan, made the following statement. My purpose in reading it here is to see how far this organization has gone in applying what he stated:

> The American Negro should have as much interest in the development of Africa as the American Jew has in the development of Israel. Not only will the renaissance of concern uncover the missing link between the American Negro and his African heritage, but it should further substantiate among other things the rich contributions Africans have made to the culture of the world. The resurgence of interest in Africa today presents a unique opportunity for American Negroes to forge an unbreakable chain with their African brethren. They should be inspired not only by great yesterdays in Africa, but even more motivated by great tomorrows. As was so aptly stated last December [1958] at the Accra conference: "Africa is a continent of the future."

I pose again the initial question: Which of the two passages I have quoted does this organization accept? I accept the second—and I believe those of you who have come from that old continent to this conference will agree. The other we reject, because we think it was written in abysmal ignorance. Apart from holding conferences and inviting us to come, I feel that AMSAC should devote itself not only to intellectual excursion but to practical education of the Negroes in America. Try to link them with their origin. They cannot be effective in the society in which they have found themselves unless, like searching roots, they reach deep into the rich soil of their birth to bring new strength and nourishment into the tree. This conference would be useless if we merely came all the way from Africa to talk to professors, lecturers, and eminent scholars. This organization must reach down to the twenty million American Negroes.

Thus, in dealing with Pan-Africanism and African unities, one of our primary concerns should be racial unity. I shall discuss others later, but here I want to point out that the reason people have been able to write as they have about the American Negro is that there is not, they claim, a strong and powerful African nation to which he can turn at any time. You mean to tell me, today—with Ghana there, Liberia there, with Nigeria soon to be there; with Sierra Leone there, Mali there, Guinea there, and the Congo this month, and the rest of them; and with the United Nations speaking on behalf of these sons and daughters of Africa—you mean to tell me you cannot lift up your head with pride, dignity, and self-respect? Can anyone dare to challenge your origin? Of course not, because there it is for all to see. You can see my color. This color—it is as they say in the Bible: The stone which the builders rejected will become the head of the corner. I am not a painter, but I know that if you use several colors and keep mixing and mixing and mixing them, the moment you add black it overwhelms the rest [laughter and applause]. It is very significant. I didn't bring it about; I merely observed it. It is black, the mythical, the unfathomable, the power that overwhelms. There is cause for pride.

Am I wrong in saying that when Perry went to the North Pole there was a Negro with him? He was the least clad, but when the others perished was it not he who brought back the details in order that people would have a report of what the explorers did?

In the North Pole he survives; in the hot equatorial desert he survives; under the sea he survives; in the air he survives. Are you to tell me he has no destiny for which the Divine Creator made him? Today the African continent is the richest in the world! The power, the first uranium, for the atom bombs used at Hiroshima and Nagasaki came from Africa, from the Belgian Congo. In our soil there are latent forces embedded by the Divine Creator. In our soil there are the richest natural gases; in Nigeria there is virtually inexhaustible oil and iron. Over in Liberia there is a hill of iron—69 per cent pure iron; in Ghana you find bauxite, manganese. There is everything in Africa! During all the time our people were being subjected to all sorts of things, these discoveries were not complete. But now that the old continent has come to life again, you see these things. Am I to believe that all these resources are meant to be used for nothing?

We come here from that vivacious continent so brimming with life, abundant sun, abundant rain—abundant mosquitoes, abundant swamps! [*Laughter*] We have everything—good, bad, and indifferent. And the good Lord who put those things there must have known his purpose. Without the mosquitoes and the swamps we in Nigeria would have been suffering from the same ills that we see in South Africa, in Kenya, and in North Africa. But now that we are beyond the reach of these, we have means of eradicating the swamps in order that our population may grow and our resources be developed to serve the African race and the human race.

Ours has been called the "dark continent." I don't know how they ever got that term. The sun rises most brilliantly there. The rain falls in buckets, not just in showers. The moon at night—very soothing and romantic. And yet they say it is the "dark continent." I just can't understand why. Perhaps because Nature closed the door, locked up everything, and refused to permit an alien eye to peer through the crevices. Perhaps it was deliberately made dark. But now, Africa is coming into her own.

We know that our continent is the richest at the moment, its natural resources the least exploited. Yet our human resources have been subjected to all sorts of things. The way I look at it is this: I think that it was for a purpose. Africa has gone through old barbaric processes. Civilization has gone from that continent right around through Asia Minor, to Western Europe, to the Americas; and now it is coming back to the roots where it started. And whereas others were not prepared to give credit to Africa for what she has contributed to humanity, the Africans now, in their own right, will have to make the world respect their knowledge, their experiences, and their contributions.

That is why such organizations as AMSAC have become so very important. Those who are responsible for running AMSAC must appreciate the importance of its role. It may be a weak organization now, but it can become an instrument of great good to this country, to Africa, and to the world. Consider, if you will, the extent of Pan-Africanism in geography alone. I purposely brought this map here. Look at the Americas; there are people of African descent in Brazil, the West Indies, and throughout the Americas. Here, in the United States, I think your latest census suggests that there are, in round figures, twenty million. All over here, all over there [indicating Africa and Americas]—that is ours. Here is Europe on our shoulders. When the Moors were in control, Spain was civilized by them. Europe could not have developed without the resources of our continent.

With the good will of the American Negroes and the people here, the combined forces of the Africans will bring stability to the world. So the twenty million American Negroes have a vital role to play. Join them with Nigeria's thirty-five to forty million; with Sudan, Egypt, the Congo, French Equatorial Africa, Ethiopia, Abyssinia, and the result will be a tremendous impact on the world by virtue of size, by virtue of population, by virtue of strategic position, by virtue of natural resources, by virtue of untapped intellectual capabilities. There are Dahomey, Togoland, Ghana, Ivory Coast, Mauritania [indicating these on map], and all the rest of them. Certainly you can't tell me that your country together with our countries in Africa cannot bring sanity to a world that has gone insane.

You have a very grave responsibility, but there appears to be a certain amount of diffidence on the part of the American Negroes, which I have noticed even though I have not been in the United States long. It is not good to be learned and allow your learning to rot. We have had similar experiences in Nigeria. There was a time when those early lawyers qualified, practiced, made money, and were quite comfortable. They were prepared to go to government functions and shake hands with all the big wheels. But they would not associate with the rank and file, the ordinary peasants, the society from which they had risen. As a result they were ineffective. But a new generation arose and withdrew from all the niceties of imperial society; we went back to the people, identified with them, transmitted our newly acquired knowledge to them and through them. So we created the ferment, became the catalyst in our society; and hence we see the transformation that has taken place.

Now if we have done it in Africa, I see no reason why you cannot do it here. Of course, you have to be loyal citizens of your state; nobody is asking you to divorce yourself from the place you built and the area to which you contributed so much effort to develop. I don't think any Nigerian or any Ghanaian or anybody from Africa would tell you that you should reject what you have in you, in your system, in the blood running through your veins. That's not it. People of British descent have a claim in Canada; people of Dutch descent have a claim in the Americas, as do the Italians, Japanese, Chinese, Indians —this is indeed the melting pot. And if they have a claim to this place, how much more have you! With such a claim, you should certainly not cease to participate effectively. What we are saying is this: we are not happy with a situation where, numerically, you can have influence in politics, in business, in education, etcetera, but where you seem to have a kind of apathy, somehow.

I understand that there are about ten American Negro millionaires. What do they do with their millions? Can they not create the same type of industries as others are creating with their millions? Can they not also create employment for their people as others are doing elsewhere? Are they not interested in the question of development on the continent of Africa? Do they not want to make more money, as others are making it? Or are they contented? One thing I know: man is never satisfied, never contented—else he is dead!

After all, was it not the Irish-Americans who made it possible for the sovereign Ireland to have her independence? You could play a similar role on the African continent. Was it not the American Jews, the British Jews, and the Continental Jews who made it possible to wring the Balfour Declaration from Britain because of the discovery of TNT by (I think) Dr. Weizmann? Duplicity in politics made it possible. On the one hand you were giving assurances to the Arabs, and on the other a declaration to the Jews; they had a fight over it, and finally the Jews got a spot on earth. The financing and development of the desert and similar projects is being done by the Jews from abroad. If they can do it in Israel, why can't you do it in Africa?

Now, everybody need not pack up and come to the continent of Africa in order to develop a vital interest. We're not suggesting that.

You already have a vital interest, and the American Negroes should recognize that the development of Africa is to their own advantage. Similarly, if the United States believes—as I have seen from various writings—that Africa is going to have a decisive effect on the world situation, then the United States may have to reconsider a number of its economic and other policies that are not to our vital interest.

Although it is not for me to say what our attitude in Nigeria will be, I believe that with good will on both sides, with a stretching of friendly hands across the Atlantic Ocean, there is every possibility of a sound and friendly relationship between our two countries.

The United States never became a real world power until after the last war. Up to then, foreign policy and world opinion were determined in Europe. When the European countries met in Berlin in 1884 to divide the African territories among themselves, no Africans were there and the United States took a purely passive interest in the matter. It was after the last war, through the activities of President Roosevelt, that you came fully into the stream of world opinion and started being effective. All this time we were nowhere. Africa did not have a voice.

Now it is going to be different. The independent African countries are going to have a voice in the management of things through the United Nations. And I can assure you—though I'm not going to say what it is—that in the 1960's Africa is going to throw a bombshell into world affairs. New factors in international relationships will have to be considered; new standards will have to be introduced to satisfy the yearning ego of the African continent. And unless those standards are met, I don't think everything will be quite all right in this world of ours.

That's where the relationship between this country and those of Africa will become very, very vital. We don't believe in signing paper pacts, which may be broken any day. But there is something more lasting than paper pacts. The understanding between the United States and black Africa is written in blood. I would say that under normal circumstances we should consider the United States as our first cousin, because all of the American Negroes here are our kith and kin. On the other hand, I would describe Great Britain as our tutor: when I have learned my lessons and graduated, I shall simply go home. But as for America, never shall I turn my back on blood of my blood and flesh of my flesh. Thus, we have a strong relationship between our two lands facing each other across the sea. Its future will depend entirely on how Negro affairs progress.

This progress is going to depend a great deal on how we in Africa handle another kind of African unity—political unity. And in this matter I say that our first need is for *national* unity. If we have national unity in Liberia, in Ghana, in Nigeria, in Congo, in Sierra Leone, in all those other places, including the North African states, then I think we shall have a real start toward Pan-African unity. It will be only a question of time!

Do not mistake me: I believe in internationalism just as I believe in interracialism. But as for internationalism, there must be *nationalism* before you can have the "inter" between nations. Therefore, when you tell us—who are engaged in the practical politics of Africa—that we should not concentrate on nationalism and the building of a nation on the African continent, we answer forthrightly: We don't agree. You cannot have interracialism unless our racial stock is respected by the world. And we will gain this racial respect only after we have established strong and thriving nations in Africa, created mutual respect among these nations, and, consequently, gained the respect of other nations for Africa. Once we attain that respected status in the world community of nations, then there will be no black man anywhere who will be treated with lack of dignity.

So to tell us to think in terms of internationalism, while national unity and national stability are not assured, is not quite sound from a Nigerian's point of view. I am sure that people in Ghana, in Guinea, in Liberia, and in all the other African countries will agree. Yet people tell us, "But look what happened in Europe!" Let me tell you, we are not going by European standards!

We are scaling the centuries! What Europe did in hundreds of years, we intend to do in decades! We intend to learn from history; and I am sure that at the rate they are going now, the African states, with God's guidance, will be able to learn from the mistakes of others. It will be impossible for us, on a newly liberated continent, to wait to be united before we do things. We can't do that! Independence is not being given to all the states at the same time. When you do have independence you begin to make use of it until others join you, and then you keep on until you have sufficient numbers to be effective. After all, it has taken seventy years for the Americas to get just the Organization of American

States! And only recently have they established a Bank for International Development and begun to think of highways and other such projects.

As an example of our aims and progress in Africa, let me tell you about some of our experiments in Nigeria. As usual, our imperial masters wanted to split our country into pieces before leaving, but we have been able to outmaneuver them and keep the whole thing together. Now, there are three things we must have in order to survive. First, we are going to have our political independence on the first of October; this we absolutely must have. Second, we must have our administrative independence. Aliens who have been controlling policy in our country and others must clear out and give opportunity to African nationals to control the policy-making posts. And third, we must have economic power in our hands. Once these prerequisites have been satisfied, we will be able to form the national unity and vitality that we desire as a prelude to interstate unity.

Any American who has gone to Nigeria, tell me: Where have you seen any place more democratic than Nigerian society? Move freely, go anywhere, associate with anybody. Eat where you like, go to a nightclub, etcetera. Nobody bothers you. And our papers are not afraid to tell you off if they disagree with you—no matter who you are. Freedom of expression!

I was in Washington recently when a motion was passed that the citizens [of the District of Columbia] there should have the right to vote for a Presidential candidate; it will take several years to get approval from enough of the states. What kind of approval is that? The Negroes in Washington, I am told, are 65 per cent of the population. And yet, unlike the citizens of Lagos, our own federal capital, those in Washington cannot vote on their own government!

In Nigeria we have three regions or states, and a Federal House, of which I am Speaker. We have taken care of our chiefs by giving them their place, where they can behave as chiefs; in the north and the west they are quite happy and contented. The younger, more virile element goes to the House of Assembly, where they can have a good fight—political war, there!—for the development of the country. We also have a Senate, composed of certain people we think can contribute in one form or another. We don't elect them as you elect senators here; they are appointed by the respective regional governments. They have a go, too, at legislation; but the most effective body is the

House of Assembly. And there you can hear my friend Tony Enahoro (who is sitting here so mild and gentlemanly) lashing out on the opposition bench.

So you see, these are the kinds of things we are doing on the African continent. Some of you need to come and see for yourselves. It is when you see our institutions in operation that you realize the developments taking place.

And when our respective states have achieved national stability, they can begin taking steps toward Pan-African union. We will, for instance, be able to develop economic unity. We came to this conference by Pan-American Airways. In Africa at present we have Nigerian Airways, we have Liberian Airways, we have Ethiopian Airways. Of all of them, there's not one that begins to compare with Pan-American. But if we work toward economic unity the African states might decide: "Well, let's put our resources together and have Pan-African Airways!" And we wake up one day and find that instead of landing at Idlewild Airport on a Pan-American jet, we are arriving in a Boeing 707 of our own! After all, this is one of the unities you would like us to have!

Similarly, you might find us doing something with currency. Nigeria used to have a common currency with Ghana, Sierra Leone, and Gambia; but because of independence they broke away. They didn't want Colonial Office interference. And now that we are becoming independent they don't want to coöperate with us again. It's all right—we have a lion's share in the world and we're not bothered. We have our own money. I brought my own here; I have English money, I have the dollar. Nevertheless, we are quite willing to coöperate with everybody; after independence there's really no reason we should not have a currency arrangement. The African states should be able to get together and decide, "Why should a pound note have one value here and another there?" There may be an agreement for common currency; and our money will become one of the hard currencies of the world because we will have the resources to back it up.

Then too, we should be able to go from Nigeria through Dahomey, Togoland, to Ghana, to the Ivory Coast, right through to Mauretania, without customs barriers. We'll remove all those things so that you will be able to travel freely from there to the Congo and the rest.

The moment Africa is completely free, there will be no bone of contention. Every country will have to rely on what it is able to produce and by exchange to derive from others what it lacks. The old process of barter which our fathers practiced will, sooner or later, be reintroduced. You'll come with your ships and take my cocoa. With my ships I'll take your machinery. No money to pay; it's all in the paperwork. Isn't that barter? And yet some say that bartering is a process of savages! No, it is civilized, because now I come with a ship, whereas formerly I would have come on foot. But whether done by airplane, ship, or leg work—barter is barter!

You see, Nigeria thinks about Pan-Africanism realistically. We hope for political union to develop as if at the apex of a pyramid. Some people are suggesting that we should invert the pyramid, that we should build the base over the apex. You know that it could not bear the weight! We believe that we should start with sound economic, institutional, cultural, and other unities as a base. We will get to know ourselves, we will get used to each other, before joining in political union at the top.

Given her independence, Africa will work things out for herself. First, of course, we must make this independence a reality. We in Nigeria will not be satisfied with our independence on the first of October while much of Africa remains in slavery. We are not satisfied to see Portuguese Africa, South Africa, Southwest Africa, and others remain under alien domination.

And as for belonging to this camp or that camp—well, as Tony Enahoro has already said, we are not bound by foreign ideological speculations. We believe we can work out ideologies for ourselves. We are African first; anything else is secondary. When Marx wrote *Das Kapital* about the circumstances of Europe, Africa was not industrialized. When Lenin went to experiment with Marxism in Russia, we were not there. We are working out our own destiny, although we are prepared to learn about scientific processes from different people. After we have settled our affairs of state, then the question of ideological differences may arise. It will be a matter of intellectual speculation.

Here in the Americas it was made quite clear in Roosevelt's Good Neighbor Policy, coupled with the Monroe Doctrine, that American states can do virtually anything among themselves—fight each other, kill each other off—so long as no external force comes and interferes. We in Africa intend to follow the same policy. I state to all nations and parties concerned that you can strangle yourselves, for all we care; but once you are out of Africa, don't come back to interfere in our affairs. This policy has worked on the American continent because, as your "Big Brother" here knows, if any one of the American countries were to fall into alien hands, that would be a source of danger to him. We will learn from that same lesson. Nigeria is not going to be independent and allow any power—any puny, decadent power—to come in and undermine its future existence.

Of course, we appreciate the contributions of the Western world in the way of science and technology. But when you come to philosophy and religion and the arts, I don't think Africa has much to learn. Those who have studied the village community, the processes by which a balance of power is kept, the establishment of chieftaincy, the election of chiefs, and so forth, know that we have our own ways. Attempts have been made to undermine our culture by various forces, but we believe that—with the independence of the African states—we will be able to recapture the spirit of ancient Africa and produce a new civilization.

We Africans have gone to universities and have tried to learn of our past. When we realized that all that had belonged to us had been concealed, that an attempt had been made to undermine our culture, it was our duty, in spite of all we had learned about the Western world, to throw aside our learning from the West. For your law—or your philosophy, as the case may be—go back to your people. When I went back to Nigeria, I went back to my people. I am from a ruling house in my division. I served in the village council. I served in the district council. I served with the native authorities. In other words, I identified myself totally with my own people. And when you identify your interests with those of your people, they have confidence in you, they trust you completely; thus the changes we have been able to initiate on African soil.

The revolution that occurred in Nigeria and other places stems from the fact that the sons of the soil got into their past history through the archives of foreign universities. You discover your art, your culture; you see the terra cottas, the brass works from Benin. You unearth so many new things once you start to investigate matters for yourself.

And today it is possible to trace African culture as it extends up to South America, North America, and on over to Europe. Throughout the world the content of our culture has been studied in private and in public museums. Those who say we have "no culture" have the objects of our culture in their homes. In fact, our cultural artifacts have spread so far that we have to "repatriate" them by buying them, by doing everything we can to get them back. Yet we have "no culture"! I tell you, there is rich cultural content on that continent! The only problem is that American Negroes have lost their link with that culture, and it is necessary for them to reëstablish this link.

It isn't merely a matter of your saying, "Oh, you must teach us." That isn't enough. You need a more vital, unbreakable link, as Mr. Biggers said in the discussion on art. It is only through such a link that you will gain your self-respect on this continent.

And so we return again to the vital role of this organization in making Pan-Africanism a reality. The interests of twenty million American Negroes are entwined with those of two hundred million kith and kin·in Africa. The American Negroes should appreciate that as long as our continent exists and thrives, as long as there are African states respected in the world community of nations, they themselves will have a full growth—which is what they require. Their full contribution will be appreciated, their role as human beings will be greater. That's all we want.

African Unity and Pan-Africanism: your African is an African, no matter where he is found.

IN RETROSPECT, the atmosphere of the conference was accented by an awareness of the rapidly unfolding drama across the Atlantic. There was in Philadelphia not only an affirmation of past and future glories; there was also a full realization of the enormity of the task of Africa's entry into a politically divided, highly industrialized society, and of the urgency of her basic problems of illiteracy, poverty, and disease. Surprising to some was the strength of the insistence upon African tradition and a peculiarly African frame of reference in Africa's modern development; upon a continuity with the past; a fidelity, in a sense, to the ancestors. The question left unanswered, and to a great extent necessarily so, was how this synthesis is to be achieved. How, for example, is the traditional solidarity of African life to be maintained in the face of increased urbanization with its seemingly inevitable growth of rootless, anonymous crowds? Every shade of opinion was evident in the cultural spectrum, and negritude proved to be an intellectual force of considerable magnitude, despite the disagreement that centered on it. As a literary and cultural influence, it provides a rallying point for reshaping cultural distortions; it serves as a weapon forcing the issue, even in the United States, if certain sensitivities inspired by the struggle against discriminaton are not ignored. The level of participation was high; it augured well to observe so large a number of intellectually astute and articulate African participants. With a heightened awareness of the development of Pan-Africanism, its imperatives and its concerns, the conference concluded. Africa must, to survive, have the assistance of the industrially advanced nations, but, for the first time in the modern era, in that ultimately decisive sphere of moral and spiritual values, Africa is on her own.

S. W. A.